CELEBRATING
50 YEARS

Texas A&M University Press
publishing since 1974

SIX CONSTITUTIONS OVER TEXAS

Publication of this book was aided by a generous gift from the Texas Supreme Court Historical Society.

SIX
CONSTITUTIONS OVER
TEXAS

Texas' Political Identity, 1830–1900

William J. Chriss

TEXAS A&M UNIVERSITY PRESS
College Station

Copyright © 2024 by William J. Chriss
All rights reserved

First edition

♾ This paper meets the requirements of ANSI/NISO Z39.48–1992 (Permanence of Paper). Binding materials have been chosen for durability.

Library of Congress Cataloging-in-Publication Data

Names: Chriss, William J., author.
Title: Six constitutions over Texas: Texas' political identity, 1830–1900 / William J. Chriss.
Description: College Station: Texas A&M University Press, [2024] | Includes index.
Identifiers: LCCN 2023041880 (print) | LCCN 2023041881 (ebook) | ISBN 9781648431715 (cloth) | ISBN 9781648431722 (ebook)
Subjects: LCSH: Constitutional history—Texas. | Constitutions—Texas. | Constitutional law—Texas. | Texas—Politics and government—19th century. | BISAC: HISTORY / United States / State & Local / Southwest (AZ, NM, OK, TX) | POLITICAL SCIENCE / Constitutions
Classification: LCC KFT1601.5 .C47 2024 (print) | LCC KFT1601.5 (ebook) | DDC 342.764009/034—dc23/eng/20230929
LC record available at https://lccn.loc.gov/2023041880
LC ebook record available at https://lccn.loc.gov/2023041881

FOR MY FATHER,
John the doctor,
AND FOR MY CHILDREN,
John and Olivia

Contents

Foreword, by H. W. Brands   ix

Acknowledgments   xi

Introduction. Constitutional Identity and Constitutional Moments   xiii

Prologue
Mexican Texas and Its Constitutions, 1821–1836   1

1 The Revolutionary Constitution of 1836   18

2 Anglos, Indians, Germans, Mexicans, and Slaves
The Constitution of 1845: The Republic and Early Statehood, 1836–1854   34

3 Rebel Constitution
Secession and Confederacy, 1854–1865   62

4 Momentary Reversal
The Republican-Free Black Axis and Reconstruction   90

5 The Constitution of 1876, the Turn Inward, and the Rise of the Judiciary   127

6 The Birth of Conservative Modern Texas, 1891–1902   172

Epilogue
Looking Backward   206

Appendix: Theoretical Constitutional History   217

Notes   223

Index   299

Foreword

H. W. BRANDS

Americans are steeped in constitutionalism. We treat our Constitution as holy writ, the product of the "Miracle at Philadelphia," to use the title of Catherine Drinker Bowen's best-selling account of the convention of 1787, crafted by an "assembly of demigods," as Thomas Jefferson called the delegates to the convention. A sturdy tradition of constitutional interpretation probes the document for its original meaning, much as Biblical literalists scrutinize the text of their scriptures for God's own word.

No such respect is paid to the constitutions of the states, including the state of Texas. Few Texans know much about the Texas constitution, except that it gets amended quite a lot: some five hundred times so far. The federal Constitution has been amended but twenty-seven times and is nearly a century older.

Yet if the Texas constitution doesn't inspire the awe accorded the American Constitution, it should inspire interest. Where the US Constitution might be seen as the happy family of Tolstoy's famous formulation, the Texas constitution is the unhappy—and therefore more interesting—one. And family it is, for the current Texas constitution has five elder siblings. The rise and fall of the first five, and the evolution of the sixth—that of the half-thousand amendments—supply the historian scope for a tale of Tolstoyan proportions.

William Chriss invokes Aristotle and Hegel rather than Tolstoy, but the story he tells has the sweep of a Russian novel and is populated by characters as colorful as any of Tolstoy's. It is a tale indeed of war and peace, not to mention loyalty and betrayal, high virtue and base interest, passion and calculation.

For students of Texas history, this has intrinsic interest, for it is the origin story of the modern Lone Star State. None has told it better, in part because no previous author has combined the legal expertise and the historical sensibility of William Chriss. To switch metaphors from Tolstoy, Chriss at appropriate moments serves as the expert analyst in a pro football telecast, making sense of the play-by-play to viewers who by themselves see only the speed and violence on the field.

For students of American history, the story of Texas constitutionalism can serve as a counterfactual foray into what might have been for the nation as a whole. The American framers had no idea their work would last as long as it did. The Constitution of 1787 was the country's second try—the first being the Articles of Confederation—and they had every reason to think constitution-writing would be a recurring endeavor. Things didn't turn out that way, and the reader of Chriss's account of Texas, where for nearly two generations constitution-writing was the second job of prominent politicians and lawyers, can begin to understand why. America's early years were spared some of the turmoil that afflicted Texas during its era of constitution-writing. By the time the turmoil hit, the American Constitution was strong enough to stand it.

No one has ever characterized the framers of Texas' constitutions as demigods, nor has their work been called a miracle. They were flesh-and-blood humans, and they crafted imperfect charters for their state. But their collective accomplishment put Texas on the path to what it is today, and for that they deserve the historical attention and reckoning William Chriss gives them here.

Acknowledgments

The author expresses his appreciation to the Texas Supreme Court Historical Society for its support of this book, as well as to Steve Schiwetz and Shannon Morris, who provided inspiration and source materials, and to the following individuals who have read prior versions of this work and offered valuable insights and recommendations for its improvement: H. W. Brands, David Oshinsky, Willy Forbath, Robert Wooster, Walter Buenger, Manuel Gonzalez Oropeza, Bill Pugsley, Marilyn Duncan, David Furlow, H. W. Perry, and George Forgie.

Introduction

Political Identity and Constitutional Moments

What is a constitution? Attorneys see it as a law that limits a state's actions. For political scientists beginning with Plato and Aristotle, constitutions, as the literal meaning of the word implies, organize a community. Historians may take this a step further. Constitutions are important artifacts shedding light on the ideologies and thought worlds of those who produced them. Both the artifacts and the ideologies change over time. This book examines Texas' six constitutions as windows into the changing political ideologies of the Texans that adopted them. Its approach to these events is amalgamated from two schools of historical criticism: the theories of "otherness" (*alterité*) and of comparative constitutionalism. Scholars of "otherness" study the process by which societal elites define themselves by marginalizing, subordinating, and dominating competing minority groups as outlandish antagonists that must be suppressed to protect good social order. Comparative constitutionalists believe that constitutions reflect the ideologies and identities of those who produced them. Flashpoints of radical political and social change are usually "constitutional moments."[1] Because identities mutate over time, combining these two perspectives allows one to see how law, the ultimate tool of social control, solidifies a culture's dominant self-conception by othering minorities.[2]

Using this perspective, the chapters that follow analyze Texas' constitutional moments. First, I argue that constitutions should be understood in the

English tradition, literally those various legal and political arrangements that combine to "constitute" a society or state, of which a written constitutional document is only one, albeit an important one.[3] Second, this book sees Texas as an imagined community, an identity produced by ideological consensus among economic, cultural, and legal elites.[4] Third, its overarching perspective is that one important way in which Texan identity was imagined and held together was by defining those who were *not* members. To cite just one example, economic and political exigencies of the 1830s and 1840s quickly amalgamated slaves, Indians, and Mexicans as dangerously savage and interconnected enemies within Anglo-Texian consciousness. No historical account of nineteenth-century Texas should ignore this fundamental psychological and ideological reality.[5]

A prefatory word about terminology is in order. "Indian" is used as a collective term of convenience for the indigenous tribal peoples of Mexico, Texas, and the surrounding Southwest, although specific tribal names (in their Anglicized linguistic form) are used whenever feasible as more precise. "Texian" describes those Anglo settlers in Texas who joined the revolt against Mexico and/or ultimately pledged allegiance to the independent Republic of Texas. "Texan," the more modern usage, describes these and all other citizens of Texas after statehood in 1845. "Tejano" refers to Texas residents of Hispanic descent, regardless of the time frame. "Mexican," except when quoted from original sources that sometimes use the term as a pejorative for Hispanic Texans, refers to citizens of, or attributes of, the nation of Mexico.

With respect to Mexicans and Tejanos, this book begins by discussing their Spanish heritage, their encounters with Anglo colonists, and the Mexican government's initiatives to limit Anglo immigration and abolish slavery in Texas. In the case of slavery, the personal correspondence of influential Texians like Stephen F. Austin, William Barret Travis, and Ben Milam makes clear that, practically speaking, the protection of a slave economy was an important part of what they were fighting for. This is not to deny that Texian leaders, some more than others, truly believed the abstract republican ideology permeating their anti-Mexican pronouncements and policies, but they believed it only for white males and largely theoretically. It is also not to deny that the simple rejection of greater central control by Mexico was an important factor in the Texian revolt. But at the most visceral level, the Texians' deepest fear was that the newly centralized Mexican government would emancipate the thousands of slaves already in Texas and, if resisted by Anglo settlers, would ally with Tejanos, blacks, and Indians to expel them. Escaped

Political Identity and Constitutional Moments xv

slaves already had a long history of cooperation in maroon communities in Florida and the lower South, and Indian attacks on the Anglo settlements remained a real threat well into the 1840s and beyond. History, it must be remembered, is human, contingent, and complex. The truth of the past is elusive and usually multifaceted, involving a myriad of perspectives, causes, and effects. Even at its simplest level, each individual actor has conscious, subconscious, and often facially contradictory motivations. History does not lend itself to oversimplification or all-encompassing theories.[6]

Once the US–Mexican War of 1846–48 defused political or military threats from south of the border, northerners soon replaced Mexicans and Tejanos as the feared agitators of racial insurrection. This situation continued through Reconstruction and culminated during the period from the end of Reconstruction in 1873–74 to the early twentieth century when class consciousness began to overlay racial fears. In the crucible of industrialization, urbanization, and social upheaval, cooperation between African Americans and poor whites became the reigning cultural and political nightmare of the Anglo elite. The successful legal and political segregation of these two groups in the early twentieth century established a new dominant identity: conservative Anglo progressivism. That worldview, or elements of it, proved robust. Some aspects of this view have been dubbed "exclusive nationalism," "jingoism," or even "machismo," and some scholars use other names.[7] It is here often referred to as "conservative modern Texas." It is an ideology characterized by a view of the world that includes belief in (1) American national uniqueness and superiority, (2) Texan uniqueness and superiority as the ultimate expression of true Americanism, (3) Anglo-American cultural superiority, and (4) government regulation of domestic profit-seeking activity only to the extent necessary to promote growth and forestall significant redistribution of wealth or power within society.[8]

Another argument made in the pages that follow is that law is an important marker of social control and political identity. Thus, properly understood, legal history is also intellectual, cultural, and political history. It seems logical that nations and states tend to write new constitutions only at important crossroads in their sociopolitical development. Thus, not only are the "whats" of these constitutions indicative of the ideological identities that produced them, but their "whens" mark the moments when conflicts over culture and politics were most acute and most meaningful.

This book deals with how Anglo Texans went about creating their political identity over three quarters of a century, and the impact of those decisions. *Six*

Constitutions over Texas moves through the nineteenth century in segments that tie historical events to their contemporary constitutions and political ideologies. The prologue gives an overview of the constitutional history of Spanish and Mexican Texas prior to independence. Chapter 1 deals with the Texas Revolution and Constitution of 1836. Chapter 2 covers the Constitution of 1845 and the period from 1837 to the Secession crisis of the 1850s. Chapters 3 and 4 discuss Secession and Reconstruction, and their respective constitutions. Chapters 5 and 6 cover Redemption, the Constitution of 1876, and the emergence of modern Texas at the turn of the twentieth century.

Like many other new perspectives, looking at history and political identity through a constitutional lens tends to complicate the conventional view of Texas history.[9] Early-twentieth-century historians propagated the image of Anglo Texas as the heroic creation of libertarian idealism, the American founders in microcosm. While that conventional history of Texas accurately described much that was noble and altruistic, it sometimes obscured other equally important parts of the story.

Readers already familiar with Texas history may well wonder why this or that person, movement, or episode is not included in this account. The answer can only be the author's judgment that it was not central to the argument, was cumulative of other evidence, or was not relevant or damning enough to require being distinguished or otherwise explained away. And it is clear that the judgments of historians are subject to revision in this regard. But this book is not intended just for the large number of Texans interested in history, or even in western or American history. Rather, this should be considered a case study aimed at a much broader audience comprising all those who seek to know more about nationhood, borders, identity, ethnicity, political hegemony, and their primary instrumentalities, law and ideology.

One of this book's central questions is: How does republicanism coexist with a bigoted political or cultural identity? Finding an answer requires an exercise in "historical anthropology"—that is, an effort to reconstruct the thought-worlds of historical actors—and thus both their self-images and the myths and stories that resonated well enough with their contemporaries to make a difference. This is an approach associated with G. W. Hegel, among others. This approach argues that understanding societies involves analyzing their dominant ideologies and how they mutate over time. Hegel argued that change is characterized by a dialectic process where the dominant ideology of a time is challenged by an opposing view, and that this conflict produces a synthesis of the two, which then provokes a new opposing view and so on through time.[10]

The eventual victory of the modern conservative idea of Texas, one that melded South and West, and that favored pro-growth capitalism over civil rights or agrarian radicalism, was a result of a long period of what Hegel would call dialectics. In nineteenth-century Texas, the process was encapsulated in the fifty-year career of O. M. Roberts. Seldom, if ever, has a historical figure been so instrumental both in creating a sociopolitical reality, and then in formulating the mythology that would summarize that reality for future generations. But this twin feat is precisely what Oran Milo Roberts managed to accomplish as Texas' paradigmatic nineteenth-century prosecutor, politician, judge, orator, rebel, senator, "redeemer," governor, chief justice, university founder, and finally its historian. Indeed, part of *Six Constitutions* is a meta-history, the history of how a history (or a mythology) came about, and how it came to be so resilient.

From 1855 to his death in 1895, Roberts was "present at the creation" of every major political act of hegemony in Texas, or else defined it after the fact, or both. One vignette of the many at hand illustrates his influence. After chairing the Texas Secession Convention and raising a regiment to fight in the Civil War, Roberts was elected to the US Senate by Texas' first postwar legislature. However, when he traveled to Washington in 1866 to take his seat in the Senate, he was met by the old Texas unionist Andrew Jackson Hamilton in the halls of Congress, who explained to Roberts that he had made his journey in vain. Hamilton warned that, like the other members of the Texas delegation, Roberts would never be seated as a Congressman because of his unreconstructed ex-Confederate views. Roberts's indignant reply was, "Jack, let me just tell you something! Me and my sort will in the near future control the destiny of Texas." He was right. As the reporter of this incident, Texas Supreme Court Clerk Alexander Terrell observed, "In 1874, after the white race had, by the election of Governor (Richard) Coke, resumed control of the State Government, Judge Roberts was appointed Chief Justice of the Supreme Court," and a mere four years later, he was elected governor.[11]

Terrell's identification of Roberts with the political victory of the "white race" after Reconstruction was apt. Earlier in the same year that he was ineffectually elected a senator, Roberts had been an influential member of Texas' postwar constitutional convention, where he stated his avowed purpose to be the formation of "a white man's…Gov[ernment]t" that will "keep Sambo from the polls." In the twelve short years from 1866 to 1878, O. M. Roberts rose from disenfranchised secessionist pariah to governor of the state. By the 1890s, he had become its preeminent historian, founding the Texas State Historical Association. And his history of Texas, and those of his associates, dominated the twentieth-century imagination as much as his actions had dominated the politics of the century before.[12]

But the victory of men like Roberts did not create a static political order. Challenged by the new ideologies of populism and progressivism, Democrats' reassertion of control over Texas culminated in the rise of James Stephen Hogg in 1890 and of his friend, kingmaker E. M. House. House and his cohorts helped elect a string of probusiness, prosegregation, but "progressive" governors from 1898 to 1906. Hogg won acclaim as an antirailroad champion of the common man but soon accommodated domestic business interests. After the Democrat-Populist fusion of 1896, the Democratic Party found a formula for lasting hegemony, one learned from the cooption of populism into progressivism: first, adopt a platform of moderate economic reform for poor whites, delivering the minimum required to maintain their allegiance to the Democratic Party; second, continue to subsidize railroads, urbanization, and industrialization; and third, play upon fears of blacks, Hispanics, and northerners to galvanize a ruling consensus among whites of all economic classes.

The six constitutions of Texas from 1836 to 1900 mark the watershed moments in this process. They epitomize the political and intellectual currents of their times.

SIX CONSTITUTIONS OVER TEXAS

Prologue

Mexican Texas and Its Constitutions, 1821–1836

THE VAST MAJORITY OF THE FORTY-FOUR REVOLUTIONARIES WHO gathered on March 1, 1836, at the little Texas town of Washington on the Brazos were Anglos from the southern United States. Only Lorenzo de Zavala of Harrisburg and Juan Seguin and three of his fellow delegates from San Antonio were Hispanic. Jose Maria Jesus Carbajal, a close associate of Stephen Austin elected from Victoria, and "Incarnation" Bascus from Goliad, may have attended also, but the historical record on this point is unclear. The men who did attend unanimously declared Texas independent from Mexico. They then framed a constitution for their new nation. Before examining the proceedings of this convention, it is necessary to place the events of 1836 within the context of the events and constitutions that came before.[1]

The 1836 Texas War for Independence occurred toward the end of what historians call "the age of revolution." The American Revolution unleashed an ideology of liberation that toppled monarchies throughout the Western world. Within fifty years of 1776, successful revolutions established unprecedented representative governments all over the Western Hemisphere (Mexico, Argentina, Gran Colombia, Chile, Brazil, Haiti), as well as in France and Greece. The ideology of democracy also liberalized domestic politics in Great Britain, Spain, and other Western European nations.[2] Hence, it is only natural to think of the Texas Revolution as part of the inexorable march of

Western civilization toward freedom. This view has much to commend it and a substantial mythology supporting it. The politics and ideology of the Texas Revolution, and the series of constitutional conflicts leading up to it, tell a more complicated story.

The Texas Revolution did arise as a product of American liberalism and Manifest Destiny, but also as a reaction to the policies of the early Mexican Republic, particularly its exertion of greater central authority over the provinces. Most objectionable among those centralist policies were Mexican efforts to crackdown on Anglo immigration and abolish slavery. Rebellion became necessary not only to fight tyranny, but also to keep Texas' doors open to immigration by Anglo Protestants and their African American slaves. The revolution and the declaration of independence and constitution it produced were imbued from the beginning with overlapping and intertwined notions of idealized liberty, free migration in search of free land, and the fear of Mexicans as the likely instigators of a dreaded slave insurrection. In this connection, it is enlightening to view the revolution from the point of view of a Mexican government, itself revolutionary but also steeped in centuries of Spanish legal tradition.[3]

In 1837, a year after the Texian rebels declared their independence, Jose Maria Tornel, Mexican Secretary of War, lamented that the rebellion had been designed to do nothing more than create an Anglo republic with even more solicitude toward the institution of slavery than in the United States.[4] Early Texas historians acknowledged that slavery was an irritant in Texian-Mexican relations but concluded that "anxiety concerning slavery [does not appear to have] played any appreciable part in producing the Texas Revolution."[5] More elegant formulations by later historians added that although proslavery sentiment was important in Texas' negotiations with the Mexican government in the 1820s, and though proslavery agitation in Texas was fierce during the early 1830s, "if any single issue could be said to have set in motion the events leading to revolution it was the Law of April 6, 1830, which prohibited further immigration from the United States and called for the collection of customs duties and garrisoning of troops in Texas." That law resulted from the report of another Mexican official on the dire state of affairs in the frontier province, Manuel de Mier y Teran.[6]

Twenty-first-century scholars, however, argue that slavery was more deeply enmeshed in the Anglo-revolutionary consciousness than earlier generations of Texas historians may have believed. By 2015, even while acknowledging that Mexicans were inconsistent in their attitudes toward slavery, historian Andrew Torget was arguing that "struggles over slavery, indeed, became the defining point of contention between those in Texas and the Mexican government during the 1820s and early 1830s, disputes that eventually became enmeshed in larger battles over federalism that drove Mexico into civil war and Texas into rebellion."[7]

Mexican government records support this view. For example, over an eighteen-month period in 1828 and 1829, Mier y Teran led a government expedition into Texas at the request of Mexican President Guadalupe Victoria. The purpose of the mission was to gather information and to determine the boundary between Mexico's northernmost province and the neighboring United States. Mier y Teran was a distinguished visitor, a man of considerable influence in Mexico City. He fought for Mexican independence in 1811 with the early rebel leader José María Morelos and again with Agustín de Iturbide in 1821, the victorious general who ultimately ejected the Spaniards and took power in Mexico. Mier y Teran was elected to the Mexican Congress and became interested in Iturbide's plans for the colonization of the northern border provinces, including Austin's colony. When Iturbide abdicated, Mier y Teran, always a nimble politician, was appointed by the succeeding junta as a brigadier general and the minister of war. When one of the members of the junta, Guadalupe Victoria, became president, Mier y Teran was a logical choice to lead the expedition to survey and report on Texas. What he found there alarmed him. The farther north and east he traveled, the less loyal he found the Anglo colonists, who, as the American frontier approached, soon outnumbered Tejanos by ten to one. In the northeastern city of Nacogdoches, Mier y Teran reported that the colonists were moronic, disloyal, and prejudiced—disdainful of Mexicans and "judging that our republic consists only of ignorant mulattoes and Indians."[8]

Mier y Teran's indictment of illegal immigration and his demand for greater border security are ironically familiar to the modern reader:

> An antipathy has emerged between Mexicans and foreigners.... If timely measures are not taken, Tejas will pull down the entire federation. The foreigners grumble about the political disorganization on the frontier, and the Mexicans ... feel themselves pushed aside for the foreigners—(and) create complications on their part in order to deprive [the foreigners] of the right to vote and to exclude them.... Meanwhile, the new settlers continue to arrive.... Among the foreigners there are all kinds: fugitive criminals, honorable farmers, vagabonds and ne'erdo-wells, laborers, etc. They all go about with their constitution in their pocket, demanding their rights.[9]

As a result of Mier y Teran's report, the Mexican government was soon debating immigration policy. Mier y Teran complained in his diary that "[f]oreigners from every nation have this frontier of our federation open to them to enter without [fulfilling] the requirements of the law. This [country] is the asylum for fugitives from the neighboring republic. Foreign agriculturalists settle where it suits them, and they take over whatever land they desire without . . . approval and in defiance of the laws of colonization and of the rights of prior ownership."[10] Officials tasked with unraveling the "Texas problem" bemoaned the fact that Anglos were flooding into the province, many illegally, and that they would soon overwhelm the loyal Hispanic population. This was particularly vexing because, from the Mexican perspective, most of the Anglos were unable to speak the official language (Spanish), unfriendly to the official religion and culture (Catholicism), and bent on exploiting the native Tejano population, taking its land and usurping its traditions. Mexican attempts to reverse this situation by strengthening the central government and clamping down on Anglo immigration (including the African slaves that accompanied them) precipitated the Texas Revolution of 1835–36.[11]

Local autonomy, in and of itself, was another *casus belli*, and special consideration of Texas' unique circumstances and protection of colonists' private property were among the justifications given publicly by the Texian rebels. What is less clear is *why* local control was so important to Anglo Texians and *what* private property they were concerned about. *What* did they want to protect or promote locally that was so inconsistent with national Mexican policy that they would ultimately turn to armed rebellion over it? *What* special circumstances or unique domestic institutions entitled Texas' local government to special deference?[12]

Slavery, at least in large part, was the *what* and the *why*. Mier y Teran well understood this as early as 1829. In his view, "The rescinding of those [antislavery] laws is the object toward which the colonists direct their efforts (for separate statehood)."[13] Close examination of the political events and rhetoric that led up to the revolt bears out the contemporary testimony of Mier y Teran and others, as well as the conclusions of recent historians like Torget. Texians engaged in significant proslavery violence and agitation in the early 1830s and whether a Mexican threat to slavery and further Anglo immigration precipitated armed revolt is fundamentally a question of Texian attitudes.[14]

The best way to answer this attitudinal question is by reference to the Texians' own revolutionary rhetoric, including their declaration of independence and constitution, and the testimony of contemporary observers. This is not to argue for a literal interpretation of these proclamations, speeches, letters, and accounts based upon twenty-first-century definitions and understandings, however. Constitutions, declarations, and words in general are ambiguous in the absence of historical and ideological context. Many political speeches and assertions are at best symbolic, at worst euphemistic, and often incomplete. Hence that historical context, beginning with Texas' Spanish and Mexican legal heritage, must be understood.

Spanish Texas and Mexican Independence

Spain forcibly acquired Mexico (then called the province of New Spain) in the sixteenth century. This northernmost border province was known to the Spaniards as *Tejas* or "the New Kingdom of the Philippines." The empire's ambitions in North America were limited to the extraction of its natural resources and the religious conversion and exploitation of its Indigenous peoples. While Spanish soldiers were exerting control ever northward from Veracruz and Mexico City into the frontier area they called *Tejas*, the crown began formulating general laws to govern that expansion. The "New Laws" Charles V promulgated in 1542 formally abolished the enslavement of Indians in New Spain, while also phasing out the peonage labor system known as the *encomienda*.[15]

Thus, almost from the beginning, Spanish authorities were forced to confront the legal and moral issues arising from the enslavement of native and then African workers. In one camp were humanists, and in the other were Catholic scholastics like the Dominican friar Bartolomé de las Casas, who debated the humanist lawyer Juan Ginés de Sepúlveda in 1550 over whether Indians possessed souls. Protestants and humanist Catholics like Ginés de Sepúlveda argued that it was permissible to subjugate native peoples for the good of the Christian state. By 1708, however, scholastics like de las Casas held sway within the Roman church, and particularly in Spain the dominant attitude toward slavery was informed by their Thomistic condemnation of permanent bondage. As Professor Torget has noted, while African slavery was technically still legal in Mexico when Spanish authorities granted permission to Moses Austin to settle three hundred American families in Texas, "the implication (was) that Americans who came to New Spain would leave behind the legal traditions of the southern United States that protected the property rights of slaveholders ... although what that would mean in practice ... was yet to be determined." And as evidence of Spain's growing disdain for the institution, Torget points to the fact that fugitive slaves from Louisiana and

East Texas often fled westward to the Spanish for protection. One may assume they knew better than anyone where they were likely to be liberally treated.[16]

Spanish law, while not absolutely prohibiting all slavery, did reflect this more liberal ideology. As Professor Gilbert Din has remarked in the context of his study of slavery laws in Spanish Louisiana, "Spanish legal tradition held that slavery was against natural reason and that slaves were human beings who possessed rights as well as obligations . . . the Spaniards long had permitted slaves to purchase their freedom, and that practice became general throughout the Spanish empire by 1708. Moreover, the government allowed slaves to engage in *coartacion*, or self-purchase, over a period of time. Overall Spanish law came down strongly on the side of slaves who sought freedom and against their masters who tried to prevent it."[17]

While many of these imperial laws applied only to Indian workers and not to slaves imported from Africa and while enforcement of all such laws was spotty, especially in frontier regions, Spain's political attitude, informed by its ideological and theological tradition, was less strident and authoritarian than the humanistic/Hobbesian tradition of conquest by *raison d'etat* inherited by the Anglo-Dutch Protestants who invaded the Americas further north.[18]

Soon Mexican independence loosed an even more radical spirit tinged with ideas from the recent French revolution and influenced by the South American peasant revolts led by Simon Bolivar in the early 1800s. Mexican revolutionaries, some imbued with Catholic antislavery ideology, and others with the antichurch egalitarianism found among many French and South American revolutionaries, radicalized the relative liberalism of Spain's legal code and her church. Father Miguel Hidalgo, Mexico's initial revolutionary leader, publicly proclaimed the abolition of slavery from the outset in 1810, as did his successor José María Morelos in 1813. Although neither of these proclamations became settled law, and although slavery persisted among some Tejanos and in some areas of Mexico besides Texas, elements of the Catholic Church in the new world had taken de la Casas's arguments for the brotherhood of all men to their logical extreme. The fledgling Mexican government would soon have to balance its need to populate the remote province of Texas against growing abolitionist sentiment among Spanish-speaking Catholics and radicals. Upon ejecting the Spaniards in 1821, the Mexican government continued to encourage immigration by Anglo-American Protestant slaveholders, but shortly thereafter it also began promulgating anti-slavery decrees. This mercurial mix of policies ensured that any future disputes over slavery in the new country's northernmost frontier would carry nationalist, ethnic, and religious overtones.[19]

Almost immediately upon coming to Texas to colonize the land his family was granted around the Colorado River, Stephen F. Austin found it necessary to plead with the Mexican government to allow his émigrés to keep their slaves. He volunteered that he had slaves in his own household and made clear to the Mexican Congress that other Anglo settlers intended to bring their slaves with them as well. Austin's attempts to insulate Texas from Mexican attacks upon Anglo immigration and the institution of slavery continued for more than ten years and formed the central theme of his correspondence with the Mexican government. As a slaveholding Southern empresario, Austin had good reason for concern. Immigration and slavery were his biggest problems. Colonization laws were constantly being amended, and from 1821 until Texas independence, the Mexican government, in fits and starts, also repeatedly tried to enact into law its abolitionist revolutionary heritage.[20]

Another important aspect of Spanish dominion (and later Mexican governance) was the enmeshment between the state and the Catholic Church. While religious differences between protestant Texians and Mexican Catholics caused Austin some initial worry, slavery soon caused him more, although the two issues were linked. Given the intensely secular perspective of the Anglo-Texian rebels and of the constitution they would adopt, the religious rhetoric that entered into Texas revolutionary propaganda was colored by the long-standing ethno-religious dispute over slavery and exploitation.[21] Indeed, religion per se appears to have had very little to do with the Texas Revolution, in that there was no significant religious violence, nor were there significant protests of the conversion to Catholicism nominally required of Texian colonists. In fact, the requirement was hardly ever enforced in any meaningful way.[22] While the Texas Declaration of Independence does contain references to Catholic tyranny (and these are important for subtler reasons), the length of time the nominal requirement of Catholicism existed without any protest and the lack of religious arguments in other revolutionary rhetoric demonstrate that the Declaration's reference was either merely incendiary window dressing or, more likely, a euphemism for something else. That subtler something else, given the ideological differences between the Mexican Catholic government and its Anglo-Protestant colonists, was probably slavery.[23]

Mexican Rule: Petitions and State Constitutions, 1821–1835

The 1836 Independence Convention at Washington-on-the Brazos was but the last of many conventions of Texians and Tejanos disgruntled by Mexican rule. From the Mexican perspective, however, that same 1836 convention also marked the end of another series of meetings, Mexican constitutional conventions and congressional sessions attempting to organize the new nation of Mexico and its border province of Texas.

Often, Mexican national legislation differentially impacted Texas. For example, what prompted Austin's very first protest to the central government was an 1822 bill introduced in the Mexican Congress prohibiting any trade or commerce in slaves and declaring that slave children born in Mexico would automatically become free at age fourteen. Before the bill could be enacted into law, Mexican president Agustin de Iturbide staged his coup. To Austin's chagrin, the new junta soon promulgated a similar law, the imperial colonization law of January 4, 1823, providing that "there shall not be permitted after the promulgation of this law, either purchase or sale of slaves that may be introduced into the empire. The children of such slaves, who are born within the empire, shall be free at fourteen years of age." In February of 1823, Iturbide was deposed, and a constitutional (*constituyente*) congress met in Mexico City later that year. On July 13, 1824, it published a new decree prohibiting the slave trade altogether. Another colonization law, passed by the Mexican national congress in 1825, left the prior decrees in effect, expressly stating that with respect to slavery, the colonists must subject themselves "to existing laws and those that might be passed in the future." This meant no more importation of slaves and gradual emancipation of those already present. Abolitionist measures were often included within legislative acts concerned with colonization and immigration. Clearly, the central government saw the two issues as intertwined, and Texians came to do so as well.[24]

With the connivance of most local authorities, Mexican, Tejano, and colonist, the Texians interpreted the latest antislavery law as nothing more than a ban on the international slave trade, similar to that authorized by the United States Constitution as of 1808. Immigrants kept bringing their slaves to Texas, the intra-Texas buying and selling of slaves continued, and few if any slaves were manumitted upon reaching age fourteen. But Austin and his slave-owning colonists knew that their strained legal interpretation and precarious economic position depended on the national authorities turning a blind eye.[25]

Fortunately for the colonists, the new national constitution would charter a weak and decentralized government. Six months after issuing the July 13, 1824, decree banning the slave trade, the same "constitutive congress" promulgated the 1824 *Federal Constitution of the United Mexican States*. That constitution, within its four corners, did not mention slavery one way or the other. The congress was presided over by the prominent liberal politician Lorenzo de Zavala, and it declared "a popular representative and federal republic" composed of four territories and nineteen strong and sovereign states, including the state of "Coahuila y Texas." That modern national republic "divided into the legislative, executive and judicial powers," nevertheless continued the Spanish practice of enshrining as its national religion "the Roman Catholic and Apostolic" and prohibiting "the exercise of any other." Following the American model, however, the new Mexican constitution provided for a bicameral national legislature with the lower house composed of deputies elected from districts of equal population and with a senate "of two senators from each state, elected by an absolute majority of the legislature of each state, one half of their number to be renewed every two years." A president and vice-president of at least thirty-five years of age and elected to a four-year term by a process similar to the American electoral college would exert the ultimate executive authority.[26]

The judicial branch comprised a Supreme Court and circuit and district courts. Supreme Court justices were required to be "instructed in the science of law" and were elected for life by a majority vote of the state legislatures by a method similar to the election of the president and vice president. Their appellate and original jurisdiction was analogous to that of the US Supreme Court. Lower court judges were appointed for life by the president from a list of three candidates "skilled in law" submitted by the Supreme Court.[27] The constitution prohibited ex-post-facto laws, arbitrary searches and seizures, self-incrimination, cruel and unusual punishment (torture), and detention without indictment. It is little wonder that Anglo rebels would, in the 1830s, come to trumpet the spirit and constitution of 1824. Modern commentators attribute the liberality of its provisions not only to the work of de Zavala, but also to the continuing influence of the Spanish liberal politician Miguel Ramos Arizpe, "the Father of Mexican federalism."[28]

Titles VI and VII of the 1824 constitution imposed several obligations upon the constituent states, including organizing their own republican governments of separated powers. On May 7th, and while the Mexican Constituent Congress was writing the new national constitution, it issued a decree formally establishing the State of Coahuila y Texas and providing for the election of its state congress. But it was not until August 15, 1824, that the newly created Constituent Congress of Coahuila y Texas assembled. It remained in session from 1824 to 1827. One article proposed for the new state constitution by this congress would have immediately abolished slavery under the promise of indemnifying owners. Austin soon learned of this amendment and dispatched his brother, Brown Austin, to Mexico to lobby the legislature to rescind this provision. Brown Austin brought with him petitions from his brother and other local officials pleading for the protection of slavery.[29]

As a result of the efforts of the Austin brothers and the Mexican need for labor and Indian protection on the northern frontier, the 1827 constitution finally adopted for the state of Coahuila y Texas dropped the abolition plan, opting for a compromise article on slavery. Article 13 of the constitution provided, "From and after the promulgation of the constitution in the capital of each district, no one shall be born a slave in the state, and after six months the introduction of slaves under any pretext shall not be permitted." Austin's immediate response was to encourage immigrants to bring their slaves to Texas right away in order to come within the six-month window allowed by law.[30]

In other respects as well, the 1827 Coahuila-Texas constitution showed solicitude toward Texian interests. Its second article trumpeted its independence from "the other Mexican United States, and of every other power whatsoever." The citizenry included "anyone now legally established in the state," each of whom enjoyed the rights of free speech, "liberty, security, property and equality." However, these rights could be suspended by the government for "moral or physical disability," for "being debtor to the public funds," for being unemployed and idle, or "for not being able to read and write." Among Mexican states, only Coahuila y Texas provided for trial by jury, the ownership of slaves (albeit not their importation), and tolerance of Anglo-American language and religion.[31]

In spite of these obvious accommodations to their traditions, the flood of Anglo colonists Austin hoped for did not come. Meanwhile, as they had done before, Texians responded to this state constitution's antislavery article by circumventing its application. They simply converted their newly born or imported slaves into indentured servants for long terms of years. In most instances, they also created terms of indenture that were so harsh that the servant would remain deeply in debt to his master even at the end of the initial term of servitude, which would then inevitably result in another long term of indenture. The state government in Saltillo succumbed to pressure from Texians and in 1828 actually legitimized such contracts as long as they were made outside of Texas with black "servants" then brought into the state. These accommodations, however, still depended upon a significant degree of local autonomy. Local officials would have to be lenient about the degree of proof needed to show that such "contracts" had been entered into in other countries with "free" blacks. Moreover, a strong central government might easily overrule the state legislature and bring Coahuila-Texas into accord with the laws and customs of her sister Mexican states.[32]

Events soon demonstrated the precariousness of Texian slave owners' labor arrangements. On September 15, 1829, a new president, Vicente Guerrero, influenced by Manuel de Mier y Teran's report and by José María Tornel, the government official who would write eight years later that slavery was the primary cause of the Texas Revolution, issued a summary executive decree emancipating every slave within the territorial limits of Mexico. Austin and the other Anglo colonists again panicked. They demanded that their state officials request an exemption for Texas from the national decree. The governor of Coahuila y Texas, J. M. Viesca, made such an appeal to President Guerrero on November 14, 1829. His argument was that the economic prosperity of the northern province of Texas required the institution of slavery—in other words, that the situation in Texas was *unique*, demanding *unique institutions*.[33]

As a further indication of the consternation caused by this 1829 decree, Austin felt it essential to keep the news secret. It nonetheless leaked out to some prominent planters. On November 10, John Durst of Nacogdoches pleaded with Austin in a personal letter, "In the name of God what shall we do—for God's sake advise me on the subject by return mail—we are ruined forever should this measure be adopted." Durst was frantic. Austin encouraged him to remain calm and not to publicize the matter until Austin had an opportunity to address it with Mexican authorities in terms of an exemption for the *unique circumstances* in Texas. The exact wording of Austin's response was telling, and it provides the key to understanding much of the euphemistic libertarian rhetoric of the revolution six years later:

> What the people of Texas have to do, is to represent to the government, through the *ayuntamientos* (local town councils) or some other channel, in a very respectful manner; that agreeable to the constitution, and the colonization laws *all* their property is guaranteed to them without exception in the most solemn and sacred manner—That they brought their slave property into the country and have retained it here under the faith of that guarantee . . . that they have taken an oath to defend the constitution and are bound to do so. That the constitution of the state expressly recognizes the right of property in slaves by allowing six months after its publication for their introduction to the state. . . .

They will defend it, and with it, their property.... If he should finally be compelled to publish and circulate it, the *ayuntamientos* must then take an unanimous, firm, and constitutional stand. The people will unanimously support them (emphasis original).[34]

When Austin spoke of "property" and "property rights" in 1829, he was talking chiefly about slaves. When he wrote of the guarantees of the Mexican Constitution of 1824 and the previous colonization laws, he meant the guarantee of local autonomy in Texas that protected Anglo immigration and Anglo institutions, jury trial and slavery chief among them.[35] Bending to the pleas of Governor Viesca, on December 2, 1829, President Guerrero agreed to exempt Texas from his 1829 emancipation proclamation, known as the "Guerrero Decree." Thus the "defense of constitutional liberty" in aid of property rights alluded to by Austin became unnecessary. For the time being, the panic was defused.[36]

Meanwhile, Austin vacillated on a number of issues, including statehood, independence, and war. He was a pragmatist, eager to do whatever the prosperity of Texas (and his colony) might require. Although he flirted briefly with gradual abolition as a solution to the increasing friction with the central government over slavery, he quickly returned to being the institution's most influential defender. Free soil would not work in Texas. As shown by his correspondence with Durst, Austin did not mince words in sounding the alarm with Mexican authorities over what would happen if their national emancipation proclamation, their Guerrero Decree, took hold in Texas.[37]

It was in this context that the Mexican government promulgated the new colonization law of April 6, 1830, cited by historians as the proximate cause of the Texas Revolution. Although historians have rightly emphasized the provisions in the law that prohibited further immigration into Texas from the United States and that allowed the quartering of troops in Texas to curtail smuggling and ensure the collection of customs duties, two important aspects of the law have received less attention. First, it also provided that existing laws against introducing more slaves into the colony were to be "strictly enforced." Second, one of the primary smuggling activities along the Texas coast involved human cargo, slaves. Texians were not only circumventing the laws by their unique form of indentured servitude, but several Texians who would become prominent leaders in the revolution were involved in the illegal importation of, and trade in, slaves. These included Benjamin Fort Smith, James W. Fannin, Monroe Edwards, and Sterling McNeil. Meanwhile, the major *entrepots* of Galveston and Anahuac/Liberty became hotbeds of proslavery, anti-Mexican sentiment. The pressure from the Mexican government continued beyond the law of April 6, 1830. In 1832, the Coahuila-Texas state legislature in Saltillo cracked down on the indentured servitude ruse by setting a ten-year limitation on the length of all labor contracts.[38]

Between 1830 and 1832, Anglo immigrants began flooding into Texas with their "indentured servants" and without much regard for the April 6, 1830, law.[39] Tempers soon boiled over. In June 1832, William Barret Travis led proslavery agitation against the Mexican customs collector for the port of Anahuac, John D. Bradburn. Bradburn had refused to return two runaway slaves from Louisiana to their rightful owners. Travis and Patrick H. Jack demanded that the slaves be returned to their masters and threatened that an armed group of Americans would invade Anahuac for the purpose of protecting their property rights. Bradburn had Travis and Jack arrested, precipitating a riot in June 1832 where Anglo colonists formed a "vigilance committee" and demanded their release. Bradburn refused and the vigilance committee declared itself a militia. John Austin then led the group's march to San Felipe to retrieve four cannons, and he sent messages to Brazoria for additional cannons to assist in an assault on the customs house. Along the way, the colonists learned of a "liberal" coup led by General Antonio Lopez de Santa Anna that promised to reinstate the Constitution of 1824. The colonists then adopted the Turtle Bayou Resolutions, declaring for Santa Anna in the hope he would return matters to their pre-1829 status. They were ultimately to be disappointed, but for the time being, they returned reinforced to Anahuac and compelled the Mexican garrison to withdraw under the promise of safe conduct to Matamoros. According to Bradburn's biographer, one of the primary reasons for Anglo dislike of Bradburn, beyond his treatment of these particular runaways, was "his enforcement of the national law against slavery.... Bradburn maintained that the exceptions granted to Austin's colony regarding slavery were not in effect outside his empresario grant; therefore Liberty and Anahuac, being in the coastal reserve, were subject to the law as written, which declared after 1829 slavery was not permitted anywhere in the republic."[40]

Bradburn knew very well why he was unpopular and he knew the psychological nexus for Texians between slavery, customs duties, and the immigration law of 1830. Anglo protests of Spanish and Mexican asylum given to fugitive slaves were nothing new. By the late 1810s, according to Professor Torget, "a steady stream of enslaved people ... fled into Texas as refugees from the U.S. cotton frontier," and on the elderly Moses Austin's first trip to Texas in 1820, he was joined by James Kirkham, whose reason for making the trip was to ask the Spanish governor for the return of three fugitive slaves.[41]

After fleeing to New Orleans, Customs Collector Bradburn set about writing a report of the entire series of incidents. In it, he alleged that Texians at Anahuac already had independence as their aim by 1831, and that upon his undertaking of his duties as customs agent, "it became necessary to name a commissioner at that port (Brazoria) to enforce the law of April 6, 1830, and also to keep an eye on the arrival of foreigners *and slaves*" (emphasis added). Again, the issues of immigration control and slavery were linked. He reported to his superiors that "one other matter which caused me much trouble and brought down the hatred of the community against me was the protection I gave to two escaped slaves." The Anglos "made much of this pretext to rise in arms against the garrison in Anahuac."[42]

Anglo colonists then held an October 1832 convention that may have promulgated some type of Texian proclamation demanding the protection of slavery, although a record of it does not survive. They also called together another convention in April 1833. The upshot of this latter meeting was quasi-official Texian sentiment for repeal of the 1830 immigration/slavery law and for separating Texas and Coahuila as independent states within Mexico. Austin penned an address to the 1833 convention at its convocation. In it, he repeated the themes that "constitutional guarantees . . . (had been dangerously) merged for the time being in military power" and that "the unnatural annexation of what was formerly the province of Texas to Coahuila . . . has forced upon the people of Texas a system of laws which they do not understand and which cannot be administered . . . to suit their condition or supply their wants."[43]

The 1833 convention went forward to propose a constitution for the new independent state of Texas written by a committee chaired by Sam Houston.[44] The convention nominated Austin to carry this plea for statehood to the Mexican capital. This proposed state constitution makes only one direct reference to slavery, that "bonded servants" and "others not liable to taxation" were not to be considered citizens. The remainder of the document reads like a paraphrase of the US Bill of Rights and a defense of the common law tradition and its prohibitions on bills of attainder, warrantless searches, suspensions of habeas corpus, and other failures of due process. But a letter Austin wrote on his journey to Mexico City to lobby for the new state constitution again confirmed that slavery was uppermost in the minds of the members of the convention that produced it. The Anahuac customs agent John Bradburn was prescient, not paranoid. Stephen Austin unburdened himself to his cousin

Henry Austin: "The sum and substance of the whole matter is that Texas must have a state government. Nothing else will quiet this country or give any security to persons or *property* for then we can take a firm stand for *rights* that were respectfully petitioned for and unjustly detained" (emphasis added).

Less than sixty days later, he wrote another letter to Wiley Martin explaining the property and rights that needed securing: "Texas must be a slave country. Circumstances and unavoidable necessity compel it. It is the wish of the people there, and it is my duty to do all I can, prudently, in favor of it. I will do so."[45]

The Texians' petition for statehood was rebuffed, and before Austin could return from his unsuccessful mission to Mexico, he was arrested in Saltillo. Shortly after Austin's arrest, a civil war erupted within the state of Coahuila. The legislature attempted to move the capital from Saltillo to Monclova, and as a result, Saltillo accused the Monclova faction of disloyalty to Santa Anna and called in the president and his army. The instability of the government caused the San Antonio *ayuntamiento*, under the leadership of Juan Seguin, to call a meeting for November 15, 1834, with other colonists from Nacogdoches and Brazoria. Oddly, the firebrands Travis and Jack, members of the central committee of this 1834 convention, opposed the notion of taking advantage of the current difficulties to declare that Coahuila and Texas had been dissolved into separate states by civil war. They may have been persuaded by Austin's continual entreaties from prison in favor of conciliation with the central government. It was in Austin's best interest to quell any further uprising in Texas and to convince the Mexican authorities that he was not a traitor. It is also possible that at this point and in San Antonio, the influence of Tejanos less enthusiastic for war still held sway. Even without Texian participation though, the civil war continued. The national government dispatched an army under General Perfecto de Cos to chastise the rump legislature still operating in Monclova under its rump governor, Augustine Viesca, the Texians' old friend. Soon, Santa Anna gave Cos command of the entire eastern portion of Mexico. Cos then delegated command of Texas to Colonel Domingo de Ugartechea. Ugartachea dispatched Captain Antonio Tenorio in January of 1835 to forcibly reopen the customs house at Anahuac. Anahuac, the location of the 1832 proslavery violence, continued to be a sore spot for the central government. Moreover, in April of the same year, Tenorio informed General Cos by dispatch that the Alabama and Coushatta Indians near Anahuac had complained that Anglo settlers were infringing upon the lands guaranteed to them by the Mexican government three years before. Tenorio asked Cos to stop "any persons from depriving these natives of the right they have acquired to their lands by their constant labor."[46]

General Cos heeded Tenorio's appeal and the Mexican Army expelled Anglo settlers from Alabama-Coushatta lands in April 1835. Although it is unknown to what extent this incident further incited the Texians, it was only two months later that they once again protested the installation of the Mexican customs inspector. At a meeting where Travis was present, a resolution was adopted demanding the removal of Tenorio's troops from Anahuac. Travis then began enlisting volunteers to actually expel the Mexican Army. On June 29, 1835, at the head of a small force with one cannon, he besieged the customs house, demanding its capitulation. Captain Tenorio surrendered his arms and retreated.[47] In the same year of 1835, Santa Anna's Mexican Congress repealed the Constitution of 1824 and centralized the government, converting what had been states into mere provinces. This action stoked the radicalism of firebrand Anglo colonists like Travis, Bowie, and Fannin, and it led more moderate men to believe that the conciliation urged by Austin was impossible.[48]

Travis's 1835 letters prove the extent to which he and his militia considered Mexican "tyranny," Anglo "rights," and slavery connected. He wrote several letters to the cautious and influential David G. Burnet throughout 1835. These shed much light on his views, as well as those of Burnet, Austin, and others. On February 6th he wrote Burnet that "many immigrants are coming into the country. A few negroes also, I understand have been landed on the coast. *But we disagree on this subject*" (emphasis added). Burnet was an immigrant to Texas from southern Ohio, a moderately antislavery man, slow to embrace the independence movement. He strongly opposed the slave trade, but was not an abolitionist, as this letter and other documents show. Travis, on the other hand, had been agitating against the central government since 1832, and protecting slavery gave him his primary justification. Its connection with constitutional safeguards, property rights, and the immigration law of 1830 is unmistakable. He soon wrote Burnet again:

> You have heard of the piracies and robberies committed by the dread Montezuma upon the property of our citizens! It is too much to have politically—it will not be borne.... I read in a No. of the *Sol* published in Mexico, that a project has been introduced in the Genl. Congress *to free all slaves in the Republic—to abolish the article of the state constitution of Coahuila y Texas, declaring colonists as citizens and abrogating that*

> article of the Colonization Law which grants the rights of naturalized citizens as Colonists. These are alarming circumstances. The law of the 6th of April is again to be renewed—indeed we stand or fall now by ourselves. I hope we may be united. The political chief Dr. Miller recommends a convention of the whole people, by means of delegates to devise measures of safety—what do you think of it? (emphasis added)[49]

It was just days after the June 1835 hostilities in Anahuac that Ben Milam, encamped with a Texian militia besieging Mexican-held San Antonio de Bexar, called the Texians to attack the town to defend their "domestic institutions" from the invading Mexican army. Writing a hundred miles west of Travis's location in Anahuac, Milam felt the same sense of alarm in describing Mexican intentions: "Their intention is to gain the friendship of the different tribes of Indians; and, if possible, *to get the slaves to revolt*" (emphasis added).

The Matagorda Safety Committee voiced the same concerns: "Being advised that danger is apprehended from the slave population on the Brazos, the Committee recommends . . . adoption of prompt measures to prevent in our section both alarm and danger."[50] Three months later on October 2nd and several leagues to the west, Gonzales militiamen fired the first shots of the Texas Revolution and repulsed a Mexican cavalry detachment sent by General Cos to retrieve two cannons previously provided to the settlers for defense against Indian attack. The psychological connection between Indians, slaves, and the Mexican authorities who threatened to loose their wrath upon the Anglo-Texians' precarious local hegemony was palpable.

1

The Revolutionary Constitution of 1836

IN 1834, TEXAS WAS ALREADY DIVIDED INTO TWO POLITICAL PARTIES. One, identified with Burnet and Austin, continued to desire conciliation with Mexico. Austin remained in this camp until his imprisonment and the events of 1834 and 1835 dampened his pacifism. The other party, the "war party," associated with Travis, James Fannin, James Bowie, and eventually Sam Houston, suspected as early as 1832 or 1833 that circumstances would soon be ripe to demand total independence. Sentiment for independence had been growing since the conflicts over slavery of 1832 and the public meetings of 1832 and 1833. Ultimately, the war party would win over many doves after the Battle of Gonzales and a convention in November 1835 at Washington on the Brazos. This convention came to be known as the "Consultation" or "*Consultado.*" Six weeks before it began to meet, Austin arrived in Texas, having finally been released from prison. His imprisonment changed his view of the Mexican government. He had begun to suspect that Travis might be right when he wrote that he had become "more and more convinced every day of the utter futility of our friend Austin's favorite plan of hanging on to Mexico."[1]

By the time of the *Consultado*, it was clear there would probably be war in Texas for independence from Mexico. Hostilities had already begun in Gonzales and San Antonio, and volunteers were in the field. Austin held titular command of the largest group, the brigade laying siege to San Antonio. In mid-November, the *Consultado* passed the "Organic Law" organizing a provisional government and the Texian militia, as well as a resolution providing for the recruitment of a regular army. The provisional government was headed by a council presided over by the war-hawk Henry Smith, who was elected governor over the more moderate Stephen Austin by a narrow margin. Sam Houston was elected major general and given overall command of the new Texas Army. On November 24, 1835, the *Consultado* also called for fielding a three-company battalion of fifty-six mounted scouts to be called the Texas Rangers. In December, although still declaring loyalty to the abrogated Mexican Constitution of 1824, the Council, through Governor Smith, called elections on February 1st to choose delegates for an independence convention to be held at Washington-on-the-Brazos on March 1st.[2]

The peace party, however, continued to hold back, even after Austin changed his opinion. For example, as late as January 1836, Burnet and his recalcitrant partisans were still being importuned by Austin to join the independence project. Burnet and others finally capitulated in the face of the Texians' December capture of San Antonio, and this caused the die to be irrevocably cast. Santa Anna invaded Texas the following spring.[3]

Understanding the causes of the revolution requires carefully analyzing the conventions and other constitutive acts leading up to it. The convention of 1833 followed the convention of 1832 that grew out of the Anahuac slavery agitation. The colonists' 1832 petition requested the repeal of Article 11 of the April 6, 1830, Immigration Law; the organization of local militia to combat Indian attacks; and most importantly that Texas be separated from Coahuila as its own state. Article 11 of the 1830 Immigration Law was the section prohibiting further immigration into Texas from the United States. Article 10, which was not directly addressed by the convention, was the section that reemphasized the validity of previous restrictions on slavery in Texas. It seems odd that the 1832 convention, called as a direct result of the proslavery agitation at Anahuac, did not mention this article specifically. However, in detailing the reasons for a break from Coahuila, the convention did express the belief "that separation from Coahuila would be to the mutual advantage of the two provinces and to the ultimate interest of the Republic. Dissimilarity of Coahuila and Texas in soil, climate, and productions, and inequality of representation rendered suitable legislation for the needs of Texas impossible." Given the pretext for the violent events in Anahuac earlier that year, there is good reason to suspect that the primary "dissimilarity" between Coahuila and Texas was the institution of slavery, and the "suitable legislation" lacking was the permanent legalization of slavery. Proslavery rhetoric was often explicitly based upon the notion of slaves as property, and on the belief that a fundamental right of free citizens was the protection of their "property." And polemics urging protection of Southern society's "domestic institutions" almost always referred to slavery because it was slavery more than anything else that made the South unique.[4]

The 1833 convention was just as euphemistic, albeit somewhat more forceful, on the issue of slavery. The convention met in April of 1833, and there is no journal of its proceedings. More than 70 percent of the delegates to this second convention had not been present at the first. One of these was Sam Houston. The convention made the same basic protests as in 1832, but this time a constitution was drafted for the new independent state of Texas. Strikingly American in structure, and like the 1824 Mexican constitution and the 1827 constitution of Coahuila y Texas, it included such features as a bicameral legislature and judges elected by that legislature. The constitution protected the domestic institutions within Texas from interference by the central government. However, it also condemned the African slave trade in a provision predictably urged by David Burnet. Although the proposed constitution did not use the word "slavery," Austin's contemporaneous letter in support of Texas statehood to his cousin Henry Austin clearly had: "Texas must be a slave country."[5]

The war party, at this point, was attempting to do two things: maximize local Anglo authority *within* the Mexican Republic, and maximize Anglo and Tejano support for this initiative. Hence it would make little political sense to specifically mention slavery in 1833, since doing so would dampen any hope of the petition for separate state government being granted and would also alienate any antislavery Tejanos and northern Anglos like Burnet. Once Burnet and others like him had signed on for the independence project, the Texians had less need for rhetorical restraint and their views on slavery were less veiled, but in 1833 the need for cohesion remained paramount. Burnet's biographer argues that he was elected president in the subsequent convention of March of 1836 because his family had been prominent in the United States "for generations" and the delegates thought this would help them win recognition and aid from the United States. It is also possible he bargained for the job by supporting independence, or more likely, he was also chosen, in part, because of his well-known reluctance to declare war, thus emphasizing the growing uniformity of sentiment for independence and camouflaging the war party's proslavery agenda. Burnet was not perceived as a proslavery man, and his election might help mollify America's northern antislavery congressmen, who were disposed to reject any dealings with an independent proslavery Texas.[6]

The Declaration of Independence

The Council's call for an Independence Convention in 1836 was sanctioned by yet another ad hoc public meeting of Texians, this one held at Columbia on the Brazos on December 25, 1835. At Columbia, Dr. Anson Jones, later to serve as the last president of the independent Republic of Texas, presented a series of resolutions demanding Texas independence and joining the Council's call for election of delegates to a revolutionary convention in the spring. While posterity has lost part of the preamble of this protodeclaration of independence, the part that survived complained of the Mexican government "driving us from Texas, and confiscating our lands and property." This fragment also made specific laudatory reference to the decentralized system of government set forth in the constitution of 1824. Hence, the 1835 Columbia Declaration contained the dual characteristics of Texian rhetoric justifying independence: the protection of private property from government seizure and the necessity for local autonomy. This is not to deny that the restrictions on immigration in the 1830 law jeopardized the conditional land grants of Austin, Milam, and the other empresarios, and by theoretical implication even the titles of their subgrantees. Certainly, such insecurity was part of the demand for protection of private property, but it lacked the visceral strength of the fear of a Spanish-sponsored, Indian-aided slave insurrection. Fear of ethnic violence imbued economic self-interest with the kind of limbic panic that could spread far more broadly and urgently throughout the culture.[7]

And the Mexicans kept irritating this psychological sore spot. For example, in the same year of 1835, the "rump legislature" at Montclova was considering yet another abolitionist law intended for application throughout Coahuila and Texas. History records the response of Travis, who called the possibility of such a law one of the "alarming circumstances" produced by "a plundering, robbing, autocratical, aristocratical, jumbled-up government which is in fact no government at all . . . there is no security for life, liberty, or property."[8] This strange belief that centralization of the abolitionist national government would ironically only produce chaos reappeared in the 1836 Declaration of Independence. The nature of the chaos feared was transparent. As early as

June of 1835, Texian firebrands were warning that the expedition of General Cos and his lieutenant, Ugartechea, would result in an army plot "to compel you to liberate your slaves."[9]

This more open discussion of the slavery question continued throughout 1836. In the heat of the revolution, prominent war party leader William H. Wharton wrote his own Texian version of the "Federalist Papers" under the pseudonym Curtius. In Number Four of this series of works, he specifically accused the Mexican government of "a sickly philanthropy worthy of the abolitionists," which led the Mexican government to "contrary to justice, and to law, intermeddle with our slave population."[10]

On March 1st, after a norther had blown into Washington-on-the-Brazos the previous night, the shivering delegates who had been elected in February finally gathered in an unfinished wooden house and elected Richard Ellis their president. Texas' official Declaration of Independence from Mexico was adopted the very next day. This document combined libertarian echoes of the Spirit of 1776 with negative racial and cultural stereotypes applied to Mexicans. The Declaration oscillated between Locke's theories of social compact and natural rights on one hand, and notions of Anglo-Protestant cultural superiority on the other, including condemnations of Catholic priests as "the eternal enemies of civil liberty, the ever ready minions of power and the usual instruments of tyrants." To reemphasize the connection between Catholicism and tyranny, the colonists added that they would not submit to "the most intolerable of all tyranny, the combined despotism of the sword and the priesthood."[11]

It was an odd recipe from which to brew revolution. While the Declaration did not specifically mention slavery, it did rely on the telltale euphemism of protection of private property. Moreover, the contrast explicitly drawn between Catholic tyranny and "liberty" is suspiciously close to encapsulating years of conflict over slavery within Mexico, especially since "liberty," in this context, often meant the liberty to own other human beings as property. The constitution ultimately adopted for the new government by the same convention provides evidence in support of these suspicions. While, in accordance with the preponderance of world opinion, it continued the 1833 convention's condemnation of the international slave trade, it specifically protected Texians' property rights in their slaves, providing that "Congress shall pass no laws to prohibit emigrants from bringing their slaves in to the republic with them, and holding them by the same tenure by which such slaves were held in the United States; nor shall congress have the power to emancipate slaves; nor shall any slave holder be allowed to emancipate his or her slave or slaves without the consent of congress."[12]

If any Texians questioned the substantive content of, or reason for, the demands for "local autonomy" and "protection of private property" from the threat of Mexican Catholic tyranny or government confiscation, here was the answer. Independence declarations and other pronouncements designed as international propaganda could afford to be discreet on the subject of slavery. The law would be direct and unequivocal. While arguing that it was the handiwork of the "People of Texas" to "secure the blessings of liberty," the constitution made the economic oppression of African American slaves among the most fundamental laws of the land.

In fact, the committee charged with reporting on slavery to the convention understood matters very much in this way. Its chairman, Samuel Rhoads Fisher of Matagorda, made plain that the committee's reasons for reaffirming the 1833 Mexican ban on the slave trade were strictly diplomatic:

> And your committee have no hesitancy in stating their views and belief of the extreme impolicy of either covertly or directly countenancing a traffic, which has called forth the indignant condemnation of nearly the whole civilized world. It is to that civilized world that we now, in our present struggle look for sympathy, and hope from that sympathy to extract assistance. Almost every nation has proclaimed against this traffic many years since, and denounced it as "Piracy;" . . . Your committee therefore respectfully suggest that, as a nation just ushered into existence, it most eminently becomes our duty and policy to adapt our measures to the genius and spirit of the age. We must be governed by the opinions of others-we must so regulate our infant steps as to deserve the kind and watchful solicitude of older Nations.

The use of quotation marks around "piracy" speaks volumes. A ban on slave trading was not a matter of suppressing real piracy, but of *appearing* not to condone what others condemned as piratical. Lest this create any domestic misunderstanding that Texas harbored doubts about slavery itself, Fisher was quick to add that "while advocating the broad and abstract principle of justice, let us not by taking a retrospective view of a doubtful and exciting question, interfere with or violate *the just rights of our citizens*" (emphasis added), by which of course he meant the right of white Texians to own slaves. This report so captured the consensus of the convention, and its dissemination to assuage Texian fear of abolition was deemed so important, that a motion was promptly made and passed to immediately order the printing of one thousand copies of it.[13]

Thus the omission of slavery from explicit reference in the 1835 Consultado and the 1836 Declaration of Independence is not dispositive. These official pronouncements, designed first for polemical use in Mexico in 1835, and then in the United States, Great Britain, and Western Europe, are understandably euphemistic due to the necessity of obtaining independent statehood in the one instance, and national recognition in the other, from nations known to harbor substantial abolitionist sentiment. The issue is concealed in the documents designed for overseas diplomatic consumption as anti-Catholic diatribe, protest against "confiscation of property," or pleas for decentralized government. The 1836 Texas national constitution that followed did not similarly mince words. Neither did the Texian rebels themselves in their correspondence penned in the heat of the moment. They knew very well what they wanted, what they were afraid of, and therefore what they were fighting for. Many genuinely believed that Santa Anna's dictatorship was an unwise form of government as a matter of theory. However, this leaves the question of *why*, in practice, it was to be feared so intensely by so many. *What* would the national government *do* with the central authority it sporadically exercised?

The Texians' answer to that question now seems obvious, although their response to centralization was incremental. Initially, Texians, including many in the war party, supported any option that would protect slave-based capitalism and economic growth. Informal skirting of the federal laws against slavery grew into formal contracts of "indentured servitude." When that loophole was closed, local autonomy and special Texas exemptions were required. As matters in Mexico deteriorated and Santa Anna took more power, the next solution was statehood as part of his promised "federal" constitution of 1824. When Santa Anna revealed himself as a centralist and dictator, war and independence became the only alternative. At that point, the war party's biggest problem became disguising their economic motivations in a rhetorical shell that doves like Burnet, antislavery men in the United States, and ultimately the governments of Britain and France could accept. The US Congress engaged in similar euphemism and avoidance during this period by, for example, prohibiting all debates over slavery on the floor of the House between 1836 and 1844.[14]

Unlike other past and future American states, by 1836 Texas had its own national mythology and this was reflected in its Declaration of Independence.

While the Texas Declaration is full of the Lockean theory of natural right and natural law, including the right to revolt and a host of other English liberties such as the rights of trial by jury, freedom of religion, and freedom from martial law, this is not the gist of its argument. Rather, the initial and longest grievance stated by the rebels was that they had been lured into Texas by the promise that they "could continue to enjoy that constitutional liberty and republican Government to which they had been habituated in the land of their birth." Precisely how Santa Anna had breached this social contract was explained in terms of his having "sacrificed our welfare to the State of Coahuila, by which our interests have been continually depressed, *through a jealous and partial course of legislation*, carried on at a far-distant seat of Government, by a hostile majority, *in an unknown tongue*; and this too notwithstanding we have petitioned in the humblest terms for the *establishment of a separate State Government*" (emphasis added).[15]

So Texas' foundational national myth combined a number of different images. One powerful and consistent image was Spanish-speaking Catholic tyranny, with all the threat and otherness that stereotype entailed with respect to slavery, jury trial, the common law, and other Anglo-Southern institutions. Another was the passing reference to Lockean liberties and the reassertion of the right to revolt, but this was in terms somewhat different from the American Declaration from which Texas' was obviously adapted. As the Texians saw it, this was not the mere severance of connections between a metropolis and a peripheral area in the way Jefferson had put the matter to Britain and the world sixty years before. Rather, this was a real Hobbesian/Lockean state of chaos that demanded immediate action because

> when, in consequence of such acts of malfeasance and abdication on the part of the Government, anarchy prevails, and civil society is dissolved into its original elements: in such a crisis, the first law of nature, the right of self-preservation, the inherent and inalienable right of the People to appeal to first principles, and take their political affairs into their own hands in extreme cases enjoins it as a right towards themselves, and a sacred obligation to their posterity, to abolish such Government, and create another in its stead, calculated to rescue them from impending dangers, and to secure their future welfare and happiness.

And the Texas Declaration expressly linked this image to the newly centralized Mexican government having "ceased to protect the lives, liberty, and property of the People from whom its legitimate powers are derived." This language is eerily reminiscent of Travis's prediction of chaos and slave revolt less than a year before.[16]

For some Texians, civilization and order were quite literally falling apart and life, liberty, and property were at risk solely because Santa Anna refused Texas separate statehood. While historians might argue that this was clearly not true in fact, it seems to have been true in the imagination of many Texians. The Declaration provides further evidence of the fear behind it. Based upon Mexican respect for Indian lands, as evidenced for example by the ejection of Anglo squatters from Alabama-Coushatta territory around Anahuac, the Texian Declaration of Independence bewailed that the Mexican government had "through its emissaries, incited the merciless savage, with the tomahawk and scalping-knife, the [sic] massacre the inhabitants of our defenceless frontiers."[17]

Unlike their Mexican Catholic neighbors, these same Texians understood quite well that neither slaves nor "savage" Indians were among the "people" for whom the convention delegates proclaimed independence, nor were they among the "people" who, according to the Constitution of 1836, "in order to form a government" ordained and established it. Although a resolution was moved in the convention to specifically affirm that "all persons (slaves and Indians excepted) residing in Texas, on the day of the Declaration of Independence shall be considered as citizens of the republic," it was tabled, presumably as an unnecessary statement of the obvious. The Texians who did constitute "the people" claimed that the centralization of government in Mexico City would produce anarchy and chaos, rather a counterintuitive claim to make against an allegedly totalitarian tyranny. Because they saw their rebuffed bid for independent statehood as their last chance to protect the institution of slavery, the chaos they now feared was a comprehensive multiethnic insurrection of "savages," red, brown, and black. This fear, easily inferred both from the documents of independence and the personal writings of some of the participants, is quite understandable in the wake of Nat Turner's well-publicized slave rebellion in Virginia only five years before, and the well-understood connection between Indians and fugitive slaves as allied enemies.[18]

Now these lurking outsiders had another ally, the Catholic national government of Mexico, which under the *centralista* Santa Anna, no longer had any patience for "special exceptions" for Texas and her slaves. To exacerbate matters, after the Immigration Law of 1830 blocked further legal Anglo settlement, the government began attempting to counterbalance the increasingly troublesome Anglo population by settling more Indians in Texas. In the early 1830s, the Mexican government began a new policy of making communal grants of Texas land to Indian tribes.[19] Although Sam Houston used his considerable contacts with the Cherokee to negotiate a quick treaty assuring their neutrality in the war for independence, rumors of Mexican-inspired Indian uprisings swept through eastern and central Texas in the 1830s.[20]

The 1836 Constitution

On the same day independence was declared, the delegates passed Robert Potter's motion to form a committee to draft a new constitution. President Ellis appointed twenty-one members to the committee from across the province, including Jose Antonio Navarro of San Antonio and the distinguished former Mexican official Lorenzo de Zavala. The next day, Sam Houston, Robert Hamilton, James Collinsworth, and David Thomas were added to the committee by general consent, and a motion was laid on the table to elect the following day a major general to "be forthwith ordered to the field" and take command of all revolutionary forces. A committee of five delegates including de Zavala was also formed to "devise . . . a suitable flag for the Republic of Texas." The Declaration of Independence had averred that "the people of Texas do now constitute a *free, sovereign and independent Republic*," and references had been made by delegates to forming a committee of the whole "on Texas," but the flag resolution was the first occasion on which the convention applied the name "the Republic of Texas" to the new nation.[21]

On March 4th, the delegates confirmed the prior action of the provisional Council and named Houston major general in command of the armed forces. The motion was made by James Collinsworth and opposed by Potter. Collinsworth was an ally of Houston's, a fellow Tennessean, while Potter had come to Texas after a scandalous career in North Carolina politics that included two terms as a US Congressman. After spending six months in jail for maiming a relative and her beau, and after having been divorced by his wife, he was expelled from the North Carolina legislature for cheating at cards and came to Texas in search of redemption. He seems to have bristled at his inability to elbow aside Houston and take a role in guiding the war effort. On March 6th, after the convention received the famous distress plea from Travis at the Alamo, Houston allies Collinsworth, Thomas Jefferson Rusk, and George Childress defeated Potter's motion to appoint a committee of five members (presumably to include him) "clothed with all the powers residing in the Convention . . . to raise and organize the militia and volunteers."

Instead the convention deferred to Houston and had Ellis merely appoint a "standing military committee" of Rusk, Collinsworth, and James Gaines from East Texas, as well as delegates James Power and William Fisher, each of whom was from areas of the state under siege. Houston left the convention and took the field the same day.[22]

The following day was taken up with discussions of land titles, which had been unsettled both by recent Mexican policies and by the rebellion, and with communications with the provisional rebel government that by this time was in complete disarray. In January, shortly after calling elections for delegates to the convention, Governor Smith, who arrived at the convention by March 7th, had been impeached by the Council, and now his lieutenant governor James Robinson wrote the convention offering to resign as well. At the same time, delegates received a letter from the Council expressing its willingness to disband in favor of the convention as well, upon "some declaration" or request to do so. The Council also offered to deliver over the government's archives "and with pleasure return to our homes and the field." The convention demurred for the time being but did take a preliminary step—it asked the Council for a list of all military officers and their ranks and dates of commission. These were apparently ready at hand from Governor Smith or others because the contemporary observer William Fairfax Gray reports that the same day the house was informed that the army had 128 officers and the navy four, including a surgeon.[23]

On March 9th, the committee on the constitution reported its first draft. William Fairfax Gray recorded in his diary that some kind of report had already been made on the 7th by committee member David Thomas of Refugio. This does not appear in the convention's *Journal*, but there is little reason to doubt Gray's witness. Thomas's report must have been brief and the draft document must have been very preliminary. Gray described it as "awkwardly framed, arrangement and phraseology both bad; ... too close a copy ... of the Constitution of the United States" because of features which "here are not applicable." Gray's diary leaves the unmistakable impression that all the proceedings recorded in the *Journal* were less formal and more rambunctious than the latter made them appear. For example, while the *Journal* records the receipt of correspondence from both the Council and the governor, Gray describes Smith handing his communiques to Potter with whispered instructions from "behind the bar" of the meeting room itself. With news of the fall of the Alamo, which reached the members on March 16th, the convention degenerated into complete chaos. Gray described the entire proceeding as having become "disorderly in the extreme, and boyish. Nearly all the members were sometimes on the floor at once, some calling 'question,' some laughing and clapping, etc. The President, by his manifest partiality, egotism, and alarm, has lost the respect of the house." Meanwhile, Collinsworth (and presumably others) had "become disgusted, [and] got drunk." The next day the convention adjourned, and according to Gray, its delegates began "dispersing in all directions, with haste and confusion. A general panic seems to have seized them."[24]

This means that the convention had barely a week from March 9th to March 16th to deliberate the committee's draft constitution before news of the fall of the Alamo would arrive and send the delegates scrambling. Opportunities to consider the constitution's provisions were sparse because of the more raucous arguments over land titles, military matters, election of government officers, and financing the war. And the committee itself had only two days to rewrite Thomas's March 7th report and propose a more formal draft to the convention. The March 9th draft was remarkably similar to the convention's final product, so it appears that delegates deferred to the committee and to the preeminent legal minds in the convention, Rusk and Collinsworth. The only significant debate dealt with land titles where one faction led by Potter argued for an aggressive policy of undoing recent Mexican grants and the other led by Rusk and Collinsworth was less radical. At issue were huge recent grants to speculators by the Coahuiltexican state, which violated existing immigration laws. Land speculation and outright fraud based on conflicting or bogus grants of the state legislature had caused so much dissension over titles and boundaries that the *Consultado* had already decreed the closure of all land offices in the province months before.[25]

The few modifications made in the draft constitution between March 9th and its final passage on March 16th are not substantial enough to indicate anything other than the few issues the convention felt important enough to require extra attention. The most extensive changes and the longest deliberations involved land titles, race, and finances. Smith and the Council had negotiated a $200,000 loan from private parties in America, but as to this and the land question, Gray reported that "[t]he business of the convention drags. There are some questions that they seem afraid to approach. They are sure to produce excitement, come up when they may. The land question is one, and the loan they are unwilling or afraid to ratify. Such miserable narrow-mindedness is astonishing." Ultimately the convention struck a compromise on the land question between the positions of the Potter and Rusk factions, and it fecklessly postponed the loan, even though the fall of the Alamo swayed a number of its previous detractors. In spite of the opposition of influential delegates, including Ellis, a resolution passed approving a loan in principle but leaving its negotiation to the judgment of the provisional government already in the process of fleeing the advancing Mexican Army. Gray and many hawks were incensed. "They have blinked the question," Gray wrote. "They have not actually rejected the loan but have not confirmed it, as the contract (offered by the lenders) required they should do."[26]

The land question was important. The constitution declared that "quieting the people in the enjoyment of their lands, is one of the great duties of this convention." The issues were resolved in committee. Instead of invalidating all recent grants from the state government and establishing a "land tribunal" urged by Potter, the committee opted to invalidate only titles issued since the *Consultado* closed all land offices, as well as the largest and most offensive grants made by the state government. It also created a General Land Office for title registration. The large grants voided were made in 1834 and 1835 to various speculators in the amount of 1,100 leagues (almost 5 million acres) per grant. The new constitution also established a presumption of ownership in favor of the "actual settler and occupant of the soil" and granted every citizen "head of a family ... one league and labor of land." This amounted to slightly over 4,600 acres per family.[27]

This kind of generosity underlined the importance of defining the citizenry entitled to receive it. On this question, and with respect to slavery, the constitution encountered the issue of racial identity. The March 9th committee draft limited voting to every "free white male citizen" twenty-one or older and mandated senatorial districts equal in population of "white inhabitants," but it neglected to actually define citizenship. Section 8 of the "General Provisions" in the draft only dealt with citizenship to be granted to future immigrants, which would only be available to "free white persons" who would reside in the state for six months, intend permanent residency, and swear allegiance to the Republic of Texas. The final constitution retained the restrictions on immigrant citizenship but added a significant section defining citizenship among those already present. It provided that all residents of the province on March 2, 1836, were deemed citizens, "Africans, the descendants of Africans, and Indians excepted." Similarly, the delineation of senatorial districts was amended to change "white inhabitants" to "free population (free negroes and Indians excepted)." Meanwhile, both the committee draft and the final version also included a proviso barring free blacks from living in Texas. The next section, Section 9 of the new constitution, not only confirmed the servitude of domestic slaves and prohibited their manumission unless sent out of the state, but it also required that "no free person of African descent, either in whole or in part, shall be permitted to reside permanently in the republic, without the consent of congress."[28]

These provisions and the remainder of the Texas Constitution of 1836 reveal a great deal about the new nation's self-image. The constitution's provisions, some of which endured for generations, trumpeted the Jeffersonian yeoman ideal, an American republic, albeit a slaveholding one, in microcosm. The law comprised a preamble, seven articles, a schedule for elections, and a Declaration of Rights. Most of the constitution's provisions were unabashedly modeled on the US Constitution. Many others were borrowed from the contemporaneous constitutions of southern states. The republic would have an elected president and vice-president, a Senate, and a House of Representatives. An independent judiciary with a supreme court and district courts was established. As in other American states, the judges were to be elected by the legislature to four-year terms, not appointed for life by the president as were federal judges in the United States.[29]

But, in other respects, the 1836 Texas Constitution was uniquely suited to the Texians who founded a new frontier republic at the edge of Anglo-American civilization. Sections of the Declaration of Rights dealt with freedom of speech and press, the right to bring lawsuits, and the right to keep and bear arms, and they were significantly broader than their US counterparts. For example, freedom of the press was balanced against the right to sue for libel, but in all such cases, the jury was empowered to decide not only the facts but also the law, an overt nod to jury nullification. The open courts provision, the only portion of the entire constitution to have survived unchanged in every subsequent Texas Constitution, guaranteed not only "due course of law" but also that "all courts shall be open, and every man for any injury done him in his lands, goods, person, or reputation, shall have remedy." And the realities of country life produced a right to weaponry beyond that found in the Second Amendment. In Texas, independent of any reference to a militia or a joint or communal right of self-defense, the constitution guaranteed that "every citizen shall have the right to bear arms in defence of himself."[30]

Moreover, these Texians were largely from the South, particularly the upper and western South, and they were Jacksonians. The constitution testified to this orientation. As already noted, the article on General Provisions was preoccupied with legislating about, and protecting, the institution of slavery.

The sections on slavery already discussed were similar to fundamental slave laws elsewhere in the South. But Texians also professed western Jacksonian ideas that were anticorporate and antimonopoly. The new constitution prohibited any legislative subsidy or assistance for "private . . . purposes," and declared illegal any monopoly or perpetuity as "contrary to the genius of a free government." And, tellingly, the 1836 Constitution specifically prohibited any "minister of the gospel or priest of any denomination whatever" holding any public office in the new republic.[31]

Anticlericalism and acrimony toward Spanish speakers, blacks, and Indians formed a mishmash of prejudice and fear that interpenetrated and infused classical Lockean/American republican theory with new connotations of meaning. Clearly, these Anglo revolutionaries resented Catholicism, but not out of Protestant religious fervor or theological quibbles. Antislavery sentiment had quickly spread well beyond Roman Catholic lawyer/theologians. There were already high-minded Protestant Christians in America and Britain spouting even more radical notions of human equality, and it would be less than a year before the first Methodist missionaries would bring the inchoate danger of contaminating the social fabric with their founder John Wesley's egalitarian antislavery ethic. For slaveholders, it might have seemed that antislavery ideology was a growing threat within all of Christian moral philosophy. Perhaps de-Catholicization would not be enough to protect Texas' peculiar conditions and institutions; perhaps complete secularization was the only sure remedy for abolitionism, and so we find that universally anticlerical ideology embedded in the 1836 Constitution.[32]

Yet one can also just detect the beginnings of another form of line drawing and alienation at work, one that would take decades to intrude itself fully on the complex mindset of conventional white Texans, a division on the basis of class. In addition to a patina of Jacksonian antimercantilism, the early Texas mindset, with all of its other pejorative categorizations, made some room for other class distinctions, even among Mexican Catholics. During the constitutional convention, one of the first matters of business was the handling of Mexican prisoners of war. While Mexican officers were to be jailed at their own expense subject to the possibility of future exchange, enlisted ranks were distributed among Texian citizens to do hard labor for their support. In addition, according to the committee report received by the convention, the Texians having custody of these Mexicans "will be compelled to treat said prisoners as Mexican hired servants." In fifty years, the dominant political culture would revisit the intersection between ethnicity and class. But, for now, the fledgling Texian government had several more pressing political and economic emergencies on their hands. Building a nation in a border area somewhere between the American homeland and unmapped Indian country would prove to be a difficult business.[33]

2

Anglos, Indians, Germans, Mexicans, and Slaves

The Constitution of 1845: The Republic and Early Statehood, 1836–1854

THE 1836 DECLARATION OF INDEPENDENCE MENTIONED INDIANS AS enemies associated with Mexican tyranny, and the threat of Indian war, even when illusory, remained high on the list of Texian fears. This threat, and Texas' vulnerable geopolitical position, impregnated the Mexican image with a savagery magnified beyond even the Alamo mythology. It similarly barbarized the white perception of black slaves while reinforcing the view of Indians as subhuman. Many Texians referred to Native Americans as "vermin" and as "red n****rs."[1] The fledgling Texan nation's precarious situation produced more than trepidation about a newly invigorated Indian–Hispanic axis. More dangerous still was the possibility of Tejano-Indian encouragement of a slave insurrection, and here Texian slave masters had reason for continued concern. The military threat from the Mexican government was blunted only temporarily by independence, and domestic antislavery sentiment, especially among Hispanics and other non-Protestants, remained. Anglo Texians' primary task was to keep the fledgling republic together as a slaveholding white community in the face of internal and external threats. Given Texians' limited military and economic power, their best hope was annexation to the United States. The constitution adopted in 1845 illustrates these realities.

In the 1840s, Irish immigrants supplied a labor force in the North that competed with free blacks. In the Southwest, Manifest Destiny created similar labor competition between the Mexican-Tejano underclass and black slaves. Here ethnic stereotypes of Hispanics were used to justify ejecting them from their lands and creating a caste of subservient Hispanic agricultural workers to augment the slave labor force. The justification used to subordinate Hispanics was similar to the justification for slavery—that brown people were inherently lazy, and that they had no right to land that they would not fully work. Just as Reconstruction would create a technically free black proletariat, Manifest Destiny created a "Mexican proletariat." And like African Americans, Hispanic workers defied these stereotypes by taking social and political action, but with little overall effect.[2]

Thus during the republic and early statehood, some of the fear previously focused on the Mexican government now came to center not only upon Indians and slaves, but upon Tejanos and small groups of abolitionist-leaning German immigrants, especially those who were Catholic, Jewish, or radical. This chapter attempts to explain how the Texas Constitution of 1845 reflected a republic-era Texian mindset that continued to sense a vague and impenetrable web of conspiracies between Indians, slaves, and Tejanos, but how the Texian perception changed to include Germans and others as part of this enemy axis.

Mexico stoked these Texian fears by intermittently invading South Texas and fomenting far-fetched plots to incite a Tejano-Indian uprising. Texians of the republic era responded by continued demands for the protection of American statehood. After annexation and statehood in 1845, the Indian threat receded as Anglo settlement continued westward under American protection. The 1846–48 US-Mexican War eliminated the threat from south of the Rio Grande, but the large African American underclass remained, along with thousands of Tejano and German residents who might provide succor to those slaves who could escape. This worry dominated Anglo-Texan fears until the 1850s.

The Mexican–Indian Axis and Anglo Fifth Columnists

After the Texian victory at San Jacinto in April of 1836, a wounded Sam Houston took ship to New Orleans for medical treatment while Texas' provisional government under interim president David Burnet took the captured Generalissimo Santa Anna to the Texas port of Velasco. There

Burnet extracted two promises—one a public treaty and the other an informal understanding. The formal Treaty of Velasco dated May 14, 1836, ended hostilities and withdrew Mexican troops south of the Rio Grande. In a separate private agreement made in order to obtain his release, Santa Anna agreed to do everything in his power to gain Mexican congressional recognition of the treaty, the independence of Texas, and the Rio Grande as the boundary between the two nations. This two-pronged diplomacy by the Texian government represented an attempt to obtain a desert buffer zone between the historical province of Texas, whose southern border was the Nueces River, and the northernmost population centers in the remainder of Mexico, which were along the southern banks of the Rio Grande. The 150-mile-wide strip between the rivers was marked on contemporary maps as the Wild Horse Desert and would soon come to be known as the Nueces Strip, a dry and largely uninhabited badlands asylum for runaways, vagabonds, horse thieves, and desperados.[3]

Once Santa Anna was released and returned to Mexico, he and the Mexican government repudiated both Velasco agreements. With Houston incapacitated by his wounds, his aide Thomas Jefferson Rusk took over command of the army, while Mirabeau B. Lamar, a cavalry commander at the Battle of San Jacinto, was elevated to the post of secretary of war. Lamar soon joined Burnet as the head of a new "hothead" or war party in Texas, drawing a natural constituency from American filibusters who kept coming to Texas to fight the Mexicans even though the war was over.[4] Stephen F. Austin, now leading the Texas diplomatic mission to the United States, was shocked when Texas' initial overtures for statehood were rebuffed by US president Andrew Jackson, who wanted a more stable government in Texas that could assure America annexation would not precipitate all-out war with Mexico. Interim Texas president Burnet responded by immediately calling elections. His hope was that by promptly establishing regular government in the new republic, and by demonstrating overwhelming public support for joining the United States, he could accelerate the path to annexation. In the September 1836 Texas presidential election, the diplomat Austin was severely beaten by the war hero Houston. The margin was more than 5,000 votes for Houston to about 500 for Austin. Meanwhile, Lamar, also claiming war hero status from his involvement in the Battle of San Jacinto, swept into the vice-presidency. He would remain a thorn in Houston's side for the remainder of the life of the republic. In the same election, voters approved the 1836 Constitution and supported annexation to the United States by an overwhelming margin of 3,277 to 91.[5]

Houston's inaugural speech as the nation's first constitutional president laid out a moderate political program that disappointed the hotheads. From his experience leading an undersupplied band of volunteers against a semi-professional Mexican army, Houston knew the precariousness of the republic's position and the dire need to obtain aid and recognition from the United States. He urged the newly elected Congress of Texas to build alliances and understandings with the surrounding Indian tribes; in his words, to "abstain on our part from aggression, establish commerce with the different tribes, supply their useful and necessary wants, maintain even-handed justice with them, and natural reason will teach them the utility of our friendship." He understood that Mexico could not be trusted, but ever conscious of the weakness of his military position, he did not seek to provoke a quarrel. Rather, he counseled "vigilance ... [and] a disciplined and valiant army." But even the moderate Houston could not resist regarding his recent victory in the revolution as proof of the moral inferiority of Mexicans and as heaping "glory on the Anglo-Saxon race."[6]

Houston's logical first step was to obtain diplomatic recognition from the United States, but here the concerns of abolitionists, soon repeated on the floor of the US Congress by John Quincy Adams of Massachusetts, threatened to turn the annexation of Texas into a debate over the fundamental question of slavery in the western territories, a question most Americans wanted to avoid. Jackson's handpicked successor, Martin Van Buren, had risen to political prominence as a northern man of southern sensibilities who adeptly side-stepped all questions involving slavery, and he wanted no part of discombobulating his 1836 presidential campaign with a divisive intersectional fight over slavery or its expansion. Texas would have to wait.[7]

Van Buren won the November election against an array of sectional candidates fielded by the Whigs, a new political party comprising remnants of the Federalists and western boosters of government-sponsored economic development. With the election safely in his protégé Van Buren's hands, Jackson finally recognized Texas on the next to last day of his presidency by appointing an American charge d'affaires to the new republic. But after that, the change in American administrations augured no improvement in Texas' fortunes. Only months after Van Buren's inauguration, the Panic of 1837 ruined his presidency and further tied his political hands. He rejected an overt proposal of annexation from Texas Secretary of State Memucan Hunt in the fall of 1837 out of continued fear that it would precipitate a war with Mexico. As a result, Houston had no choice but to appoint diplomatic emissaries to Great Britain and France for the purpose of obtaining recognition and support elsewhere. Nothing came of these overtures until after Houston's first term as president ended. In 1839 King Louis-Philippe appointed Duboise de Saligny as charge d'affaires to Texas, thus accomplishing French recognition. Britain followed suit in 1842, but only after exhaustive negotiations to obtain an anti-slave-trade treaty from the Texas government in exchange.[8]

For the two years of the Houston administration from December of 1836 to 1838, little was accomplished other than American recognition and the passage by the Texas Congress of a boundary act that greatly extended the perimeters claimed by the nascent republic. Houston's idea was to take within Texas all of the lands east of the Rio Grande from Matamoros to Colorado, west of the old Louisiana Territory, and south of the Oregon country claimed by Britain, the United States, and Russia. The result was that Texas claimed an area that included most of modern New Mexico and much of Colorado, territory approximately three times larger than the region in central and eastern Texas inhabited by Anglo settlers. In essence, Texas claimed all the land not already part of the United States that lay between the Rio Grande and the Arkansas River all the way to the Rocky Mountains. Houston's plan was to create so big a plum that the United States could not resist picking it, but the domestic political situation in the United States still prevented annexation. When Houston's term as president ended late in 1838, the 1836 Constitution's provision preventing Texas presidents from succeeding themselves resulted in the easy election of Vice-President Lamar as the nation's second president with little immediate hope of making Texas a state.[9]

Lamar and Burnet despised Houston and the feeling was mutual. Houston called Lamar a dog and Burnet a "canting hypocrite whom the waters of Jordan could never cleanse from . . . political and moral leprosy."[10] For his part, when he succeeded Houston as president, Lamar initially agreed to purchase Houston's furniture from the governor's residence but then refused to pay and unceremoniously returned the accoutrements to Houston in a shameful condition of disrepair.[11] Vice-President Lamar had opposed Houston's policy toward both the Indians and Mexico. During Houston's administration, Lamar, Burnet, and Edward Burleson led a hot-head party that stood for the extermination of the Indians, aggression toward Mexico, and the humiliation of Houston. The Houston faction favored negotiation and alliance with as many of the Indian tribes as possible, and a defensive posture toward Mexico until annexation brought US military protection. Predictably, the Texas Congress rejected much of this policy.[12]

One thing that played into the hothead party's hands was the influx of Indians from US Indian Territory into disorganized Texas. In addition to those Indians already residing along the Red River and in northeast Texas, the US policy of extermination or relocation of Indians drove substantial numbers of Cherokees, Delawares, Shawnees, Seminoles, Choctaws, and Creeks into Texas. Some of these moved on into the western borderlands formerly occupied almost exclusively by the Comanches.[13] President Van Buren attempted to soften US Indian policy when he took office in 1837, which gave Houston a window of opportunity to reopen negotiations with the Indian tribes to guarantee them lands within the republic, but his attempts at conciliation continued to be blocked in the Texas Congress. As independence lured new Anglo settlers into Texas, by the end of Houston's term the Texas Congress had made it impossible for him to provide any of the tribes with the land necessary to pacify them. Once Vice-President Lamar succeeded Houston as president in 1838, it was clear that the hotheads in Texas politics had the upper hand. Indians had good reason for concern.[14]

Like many of his contemporaries, Lamar was anti-Indian and anti-Mexican in outlook. He considered nonwhite, non-Anglo peoples savages.[15] Late in 1838, when it became clear that Lamar would succeed Houston, Caddoes, and Wichitas began raiding western settlements, while Comanches did the same along the Colorado River. Thus, by the time of his inauguration, Lamar had fortuitous grounds to call for a larger standing army and to demand immediate punitive expeditions against the Indians. His policy for the two years of his term in office would be to eject them from Texas or to exterminate them, if possible.[16] At his inauguration, he immediately called for a military buildup against the Indians as illegal immigrants who threatened further Anglo settlement.[17]

When a prominent Nacogdoches Tejano named Vicente Cordova led a number of Tejano bandits and a few Indians against President Lamar's newly created army in 1839, members of the Texas Senate concluded that this was additional evidence of the local Indian tribes being in league with Tejanos and Mexicans to overthrow the new Texas government. They may have been right. It appears that General Vicente Filisola of the Mexican Army had been conspiring with Cordova and his lieutenants to recruit Tejano and Indian allies for a forthcoming Mexican invasion.[18]

Using as pretexts this insurrection in Northeast Texas and the fact that some Cherokees had cooperated with the Mexican Army during the revolution, Lamar took the opportunity to write a letter to Chief Bowles of the Cherokees demanding that the entire tribe leave Texas immediately. This letter was delivered to Bowles by an Indian agent appointed for the purpose, Martin Lacy, who was accompanied by an ambitious young immigrant from Tennessee, John H. Reagan, later Texas District Judge, US Senator, and Texas Railroad Commissioner. Reagan never forgot the impression of calm dignity Bowles's demeanor conveyed. When the chief refused Lamar's ultimatum, the new president dispatched Burleson and General Thomas Rusk to attack the Cherokees in their towns in northeast Texas. This Texian Army mercilessly exterminated them and then turned to attack the Shawnee Nation, whom Lamar had duplicitously promised to leave alone in exchange for their neutrality. As a result of these campaigns, the Indian tribes were essentially removed from northeast Texas. Houston tried to defend his friends the Cherokees in the Texas Congress, but he was ignored.[19]

Even though the Cordova Tejano-Indian uprising in Northeast Texas justified the fears of Anglo Texians, Sam Houston maintained his policy of conciliation. In a letter to Anna Raguet in May of 1838, he responded to her report of an Indian raid in the vicinity of her home in Nacogdoches. Houston expressed "regret that my friends should be visited by the Indians, or that any cause of alarm should exist," and he continued that "until our citizens learn prudence, we must be afflicted by such visitations. The Bowl is here and has every disposition to keep peace and do all that is right and proper. I am satisfied if anything improper or hostile should arise it will be owing to the conduct of bad men."[20] Most Texans would have agreed only if Houston was referring to the Mexicans as the "bad men." Indeed, once the Cordova raids had begun, it is clear that in Nacogdoches, Indian wars, relations with the Cherokee, and disturbances and rebellion fomented by the Mexicans "formed the all-engrossing theme" of polite Anglo conversation, as two contemporary correspondents put it to the same Ms. Raguet a few months later.[21]

But within two years, Houston was still describing the Lamar administration as one of "vicious stupidity" that had led the new republic to ruin because "the expenses of this year are appalling to those who do not wish to be buried by taxation." He was referring, in significant part, to military expenditures to fund Lamar's expeditions against the Mexicans and Indians.[22] Houston repeated the same sentiments to Texas Senator Robert Irion in January of 1840, claiming that "no patriot can anticipate the future prospects of Texas without the most acute and heavy anguish." His complaints included financial extravagance, corruption, and the location of the seat of government in Austin, "this accursed place."[23]

Although Lamar's 1839 war against the Cherokees and Shawnees raised the possibility of retaliation, the government's attention was forced to turn elsewhere, to the Comanches in the West, who had intensified raids on western settlements for horses, loot, and captives. Somewhat surprisingly, in January of 1840, a small group of Comanches came to San Antonio offering to negotiate. The local military commander was Colonel Henry Wax Karnes, a revolutionary war veteran who had been in command since 1837 when Houston had ordered him to negotiate with the Comanches west of San Antonio. Although it is likely Houston expected him to use Tejano intermediaries for this purpose, Karnes was too suspicious of the Indian tribes and the Tejanos to do much to appease Indians or work with Tejanos. Tejanos had sensed the opprobrium exhibited by leaders like Karnes for some time. For example, Francisco Ruiz of San Antonio had offered a bill in the Texas Congress as early as 1837 to protect Tejano property from Anglo squatters, but the measure was defeated amid fears of a Tejano-Indian conspiracy.[24]

By 1840, Lamar's Congress had authorized Karnes to raise eight companies of Texas Rangers, and Karnes had already led a small detachment of them in a retaliatory raid against two hundred local Comanches a few months before. He now encouraged the Comanche peace envoys that had appeared in San Antonio to depart and return only when they were ready to bring and release all their Anglo captives, which Karnes believed to approximate about a dozen. In response to the invitation, a large Comanche delegation returned in March, including women and children. What ensued came to be known as the Council House Fight that famously stoked Texian fears of an Indian uprising. While the result of the battle was indecisive, it produced even more strenuous cries in the newspapers for vigorous action against the Indians.[25]

An Indian war quickly expanded throughout the frontier with Texas Army regulars and Texas Rangers conducting raids farther north against the Wichitas, Cherokees, Shawnees, Kickapoos, and Caddoes. As a result of these efforts, Texas Rangers like Captain Jack Hays quickly became popular heroes and Lamar's policies ejected the vast majority of the Indians from the Central Texas borderlands in the Hill Country. Flush with apparent victory, Lamar endorsed another expedition farther westward, this one aimed at annexing Santa Fe in disputed Mexican/Texas territory. This expedition, after suffering casualties at the hands of Comanche raiders, was so ill-equipped and exhausted by the time it reached New Mexico that it was forced to surrender to Mexican authorities before even reaching Santa Fe.[26]

The exorbitant cost of these campaigns helped Sam Houston win election to his second term as president in December 1841 on a platform of peace and fiscal restraint. The Houston platform was quickly mooted by Santa Anna's return to power in Mexico in 1842, and in an effort to further rehabilitate his political fortunes, the old generalissimo ordered General Rafael Vasquez to invade Texas and seize San Antonio. In March of 1842, Vasquez and his troops entered San Antonio, captured and looted the government buildings there, suspended the operation of the court system, and returned to Mexico with several Anglo captives. Houston ordered General Alexander Somervell and a small Texian Army to take command of militia forces gathering at San Antonio and conduct a punitive expedition into Mexico. Somervell was an ineffective commander, and he was unable to discipline the assembled volunteers and prevent them from looting Tejano properties and businesses in San Antonio and the surrounding area. Chaos reigned, and the well-informed Mexicans invaded Texas again under General Adrian Woll, capturing San Antonio for a second time in September of 1842. Houston again ordered Somervell to assemble volunteers and act. The second capture of San Antonio motivated the militiamen to better discipline, although the mixed regular/militia force was still bloated with "volunteer" looters and brigands. This time Somervell managed to march his command all the way to Laredo. The army was able to plant the Texas flag and loot the place, but this only resulted in massive desertions. Only five hundred loyal troops followed Somervell across the Rio Grande to Guerrero in Mexico. There Somervell completely lost control and 189 of the remaining men mutinied in support of Colonel William S. Fisher, who had taken part in the Council House Fight. Fisher proposed to loot Mier on the southern bank or the Rio Grande, but General Pedro de Ampudia attacked the Texans and forced them to surrender in December of 1842. The Mexican commander chose to deal with the Texan prisoners in the manner of the Roman Republic, by decimation. Seventeen of the approximately 170 Texan captives were chosen by lot for execution. A gourd filled with seventeen black beans and nine times as many white ones was passed among the Texans. Those with the misfortune to draw a black bean out of the jar were executed by firing squad.[27]

Throughout this period, while trying to assuage the newspapers with reports of the efforts, albeit ineffective, of his army, Houston continued to importune the Congress and the people of Texas with arguments that

Lamar's aggressive Indian-Mexican policy had been unsuccessful and fiscally irresponsible. Meanwhile, Houston also conducted secret diplomacy with a number of Indian chiefs, particularly among the Caddoes, Wichitas, and Cherokees. After the disaster at Mier, his conciliatory policies began to look wiser to a larger number of Texans because the population had become increasingly insecure, economically and militarily. In January of 1843, the Texas Congress finally acceded to Houston's requests by passing a version of his old plan to create trading houses on the Indian frontier and to outlaw raiding of any kind on both sides. They also endorsed his plan to establish by treaty a line of demarcation between Anglo settlement and Indian lands. This resulted in a tentative peace in 1844, which was broken only by an extemporaneous fight near Fredericksburg between some Comanches and a small company of Rangers led by Major Jack Hays and armed with new Colt revolvers. Although out-numbered four to one, this group was able to dispatch over sixty Comanches. Without the continued lull thereafter in anti-Indian and anti-Mexican violence, it is unlikely that Houston and his successor Anson Jones could finally have successfully treated for annexation with the United States in 1845.[28]

In addition to dread of a Mexican/Indian alliance and the slave revolt it might precipitate, Texians of the late 1830s and early 1840s feared the small domestic population of free blacks. They also had to make sense of a growing number of local white abolitionist schemers and dreamers, the kind of cultural turncoats likely to accelerate xenophobia. While any remaining free blacks within the state were expelled from Texas by an 1840 decree of Lamar's congress, such omnibus measures might not be effective against white anti-slavery men harder to identify.[29] Stephen Pearl Andrews, for example, came to Texas from Massachusetts via Louisiana. Like many northerners, he believed that slavery had served the useful purpose of evangelizing African Americans but, having served that purpose, should soon stop. He settled in Houston in 1839 and began practicing law, the vocation he had earlier pursued in New Orleans. He also managed to obtain a commission for himself from the government of the republic to translate Texas laws into Spanish. Andrews was a temperance activist and in 1839 went to New York to visit the influential abolitionist/temperance reformer Lewis Tappan.[30]

While visiting in the North, Andrews came up with an abolition scheme for Texas and began publicizing it upon his return to the port of Houston in 1842. With the support of Tappan and others, he organized a mass meeting at the Houston courthouse where he convinced a number of Texians that his plan would result in British financial and military support for the young republic. He then went to Galveston and arrived there on March 13, 1843, with what his biographer Madeleine Stern described as "a boat-load" of supporters.[31] He first canvassed local planters and businessmen for support and then called another mass meeting with assistance from Andrew J. Yates, a fellow antislavery attorney from Connecticut who published a Galveston newspaper. Andrews's mass meeting in Galveston was aborted by a proslavery band led by a South Carolina lawyer named Cole who forced him off Galveston Island onto a boat commandeered for that purpose. Andrews didn't give up. He proceeded to England with Lewis Tappan and enlisted John Scoble and others in an effort to obtain from the British government promises of military support and the funds necessary to compensate slave owners if Texas would agree to emancipation. This scheme came to nothing, and by the time Andrews returned to the United States, the issue was mooted by President John Tyler's decision in 1844 to negotiate annexation with the Texian government. Andrews never returned to Texas but spent his remaining years in Boston, where he continued to engage in abolitionist politics, exposing to public scandal some of the residents there who illegally still owned slaves.[32]

The reason that Andrews's schemes were met with such interest upon his initial return to Houston was not so much because of his advance work, but because Texians were particularly worried in 1843 that they might never be annexed to the United States. Thus they came to consider the only practical alternative, a British-supported independent republic. While England had already extended diplomatic recognition to Texas, Lamar's misadventures left the Houston administration badly needing money to keep operations afloat and defend the frontiers from Mexico and the Indian nations. To secure British financial aid, compensated emancipation was the likely price, and one that many Texans were willing to meet so long as England footed the lion's share of the bill.[33]

In this vein, the attendance at Andrews's Houston meeting was enhanced by an editorial in the Houston *Telegraph and Daily Register* arguing that safety from further Mexican aggression might be obtained from Britain in the same way that Britain had protected Uruguay from Brazil in 1838 after Uruguay had abolished slavery. By historian Charles Shively's reckoning, this editorial, combined with the public mood, caused a "spontaneous outburst" that was "engineered or directed by no one or by no party in particular, but by the people *en masse*." Of course, it was this spontaneous popularity that made Andrews dangerous enough to justify his being run out of Galveston before he could hold a meeting. It is precisely this kind of internal threat to the dominant ethos that precipitates prompt, vigorous, and often violent response.[34] Still, the antislavery views of renegade whites like Stephen Pearl Andrews were by far the exception and not the rule. In Texas after independence, domestic white antislavery was sporadic, rare, and almost always Catholic or German, but this had the effect of making it all the more mysterious and foreboding to the Texian imagination.[35]

Annexation, the Constitution of 1845, and the Mexican War

Although an indecisive President John Tyler ultimately supported it, a treaty annexing Texas as a federal territory was defeated in the US Senate in 1844. Under the proposed treaty Texas' debts would be assumed by the federal government in exchange for ceding her public lands. Although the bid to make Texas a territory failed, James K. Polk, the Democratic candidate for president that same year, pledged to annex Texas as part of his campaign platform. He was motivated in part by concern that Texas would become a powerful independent nation to the west supported by England, France, or Spain. Houston's annexation strategy had gained some traction with the Democratic nominee.[36]

When Polk won the presidency on a platform of territorial expansion, President Tyler saw this as a mandate to try again to annex Texas before his own term ended. In the face of northeastern sentiment against it because Texas was a slave state, on March 1st, the US Congress nevertheless passed a joint resolution in favor of annexation, although in the Senate, the margin was perilously close, a vote of 27 to 25. Because the latest congressional act was merely a joint resolution of both houses rather than a treaty submitted by the executive, this slim majority in the senate sufficed instead of the two-thirds vote required to ratify a treaty. And unlike the failed treaty, under this resolution, Texas was allowed to keep her public lands (referred to in the resolution as "vacant and unappropriated") but therefore had to pay her own debts. The resolution also contained an interesting proviso that Texas could form four new states out of her own territory to apply for separate admission to the Union "which shall be entitled to admission under the provisions of the Federal Constitution." Given that Texas claimed territory extending northwestward all the way into what is now Wyoming, this provision also provided that any states formed above the Missouri Compromise line must be free, while those below the line "shall be admitted into the Union, with or without slavery, as the people of each State, asking admission shall desire." In order to be admitted to the Union, Texas would have to fulfill the requirement of republican state government contained in Article IV, Section 4, of the US Constitution by providing Congress evidence of its adoption of an appropriate constitution for the new state. After the passage of the federal resolution, Texas President Anson Jones issued a proclamation dated May 8th calling for the election of deputies to a state constitutional convention beginning on the auspicious date of July 4, 1845.[37]

Since the Van Buren administration, Mexico had threatened war if the United States annexed Texas. Texas was already deploying its militia in the disputed Nueces Strip, and immediately upon his inauguration in March of 1845, Polk knew he must prepare for a bellicose Mexican response to the annexation resolution. In fact, on March 6th, two days after Polk's inauguration, the Mexican ambassador left Washington in protest. In April the War Department ordered General Zachary Taylor to depart his headquarters at Fort Jessup, Louisiana, with the US Third Infantry Regiment and join the Texas militia in the Nueces Strip. Negotiations between the United States and Mexico continued, and Texas even signed a separate peace treaty with Mexico in June 1845. But already under orders, a few weeks after that treaty was signed, Taylor and his troops took ship from New Orleans and arrived in Corpus Christi on the southern bank of the Nueces River. Taylor's army was reinforced by the US Seventh Infantry Regiment a month later.[38]

While the three republics (Mexico, Texas, and the United States) maneuvered for advantage in the Wild Horse Desert, fifty-six Texans were elected delegates to the convention that would write Texas' first state constitution. They assembled in Austin on July 4th and unanimously chose Sam Houston's old lieutenant, Thomas Jefferson Rusk, president of the convention. Only one of the delegates was a native Texan, and he was also the only Hispanic, José Antonio Navarro. Navarro and Rusk were two of only six delegates who had signed the Texas Declaration of Independence nine years before. Rusk came to regard John Hemphill, James Pinckney Henderson, Abner S. Lipscomb, Hiram G. Runnels, James S. Mayfield, James Love, and John Caldwell as the ablest delegates. Given their distinguished backgrounds and Rusk's legal acumen, this is not surprising. Hemphill and Lipscomb were experienced jurists who served as members of the Texas Supreme Court for decades. Hemphill was already chief justice of the republic at the time of the convention and continued to serve the state in that capacity until 1858. Lipscomb, a protégé of Mirabeau B. Lamar, had earlier served twelve years as chief justice of the Alabama Supreme Court, would be appointed associate justice in Texas after annexation, and served until he died in office in 1856. Rusk appointed these two men to important posts in the convention: Hemphill was selected chairman of the judiciary committee that worked on provisions concerning the judicial branch and land titles, while Lipscomb headed the committee on framing an ordinance adopting Texas' annexation as a state.

Love, like Judge Abner Lipscomb, was an early political ally of Mirabeau B. Lamar and an enemy of Sam Houston. A former US congressman and Speaker of the Kentucky House of Representatives, Love had come to Galveston in 1838 to practice law. Caldwell, another Kentuckian, was a second-generation Irish American who came to Texas in 1831 and ultimately settled in Bastrop County near Austin, which was then the Indian frontier. A lawyer, he was elected several times to the congress of the republic and then to the new state senate. Characteristically, among these prominent men clamoring for joinder to the United States, only Caldwell, an ethnic Texan residing among the Germans and Tejanos of the western frontier, would remain loyal to the Union a mere fifteen years hence.[39]

The most pressing and contentious matters facing the convention were a proposed bill of rights and the complex issues surrounding land. These issues included quieting title to private lands and dealing with unsurveyed public lands within the territorial boundaries of the republic. Texas had won this vast acreage on the western frontier by conquest from Mexico, but either it had not yet been granted or sold to private owners, or the government had been presented with invalid, conflicting, or overlapping claims to portions of it. Under the terms of the US annexation resolution, the federal government made no claim to these "public" lands and, although unquantified and unsurveyed, they were the property of the new state as the republic's successor in interest. In fact, the lands were beyond the effective reach of any Anglo government and were sparsely occupied only by Comanches, Apaches, Tonkawas, and a few Tejanos. Even in the densely populated areas to the east, private title disputes were all too common in a nascent republic with limited recordkeeping capability where land might be claimed through Spanish royal grant, Mexican land grant, purchase from a Mexican grantee or empresario, bounty for military service to the republic, inheritance, mere possession, or some combination of these. Indeed the longest report of any convention committee was that of Hemphill's on the question of lands. But the issue that occupied most of the convention's deliberative time and attention was a new bill of rights.[40]

When the delegates convened on July 4th the first order of business was to elect Abner Lipscomb as president *pro tempore*. Hemphill then moved that the delegates be called by counties so that the roll could be established, and Rusk was elected permanent chairman of the convention. Rusk delivered an address pointing out that "the history of the world may be searched in vain for a parallel to the present instance of two governments amalgamating themselves into one, from a pure devotion to that great principle, that man, by enlightening his intellect, and cultivating those moral sentiments with which his God has impressed him, is capable of self-government." He exhorted members not to vary from the welcome terms of the federal annexation resolution, extolled the virtues of "republican government," and cautioned the delegates to be careful to avoid "the introduction of new and untried theories." The text of the federal annexation resolution was reported to the convention in a letter from Texas president Anson Jones. Lipscomb was then appointed to head a special committee of fifteen to draft an ordinance effectuating Texas' accord with the resolution. On the same day, Lipscomb's committee reported a brief ordinance "assenting to the proposals thus made."[41]

The following day, bearing witness to the importance the delegates placed on the military protection of the United States, John Caldwell proposed an ordinance requesting that the President of the United States "occupy without delay, the frontier of this Republic with such troops as may be necessary for its defense" for the reason that "there are many tribes of Indians, belonging to the United States of America, located within and adjacent to the territory of Texas."[42] Only then did the convention proceed to form various committees and to deal with other procedural matters, one of which was the selection of George Fisher of Houston as interpreter for José Antonio Navarro, the only native Spanish-speaking delegate. On July 7, the special committee to which Caldwell's ordinance for US troops was referred reported a substitute resolution making no reference to Indians but rather to "the frontier and exposed positions in this Republic." Navarro moved to strike out the word "frontier," but this was overwhelmingly defeated. The committee substitute was adopted, and it stands to reason that the reference to Indians in the original was deleted lest the US become concerned that it had annexed not a well-populated Anglo republic but a frontier territory under persistent Indian attack.[43]

The next few days of the convention were taken up with procedural questions, including delegate credentialing and publication of the convention's proceedings. On July 8th, James Love introduced a resolution that the Committee on General Provisions headed by Isaac Van Zandt be charged with drafting a bill of rights to be "prefixed to the Constitution." This was a departure from the 1836 Constitution, which possessed only a "Declaration of Rights" at the end. The resolution was adopted, and three days later, on July 11th, Van Zandt reported the proposed bill of rights to the convention. It began with a declaration that "all political power is inherent in the people; and all free governments are founded on their authority, and instituted for their benefit." It went on to claim that "all free men" have equal rights. Other provisions prohibited religious tests for public office, guaranteed freedom of religion and freedom of speech and the press, and guaranteed the procedural rights available to criminal defendants under the US Constitution. Van Zandt's draft carried forward the "due course of law" provision of the 1836 Constitution, as well as its prohibition of imprisonment for debt, and its prohibition of "perpetuities or monopolies" as "contrary to the genius of a free government." The initial proposed bill of rights was considered so important as to cause the Convention to authorize the printing of five hundred copies of the committee report immediately. This Bill of Rights was passed on its third reading on August 19th.[44]

The committee on the organization of the executive department made its report, recommending that the supreme executive should be entitled the "Governor of the State of Texas," who would be the commander in chief of the army and navy "of this state, and of the militia, except when they shall be called into the service of the United States." The governor was to be allowed to convene the legislative branch at the capital or elsewhere if the capital "shall have become, since their last adjournment, dangerous from an enemy."[45] Within the executive article of the new constitution would also be found the organization of the state militia, which was to be accomplished by the legislature but commanded by the governor with authority to "call forth the militia to execute the laws of the State, to suppress insurrections, and to repel invasions." Delegates debated the relative power or weakness to be desired in the governorship, ultimately deciding in favor of strengthening the office in accordance with the prevailing trend of reform in other states. There was much to borrow from these models because in the 1840s many states revised their constitutions along Jacksonian lines, beginning with the notorious Dorr Rebellion and convention in Rhode Island in 1842. This populism dovetailed with both Jacksonianism and a general sentiment toward social reform. Texas delegates cited the constitutions of no less than twenty states, north and south, in their debates.[46]

The judiciary committee headed by Hemphill reported a proposed article organizing the judicial branch on the same day, July 11, 1845. It proposed that the judicial power be vested in one Supreme Court, and in district courts and such other inferior courts as the legislature might create. The Supreme Court was to be composed of one chief justice and two associate justices, a reduction in number from the court that served the republic. All judges would be nominated and appointed by the governor with the advice and consent of two-thirds of the senate. The district courts were to have original jurisdiction in criminal cases and in all civil cases where the matter in controversy was greater than one hundred dollars, whereas the Supreme Court was to possess appellate jurisdiction only. The proposed judicial article specifically prohibited any judge from sitting in cases where he "might be interested, or where either of the parties may be connected with him by affinity or consanguinity, within such degrees as may be proscribed by law, or where he shall have been of counsel in the cause."[47] The system of appointment inaugurated by the 1845 constitution only lasted five years. In 1850 an amendment passed to change the selection system to one where all judges were thenceforward to be elected.[48]

When the convention reconvened on Monday, July 14th, delegate A. S. Cunningham proposed that the judiciary committee headed by Hemphill be instructed to inquire into the expediency of inserting into the Constitution "a clause providing for the appointment of an officer in each judicial district" for the purpose of inquiring into and bringing before the district court "all cases in their respective districts, of land titles forfeited under the laws of Coahuila and Texas, as well as all lands escheated under any of the laws heretofore existing within the Territory of Texas." This measure passed and was an indication of the continuing problems with land titles upon which Hemphill's committee would eventually report.[49]

The next business taken up by the convention was Hiram Runnels's committee report on the organization of the legislative branch. The first problem addressed was how to constitute the electorate for legislative representatives. Runnels's committee determined that qualified voters should include "every free white male person who shall be a citizen of the United States, or who is, at the time of the adoption of this Constitution, a citizen of the now Republic of Texas" and who resided in the state for a year preceding the relevant election, "Indians not taxed, Africans and descendants of Africans excepted."[50]

A few days later, during a discussion on possible amendments to various draft provisions, an argument arose over the use of the word "white" as a qualification for citizenship or voting. President Rusk stated he "hoped" the word would be stricken because US courts had already determined that everyone other than Africans and their descendants were white, and so the use of the word might unfairly cause it to "be contended that we intend to exclude the race that we found to be in possession of the country when we came here." Runnels then denied that his drafting committee had any such thing in mind. Oliver Jones rose to support striking the word out on the same grounds as Rusk, that it might be unfairly interpreted to deny the vote to Tejanos or assimilated Indians. Indeed, he recalled, he had seen plenty of people object to "Mexicans, descendants of Indians, and even to [other] persons of a somewhat dark complexion, caused by the heat of a south." Navarro, the convention's only Hispanic delegate, then rose to perform the coup de grace, explaining that he "was as much opposed to giving the right of suffrage to Africans or the descendants of Africans as any other gentleman" and "hoped the Convention would be clearly convinced of the propriety and expediency of striking out this word. It is odious. captious and redundant; and may be the means at elections of disqualifying persons who are legal voters, but who perhaps by arbitrary judges may not be considered as white."

The liberality of delegates like Rusk and Jones and the influence of Navarro on this issue is remarkable in light of what his biographer describes as "a time when general animosity toward Tejanos was intense" and when "the loyalties of almost all Tejanos were highly suspect after the Mexican raids of 1842." Equally interesting is the way in which Navarro defended Tejano rights by joining in Anglo subordination of Africans.[51]

On July 16th, Edward Clark, chairman of the committee on education, reported a unique section for the new constitution. It read that "a general diffusion of knowledge being essential to the preservation of the rights and liberties of the people, it shall be duty of the Legislature . . . to make suitable commissions for the support and maintenance for public schools." It also provided that schools should be supported by the legislature through taxation on property and by the allocation of public lands for the building of public schools. The proposed article was laid on the table for future consideration but was nonetheless considered of sufficient importance to require that five hundred copies be immediately printed and distributed.[52]

On July 28, Van Zandt's committee reported a substantial number of proposed general provisions, two of which dealt with prohibitions on dueling. Another prohibited lotteries, while yet another contemplated that the legislature would have the power to exempt certain properties, including homesteads, from execution to pay any judgment against the owner. While legal historians have pointed to Spanish and Mexican antecedents as explaining this new (and unique among contemporary American constitutions) homestead law, tellingly Van Zandt's report also evidenced a strong dislike for corporation and banks. Any corporation was to exist only for a specified term of years, with the sole exception of public utilities. Clearly more was at work than adherence to Spanish and English precedent. Articles were also proposed for processes for impeaching public officers and for scheduling the transition from republic to state. The report was adopted.[53]

On the following day, the convention debated the important question of slaves. Van Zandt's report on this subject contemplated a specific article on the institution of slavery. It began with a prohibition on the legislature passing any law "for the emancipation of slaves without the consent of their owners, or without paying their owners previous to such emancipation a full equivalent for the slaves so emancipated." Van Zandt also suggested a prohibition against preventing owners from bringing slaves into the state "so long as any person of the same age and description shall be continued in slavery by the laws of this State." Continuing the eighteenth- and early-nineteenth-century practice of passing laws prohibiting the mistreatment of slaves, the proposed article contained provisions guaranteeing slaves a right to trial by jury in felony cases, and prohibiting any person from maliciously dismembering or depriving a slave of life. However, an exception was allowed if the slave had been involved in "insurrection." The usual requirement that the proposal lay on the table a day for deliberate consideration was suspended, and the resolution was immediately adopted. Thus the provision in substantially the same form made its way into the Constitution of 1845. As others have shown, provisions like these, coming as they did on the heels of slave rebellions in various states, beginning with Stono's Rebellion in South Carolina, were less about benevolence than about preventing uprisings caused by indiscriminate master cruelty. This explains the freedom granted under Texas law to kill slaves with impunity only on account of "insurrection."[54]

On the same day, Hemphill's committee on the judiciary made its report on land titles. The primary focus of the report was to quiet titles and to prevent the federal courts from intruding upon or superseding the establishment of title by prior acts of the republic.[55] Hemphill ended the report by rejecting the proposal that a special judicial officer should be appointed in each judicial district for the purpose of inquiring into land titles, the committee having determined that it should be left to the legislature how to handle this problem. The 1836 convention had rejected a similar proposal for a special "land tribunal."⁵⁶

The convention spent substantial time debating the rights of women. Hemphill's judiciary committee determined to continue the Spanish legal tradition, adopted by the republic, of community property. As chief justice of the republic, Hemphill, a scholar of Spanish Law, was devoted to amalgamating English common law traditions with Texas' Spanish legal heritage, borrowing the best of both. The initial judiciary committee report provoked a substitute proposal that was ultimately adopted. It provided that all property of a wife owned or claimed by her before marriage or acquired after marriage by gift or inheritance was her separate property, and it called upon the legislature to pass laws providing for registration of the wife's property.⁵⁷ One delegate proposed an amendment that all land and slaves owned by the wife before marriage "together with the increase and profits of the same" should be considered separate property as well. This was rejected as being inconsistent with Spanish community property tradition, as well as constituting an apparent attempt to allow women to continue to maintain as separate property an increase in their slave holdings by birth of new slaves after marriage.⁵⁸

On August 1st, Hemphill's committee reported further on land titles, specifically the composition and identification of public lands. The problem was the issuance of fake land certificates and other forms of swindling that had clogged the courts with, among other things, headright claims to land issued to fictitious persons.⁵⁹ Ultimately, James S. Mayfield offered a provision that was designed to invalidate imprudent colonization contracts made by the Republic of Texas for some of the vacant public lands. His provision allowed the legislature to pass laws providing for "the mode and manner by which all colonization contracts . . . shall be vacated and fully annulled." The sense of the convention was that such contracts made by the republic were unconstitutional, and the provision was passed on August 23rd, clearing the way for the state to assume ownership of lands unoccupied but previously granted improvidently to speculators by the cash-poor Texan nation.⁶⁰

Finally on August 28, 1845, after assurances by a special committee chaired by Hemphill that the convention's record-keeping had been correct and that the copy of the constitution thus compiled was also correct, the constitution was circulated to the delegates in final form and unanimously adopted.⁶¹

The constitution proposed by the convention to the white male voters of Texas contained a preamble and thirteen articles, the last being a schedule for the proceedings necessary to consummate annexation. This required a

John Hemphill, Chief Justice of the Republic of Texas and influential member of the 1845 constitutional convention *(Published with permission of the Tarlton Law Library, Jamail Center for Legal Research, University of Texas School of Law)*

popular election to be held in October 1845 across the state, not by secret ballot, but *viva voce*. County officials were instructed to submit their returns from this election to President Anson Jones, who, if "it should appear from the returns that a majority of all the votes given is for the adoption of the constitution, then it shall be the duty of the president to make proclamation of that fact, and thenceforth this constitution shall be ordained and established as the constitution of the State." The republic's president was also authorized to make the same fact known to the president of the United States. It then befell the Texas president to call further elections for the third Monday in December to fill the offices of governor, lieutenant governor, and members of the Texas Senate and House of Representatives. As per the report of Hemphill's committee, the members of the judicial branch would be appointed to six-year terms by the new governor and confirmed by a two-thirds senate vote, this system remaining in effect until the constitution was amended to return to the practice of electing judges in 1850. Once the republic's president received word that the US Congress had accepted the new Texas constitution, the president's last act would be to convene the newly elected legislature and hand over all public records and property in his possession to the governor.

As part of this transition, all laws of the republic not inconsistent with the new constitution, the joint annexation resolution, or the US Constitution would remain in effect unless and until they expired of their own accord or were changed by the state legislature.[62]

Significantly, the first article of the 1845 constitution was the Bill of Rights. Article II required separation of powers between the three branches of government, and Articles III, IV, and V organized the legislative, judicial, and executive branches, respectively. Article VI provided for a state militia. Of particular interest are Article VII (General Provisions) and the inclusion of Articles VIII (a specific article covering slavery) and X (a specific article requiring a public school system). Article XI concerning land titles and Article XII establishing the General Land Office were related to the education provisions that allocated portions of the public lands for the support of public schools. Article IX governed the impeachment of state officeholders, should that become necessary. This format would provide the basic rubric for all future Texas constitutions.[63]

That the convention established a bicameral state legislature and defined its powers is no surprise. From the perspective of defining Texan identity, however, the qualifications for voters who could select the members of these two houses are of greater interest. The convention debates over the petty details of the matter do not obscure the consensus among the delegates reflected in their final product. The convention was careful to set out residency requirements (six months residency in Texas prior to acceptance of the constitution) to avoid interlopers and vagrants from meddling in the coming elections, including a proviso that "no soldier, seaman, or marine, in the army or navy of the United States, shall be entitled to vote at any election created by this constitution." In de facto terms, the residency requirements meant that recent immigrants from Mexico, or those Tejanos who did not own property and thus could not establish residency in Texas of sufficient duration, could not vote either. More telling was the requirement that all electors be free, male, and twenty-one years of age, "Indians not taxed, Africans, and descendants of Africans, excepted." Women, blacks, and Indians not amalgamated within the white community were de jure excluded.[64]

Articles X, XI, and XII, as well as some of the "General Provisions" of Article VII, show a preoccupation with the white yeoman farmer ideal and a heightened mistrust of banks and other incidents of northeastern commercial power. The 1836 Constitution had placed no restrictions on the power granted to the legislature to "grant charters of incorporation, patents and copy rights," other than the provision, carried over into the 1845 Constitution, that "perpetuities or monopolies are contrary to the genius of a free government, and shall not be allowed." The 1845 convention deemed this limitation insufficient. It specifically directed, in two new constitutional provisions, that Texas be made unfriendly to eastern banks and commercial interests. Section 30 of Article VII specifically prohibited any "corporate body . . . with banking or discounting privileges," and Section 31 prohibited any corporate charter being issued at all except upon a two-thirds vote of both houses of the legislature.[65]

While both the constitutions of 1836 and 1845 prohibited imprisonment for debt, the 1845 convention thought this insufficient to protect working whites from financiers and creditors. Rather, by 1845, sentiment in Texas (and likely elsewhere in the South and West) had grown sufficiently anticommercial and antibank as to impel the convention to add provisions authorizing the legislature to "protect by law, from forced sale, a certain portion of the property of all heads of families . . . not to exceed two hundred acres of land," and to prevent a married man from alienating the same "unless by the consent of the wife," and to "exempt from taxation two hundred and fifty dollars' worth of the household furniture, or other property belonging to each family in this State."[66] These were telling additions to Texas' fundamental law. They demonstrate a strong desire to maintain the integrity and economic independence of white small farm families. Suspicion of the unwholesome and deleterious influence of northern and eastern bankers, lenders, and commercial creditors would continue through the end of the century, rising precipitously during the secession crisis and only intensifying as the state grew and developed after the Civil War.

While the emergence of this economic trepidation bears mention, in the Texas of the 1840s fear of Indians, Tejanos, slaves, and their possible domestic allies still reigned supreme. Although the first section of the Bill of Rights did not limit the polis to free white males, but rather intoned that all political power is inherent in "the people," it was known to all that many were excluded. From the provisions of Articles III and V excluding from the electorate "Indians not taxed, Africans, and descendants of Africans" to the second section of the Bill of Rights declaring that only all "freemen" forming a social compact "have equal rights," the intention was clear.[67]

Also important to these white men were religious liberty and the condemnation of any state religion (and what else could they have meant but the Hispanic Catholicism of their recent experience). Immediately after the first two provisions of the Bill of Rights setting out the Lockean theory of liberty, equality, and social contract, the next two sections outlawed any "religious test . . . as qualification to any office" and that any man "be compelled to attend, erect, or support any place of worship, or to maintain any ministry against his consent," further demanding that no "human authority ought, in any case whatever, to control or interfere with the rights of conscience in matters of religion; and no preference shall ever be given by law to any religious societies or mode of worship." As previously demonstrated, this white-only, anti-Catholic ideal was supplemented to an extent unprecedented in the 1836 Constitution with strengthened provisions against the machinations of corporations, banks, and other northern commercial interests.[68]

Perhaps as xenophobic as any provision of the Constitution of 1845, Section 13 of Article VII's "General Provisions" required that no "member of Congress nor person holding or exercising any office of profit or trust under the United States, or either of them, or under any foreign power" could hold any office in the new state of Texas. Both northern politicians and any Tejanos who had held office under the Mexican government were excluded from public office by this provision. But slaves and those who might succor them remained the greatest danger to the white majority, meriting the entirety of one of the constitution's fourteen articles. The 1836 Constitution had provided that (1) slaves brought to Texas prior to the revolution remained slaves in the republic; (2) the government could not prohibit Anglo immigrants from bringing more slaves with them, nor could it emancipate slaves; (3) no master was allowed to emancipate his own slaves and allow them to remain in Texas without consent of Congress; (4) "no free person of African descent, either in whole or in part, shall be permitted to reside permanently in the Republic, without the consent of Congress"; and (5) the importation "or admission of Africans or negroes into this Republic, excepting from the United States of America, is forever prohibited, and declared to be piracy."[69]

The 1845 state constitution omitted as unnecessary the first provision confirming existing slave ownership, but it made substantial changes in other respects that indicate a refinement in Anglo attitudes. During the republic, the Texas Congress could not emancipate slaves, nor could owners unless they sent their slaves out of state. However, the 1845 Constitution limited the state legislature's power of manumission only if it attempted to emancipate slaves "without the consent of their owners, nor without paying their owners, previous to such emancipation, a full equivalent in money." Hence a notion of compensated voluntary emancipation was now within contemplation.

Indeed, the legislature was specifically authorized "to pass laws to permit the owners of slaves to emancipate them, saving the rights of creditors, and preventing them from becoming a public charge."[70]

Likewise, although the 1845 Constitution continued the right of white American immigrants to bring their slaves to Texas, it limited this right to the importation of such slaves only "so long as any person of the same age or description shall be continued in slavery by the laws of this State." The new constitution also granted the legislature new "power to pass laws which will oblige the owners of slaves to treat them with humanity; to provide for their necessary food and clothing; to abstain from all injuries to them, extending to life or limb; and, in case of their neglect or refusal to comply with the directions of such laws, to have such slave or slaves taken from such owner and sold for the benefit of such owner or owners." Other apparently tolerant provisions guaranteed slaves a jury trial in felony cases and outlawed murdering or dismembering slaves.[71]

While some of the Anglo elite may have been legitimately concerned about the mistreatment of African Americans or the possibility of their false enslavement, the overriding concern expressed in these provisions is perhaps less obvious to the modern mind. The constitution also required that "laws shall be passed to inhibit the introduction into this State of slaves who have committed high crimes in other States or Territories," and it contemplated that laws would be passed preventing "slaves from being brought into this State as merchandise only." Taken together with the other constitutional requirements, these sections reveal a different motivation. Telling was the express permission granted to masters to "maliciously dismember, or deprive a slave of life . . . [only] in case of insurrection by such slave." The primary purpose of the entire article on slavery was, like slave codes in other states, to minimize the possibility of slave insurrection, while holding open the possibility of gradual compensated emancipation. The theory was that prior slave revolts had resulted from a combination of overly harsh treatment and a population of recently imported African slaves insufficiently acculturated to plantation life. It is in this context that the prohibition on bringing slaves from anywhere but the United States itself, and the authorization extended to the legislature to "pass laws to prevent slaves from being brought into this State as merchandise only" make sense. Attitudes about slavery and African Americans became more sophisticated, but they were no less oppressive.[72]

The referendum of October 1845 was a foregone conclusion. On October 13th, annexation passed 4,254 to 267, the constitution was ratified 4,174 to 312, and voters elected James Pinckney Henderson governor and Albert Clinton Horton lieutenant governor. By May 1846, negotiations to avert war between the United States and Mexico over annexation failed and war ensued. The constitutional identity of the new American state of Texas continued to exhibit fear of slave insurrection and unease over Indians, Mexicans, and fifth columnists that might assist or foment it, but even as the threat from south of the Rio Grande and west of the line of white settlement receded, constitutional provisions began to betray new fears of northern and eastern commercial interests. An important aspect of Texas constitutional identity was the southern and Jeffersonian ideal of the yeoman farmer opposed to bankers and financiers. And with the Mexican threat eliminated by annexation and victory in the Mexican War, the 1850s would see Anglo Texans shift their fears of a slave revolt from instigators south of the border to those within the state.[73]

Tejano and German Domestic Threats of the 1850s

After Texas achieved American Statehood and federal protection, Anglo-Texian fears naturally turned inward. Frederick Law Olmsted, in his *Journey through Texas*, written in the early 1850s, claimed that during the late 1840s and early 1850s, it was significant numbers of Tejanos and Germans that posed the biggest threat to slavery in Texas. Many modern historians reply that the Tejanos had too many problems of their own with the Anglo majority to do much against slavery and that German antislavery sentiment is overblown.[74] However, careful study of Olmstead's journal belies this conventional wisdom as overly dismissive. Written in 1853 and 1854, it is the best contemporary account of German-Texan and Tejano antislavery sentiment.

Olmsted was a liberal sympathetic to the European radical democratic revolutions of 1848, and some modern historians seem to believe that all abolitionist or liberal accounts of slavery and antislavery in Texas are to be viewed with suspicion.[75] However, while Olmsted's political views might seem to justify such doubts, a careful reading of his text makes it difficult to believe the charge of exaggeration. Olmsted, like Thucydides, was careful to demonstrate that he did not accept one or two similar stories as historical truth. For example, while he made the general statement that there was danger "to slavery in the west by the fraternizing of the blacks with the Mexicans. They helped them in all their bad habits, married them, stole a living from them, and ran them off every day to Mexico,"[76] lest the reader think he is merely making a bald assertion, Olmsted carefully confirmed it. He did so by use of both corroborating accounts and cultural norms expressed in jokes and other commonplaces. One of the most persuasive passages in the whole book is the corroboration he provided of this view of Mexican and Tejano antislavery sentiment. Later in his travels, speaking with a black runaway in Mexico, Olmsted reported, largely in the man's own words:

> Runaways were constantly arriving ... he could count 40 in the last three months ... being made so much of by these Mexican women that they spent all they brought very soon ... The Mexican government was very just to them; they could always have their rights protected as if they were Mexican born ... Some of them had connected themselves by marriage with old Spanish families who thought as much of themselves as the best white people in Virginia. In fact, a colored man if he could behave himself decently had rather an advantage over a white American, he thought. The people generally liked them better. These Texas folks were too rough to suit them.[77]

Olmsted went even further, though, in explaining why he believed statements like these. It was because

> they were confirmed also in all essential particulars by every foreigner I saw who had lived or traveled in this part of Mexico, as well as by the Mexicans themselves with whom I was able to converse on the subject. It is repeated as a standing joke—I suppose I have heard it fifty times in the Texas taverns and always to the great amusement of the company—that a n****r in Mexico is just as good as a white man, and if you don't treat him civilly he will have you hauled up and fined by an *alcalde*. The poor yellow-faced, priest-ridden heathen actually hold in earnest the ideas on this subject put forth in that good old joke of our fathers—the Declaration of American Independence.[78]

This refrain was repeated wherever he went. When passing through the area around San Marcos, Olmsted reported that "the difficulty ... which will go far to prevent this from becoming a great enslaved planting country *was again brought to our notice* by complaints of the loss of negroes who were supposed to have fled to Mexico" (emphasis added).[79] When discussing the political sentiment in southwestern Texas, Olmsted reported that "the loss and annoyance from this running of slaves to Mexico has been so great in Central and Western Texas as to lead to many propositions. . . . Several conventions and public meetings have been held. . . . Among other plans, it is proposed that a body of 100 rangers be organized, to be equipped at the expense of those interested and stationed upon the Rio Grande for the purpose of awing or catching the runaways." Another meeting proposed a one-cent premium to be charged for membership in a voluntary master's organization, with the money to be used to increase the reward paid to bounty hunters, thus supposedly increasing the deterrent to slaves running away. Contemporary witnesses well knew there was an underground railroad in Texas. It did not lead northward but south to Mexico.[80]

Olmsted was fully aware of a divergence of opinion in the German community about slavery, and he did not ignore this fact or exaggerate the radical end of the spectrum.[81] He was also careful to distinguish between a more liberal Mexican view toward slaves, and a more ambivalent German one. If anything, his prejudices and personal friendships with radical Germans should have caused the reverse emphasis. Reading it against the author's own interests and prejudices, his account is believable as written. Catholic, Tejano, and German antislavery in Texas generated almost as much angst among Texians as Indian uprisings and Mexican incursions, but soon old enemies south of the border and the new ones inside the state would be eclipsed by foreign strangers as the primary source of Texan fears. As chronicled in the next chapter, in the Texas of the 1850s, southern solidarity against the Yankee of the North became more important than American Anglo-Protestant identity.

3

Rebel Constitution

Secession and Confederacy, 1854–1865

ANGLO TEXANS SOON FEARED THE ANTISLAVERY NORTH MORE THAN their old Mexican and Indian enemies. The frontier with Indian country receded ever westward, especially after the stampede of Anglo-American immigrants who settled in Texas after annexation and those who merely passed through on the way to the California gold fields. The Mexican question was settled by the US-Mexican War and the 1848 Treaty of Guadalupe Hidalgo, which vastly expanded American sovereignty to the southwest. These political and demographic realities combined to push the Mexicans and Indians farther and farther away, both physically and psychologically.[1]

As it became clearer that the Indian nemesis was receding and that the domestic slave economy was threatened more by northern activists and politicians than by Hispanics or Germans, the Texan mind began transferring negative racial, ethnic, and religious characteristics from the old *bête noir* to the new. By the time the secession crisis hit in 1860–61, the Texan stereotype of Americans in the North had come to look much like the Mexican/African/Catholic enemy of the 1830s and 1840s. The ideological transformation became so complete that northerners, in a convoluted and symbolic way, even took on darkness and papism as attributes of strangeness in the Texan imagination. Texans' new challenge was to maintain their white proslavery identity in the face of increased interference from the free-soil North.

Abolitionist Infiltrators and Unionism

The 1850s saw isolated Methodist, Episcopalian, and Presbyterian clergymen from the North foment controversy in Texas over slavery. For example, in 1859, Solomon McKinney and a man known to history only as Blount, both Northern Methodist ministers, were run out of Dallas by an angry mob that accused them of abolitionism. The actual extent of their antislavery sentiment is unknown because they protested their innocence and were condemned solely for being part of the northern wing of the Methodist Episcopal Church. Methodists in the South, upset by their church's stand against slavery, had withdrawn to form their own denomination, the Methodist Episcopal Church-South, in 1844. At the Methodist Episcopal national convention in 1848, which many Southerners boycotted, the Northerners refused a Southern "plan of separation" that would have prevented them from organizing churches in the South. The Northerners were anxious to protect southern churches, primarily in Missouri, Texas, and Arkansas, that remained loyal to the national denomination. Soon all of their ministers in these slave states came to be regarded as outside agitators. The national Methodists put Rev. Anthony Bewly in charge of the Texas mission district in 1855. From then until the ejection of McKinney and Blount from Dallas in 1859, the activities of the northern Methodists in Texas centered on Bonham in North Texas, which was a major settlement at the time.[2]

Ironically, northern Methodists eventually began withholding support from Texas when they came to believe Bewly too soft on slavery. But, in fact, Bewly found himself caught between his national hierarchy, who expected vocal abolitionism, and his local circumstances, which required caution. He was unable to satisfy either. In 1859, local southern Methodists went to their annual Texas convention in Timber Creek near Bonham and voted to exile Bewly and his assistants, William Butts, James Harrer, and Thomas Willette, as tainted by northern influence. Bewly and Butts quietly defied the order and remained in North Texas, but they could only hold services in secret. The precarious situation caused furious debate in the press organs of both the southern and the northern Methodist sects. Eventually, Bewly and Butts departed for the North, but in a singular case of faulty timing, a few months later and shortly after John Brown's raid on Harper's Ferry, Bewly's bishop dispatched him and Willette back to Texas. Antislavery sentiment among frontier Germans and Hispanics in southwest Texas was well documented in contemporary accounts, including Bewly's. When the bishop had asked about the prospects of attracting converts in Texas, Bewly said he thought it unlikely he could do any good "except that Germans on the Nueces and West of the Colorado had expressed a desire for the preaching of the Methodist Episcopal Church." The bishop sent him south anyway.[3]

Unfortunately, at just the time that Bewly returned to Texas, unexplained fires broke out in Bonham and a six-year-old child died under mysterious circumstances. Rumors immediately spread through North Texas of a Methodist-inspired slave revolt. Bewly was lynched in 1859 by a group of Fort Worth vigilantes, although the only real evidence against him was a letter that some historians are convinced was forged. Witnesses nonetheless came forward to testify that they overheard Bewly talking of plans to start an insurrection. Although letters he wrote to his family while awaiting execution vehemently deny that he was involved in any such plot, Bewly's personal abolitionist leanings are without serious doubt.[4]

Certainly from the 1850s well into the Civil War, conventional Anglo Texans believed they had growing reason to fear outside abolitionist agitators. For example, secessionist editors in South and West Texas, like Henry Maltby of the Corpus Christi *Ranchero*, testified to the truth of Frederick Law Olmsted's accounts of their antislavery Tejano neighbors. "Not only [do Mexicans] consider a n****r equal with themselves," wrote Maltby in 1863, "but they actually court the company of the Negroes."[5]

But even more unsettling were abolitionist fifth columnists that began to appear in the mid-1850s that were not Tejanos, Germans, or "crackpot" ministers of the gospel. In 1855, Lorenzo Sherwood, a member of the Texas state legislature, made the mistake of publicly lecturing that body that even if slavery might be necessary until the end of the century, it "could not be maintained permanently in a democracy." Sherwood was immediately denounced on the floor of the house, excoriated in the newspapers, and forced to resign by his constituents. Their outrage was spontaneously expressed at a hastily called public meeting in Galveston organized by the prominent local lawyer and editor, William Pitt Ballinger. Sherwood wanted to address the meeting and explain his position, but Ballinger warned that if he or any of his supporters tried to do so, then that would constitute "the occasion for the definite and final settlement of that issue, both as to you and to them." Sherwood was no fool. He resigned, but the remote possibility remained that Tejanos or radical activists might destabilize Anglo hegemony over Texas' enslaved African population. These eruptions of domestic abolitionism served to heighten suspicion of any who too loudly professed loyalty to the national government. They would become known as "unionists."[6]

In the late 1850s, states' rights ideology became so virulent as to amount to southern nationalism. Unlike abolitionists, who were seen as crackpots, Texas unionists were more traditional, more numerous, and therefore more politically and psychologically dangerous. Unionism developed as a response to states' rights extremism and parallel to abolitionism, but it drew from a much broader demographic constituency in Texas. As historian James Marten has demonstrated, most unionists were neither oddball dreamers nor radical German artisans, but rather, "older, more settled, and more economically independent than their secessionist counterparts. They rejected southern nationalism not because they rejected the South and wished it ill, but because they believed disunion would destroy a southern economy and society that had been very good to them, because they distrusted the motives of secessionists, and because they refused to acquiesce in the destruction of their Union."[7]

Very few Texas unionists were overt antislavery men. Such abolitionists as there were in the 1850s and 1860s, with few exceptions, manifested their beliefs quietly and as best they could. They declined to be more bellicose because activists like the German radical Adolph Douai were invariably driven from the state or, as in the case of Reverend Bewly, suffered worse. Most abolitionists and unionists thought better of voting in the secession election of 1861 because "secret" balloting was nonexistent, and Tejanos would likely be barred from voting by their ethnicity anyway.[8] Most public unionists were not abolitionists but whiggish independent Democrats or Know-nothings, including Sam Houston, Ben Epperson of Red River County, and John Hancock of Austin. The unionists controlled nineteen newspapers according to one of their number, *The Washington American*. The other unionist newspapers included the *Galveston Weekly News*; *The Alamo Express*, edited by James P. Newcomb; and the pro-Houston *Southern Intelligencer*. By far the most influential of the unionists was Sam Houston, the paradigm of the moderate national-union Democrat who approved of the institution of slavery but rejected southern states' rights extremism.[9]

After the demise of Know-Nothingism and the rigid enforcement of states' rights orthodoxy within the Democratic Party of the 1850s, these unionist politicians and editors supported John Bell's Constitutional Union ticket in 1860, and according to historian Frank Smyrl, "All ten counties giving over

40% to the unionist candidate were definitely western if not frontier counties, some containing a sizeable number of Germans." These numbers were subjected to more rigorous statistical analysis by Dale Baum almost twenty-five years later, and he agreed with Smyrl that unionist sentiment was strongest among Spanish speakers and recent German immigrants. While many Germans and Tejanos in western Texas and around San Antonio vigorously opposed slavery, a far greater number opposed secession on other grounds. Their chief reasons were the simple fact that among these citizens slavery was virtually unknown, and the economic reality that the federal army's western forts were important consumers of their surplus farm produce. And the prominence of Hispanic San Antonio and southwest Texas as hotbeds of unionism is confirmed by other incidents and personages absent from many conventional accounts. For example, as soon as it became known Lincoln had won the presidential election of 1860, it was in heavily Hispanic San Antonio that unionists called a meeting to respond to the secessionist sentiment growing across the state. And the most radical unionist state legislator hailed from the Mexican border, John L. Haynes from Rio Grande City.[10]

Even so, the careers of German newspaper editors Ferdinand Flake and Ferdinand Lindheimer illustrate a degree of ambivalence about secession within their particular communities. Flake was a newspaper editor in Galveston. He and Lindheimer were both Democrats because of their understandable dislike for Know-Nothings' virulent nativism. Flake vehemently opposed the slave trade and probably harbored some doubts about the morality of slavery, but he owned a slave. Lindheimer, a conservative assimilationist, also opposed the slave trade but only because he feared a massive influx of slave labor that would take away German jobs. He edited the *Neu Braunfelser Zeitung*. These two prominent German editors spilled much ink debating who was a "true" and who was a "bogus" Democrat, and even the more liberal Flake came to accept Secession once it was a *fait accompli*. One the other hand, while Lindheimer more quickly adopted a secessionist stance, historians have argued that his real sympathies lay with the Union. Similar ambivalence and multiple shades of antislavery sentiment also obtained in the broader German community. More recent immigrants and those living in closer proximity to frontier and heavily Hispanic areas tended to be more radical.[11]

The political spectrum began and ended much farther to the right among the overwhelming majority of Anglo Texans in the settled areas to the east. Within that community, the only real controversy over slavery was disagreement over the extent to which slavery should be *expanded*. At the 1857 Texas Democratic convention, a resolution was offered, proposing that Texas lobby the federal government to remove the 1808 ban on slave trading. This caused something of a groundswell within the Democratic Party and resulted in a similar resolution being introduced in the next legislature. Cooler heads prevailed, and it was referred to committee where it died due "to the controversial nature of the proposition," even in the rest of the South. As distinguished from unionism, overt antislavery existed in Anglo Texas only if one counts opposition to *reopening the slave trade* as "anti-slavery."[12]

The Secession Crisis and Its Rhetoric

The contest between xenophobia and liberalism during the revolution and the republic continued in the debate over Texas secession, but the nature of the dialectic changed drastically in 1859 and 1860. The Mexican, Indian, and Tejano villain was rapidly replaced with a new enemy, the northerner, whose strangeness became so palpable as to cause his fellow Americans in Texas and the South to consistently refer to him as a "black" Republican.[13] The dominant political identity enshrined in the Secession Constitution of 1861 defined the white Anglo establishment as distinctly southern and cast in relief against the dark enemy of the North.[14]

The unionists, on the other hand, rebutted the secessionists by arguing that the lessons of Western civilization taught that disunity and extremism were dangerous and unwise. As a practical matter, they counseled caution. But secessionists, in defending their vilification of the North, took a different rhetorical tack. Typically, they confined themselves to narrow appeals to sectional self-interest and antinorthern bias, and with this they won the day, largely by demonizing the North. In addition, although most of the protagonists on each side, including Houston, were trained as lawyers, the secessionists were much more likely to use legalism and allusions to the Declaration of Independence and the "Spirit of 1776." Conversely, although some of the secessionists were at least as familiar with world history and the classics, as were Houston and his partisans, their rhetoric was much less likely to allude to it. The most important reason for this was the difficulty of combining an argument fundamentally based on xenophobia with an argument based on the lessons of another ethnicity's history. Thus secessionists were forced by the very internal logic of their own arguments to limit their historical evidence to recent Anglo-American history. Unionists operated under no such ideological constraint and moreover, many of them were recent German immigrants, Tejanos, or otherwise not Anglo-American. For them, the lessons of Greece, Rome, and the Renaissance rolled off the tongue.[15]

But upon reflection, the whole phenomenon of Texas secession is, in Walter Buenger's words, a riddle. While Texans heavily favored joining the Union a mere fifteen years earlier and reaped substantial economic benefit as a result, by 1860 secessionism quickly appeared at the grassroots in most counties of the state. And yet, as Buenger has pointed out, the process was simultaneously and "openly led by the pillars of the community."[16] What rhetorical devices did these "pillars of the community" use in their public proclamations and official declarations? What does this rhetoric tell us about their self-referential internal narratives as actors and prodders, about the audience that responded so enthusiastically to their entreaties, and about the identity that would be enshrined in the victors' Constitution of 1861?

A reasonable starting point in answering this question is the oratory of Houston's electoral nemesis, Hardin R. Runnels. Runnels, whose uncle Hiram was a delegate to the 1845 convention, defeated Houston in the gubernatorial election of 1857 when Houston had run as an independent. Houston, a few years after his reelection to the U.S. Senate in 1852, began flirting with Know-Nothingism because his vote against the pro-slavery 1854 Kansas-Nebraska Act alienated him from mainstream Democrats. Although a slaveholder, Houston, like his mentor Andrew Jackson, venerated the Union and the delicate balance of compromises that he believed held it intact. The Kansas-Nebraska Act was doubly odious to Houston not only because it repealed the Missouri Compromise and portions of the Compromise of 1850, but because it threatened to organize into US territories land already given to Indian tribes. It was not long after this vote that the states-rights and slavery-expansion Democrats in Texas began calling for Senator Houston's political scalp, and he in turn experimented with Know-Nothingism. But in 1856, even the Know-Nothings endorsed the Kansas-Nebraska Act and nominated Millard Fillmore rather than Houston for president. So Houston, without a party and annoyed with national politics, decided on a maverick run for governor against Runnels, who had already been nominated by the Democratic state convention for the office. Houston lost the election by nine thousand votes but remained in the Senate until his term there expired in 1859.[17]

In that year, Houston again ran for governor, this time as a maverick "Union Democrat" unendorsed by the state party convention. He unexpectedly succeeded in ousting Runnels from office. So Runnels, the bitter outgoing incumbent, was a natural bellwether of anti-Houston and radical proslavery sentiment. On Thursday, November 10, 1859, three months after he had lost the election to Houston, Runnels delivered his written biennial message to the Texas legislature. Forty-one days after this written message, on Wednesday, December 21, 1859, Runnels also delivered a valedictory address to the legislature as Texas' departing governor. Houston and his newly elected lieutenant governor, Edward Clark, were seated in the chamber and heard this address.[18]

Runnels spent the first two-thirds of his written November 10th "State of the State" speech on a variety of policy issues.[19] Before moving to the subject of secession in the last third of this document, he lamented the deplorable condition of the Texas frontier beset by bandit raids, and then eulogized the recently deceased Sen. J. Pinckney Henderson, the states' rights firebrand whom the legislature had elected to replace Thomas Rusk in the Senate when the latter committed suicide in 1857. Runnels's eulogy of the fire-eating Henderson was a logical *segue* into a tirade against the free-soil North.[20]

Runnels's remarks that began with Henderson's eulogy and ended with an exposition of states' rights are little more than repeated warnings that Texas and the Constitution "are in danger of being overwhelmed by the seemingly resistless tide of sectional and religious fanaticism." Runnels saw the Black Republicans as intellectual heirs to the evil Federalists of the late eighteenth and early nineteenth centuries, henchmen of the eastern commercial interests who had always been "at open warfare with the rights of property and the constitutional laws by which it is protected." His address describes abolitionism as "fanatical pretensions," resulting from a loose construction of the Constitution claiming "for the General Government more extensive powers than are warranted by that instrument."[21]

At the end of his speech, he resorted to nineteenth-century American legalism, claiming that the "unconditional submission" to the Union urged by the neo-Federalist Republicans resulted from "a higher law construction" that "makes the agent superior to the principal." He then referenced the Dred Scott decision, lamenting that the North would not be deterred from abolitionism even by pronouncements from the highest court of the land: "When the courts have intervened and determined the question, the South is not allowed to benefit of that decision, but an appeal is taken to the people with the revolutionary object of depriving us of that protection of the property of our citizens to which the Constitution entitles them."[22]

His message concluded by recommending a "clear and unequivocal expression of opinion by the legislature on the subject.... Equality and security in the Union or independence outside of it, should be the model of every Southern State."[23] Runnels justified this conclusion by a complex but important historical argument that traced the pedigree of the "anti-Democratic" faction within the United States. Beginning with a history of the Federalists, and heaping upon them the charge of treason in connection with the War of 1812 because of their traditionally pro-British sympathies, he claimed that characteristic policies of these early "Anti-Democrats" included the tariff, the bank, and the restriction of slavery.[24] He described the Whig party as the intellectual successor to the Federalists from the election of 1836 until 1852, at which time arose other incarnations of the opposition. As Runnels declared, "By whatever names the opposition to the regular Democratic organization may have passed for half a century, whether it is Anti-masons, National Republicans, Whigs, Know-Nothings, Union Men or Higher Law Men, the radical difference of opinion which has existed in regard to the nature and powers of the government, has manifested itself in that federal and latitudinous construction of the Constitution, so often and so long repudiated for its dangerous tendencies."[25]

In rebuttal to this "federal and latitudinous construction," he invoked the figures of Jefferson, Franklin, "and other sages and heroes," reminding his readers that their Declaration of Independence was the reluctant culmination of repeated arguments and entreaties to the British crown for less government and more respect for constitutional rights. "This," he said, "I regard as analogous to the position of the States' Rights Democracy of the South and of the Union."[26]

In his later valedictory message of December 1859, Runnels echoed the same themes of abolitionism as a fanatical politico-religious heresy, Black Republicanism as an outgrowth of anti-Jeffersonian Federalism, and the consonance of his own views with the American "Spirit of 1776." He began his inevitable defense of states' rights by reminding the legislature of his recommendation two years earlier that it should organize a militia for public defense "in view of the impending sectional difficulties." He argued:

> It is now clearly demonstrated by the history of the past five years that a deep unchangeable determination exists in the northern states to assail our dearest political rights, and if possible, destroy our domestic institutions. This determination has its foundations in a difference in the manners, feelings and opinions of the northern people upon the subject of Negro slavery. They believe it to be a moral, social, and political evil. This belief strengthened into a conviction that has been incorporated

with and now constitutes the sole of their religion and the mainspring of their morality.[27]

Runnels's allusion to religion should not be overlooked. Although legalism, recent American history, and constitutional libertarianism play a role in these speeches, they are clearly handmaidens to the overarching theme: terror of a northern bogeyman, who like his Mexican Catholic predecessor, now also became an authoritarian religious heretic.[28]

Upon Runnels' departure from office, the man who took over leadership of the anti-Houston faction in state government was Texas Supreme Court Justice Oran Milo Roberts. O. M. Roberts had a long career in Texas politics prior to Secession. Raised in Alabama, Roberts learned Greek and Latin in grammar school and began studying the law with a local practitioner in Ashville, Alabama when he was only seventeen. After attending college and studying law, Roberts moved to Texas in 1841, at age twenty-six. He was an outstanding debater in college, and he used these skills in his East Texas law practice, centered upon the city of San Augustine.[29]

In 1844, he was appointed district attorney and then, in 1846, state district judge, and it was from this position that he conducted his political activities. He was thoroughly involved in Democratic Party politics throughout the 1840s and 1850s, having run unsuccessfully for Congress in both 1851 and 1853. Around 1855 he became involved in criticizing Sam Houston and the rising Know-Nothing Party in Texas, and he was ultimately elevated to the position of Associate Justice of the Supreme Court of Texas in 1857. As a political agitator for states' rights and secession, Roberts appears to have been guided by regional prejudice, his personal political philosophy, and his religion. He was a devout and fundamentalist Protestant Christian.[30] As early as his first years in Texas, Roberts wrote articles on educational and religious subjects.[31] In 1858, he wrote an essay that foreshadowed the traditional Anglo-Protestant morality that would reappear in his later works: "The society of Europe and America is based on a few leading ideas generally regarded ... as axiomatic truths. Some of these are First, the Christian Religion; Second, a man shall have one wife; Third, every male person shall look out and provide for himself and his family."[32]

The appearance of Know-Nothingism in the late 1850s provided Roberts his first opportunity to speak out publicly in behalf of the Texas Democratic Party against any form of "whiggishness." The other major leaders of the states' rights Democrats in the 1850s were Runnels, his lieutenant governor F. R. Lubbock, US Senator J. Pinckney Henderson, Louis T. Wigfall (also a

US Senator), and John H. Reagan.[33] As early as the late 1850s, the anti-Unionist rhetoric of these individuals, Judge Roberts, and other Democrats like Thomas Rusk set the pattern for the oratorical style of later secessionists. For example, in 1855, Rusk made a speech condemning the North as follows: "Their secrecy is highly objectionable. No party can be safely trusted with power who does not openly avow their principles, the oaths which it is understood they take are illegal, tyrannical, and at open war with the fundamental principles of our government . . . at the north, as all elections show, they are abolitionists. At the south they profess to be pro-slavery men. . . . The whigs are disorganized if not disbanded; no one can mistake the rock upon which they split."

As with Runnels's speeches, Rusk's references to cabals, secret oaths, and unrestrained hierarchy obviously recalled papism, and these tropes would become more sinister as other secessionists began to fill in the caricature with more color, detail, and imagination. Speaking to fellow Democrats, Roberts recommended, "If we desire to succeed as a party. . . . We must drive out of our ranks that cursed faction of freesoilers and abolitionists who, determined to rule or ruin, have . . . jeopardized the Union." While this early speech only accused the Know-Nothings of being abolition-tolerant chameleons and former Whigs, demonization of the North would intensify in the years to come.[34]

Roberts gave a similar anti-Know-Nothing speech in Henderson, Texas, on August 24, 1855. In it, he quoted Macaulay's essays in comparing Puritans and Pharisees to Know-Nothings. He used this analogy to create fear in his audience that Massachusetts, "the breeding ground for Federalism and Puritanism," was responsible for the Know-Nothings blurring the distinction between church and state. Thus Roberts, even if unconsciously, recalled to his audience the odious specter of papism, power-grabbing and pharisaical. He quickly moved on from this brief historical analogy to demonize "the north, the Puritans, the Federalists, Massachusetts, northern preachers, and the Know-Nothings." This passage further reveals the religious leitmotif running through the condemnation of federal whiggishness and "loose constructionism" common to the rhetoric of Runnels, Roberts, and other secessionists. Through loose constructionism, nonfundamentalism, nonliteralism, anti-Masonism, and power-grasping tyranny, the antislavery Northerner had become not only "black," but simultaneously a slave-coddling papist/puritan and an uncivilized brigand with no respect for, or fear of, the written word, whether scriptural or constitutional. Although the Know-Nothings were themselves anti-Catholic, Roberts equated them figuratively with all parties throughout Christian history who exalted power, custom, or tradition over those who recognized no authority but the strict and limiting construction of the written word. He ranged them among the bogeymen of fundamental Southern Democratic Protestantism: whigs, Federalists, papists, Puritans, abolitionists, and ... northerners.[35]

Roberts drew distinctions between the Democratic Party of "the word" and the authoritarian Federalist/Whig/Know-Nothing opposition. His exposition of its ideological pedigree mirrored that suggested by Runnels to the Texas Legislature four years later. Like Runnels, Roberts targeted the National Bank, Federalists, domestic manufacturers, loose interpreters of the Constitution, and abolitionists. He portrayed these elements of society as traitors to the separation of church and state, repeating, "Know-Nothingism is an offshoot from this same old stock of Puritan nationality." He thus railed again at the northerner as a religious heretic, as a nonliteralist, as an exalter of human power and hierarchy over the sanctity of written text. While the papist had become a "puritan" for geographical effect (the puritan connection with abolitionist Massachusetts), the theological objections were the same. Roberts's historical analogies were designed to demonstrate a continuous lineage of evil political and religious heresy from the repressive Puritans, through the big government Federalists and Whigs, to the Know-Nothing "American Party" of the 1850s. The Jacksonian trepidation over eastern commercial interests that surfaced in the 1845 constitutional convention had now, in the space of only ten years, become full-blown hysteria.[36]

Roberts's efforts in 1855, along with those of the other Democrats, soundly defeated the Know-Nothing candidate for governor, sitting Lt. Gov. David C. Dixon. They also handed Sam Houston, running as an "independent unionist," his only electoral defeat in the gubernatorial election two years later.[37] By the time Houston returned to win the 1859 gubernatorial election as an "Independent Democrat," Secession as a political agenda had progressed rapidly from the inchoate ruminations of states' rights Democratic Party leaders to a broad-based movement. That movement was touched off by Lincoln's election in 1860. By then, Oran Milo Roberts had decided to vie for leadership of this groundswell of public sentiment. In 1860, he gave his first blatantly secessionist speech in Austin, at the end of a day's work as an associate justice of the Texas Supreme Court. The speech came about as a result of an odd combination of circumstances, in that the other associate justice of the court, James H. Bell, had announced at a unionist meeting in Austin three days earlier that he intended to make a pro-Union speech on December 1. Roberts took this as an opportunity to contradict Bell's oration and announced that he would give a rebuttal against the Union "at the same time and place."[38]

Roberts's speech assailed "the revolutionary party of the north" that had "advanced step-by-step toward the destruction of our domestic institutions." The several pages of handwritten text continued along the same lines as his speeches of the mid-1850s and Governor Runnels's 1859 messages to the legislature.[39] Unlike Roberts's oration, Judge Bell's antisecession speech was full of literary analogies. Bell, like Houston, had just defeated a firebrand Democratic Party machine candidate, Constantine W. Buckley, and Houston and Bell had long been friends. Bell's speech quoted Edmund Burke's observation that "timidity where the welfare of one's country is concerned, is heroic virtue." In addition, he cited the opening Canto of Shelley's *Revolt of Islam*, Shakespeare's *Romeo and Juliet*, and the rabble-rousing demagogues Jack Cade and Wat Tyler from Shakespeare's *Henry VI*. Judge Bell's point was to discourage hasty mob rebellion against the rule of law.[40]

Roberts's speech of December 1, 1860, on the other hand, had no need of similar culture. It simply ran through the traditional litany of legal and constitutional arguments in favor of a state's right to secede from the Union. Characteristically, Roberts did not reach for historical support more remote than his own Anglo-Saxon origins. In a passage echoing his essays on Christiantity, he set forth his familiar personal ethic: "European society, since the extinction of villenege and serfdom, has assumed and rests upon this basis. That every person of lawful age must provide for himself and the liberty and means of doing [it] . . . is controlled by the few—the governing class."

The rest of the speech refers to the need for cooperation with Texas' "sister southern states, whether it be in or out of the union," to the northern "virulent antipathy" toward slavery, to the North as "a set of fanatics," to the dangers associated with "an infuriated mob of free Negroes," and to an evil liberal construction that "induces a continual effort to find powers in the constitution that are, in fact, not expressed." Roberts concentrated on constitutional legitimation as a rational persuasive device, and then counted on conjuring up a "fanatical," authoritarian, loose-constructionist, Negro-inciting Northern bogeyman to do the rest.[41]

On the unionist side, besides Houston and Bell, the major proponents were Houston's friends Ben Epperson, D. B. Culbertson, and most significantly, US Congressman A. J. "Colossal" Hamilton and newspaperman George W. Paschal. John H. Reagan, a moderate Democrat, originally sought to defuse

Rebel Constitution

Oran Milo Roberts (right) and **James H. Bell** (below) Texas Supreme Court Justices who debated Secession in Austin in 1860 (Published with permission of the Tarlton Law Library, Jamail Center for Legal Research, University of Texas School of Law)

talk of secession, and had generally unionist sympathies, but he quickly gave way to the popular will and became a secessionist.[42]

James Throckmorton was also influential. A member of the Texas Senate and one of the mere handful of delegates to the Texas Secession Convention who voted "no" on the ordinance of secession of February 1, 1861, his statement at the time was "Mr. President, in view of the responsibility, in the presence of God and my country and unawed by the wild spirit of revolution around me, I vote no!" When spectators hissed him from the gallery, he added, "When the rabble hiss, well may patriots tremble."[43]

Throckmorton went on to fight in the Civil War as a captain in the Sixth Texas Cavalry, putting his unionist views behind him. Throckmorton, Epperson, and many of Houston's other lieutenants exemplified the historical evolution of naturally whiggish politicians into Know-Nothings and then unionists, in just the fashion O. M. Roberts and Harden Runnels had denounced. They represented the loyal opposition in the Democratic South. Unfortunately, few ready examples of their polemics during the height of the secession debate survive, but the speeches and writings of Hamilton and unionist editors like Paschal were somewhat better chronicled, and some examples of Houston's unionist oratory survive. In the election of 1859 that seemed fleetingly to endorse his unionism, Houston gave only one formal campaign speech. It was on his home turf in Nacogdoches, Texas, and Paschal's friendly *Southern Intelligencer* published the entire text in a July 23, 1859, special edition appropriately titled *The Campaign Intelligencer*. The newspaper described the speech as "a stunner from which the secessionist and reopen the African slave trade opposition cannot recover. They have no man with the brains to answer it." With respect to the gubernatorial election, *The Intelligencer* was right, but as to secession, "brains" would soon hold little sway.[44]

By the fall of 1860, there were already moves afoot in the legislature to call a convention to secede. The tide was fast turning against the unionists. Houston's strategy was to deny the legislature's authority to dissolve Texas' ties with the Union. While he maneuvered against Roberts and the legislature for more time, he was quietly recruiting surrogate orators like Justice James H. Bell and encouraging his other friends in politics to speak out as well. Some had long already been stumping against the party machine, however, and needed no encouragement. For example, Andrew Hamilton gave a speech in Austin on July 31, 1858, in support of Bell's independent campaign for the Supreme Court. Its rhetorical style presaged the language both he and Bell would later use to defend the Union. In both situations, it was necessary

Rebel Constitution

George W. Pascal, prominent unionist newspaper editor (right) and **J. Pinkney Henderson**, firebrand secessionist governor and senator (below) (Published with permission of the Tarlton Law Library, Jamail Center for Legal Research, University of Texas School of Law)

to attack the Democratic Party machine, in the first instance because it had nominated the incompetent party hack Constantine Buckley for the Court, thus precipitating Bell's independent candidacy, and in the latter case because the convention endorsed John C. Breckinridge, the schismatic secessionist "Democratic" candidate in the presidential election of 1860. On this particular occasion in the summer of 1858, Hamilton showed up at a picnic/barbecue sponsored by the party regulars and began to speak against them and their candidate Buckley.[45]

Editor Paschal of the friendly *Intelligencer* reported that the "organizer" clique of the party, whom he also referred to as "organ-grinders," underestimated Hamilton's eloquence and lungpower. They had erected a "temple of liberty too near the organ . . . ever ready to grind out denunciations against all who will not bow the supplicant's knee to Baal." Paschal, in extolling Hamilton here and later, often referred to his strong manly physique, built by proudly tilling fields "which the silk-stocking gentry think degrading to all but an imported African." Hamilton began the speech by congratulating his listeners for having the courage to gather within sight of the "organizer" meeting and to "question the infallibility of the Star Chamber" of this "self constituted junto." Paschal himself then rose to speak in support of Hamilton, but wearing his editor hat a few days later, reported tongue in cheek that "it becomes us not to chronicle that gentleman's (his own) speech. . . . And the speaker is too hoarse this morning to prompt us."[46]

Hamilton gave a similar antiestablishment speech in the Austin federal courthouse during the 1859 campaign. He again made reference to his yeoman origins, arguing that the regular party's adoption of a platform supporting reopening the slave trade was an affront to the work ethic of white laborers. He warned that he "would never consent to a system which would reduce white labor to nothing and Africanize the South." He denounced the move to reopen the slave trade as "an undisguised secession measure . . . aimed at nothing short of overturning the government." Hamilton went on to announce his candidacy for Congress from Texas' western district and to endorse the election of Houston as governor.[47] A few weeks later, he conducted a series of debates with his "organ-grinder" opponent, Thomas N. Wahl. In these, Hamilton played upon the same themes and at one venue concluded with a testimonial to Houston that the *Intelligencer* reported had made "old and gray bearded men spring from their seats and bound into the air."[48]

Like Houston, Hamilton won his election, but on January 26, 1860, in his first speech on the floor of Congress, Hamilton engaged in the very demonization of the North epitomized by his secessionist opponents. Reminding his colleagues of the uniqueness of Texas' affection for the Union, he warned that the election of a "Black Republican" Speaker of the House would further the cause of disunion. He saw himself and other Southern Jacksonian unionists as the ultimate conservatives, caught between radicals on both sides: "The Union sir is being dissolved now. It may be in the power of the conservative elements of this House to arrest it; but that cannot be done by the election of a Black Republican Speaker. I believe that I represent as conservative a constituency as any gentleman upon this floor; a people who are devoted to the Union; a people, sir, who have, I think, manifested that devotion by . . . yielding up what no other State in the Union has yielded, a separate nationality."[49]

Like Houston and Hamilton, during the run-up to the Secession crisis in the late 1850s, the *Southern Intelligencer* steadfastly advocated Jacksonian unionism. From 1856 to March of 1860, the "proprietors" identified themselves as Baker & Root, while the editor and primary propagandist was George W. Paschal. [50] A self-professed constitutional lawyer, he was instrumental in convincing James Bell to run for the Texas Supreme Court and in whipping up popular sentiment against the party machine's candidate Buckley.[51]

Although a unionist, Paschal considered himself a loyal and "true" Democrat opposed to sectionalists, secessionists, and northern or Mexican abolitionist agitators who might whip up their vengeance. He regularly blamed threats to the Union upon the equally extreme views of Free-Soilers on the one hand and Southern fire-eaters on the other. Thus in 1856 he excoriated southern extremists for exaggerating threats of a northern-backed slave rebellion, and in 1859, he extolled Judge John Reagan for denouncing the troublemakers, "the re-open-the-African-slave trade free booter-filibustero-secessionists." Like Reagan, Paschal considered himself a "States-Rights Union loving Democrat . . . who preaches no doctrine South which he might not preach North." From 1856 to 1859, Paschal was consistently critical of the southern radicals (whom he dubbed "salamanders") who favored reopening the slave trade and invading Cuba solely to make it a new part of the southern slave plantation system. The November 19, 1956, *Southern Intelligencer* attests Paschal's dislike both of exaggerated reports of slave uprisings and outside abolitionist agitators. He wrote that "the contemplated negro insurrection which was developed at Lavaca a few days ago has been traced to an 'Ohio Yankee' . . . who confessed his participation, and received a hundred lashes of the 'discipline' over which he may shed lugubrious tears at the first abolition meeting which he shall attend—No Mexicans have been implicated at this time." Even the reporting of the secessionist elite's most well-placed opponents testified to its fear of a Yankee-Mexican-slave insurrection conspiracy.[52]

When it became clear that Houston would be the only viable candidate to unseat the sectionalist Runnels as governor, Paschal's rhetoric intensified apace with Hamilton's and he made peace with Houston, whom he had opposed in the 1850s as a Know-Nothingish traitor to the Democratic Party.[53] In 1860, Paschal was instrumental in organizing Union clubs throughout the state. Their purpose was to thwart the election of either the Republican Lincoln or the Dixiecrat Breckinridge by any means. These clubs agreed to endorse the candidacy of four uncommitted Constitutional Union electors from Texas, Paschal and William Steadman at large; and Ben Epperson and John H. Robson from the eastern and western congressional districts, respectively. While most of the clubs also endorsed the national Constitution Union ticket led by Tennessee's Whig Senator John C. Bell, they agreed to vote for the uncommitted "Union ticket" of electors "content to leaving them uninstructed as to how the vote of the State shall be given, except that they should so cast it, if necessary, as will defeat the nominees of the Chicago (Republican) Convention." Meanwhile, the old-line Democrats formed "Douglass and Johnson Clubs," yet these also endorsed the same Union electoral slate with instructions to vote for the candidate "shown to be most available against Lincoln."[54]

The Constitution of 1861

In November of 1860, shortly before his debate with Justice Bell over Secession, Roberts had already drawn up the "First Call upon the People of Texas to Assemble in Convention" with a group composed of W. P. Rogers, Attorney General George Flournoy, and Texas Ranger Col. John S. "Rip" Ford. This "Call" was copied by Roberts and sent later in the month to Rogers, who had left for Houston to organize a mass meeting. At that meeting, a resolution passed endorsing the Call. Roberts mentioned these events briefly in his December capitol speech, and the Call was printed and published shortly thereafter. The Call, like the secessionist pronouncements before it, merely listed the affronts recently suffered at the hands of the Black Republicans of the North. In response, a convention was indeed convoked by the Texas Legislature over Governor Houston's objection, but the legislature agreed to Houston's fallback position that even if Secession passed the convention, it should still be submitted to a popular referendum.[55]

More evidence of the emerging ideological identity of the prosecession party in Texas is contained within the journal of that convention, which met at the end of January 1861. The convention began, after some preliminary matters involving the election of Roberts and other officers, the seating and credentialing of delegates, the adoption of rules, and the like, by asking its president O. M. Roberts to appoint various committees. On January 29th, Roberts appointed a committee to confer with Governor Houston on "the subject of federal relations." The committee was composed of John H. Reagan, John Stell, Peter W. Gray, William P. Rogers, and Thomas J. Devine. Roberts also appointed a committee of twenty to "present business to this Convention for its consideration." It is a testament to Reagan's incredible knack for political survival that he, a conservative unionist only a few years before, was among the most respected secessionist leaders at the convention. The next day the committee reported "in secret session" the response of Houston, which was oblique. While Houston assured the committee that "whatever will conduce to the welfare of our people will have my warmest and most fervent wishes," his written reply of the following day, January 31, 1861, insisted that a vote by the citizens of Texas was still necessary before any decision could be made about "federal relations."[56]

The convention met the next day, February 1, 1861, and promptly passed a resolution seceding from the Union by a vote of 166 to 8. Convention President Roberts signed it first, followed by the remaining secessionist delegates.[57] On February 2nd, in anticipation of the required plebiscite, a resolution passed endorsing "a declaration of the causes which impelled the state of Texas to secede from the federal union," drafted by John Henry Brown, George Flournoy, John Wilcox, M. D. Graham, and A. P. Wiley. This document occupies several pages of the journal of the convention, but unlike Jefferson's majestic 1776 document, this declaration included only a chronological examination of those recent grievances "and other wrongs we have patiently born in the vain hope that a returning sense of justice and humanity would induce a different course of administration" by the federal government. Chief among these was that the states of the North "in violation of that good faith and comity that should exist between entirely distinct nations" had become "a great sectional party" bent upon controlling Texas and the South "based upon the unnatural feeling of hostility to the Southern States and their beneficent and patriarchal system of negro slavery, proclaiming the debasing doctrine of the equality of all men irrespective of race or color." No one reading this declaration can have any illusions about whether slavery was the right among "states' rights" that Roberts and his allies wanted to protect. Like Vikings of old, the northmen that Roberts feared had even "invaded Southern soil and murdered unoffending citizens," and like religious zealots, they from "a fanatical pulpit have bestowed praise upon the actors and assassins in these crimes."[58]

But this was not all. Other old enemies were included in the indictment of northern perfidy. The declaration's complaints included: "The federal government, while but partially under the control of these our unnatural and sectional enemies, has for years almost entirely failed to protect the lives and property of the people of Texas against the Indian savages on our border, and more recently against the murderous forays of banditti from the neighboring territory of Mexico."

The vestigial appearance of Mexicans and Indians in the secessionists' nightmare vision is telling. It testifies to the way in which alienation proceeds incrementally and new enemies grow out of old ones. The Secession declaration opted decisively for the xenophobic side of the double-edged 1836 Texas Declaration of Independence, away from the philosophical ambiance of 1776, and toward the visceral provincialism and fear that ultimately led to civil war.[59]

The final straw was that the northern states "by the combined sectional vote of the 17 non-slave holding states . . . elected as president and vice president of the whole confederacy two men whose chief claims to such high positions are their approval of these long continued wrongs." In a superficially correct but nonetheless unsettling construction of the principles behind the Declaration of Independence, the convention held it as undeniable that American governments "were established exclusively by the white race, for themselves and their posterity," and that in such "free" governments "all white men are and of right ought to be entitled to equal civil and political rights." This "Declaration of Causes" was again signed first by Roberts as president of the convention, and then the arrangements for the popular vote were made in secret session under his watchful eye.[60]

When the Texas convention reconvened on February 4th, it appointed seven commissioners to the Confederate Convention being held in Montgomery, Alabama, John H. Reagan, Louis Wigfall, John Hemphill, T. N. Waul, John Gregg, W. S. Oldham, and William B. Ochiltree. Then the delegates resolved to recess until March 2nd in order to organize the popular vote. Gregg moved that, assuming secession passed the electorate, when the convention reconvened, "as few changes should be made in our State constitution and laws as can be made in order to fit our government for the condition of separation from the United States." Later events would show that he correctly expressed the sense of the members, but the motion was tabled until after the plebiscite as premature.[61]

Secession was approved by Texas voters by a margin of 46,153 for and 14,747 against, although the real balance of sentiment on the issue was probably not reflected in an election where secret balloting did not occur and many unionists did not vote.[62] After victory in the election, the convention reassembled on March 2nd, but a quorum could not be achieved until two days later. On March 4th, it passed an ordinance seceding from the Union and adopted another ordinance demanding the withdrawal of all federal troops. It also resolved to have Roberts appoint a ten-member committee "on the Constitution." The next day the delegates overwhelmingly voted to join Texas to the Confederacy. A committee of five was appointed to inform Governor Houston that the convention had reassembled, had counted the popular vote, and had determined that Secession was an accomplished fact.[63]

On March 6th an ordinance was read for the continuation of the existing state government so long as its officials would swear allegiance to the Confederacy. It was promptly referred to the constitution committee along with all other resolutions from the 6th to the 14th that dealt with composition of the new government. Meanwhile, the committee dispatched to Governor Houston reported on March 7th that his response was less than enthusiastic. Houston held that the sole reason for the convention was to submit Secession to popular vote, and that having done that, the delegates should all go home and leave Houston and the Legislature "to take into consideration the important issues arising out of the severance of our connection with the United States," including calling another convention for the purpose of framing a new constitution. The clear implication was that Texas, if no longer in the federal union, should remain independent—Roberts's convention had no authority to join the new republic of Texas to any other confederacy of states. On March 8th, Roberts came down from his chair and proposed his own resolution in response to Houston's recalcitrance. The resolution, which passed unanimously, provided that the convention "not only had the power" to pass a secession ordinance, but to do anything else necessary "in the present emergency," including joining the Confederacy. As an example of what Roberts meant, the next day the convention adopted an ordinance authorizing one Major Ben McCulloch to purchase one thousand Colt revolvers and one thousand Morse's rifles "for frontier defense" and to "pledge the full faith of the State of Texas for . . . any . . . purchase."[64] Later the same day, proof arrived that the convention was not wrong to anticipate trouble on the frontier upon the withdrawal of US troops. A report was received from Uvalde that a raiding party of fifteen to twenty Indians had attacked Henry Adams's ranch on the Nueces and killed him and a Mr. Henry Robinson, who had been found "scalped and their hearts cut out, etc."[65]

On March 11th, Gregg's resolution to keep much of the 1845 constitution intact was passed in slightly altered form. It continued to contemplate only such changes as were made necessary by secession, but now also allowed those related to "our connection with the Confederate States of America." This illustrated the constitutive act the convention saw itself as undertaking. There would be no "new constitution" because, from the delegates' states' rights perspective, the body politic was not changing. Instead, the unit of fundamental sovereignty created by the Constitution of 1845, the State of Texas, was merely withdrawing from one confederacy and joining another.[66]

On the 14th, the constitution was amended to broaden the power of the legislature to raise and borrow money to defray "the extraordinary expenses arising from the condition of public affairs," while a suggestion to open for other uses the public lands dedicated to public education in 1845 was rebuffed. Meanwhile, the amendment to the constitution changing the loyalty oath required of state officers to one including adherence to the Confederacy was passed on the third reading. Thereafter the state officers were administered their new oaths of office, an oath that Governor Houston refused to take, with the result that he was removed from office. All members of the legislature took the oath and assembled on March 18th.[67]

Given the desire to use the 1845 Constitution as a model, the amendments required by the current situation were left largely to the committee to which they had been referred. The 1861 Constitution was only sporadically discussed by the full complement of delegates and only for the one-week period from March 18th until the convention adjourned on March 25th. While the delegates specifically ratified the Constitution of the Confederacy on March 24th, no vote was taken ratifying a new constitution for Texas. Rather, the constitutional structure of 1845 remained, and the few amendments reported by the committee were voted upon, including those changing the loyalty oath and expanding fundraising procedures. Most important from the perspective of constitutional identity were the few changes made to the provisions on slavery. The three-section article in the 1845 Constitution was amended and completely reorganized into six new sections, the most significant editing work done on the entire document. Gone were the provisions governing and circumscribing the right of owners to emancipate their slaves. In their place was inserted a total prohibition of any form of emancipation, gradual, public, private, compensated, uncompensated, or otherwise. No slave in Texas would ever be set free, not by the legislature, even with the master's consent (as the 1845 Constitution had allowed if compensation were paid), and not privately by any master so inclined. In other respects, the slavery article remained essentially the same (e.g., discouraging inhumane treatment), but in addition to insurrection, the circumstances where a white might kill or dismember a slave with impunity now included rape or attempted rape "on a white female."[68]

These provisions should be understood as fortifying the white establishment against the increasing danger of slave insurrection that war with the North might generate. White slaveholders, while still exhorted to treatment humane enough to avoid a Nat Turner's rebellion, were given a freer hand in protecting their sexual hegemony in the more precarious demography that sending troops to war would bring. This fear of Freudian proportions has been debated and commented upon extensively by others for decades. They have argued that fear of black male sexuality emerged with force among whites in the decades after the Civil War, and this may be true. Yet this makes its appearance in antebellum Texas' constitution all the more telling, perhaps even unique. It is not unreasonable to perceive a subconscious fear of the domestic traitor most horrifying to the white male slaveholder, an unfaithful wife. The situation was becoming precarious indeed, especially on the frontier where runaway slaves had well-established allies and asylums among the Indians and Catholics to the south and west.[69]

After the convention adjourned, one of its committees published an "Address to the People of Texas" dated March 30, 1861, that appears as the first appendix to the journal. This proclamation, authored by a committee of three members of the convention, Pryor Lea of Goliad, John Henry Brown of Bell, and John D. Stell of Leon, recapitulated the same arguments made by Roberts and others. In its ten pages, there are no references to classical political theory or even to the black North. Rather, this address blandly states that "the political crisis arose from an irreconcilable diversity of opinion between the northern and southern portions of the United States of America as to relative rights." In support of this, the committee assembled the same examples from recent history and the same theories of interstate compact and constitutional law repeated before. Secession was treated as a political fact requiring only legal and procedural justification. Indeed, the committee advised that "it would be out of place and time in this address to recite the causes justifying secession." Instead, the committee merely described the purported legality of the convention's activities and the validity of the secession plebiscite. The new Texan identity was complete. The Houston party and its voice of moderation were silenced. Indians, ever pushed westward and out of the state, would constitute only a receding and occasional threat, and Mexico was emasculated by the war of the 1840s. As Stephen F. Austin had predicted three decades before, Texas must be a slave state. Whites continued to fear that the oppressed might rise up and slay their masters in their beds, but now the slaves' most dangerous allies were the traitorous ethnic unionist from within and the barbarian "black" Norseman from without, both susceptible to the religious zeal of a "fanatical pulpit."[70]

Houston, ever the maverick, refused to change with the times. With the issue no longer in doubt and his own political career ruined, he gave one final public speech on the subject of Secession on Sunday, March 31, in Brenham, Texas. Unlike his earlier political efforts to muddy the waters, and his legalistic defenses of his now lost position, it was brutally candid. His arrival in the town caused quite a stir among secessionists. They called him out into the street from the courthouse where his few remaining admirers had asked him to deliver a brief address. Hugh McIntyre, a local secessionist but also an old friend of Houston's, emerged from the courthouse and quieted the crowd by climbing upon a nearby table and drawing his pistol. They soon heeded his warning not to molest Houston: "You ruffians keep quiet, or I will kill you."[71]

Houston then came out behind McIntyre and delivered his remarks. It cannot be known whether it was the speech he intended to give inside the courthouse, or whether it was an extemporaneous plea to the crowd, or some combination of the two. In it, Houston appealed to the wisdom of calmer, greyer heads:

> I declare that Civil War is inevitable and is near at hand . . . when it comes the descendants of the heroes of Lexington and Bunker Hill will be found equal in patriotism, courage, and heroic endurance with the descendants of the heroes of Cowpens and Yorktown. For this reason I predict that the Civil War which is now near at hand will be stubborn and of long duration. When the tug of war comes, it will indeed be the Greek meeting Greek. Then, oh my fellow countrymen, the fearful conflict will fill our fair land with untold suffering, misfortune, and disaster.

The soil of our beloved south will drink deep the precious blood of our sons and brethren. I cannot, nor will I close my eyes against the light and voice of reason. The die has been cast by your secession leaders, whom you have permitted to sow and broadcast the seeds of secession, and you must ere long reap the fearful harvest of conspiracy and revolution.[72]

It is fitting that one of the portraits of Sam Houston that adorns the governor's office at the Texas state capitol is Washington Bogart Cooper's "Sam Houston as Marius among the Ruins of Carthage." In it, Houston is depicted wearing a Roman toga and standing among the broken column capitals of that ancient enemy of Rome. History tends to run together in the popular imagination, and so it mattered little to Cooper that Houston's career bore little resemblance to Marius's. Likewise, few of Houston's listeners realized that when he admonished the Brenham crowd that "the die is cast," he was referring to the reported comment of Julius Caesar when he crossed the Rubicon.[73] Unlike Caesar, Houston would not cross. When President Lincoln offered him federal troops to keep Texas in the Union, Houston asked a few close friends for advice. All but Epperson counseled against assuming the role of *imperator* in a domestic civil war. A tired Houston, ten years older than Caesar was at his crucial decision point, accepted their advice. "Gentlemen," he concluded, "I have asked your advice and will take it, but if I were ten years younger, I would not."[74]

Finding the constitutional identity of Civil War Texas requires analyzing not only the 1861 Constitution but the official proclamations of the Texas Secession crisis that accompanied and informed it. As in the similarly revolutionary context of 1836, formal declarations carried more obvious political valence than the written constitutional provisions they produced. They lent meaning to written constitutions because they reveal the thought-worlds of those who interpreted them and would continue to do so. In times of unrest, declarations of independence (or in this case, declarations of secession) define the constitutive moment of the polis as much as the legal provisions that ensue. This is especially true among revolutionaries who see themselves as conserving the existing order against an outside threat, in this case both the "fanatical" North and domestic compromisers and appeasers, chief among whom was Houston. Hence the secessionists preserved the Constitution of 1845 because they believed they were being faithful to the bilateral terms under which it had accomplished union with the North, making only those changes necessary in light of "the condition of public affairs."

This analysis also helps explain why the unionists' words, no matter how eloquent, could not stem or contain the wildfire of popular sentiment for Secession. In the few short years since annexation, anti-North feeling ran so deep and was so ingrained in Texas Democratic Party ideology that Houston's and Hamilton's secessionist opponents, no matter how eloquent or well-educated, needed to do little more than touch upon it and give it vent. The nature of the popular opinion they inflamed was not amenable to statesmanlike views of the distant past and centuries of Western constitutional tradition. It was visceral, emotional, and immediate, produced by recent events and engrafted upon decades of terror of Mexicans, Catholics, Indians, and slaves. The attempt by Houston and others to calm this rebellious temperament by appeals to reason, logic, and the broader, quieter lessons of history fell upon deaf ears. This surprised few of his contemporaries. After his own unionist speech in 1860, Judge James Bell wrote his supporters:

> I spoke . . . with full knowledge of the fact that the expression of my opinions would subject me to be denounced as a freesoiler and an abolitionist by those who think that the greatest political offense of which a man can be guilty is to differ from them in opinion. I am perfectly willing to take my full share of abuse from those who wish to plunge hastily into revolution . . . if by this means, I can be instrumental in persuading the people to act with calmness and moderation in this great crisis of our affairs.[75]

The rubric of ideological history moots the question of whether rhetoric, in this instance, was causative or merely incidental. The important lesson it teaches is that because politicians use arguments that win approval and discard those that do not, studying the recurring themes in those arguments tells us what both the speakers and listeners *thought* they were doing at the time, and what they *thought* was at stake. Along with the foundational laws thereby produced at critical junctures in a state's history, it gives us the crux of the political battle as it was waged in the minds and hearts of men. If one assumes some continuity in this aspect of human nature, this kind of ideological history also tells us what polemics tend to work, given a particular cultural milieu or ethos. The appeal to tradition and moderation against the temptations of faction and prejudice requires a calm reflective audience to sink in. Thus, inevitably, in times of crisis it seldom does. Long views do not sell well in the heat of the moment.

Just as important is the necessity for such a viscerally persuasive argument to attribute to new enemies the same characteristics as old ones. The northerner suddenly became a "black" Republican, a papist/Puritan religious heretic in pursuit of power at the expense of constraining sacred texts, an ally of the Mexican, and an instigator of slave rebellion. Unionists' political strategy of privileging caution over fear and retribution did not work. The secessionists had no need for abstract arguments or calm logic. It was enough to paint the northerner as vaguely similar to the loose constructionist Federalists or Puritans of the North and the Catholic "tyrants" of the Texas Revolution.

To quote Cicero, *"silent inem leges inter arma"* (the law falls silent in times of war), and Civil War Texas' constitutional identity was already set by 1861. Others have well chronicled the legal history of Texas during the war, so little need be said here,[76] except that throughout the Civil War, Confederate Texans would continue to be paranoid of outside infiltration and fifth columnists. This is illustrated by the trial of William G. Gamble by a Confederate military tribunal in San Antonio in 1862. Gamble, a bookseller, was tried for his life on a charge of "keeping and circulating abolition books." His defense, which ultimately succeeded, was that he was ignorant of possessing any book that may have contained "that false, unjust and slanderous vituperation of Southern Institutions, with which Cockney English writers are accustomed to cater to the jealous appetites of . . . their countrymen."[77]

Once the war was lost, a period of political confusion and constitutional schizophrenia would ensue. Presidential Reconstruction did little to change the ideological synthesis struck in 1861, but Congressional Reconstruction would briefly reverse the political polarity, subordinating the dominant ethos of the secessionists. In less than a decade their ideological hegemony would reemerge in response to new political challenges that arose after Reconstruction had ended and the federal troops that enforced it had departed.

4

Momentary Reversal

The Republican-Free Black Axis and Reconstruction, 1865–1874

AFTER THE CONFEDERACY'S DEFEAT IN THE CIVIL WAR, FEDERAL troops remained in the southern states to administer their readmission to the Union on terms acceptable to the national government. President Lincoln proposed a policy of accommodation that was followed by his successor Andrew Johnson. A loyalty oath was to be administered to all but the most prominent former rebels in exchange for amnesty, and their states, to rejoin the Union, were required to ratify the Thirteenth Amendment abolishing slavery and to reconstitute their governments accordingly. This "Presidential Reconstruction" proved easier to comply with than the "Congressional Reconstruction" that followed. Congressional or "Radical" Reconstruction resulted from Congress's dissatisfaction with President Johnson's lenient policies and followed the passage of the Fourteenth Amendment, which guaranteed the fundamental equality before law of the newly freed African American population.

The Texas constitution adopted during Presidential Reconstruction allowed readmission to the Union and reflected but a few new political realities, chief among which were the emergence of a significant emancipated black population, the beginnings of a state Republican Party, and a consensus in favor of economic development and closer integration into the national economy. But Congressional Reconstruction then radically reversed the balance of political power in Texas, requiring another constitutional convention in

1868. This convention not only penned Texas' fifth constitution, but also empowered free blacks, hamstrung the old Democratic establishment, and even generated a proposed constitution for a partitioned liberal state of "West Texas" that was almost adopted, following the example set by West Virginia in the Civil War. It would take the better part of a decade for Reconstruction to end and for Democrats to regain control.[1]

Presidential Reconstruction and the Constitution of 1866

President Lincoln had offered amnesty to southern rebels as a wartime measure aimed at sapping Confederate manpower, but this did nothing to hasten the end of hostilities. After the war, his successor adapted this measure to readmitting southern states to the Union. President Andrew Johnson's amnesty proclamation of May 29, 1865, was quite conciliatory. In it, he offered ex-Confederates total amnesty and restoration of property (excepting slaves and property properly confiscated during the war) in exchange for a simple oath of loyalty to the laws of the nation, especially the laws emancipating the slave population. Anyone could avail himself of this generous bargain, except the following small class of high-ranking ex-rebels:

> Civil or diplomatic officers or . . . foreign agents of the . . . Confederate government; . . . all who left judicial stations under the United States to aid the rebellion; . . . all . . . military or naval officers of said pretended Confederate government above the rank of colonel in the army or lieutenant in the navy; . . . all who left seats in the Congress of the United States to aid the rebellion; . . . all who resigned or tendered resignations of their commissions in the army or navy of the United States to evade duty in resisting the rebellion; . . . all who have engaged in any way in treating otherwise than lawfully as prisoners of war persons found in the United States service . . . , all persons who have been, or are absentees from the United States for the purpose of aiding the rebellion; . . . all military and naval officers in the rebel service, who were educated by the government in the Military Academy at West Point or the United States Naval Academy; . . . all persons who held the pretended offices of governors of States in insurrection . . . all persons who left their homes within the jurisdiction and protection of the United States . . . for the purpose of aiding the rebellion; . . . all persons who have been engaged in the destruction of the commerce of the United States upon the high seas, . . . from Canada, or . . . upon the lakes and rivers that separate the British Provinces from the United States; . . . all persons who, at the time when they seek to obtain the benefits hereof by taking the oath herein

prescribed, are in military, naval, or civil confinement, or custody, . . . all persons who have voluntarily participated in said rebellion, and the estimated value of whose taxable property is over twenty thousand dollars; (and) all persons who have taken the oath of amnesty as prescribed in the President's proclamation of December 8th, A. D. 1863, or an oath of allegiance to the government of the United States since the date of said proclamation, and who have not thenceforward kept and maintained the same inviolate.

So, other than Confederate army generals, high naval officers and civil officials, commerce raiders, graduates of West Point or Annapolis, deserters, and the very rich, the vast majority of rebels, even rebel soldiers, were eligible for a full pardon and citizenship in the reconstituted Union. And even those ineligible could still apply for special pardon directly to the president.[2]

President Johnson adopted the same litmus test for political participation in reconstructing the government of Texas. He appointed Andrew "Colossal" Hamilton, the old Texas unionist, provisional governor of the state. Hamilton had fled north in 1860 and obtained a commission as a Union general during the war. He was now directed to organize a constitutional convention of delegates elected by, and composed of, Texans who had rightfully taken the amnesty oath. On July 25th, Governor Hamilton issued a proclamation urging Texans to cooperate with Reconstruction and proposing a constitutional convention as soon as practicable. Four months later, the governor directed county election boards to be formed to supervise an election of delegates on January 8, 1866, to attend the convention scheduled for February 7th in Austin.[3]

Sixty-three delegates were elected and assembled at the appointed time. They elected James Throckmorton, the conservative unionist Democrat turned Confederate officer, as president of the convention. Throckmorton defeated Hamilton's liberal unionist ally Albert H. Latimer, as well as hardline secessionists Hardin Runnels and William M. Taylor. The results of this election revealed the political division that would continue for the remainder of the convention. On the first ballot, Latimer held a plurality of twenty-four votes to Throckmorton's twenty-two, but once the other twenty-two voters abandoned the reactionary candidacies of Runnels and Taylor, Throckmorton received virtually all their votes and won the runoff against Latimer by forty-one to twenty-four.[4]

Thus commentators have tended to view the convention as roughly evenly split between three factions: liberal unionists allied with Governor Hamilton,

Andrew "Colossal" Hamilton, moderate unionist, and Texas Governor and Congressman (Published with permission of the Tarlton Law Library, Jamail Center for Legal Research, University of Texas School of Law)

who took the name "the Union Caucus"; conservative or Democrat unionists led by Throckmorton; and the essentially unreconstructed secessionist Democrats like Runnels, Taylor, and Oran Milo Roberts, none of whom apparently balked much at taking the loyalty oath, although Runnels felt compelled to apply for special pardon from President Johnson before doing so. The balance of power held by the Throckmorton faction and the conservative unionist bent of the entire convention can be seen in its actions with reference to Sam Houston, who had died in 1863 at the nadir of his popularity. On March 24th, delegates unanimously resolved that Houston's death had been a "national calamity" and that the current governor should procure a portrait to hang in the capitol "to commemorate his distinguished service and perpetuate his memory." Three days later, a nearly unanimous vote, this one with only reactionary Democrat Amzi Bradshaw in the minority, enacted an ordinance requesting that Governor Hamilton pay to Houston's widow Margaret the sum of $1,925, her late husband's unpaid salary for the years of his gubernatorial term of which he had been deprived by Secession. This ordinance and twenty-eight others representing the statutory actions of the convention were appended to the official version of the constitution published by the state printer Joseph Walker. The convention deemed them legislation of "the people of Texas in convention assembled."[5]

Upon his election as president by the convention, Throckmorton addressed his colleagues and urged them to put behind them the "recent past, with all its painful associations and recollections," and in a spirit of harmony, to focus on "the general good of our own State . . . and the promotion of the general interests." Two days later, Governor Hamilton delivered his own written message to the chamber. In it, he outlined the most pressing issues facing the delegates: (1) the state's Civil War debt; (2) the plight of the freedmen; and (3) "a formal and solemn recantation" of the "heresy" of Secession. He also took great pains to defend himself against accusations of foot-dragging in calling the convention. He denied that he had tried to exclude as many ex-confederates as possible by insisting that all electors and delegates be checked and double-checked for eligibility to take the loyalty oath. Hamilton then confessed to having no particular suggestions for revamping the organs of government, other than to demand debt relief, denunciation of the right to secede, and a liberal policy toward the newly emancipated.[6]

While the governor left the details of debt relief to the delegates, he expressed strong and specific views on the rights of former slaves, but he harbored no illusions. Hamilton admitted that he knew from many of the delegates' campaign promises that the majority of them would find his opinions unacceptable. Yet, he declared, "the present is not a time for any true man . . . to dissemble his honest convictions and opinions, out of an unmanly apprehension that his views will not accord with the immature and timid judgment of those who are yet wedded to the prejudices of the past." So, he argued plainly for the extension of more than mere technical freedom to former slaves, but "civil rights, on an equality with the white population of the State." By this he meant the right to sue and testify, to own property, to be treated equally when accused of crimes, and, in a limited sense, the right to vote. Hamilton was no believer in what was then termed "social equality." He agreed with his opponents and many of his allies that blacks were not "qualified by their intelligence to exercise the right of suffrage," but he argued for some limitation on suffrage (perhaps a literacy test or poll tax) that would effectively disenfranchise freedmen, but not overtly on the basis of race. He also argued that the lack of education that justified withholding the franchise should be ameliorated and would not last forever. In all this he represented the left of the contemporaneous political spectrum in Texas, the mainstream of southern Republicanism, and a narrow plurality but distinct minority of the convention. Hamilton's address provoked an immediate response in the form of a resolution by conservative farmer J. K. Bumpass that the convention alter or amend the 1861 constitution "only so far as is actually necessary to enable the state to resume its former friendly relations with the United States." The resolution was referred to committee, where it was consigned to oblivion.[7]

As in prior conventions, committees proved to be the order of the day. Thirteen committees were appointed, the most important being the "Committee on Condition of the State" chaired by the old unionist editor A. B. Norton and the "Committee on General Provisions of the Constitution" under conservative unionist John Hancock. Other committees considered proposals regarding the judiciary, the executive, the legislature, education, and public lands. It is a mark of the strength of the conservative elements of the convention and his own legal prestige that O. M. Roberts was made chairman of the Judiciary Committee.[8]

On Monday, February 12th, Judge C. A. Frazier offered a resolution that the Judiciary Committee should take under consideration the question of establishing a separate criminal appellate court, thus leaving the Supreme Court with a docket of only civil cases. This resolution was adopted.[9] On February 13th, the convention passed a resolution by W. E. Jones of Bexar County instructing the Judiciary Committee to consider increasing the number of Supreme Court justices to five, "who shall hold the court at but one place, and be in permanent session." They were also to "consider the propriety of compelling the district judges to hold their courts four times a year in each county."[10] Ultimately, Roberts's committee omitted the separate criminal court of appeals but obtained passage of a judicial article that modified the system in effect since 1850. In that year a constitutional amendment replaced judicial selection by gubernatorial appointment with elected judgeships. In an effort to preserve the "leading features" of the existing system but make such improvements to the Judicial Department "as would secure its efficiency," the committee increased the number of Supreme Court justices from three to five, with the five electoral winners selecting their own chief. All the members of the court had their terms increased from six to ten years, and district judges had their terms extended from six years to eight. While the earlier constitutions authorized the legislature to create inferior judicial officials to be elected in counties, such as constables and justices of the peace, this convention opted to create an entirely new unified system of county courts led by new county judges with jurisdiction of probate matters, misdemeanor and petty offenses, and civil cases involving less than five hundred dollars, an innovation whose essential terms remain in effect to this day.[11]

While the judicial article elicited little rancor, one issue that did provoke dissension was partition of the state. On February 14th, W. E. Jones first broached the subject of treating western Texas as a unique district. He proposed that the Committee on the Condition of the State report upon the propriety of "selling the government of the United States all of the territory of the State, lying west of a line commencing at some suitable point below the mouth of the Pecos, on the Rio Grande and running thence to the northwest corner of the most western county lying on Red River or some other suitable point." Jones's idea was to use the proceeds of the sale as a permanent school fund, but his resolution also asked the committee to consider dividing the eastern part of the state into three separate states for readmission into the Union.[12] Soon after that proposal, the convention adopted a resolution moved by O. M. Roberts, instructing the Committee of Indian Affairs to report upon the idea of ceding to the United States for fifty years the same western territory contemplated by Jones's motion. Roberts's idea was to create a buffer zone against Indian attack. His proposal was referred to committee in lieu of the Jones proposal. Several days later a similar proposal by Edward Degener, a German unionist from the hill country, to cede western lands to the United States was also referred.[13]

Ceding a portion of the state to the federal government was vetoed by the Committee on Indian Affairs. It instead reported a resolution demanding that the federal government protect the frontier, and a separate resolution asking Governor Hamilton to appoint three commissioners to treat with the Indian tribes of the frontier and one commissioner to go to Washington to make known "the true condition of the frontier of Texas, and to procure the consent of the general government for the State of Texas to enter into said treaty." These enactments made their way into the final ordinances of the convention appended to the constitution as published. They became Ordinances Nos. 7 and 8, alerting the President of the United States to "extensive raids by Indians," demanding immediate federal aid, and authorizing the governor to send an emissary to Washington.[14] The convention also adopted an ordinance providing for the circumstances under which "actual settlers in the frontier west of the Pecos and upon the unsurveyed school lines might be provided with 320 acres of land upon paying the fees for surveying the same."[15]

All of these measures were designed to consolidate white control of the Indian frontier of the West, even at the expense of the territorial integrity of the state. Although the proposals for separating the western frontier from the remainder of the state and for creating three new states in the eastern part of

Texas were rejected, significant groundwork for some form of state division was laid and the idea would be resurrected during Radical Reconstruction. There was strong sentiment among conservative East Texans for multiplying Texas' influence in Congress by making new states, and many Central and Southwest Texans fantasized about a new state in West Texas devoid of the ex-Confederate majority elsewhere. Indeed, although there is no mention of it in the constitution itself, the convention did adopt by a vote of thirty-one to seventeen an ordinance "To Provide for a Division of the State of Texas." In it, the legislature was vested with the power to "give the consent of the State" to erect a new state or states, and to pass all laws necessary thereto. The ordinance and the method of its passage produced a sharp rebuke from twelve delegates led by John K. Bumpass and Middleton T. Johnson, conservative Democrats. The measure was passed on the last day of the convention after a voice vote suspending the rules ordinarily requiring three readings of a bill before passage. The Union Caucus voted unanimously in favor. The dissenters decried this act as suicidal. They feared a general social collapse in the wake of war and Reconstruction, which they called federal "military despotism." In that postapocalyptic world, they claimed, Texas must have territory and population sufficient to defend itself and "seize once more the old Star of Texas, and raise it above the common ruin by which it may be surrounded; or, like the brave defenders of the Alamo, go down defending Texas as it was."[16]

Other important work of the convention was dealt with by ordinance, rather than by constitutional amendment, including the questions of nullifying secession, fixing the time for the next general election, and ratifying the constitution. "Ordinance Number 1," the first one passed by the convention, acknowledged the supremacy of the federal government, declared the Act of Secession null and void, and "distinctly renounced" any right of Texas to secede from the Union. Ordinance Number 2 declared all state war debt void and forbade the legislature from ever making provision to pay it. Ordinances 3 and 4 called for an election on the fourth Monday of June of 1866 to fill all state and county offices. The constitution would be ratified at the same election pursuant to the other election laws already in force, with precinct and county election officers making returns within five days of the election to the judge of the judicial district in which such ballots were cast.[17]

Thus the Hamilton faction was able to attract enough conservative unionists to repudiate the state debt and disavow the right of secession, but the Union Caucus was unsuccessful in securing a declaration that secession was null and void ab initio. Conservative Democrats were able to lure enough unionists away from that extreme position to defeat it. They argued that "ab initio" would annul all the marriages, contracts, and other business done in the state during the war. Instead, in addition to Ordinance 1 renouncing the right to secession, the delegates adopted another ordinance making clear that the actions and laws of the state government were deemed "in full force" to the extent not in conflict with federal law.[18]

However, when it came to economic development, the Hamilton faction was successful in combining with conservative unionists to begin the constitutional system of railroad subsidy. The constitutions of 1845 and 1861 dealt with corporations only by way of limitation and with railroads not at all. The word railroad was not used in either document, but each established that no corporation could be chartered for the purpose of lending money, whereas any other corporation could only be created or dissolved by a two-thirds vote of the legislature, and none of its stock or property could ever be owned wholly or in part by the state. This included railroad companies.[19] But railroad building had proved crucial to the superior economic power of the North demonstrated during the Civil War, so on March 8th, the Committee on Internal Improvements led by Isaiah Paschal, a unionist lawyer, proposed a new section dedicated to railroads within Article VII's general provisions. As finally enrolled, this became Section 36 of the article. The original committee proposal included not only an endorsement of internal improvements, but also "mining and manufacturing." This was removed from the text as enrolled, but in all other respects the provision ultimately approved corresponded closely with the original proposal, which elicited little debate. John Ireland of Guadalupe County, who would later become governor in the 1880s under the nickname of "Oxcart John" because of his opposition to railroads, did propose an alternative substitute on March 30th acknowledging the duty of the legislature to encourage internal improvements but prohibiting them from "creating any debt against the state, without providing, at the same time, for its payment."[20]

As adopted over Ireland's objection, the new internal improvements section of Article VII provided that it was the legislature's responsibility to encourage internal improvements, and it authorized that body to do so by guaranteeing the bonds of railroad companies to the maximum extent of $15,000 per mile of track laid. There were other limitations placed on railroad companies receiving these subsidies, violation of which would cause forfeiture of the railroad's property. The constitution also granted the state a first lien on all rails, rolling stock, depots, and franchises of any railroad company receiving a subsidy. And guaranteeing the bonds of any railroad company required a two-thirds vote of the legislature. Simultaneously upon passage of this amendment, the convention repealed the other railroad laws passed by the legislature in the 1850s, an action that would produce some litigation in the 1880s by companies caught between the old legislative scheme and the new one. In addition to bond guarantees, the new constitution enshrined within its education article the policy of subsidizing railroads by donating to them alternate tracts of public land along their rights of way. Portions of this scheme were already enacted by statutes passed in the 1850s, but the new constitution provided for the first time that "all the alternate sections of land reserved by the State out of grants heretofore made, or that may hereafter be made, to railroad companies or other corporations of any nature whatever, for internal improvements, or for the development of the wealth and resources of the State, shall be set apart as a part of the perpetual school fund of the State."[21]

Meanwhile, knowing of congressional support for transcontinental railroad building during the war, the convention passed an ordinance recommending to the US Congress that it "cause a South Branch to the Union Pacific Railroad to be immediately constructed through the Indian Territory." The construction of such a rail connecting the Union Pacific hub at St. Louis to Texas' railroad net and navigable streams was deemed "imperative in developing the vast resources of the territory [Texas] . . . and an important means of bringing into more intimate, harmonious, and advantageous relations, the people of the section embracing these roads, not only with each other, but with those of the remainder of the United States." Hamilton Stuart, a conservative unionist editor from Galveston and an old friend of Sam Houston's, made the proposal. The vote was an overwhelming forty-two to seven, the dissenters including some of the most unreconstructed conservative Democrats present, O. M. Roberts, Amzi Bradshaw, and T. N. Waul. They were joined by Alexander Phillips, another former ally of Sam Houston, but one who was speculating shortly after the convention, if not before, in a competing railroad venture to the Pacific.[22]

While delegates shared broad agreement on infrastructure improvements and integration into the national transportation network, they were most sharply divided on the question of racial inequality. In response to Governor Hamilton's plea for limited "equal" rights for blacks, four days later "Oxcart" John Ireland moved to charge the Committee on General Provisions to report a constitutional proviso "declaring that all marriages . . . between the white races and Africans, and descendants of Africans null and void." The motion passed, but only two days later the committee chaired by Democratic unionist John Hancock reported back unanimously that such a provision was unnecessary because the laws already passed by the legislature "prohibit such intermarriages, and . . . it is not apprehended that the moral sentiment of the country will allow a repeal of these laws."[23] Some weeks later, O. M. Roberts felt compelled to introduce an ordinance declaring that "the permanent preservation of the white race being the paramount object of the people of Texas," the legislature should be empowered to do anything to "the African race within her limits, as may be necessary . . . to secure their ultimate removal or colonization, so as to give place to an unmixed white race." The matter was referred to a committee not to be heard of again, but liberal Republican agitation for modest civil rights would continue to produce appeals to fear and bigotry. The balance of power lay with the Throckmorton faction resigned to accept the end of slavery, anxious to do the minimum necessary to reconcile the state to the Union, and interested in doing no more.[24]

On February 17th, the Committee on the Legislative Department chaired by secessionist James W. Henderson reported amendments to the legislative article of the constitution. These amendments were crucial in the debate over civil rights because the qualifications for citizenship and voting in Texas had always been stipulated in the legislative article. The committee recommended disqualifying all persons of African descent from voting and holding legislative office, and its recommendations were adopted. In this, the 1866 Constitution reworked previous restrictions on citizenship based on both race and slave status and now made them purely racial. The old system had excluded "negroes" and slaves and their descendants from citizenship in the state, while also restricting voting and office-holding to citizens. The new system eliminated the concept of state citizenship in favor of state residency for a term of one year as a prerequisite to vote, and the new system extended the necessary residency of representatives and senators from two years for the House and three for the Senate to five years for both houses. Faced with a large population of free black citizens and having abandoned the state citizenship qualification for voting, the new constitution expressly declared "Africans" and their descendants unable to vote by reason of race alone. Facing an influx of "carpetbaggers" in addition to the newly freed black population, the convention also proscribed white newcomers and blacks from holding office. In addition to the residency requirements, the new Article III expressly specified for the first time that representatives and senators must be "white." And because the residency qualifications required *continuous* residence in Texas, any unionist who had fled the state during the war could arguably also be disqualified from office or even from voting for the foreseeable future.[25]

A week after the committee reported, the frontier German Edward Degener submitted an impassioned minority report based upon both political expediency and human rights. He described for the delegates his attempts in committee to liberalize voting rights. First, he had proposed a literacy test as a racially neutral way of restricting black voting. Then he had proposed that literate black male suffrage be delayed ten years and extended only to those reaching the age of twenty-one after 1876. Finally, he had put forward another version extending immediate black male suffrage only to those born free, excluding all former slaves from voting forever. All these ideas were rejected, even though like Hamilton, Degener tried to convince the committee that gradual enfranchisement was wise because any objection based on alleged ignorance "as applied to the present generation of blacks . . . cannot apply to the next . . . and as we are legislating for generations to come." Unlike Hamilton, however, Degener really believed in at least some form of racial equality. He argued that any objection based on the alleged ignorance of black voters was simply wrong because "the same objection can with equal force be urged against a certain class of white men, but no one pretends, in their case, that the objection is valid."[26]

Degener continued that it was also impolitic to restrict black voting. The Congressional Committee on Reconstruction had passed a new constitutional amendment tying representation in Congress and allocation of federal tax burdens among the states to the number of voters, not raw population. While Degener could not have predicted that this amendment would never be ratified, it was a harbinger of the Fourteenth and Fifteenth Amendments that soon would. Still, his strongest and longest argument was based upon democratic principles. "The colored people of our State constitute an important part of the body politic," he pleaded. He reminded his colleagues that as free men, no longer slaves, African Texans "will be called upon to sustain an equal share of the public burdens . . . they will be taxed to support the government . . . as property holders, they will have a permanent interest in the welfare of the state, and if ever the necessity should arise, they will be required to shed their blood in defence of our common country. Who then will say they should be deprived of the rights of citizenship?"

Degener's report was read "to come up in order," and it was ignored by all but the Union Caucus when the majority report disenfranchising all Blacks was approved with only minor changes a few weeks later.[27]

The views of the more radical members of his Union Caucus notwithstanding, Governor Hamilton had recognized in his message to the convention that black suffrage was a lost cause, at least in the near term. So, the real battle on civil rights was always likely to be fought over Hamilton's more modest proposals regarding jury service, access to education, the right to sue and be sued, property ownership, and other rights less threatening to the Throckmorton faction that held the convention's middle ground. The vehicle quickly agreed upon for addressing African American rights was a new Article VIII in the 1866 Constitution. Article VIII had been reserved for the question of slavery in the 1845 and 1861 constitutions, and since that subject was now moot, the Committee on General Provisions recommended replacing it with a new article on "freedmen." The proposed new article contained two sections, one explaining slavery's demise, and one setting forth the rights of the newly emancipated.[28]

The proposed first section accepted the illegality of slavery, while making clear that from Texas' perspective its abolition was involuntary, "having been terminated within this State, by the Government of the United States, by force of arms, and its re-establishment being prohibited, by the amendment to the Constitution of the United States." In light of this inescapable reality, the committee recommended that the first section of the article should further provide that "freedmen and their descendants, shall be protected in their rights of person and property by appropriate legislation; they shall have the right to contract and be contracted with; to sue and be sued; to acquire, hold and transmit property, and be subject to no penal laws based upon inequality or distinction of race."

This section was adopted with only two changes, one substituting of the word "Africans" for "freedmen," and the other limiting their equality in criminal courts. As ultimately passed, Article VIII provided only that all criminal prosecutions against blacks "shall be conducted *in the same manner* as prosecutions, for like offences, against the white race, and they shall be *subject to like penalties*" (emphasis added). Someone must have pointed out the problem with the original proposal: that there still were, or soon would be, many "penal laws based upon inequality and distinction of race," such as the miscegenation statutes. The journal of the convention does not reveal precisely how this change was made, so it likely was part of deliberations the convention conducted as a "committee of the whole," where the journal indicates O. M. Roberts succeeded in obtaining approval of some unspecified modifications to the original committee report with the support of Throckmorton.[29]

Section 2 of the new Article VIII dealt with the subject of African Texans as witnesses in court. As ultimately adopted, it guaranteed blacks the equal right to testify and be heard only in cases, civil or criminal, involving *their own* persons or property. In all other cases, "the Legislature shall have power to authorize them to testify as witnesses . . . under such regulations as may be prescribed, *as to facts hereafter occurring*" (emphasis added). This was another retreat from the original committee report, which had affirmed blacks' rights to testify against white people so long as "it shall be in open court." Republican Edmund J. Davis had attempted to make the committee version even more liberal by making it applicable in all cases, not just those where blacks were parties. This lost on voice vote (i.e., based on the chair's perception that more delegates yelled "nay" than "yea," and with the number of votes yea and nay not counted or recorded). W. E. Jones of San Antonio reurged Davis's proposal, restricting the right to testify to those facts occurring after emancipation, but this also failed with all but the most liberal unionists voting with the conservatives against it. Emboldened by these failures, former Confederate general Hinche Mabry then moved to strike out the entire section, but this was beaten back by a coalition of Republicans and Throckmorton Democrats, sixty to fifteen. Edward Degener moved another liberalizing amendment to simply provide that "no person shall be excluded from giving evidence, on account of his race or color," and this was predictably laid on the table. After further wrangling, it was President Throckmorton who left the chair to suggest adding to the end of W. E. Jones's proposed language, "as to facts hereafter occurring," in order to prevent blacks from testifying as to anything that happened before 1866, except in their own defense. This limitation passed because, unlike Jones's original proposal, it was not attached to a general right to testify in all cases. A. B. Norton made one last attempt to substitute an article generally providing for the equality of all persons before the law. This was tabled by a vote along the same party lines that defeated the proposal of E. J. Davis, and the final compromise article was engrossed as officially adopted.[30]

Although voting rights were clearly a step too far for a majority of delegates, these debates show that slavery's demise did require the new constitution to accommodate blacks within the body politic. As witnessed by the sections limiting office-holding and access to courts, it did so modestly and for the most part merely substituted discrimination based on race for outright servitude. The debate over education mirrored this paradigm. The education article of the 1845 and 1861 constitutions had contained only four short sections. In 1866, the treatment of blacks, the constitutionalization of railroad building, and the details of public school funding expanded the article to eleven sections. The 1845 and 1861 injunctions to the legislature to maintain free public schools were maintained and a mandate to establish a major university at the earliest possible date was added, but now provision also had to be made for free blacks. So, the education article was amended to make clear that the public school fund was "exclusively for the education of all the *white* scholastic inhabitants of this State, and no law shall ever be made appropriating said fund to any *other* use or purpose whatever" (emphasis added). Conservative Andrew McCormack, a former member of the Confederate Congress, suggested conditioning the school fund's exclusive use for whites upon keeping "the white schools and colored schools . . . separate and distinct," but a large majority tabled this measure as either unwise or unnecessary and better left to the legislature. A left-handed method for funding schools for black children was enacted by adding a new Section 7 that authorized the legislature to levy taxes to fund education but required that "all the sums arising from said tax which may be collected from Africans, or persons of African descent, shall be exclusively appropriated for the maintenance of a system of public schools for Africans and their children." Only after this meager compromise had been reached did Edmund J. Davis succeed in appending to Section 7 that "it shall be the duty of the Legislature to encourage schools among these people."[31]

At the time, some argued that the 1866 Texas Constitution was the most liberal among the southern constitutions adopted during Presidential Reconstruction. That observation finds support in the state's unique characteristics during and after the war: as western as it was southern, relatively undamaged by the war, and with a concentrated and identifiable unionist minority led by an experienced albeit outnumbered, prounion domestic elite. However, the governmental rubric enacted in 1866 guaranteed that time would be on the side of the ex-secessionists. The newly emancipated could not vote and would surely remain segregated, largely uneducated, wholly economically subservient, and physically and legally vulnerable. This left their white liberal patrons badly outnumbered by secessionist Democrats and conservative unionists who would certainly combine to reassert a traditional Democrat regime once readmission had been accomplished. As the convention itself explained in a valedictory message to President Johnson, it had met his minimal requirements for readmission, even though some of them had required abandoning "long cherished sentiments of the Southern people." In return, the delegates expected "that equality of position which rightfully we are entitled to," and no further "attempt to maintain control over any portion of their territory by the military power." The elections ordained by the convention were held on June

4, 1866. The constitution was ratified, but the Hamilton forces were predictably routed by a coalition of conservative union and secessionist Democrats led by Throckmorton and Roberts. Throckmorton was the party's nominee for governor and trounced his Union Party opponent Elisha M. Pease, whom the liberal group had nominated when Hamilton demurred. And the new state legislature elected O. M. Roberts and reluctant secessionist David G. Burnet the state's US senators. President Johnson was satisfied. He responded by issuing a proclamation on August 20th declaring that Texas' rebellion was over and that the situation had been normalized.[32]

Congressional Reconstruction and the Constitution of 1869

Unlike the president, radicals in Congress and liberal unionists in Texas were not satisfied. The Fourteenth Amendment requiring equal treatment of all persons regardless of race passed Congress only nine days after the 1866 Texas election. But ratification of that amendment might be a long process, and in the interim Texas conservatives reaped rapid political advantage from their takeover of the new state government. After the disastrous June 4th elections, lame duck Governor Hamilton departed for Philadelphia to attend a Convention of Southern Loyalists held in September. He was joined by E. M. Pease, Edmund J. Davis, George W. Paschal, and other members of the old Union Caucus that had run its unsuccessful 1866 candidates under the banner "the Union Party." After their June defeat, these former liberal unionists turned more radical, now favoring the only platform that could reverse their electoral fortune, immediate black suffrage. Hamilton remained in the North and undertook a speaking tour, during which he espoused ever more liberal views, culminating in his decision to join other unionists in founding the Southern Republican Association. This group of newly organized southern Republicans began agitating for congressional action to override Johnson's lenient policy and to eject the unreconstructed Democrats from control of Texas. Meanwhile, Throckmorton's middle ground was absorbed within the traditional Democratic Party once the need to obtain reintegration into the national economic and political system was satisfied. The secessionists and the Democrat unionists, after all, had agreed at least in principle on most political and social issues: economic recovery, low taxes, small government, and the subjugation of the African race. The more liberal unionists were forced ever leftward, recognizing that their only hope was federal intervention to change the domestic political landscape. They became loyal Republicans.[33]

Meanwhile, the reunified Democrats made clear they were bent on a return to the prewar status quo, excepting only the legal institution of slavery. In his 1866 campaign for governor, Throckmorton vowed opposition to any form of black suffrage or social equality, and this explains his victory over Pease by a margin of four to one and the Democrats' complete takeover of the Texas Legislature. That body wasted no time subjugating freedmen. Laws were passed limiting the right of African Texans to testify in court, segregating them in public transportation, and prohibiting them from holding any office or serving on any jury. Perhaps most oppressive was the legislature's enactment of new black labor laws that provided that workers could only be hired through the heads of their families, that workers could not leave their "place of employment" without their employer's consent, and that "it is the duty of this class of laborers to be especially civil and polite to their employer, his family and guests." African American workers were to be "free" in name only. And in a coup de grace, this the Eleventh Texas Legislature rejected the Thirteenth Amendment as if its passage had not been a condition of readmission to the Union, and then it voted down the Fourteenth Amendment by a vote of seventy to five in the house, with only one dissenting vote in the senate.[34]

At the national level, the success of radical Republicans in the congressional elections of November 1866 portended a reaction to these affronts and the demise of President Johnson's policies. The sitting Republican Congress had already refused to seat southern senators and congressmen, including Roberts and Burnet, as unreconstructed Confederates, and in March 1867, the new Congress passed two Reconstruction Acts over Johnson's veto.[35] Because "no legal State governments or adequate protection for life or property now exists in the rebel States" (other than Tennessee, which had promptly ratified the Fourteenth Amendment), Congress placed the ten other Confederate states under martial law. These states were divided among five military districts, each to be commanded by a federal general until such time as each respective state: (1) approved the Fourteenth Amendment; (2) held an election for delegates to a new constitutional convention where all adult males, regardless of race or previous servitude and resident in the state for a year, must be eligible to vote and to serve as delegates unless disenfranchised as rebels; and (3) ratified a new constitution "in conformity with the Constitution of the United States in all respects," approved by Congress, and providing for adult Black male suffrage. Only then would the rebel states be entitled to representation in Congress. Moreover, since the text of the Fourteenth Amendment disqualified from state or federal office any prior state or federal officials who "engaged in insurrection or rebellion," this same class of ex-Confederates was also disqualified from voting for convention delegates or serving as same.[36]

The result was tonic to the liberal Texas unionists, now called Texas Republicans. The national legislature had wrought what they could never accomplish, reconstituting the electorate in their favor and excluding from office all the most popular and politically active ex-Confederates like Throckmorton, Runnels, and Roberts. The second of the congressional Reconstruction Acts granted General Philip Sheridan, appointed commander of the Fifth Military District comprising Texas and Louisiana, exclusive power to "cause a registration to be made" of all eligible voters who would take what came to be called "the ironclad oath" averring their qualifications. This placed the determination of who was disqualified by prior Confederate sympathies totally in the hands of the national army. Sheridan was also given control of all details of the election for constitutional convention delegates, including voter registration and identification, and the appointment of election superintendents.[37]

At the urging of Texas Republicans, Sheridan went much further. Using the full martial authority delegated to him by Congress, he also removed Governor Throckmorton and other state officials as disloyal impediments to Reconstruction. In August of 1867, Sheridan replaced Throckmorton with E. M. Pease, the loser of the 1866 election. Soon Republicans and unionists were appointed to replace other Democrats recently elected. Meanwhile, one final provision of the Reconstruction Acts required that, in order to be effective, the elections for delegates and to ratify the new constitution had to see a majority of those registered to vote in Texas actually cast ballots. In this the Democrats perceived an opportunity, even while in retreat before military administration. If those eligible among them registered but then stayed home, they might obstruct the entire process, hoping that the resulting delay might produce relief from Congressional Reconstruction. They were unsuccessful. A sufficient number of voters did turn out at the election ordered for February of 1868 by Sheridan's successor, Gen. Winfield S. Hancock. They elected a convention delegation that was radical to an extent unique for Texas politics, composed of only twelve Democrats but seventy-eight Republicans, nine of whom were African American. The boycott strategy of the old-line Democrats backfired badly.[38]

The delegates assembled in Austin on June 1, 1868. As often happens in the wake of success, the ascendant Republicans were already fracturing between radicals like Edmund J. Davis and Morgan Hamilton and more moderate delegates such as Morgan's brother Andrew Hamilton and provisional governor E. M. Pease. Yet the moderate faction was still far to the left of where the Union Caucus had been in 1866. The new split between the Hamilton brothers and between their respective factions showed in the election of the convention's president. Upon a temporary chair being elected, Andrew moved to proceed to elect a permanent chair. Morgan disagreed, claiming that it would be better to "inform the Commanding General of the presence and temporary organization of the convention before proceeding further." Morgan's suggestion was ignored and Andrew's motion was passed on voice vote, whereupon nominations opened. Morgan nominated radical Republican Edmund J. Davis. Andrew nominated his close friend and fellow moderate, Judge Colbert Coldwell. Davis won forty-three to thirty-three.[39]

While this was some reflection of the respective voting strength of the two Republican factions, which were roughly even, there were other alliances and rivalries at work. Historian Carl Moneyhon performed a cluster analysis of voting patterns within the convention and concluded that it would be more accurate to posit four Republican factions, rather than two. He identified the following: (1) a bloc of ten Republicans generally loyal to Pease and Andrew Hamilton; (2) a bloc of eight East Texas Republicans pro-multi-state division but anti-black and led by James W. Flanagan; (3) a bloc of nine western radical Republicans affiliated with E. J. Davis; and (4) a bloc of eight Republicans led by African American George Ruby and preoccupied with freedmen's rights. On most issues, these four subfactions split according to geographic and economic interest, but they were not precisely arranged as subcategories of the dichotomy between moderates and radicals, though the first two were generally more moderate and the latter two more radical. However, this faction analysis leaves out forty-three of the seventy-eight Republican delegates altogether, not to mention the twelve Democrats. And the more important point is that the *consensus* of the Republican delegates was far to the left of the men of 1866. The Republicans dictated the results of the process and a majority of them favored state division, a strong governor and state government, government support for railroads, black suffrage, public education, and civil rights. The most contentious other question to be dealt with by the convention was the continuing and rather symbolic dispute over the ab initio doctrine.[40]

On its third day, Governor Pease submitted an opening message to the convention. In it, he outlined the deficiencies of Presidential Reconstruction, extolled federal intervention, and outlined a moderate program of reform. Pease lamented the situation of his government as "one of extreme difficulty and embarrassment" because his appointment was so distasteful to most whites and required the intervention of the army, without whose cooperation "efforts to execute the laws and preserve the public peace can avail but little." He further complained that crime and lawlessness, including people "taking the law into their own hands," were more prevalent in Texas than ever before. His prescription for order was prompt "resumption of our relations with our sister States," and the primary obstacles to this had been the refusal of the white majority to accept disenfranchisement of rebels on one hand and enfranchisement of newly emancipated blacks on the other. Pease chastised the Democrat legislature for antagonizing Congress by rejecting the Fourteenth Amendment "so contemptuously" and thereby precipitating the current state of affairs.[41]

His specific proposals for reform included a moderate stance on the ab initio question; equal civil and political rights for blacks, including the vote; disenfranchisement of enough ex-Confederates to ensure that unionists would continue in power; "liberal provision, by taxation upon property" for free public education for all; homesteads for all; and stimulus for immigration and economic development. He opposed any division of the state on the grounds that two or three state governments would cost two or three times as much as one, would hamstring efforts to properly fund education and economic development, and would delay readmission to the Union. Instead of division, he resurrected the argument in favor of selling the sparsely populated and mostly public lands of West Texas to the United States, including El Paso. He argued that this section would be of far more use to the Indian policy of the nation than to that of the state, and that "it would be more valuable to them than it can ever be to this State," perhaps the one statement in Texas history most proved wrong by subsequent events, given the discovery of vast oil resources there in the twentieth century.[42]

Pease's discussion of the ab initio dispute was conjoined with his recommendations concerning state debts, and this was no accident. He encouraged the convention to make provision for paying all debts incurred by the state prior to the war, and to only prohibit the payment of such war debts as were "incurred in aid of the rebellion." The language he used was important. If the convention accepted Pease's formula, it would ratify all debts of the wartime state government incurred for railroads and other contracts and improvements, so long as they were not directly involved in the Confederate war effort. And here was the key to the mystery of why such a semantic dispute as the one over ab initio elicited such controversy among the Republican leadership. The radical proponents of extreme ab initio wanted all acts of the wartime government declared void, with the effect that prior loan subsidies to railroads, which tended to benefit the eastern and northern sections of the state, would be canceled and their debts immediately repaid in federal dollars. One case in point was a dispute among delegates over the validity of an 1864 law allowing railroads to pay their state debts in Confederate warrants. Railroads whose debts were called in dollars would likely fail, only to be replaced by others more attractive to Davis's radical supporters concentrated in the central and western parts of the state. While for many ab initio represented a litmus test of radicalism, the primary practical effect was on railroad building and government subsidies because even the moderates agreed that all laws inconsistent with federal law or in aid of the rebellion were void ab initio. It is here that Moneyhon's cluster analysis of geographic voting blocs of delegates is most telling. After a long series of parliamentary battles, the radicals ultimately lost the ab initio fight because of a combination arrayed against them of Democrats, Pease Republicans, and East Texas "Flanagan" Republicans. The tipping point was the support of the Flanagan faction for existing railroads concentrated in their home base.[43]

President Davis appointed the usual array of standing committees, the most important of which were the committees on education, internal improvements, public lands, and federal relations (which had jurisdiction over the ab initio question). The issue that most occupied the first three months of the convention was ab initio, on which the radicals eventually lost. Most of the remaining days and hours of the summer of 1868 were taken up with a tedious factional fight over printing contracts and newspaper subscriptions, expenses of the convention, disputes over rules and parliamentary procedure, ordinances addressing special local needs, resolutions supporting various railroad projects and other enterprises, and the subject of the state penitentiary. After debate and committee referrals for almost three months and with little other than ab initio resolved, tentative majorities began to coalesce on important subjects before the exhausted delegates agreed to recess at the end of August to reconvene in December.[44]

For example, the internecine squabbling over ab initio aside, the summer session witnessed a broad consensus among Republicans for the protection of middle-class mechanics, farmers, and merchants; for supporting railroads and European immigration; for universal public education; and for black suffrage and civil rights. With respect to the protection of mechanics and small farmers, many proposals were referred to the Committee on the Judiciary. For example, James Flanagan, on the fifth day of the convention, proposed that the Judiciary Committee consider suspending all sheriffs' sales for the satisfaction of judgments or other liens. Four days later, the majority committee report suggested the delegates ought not to legislate for only the debtor or the creditor portion of the community because the convention represented the "whole political element of the state for a certain and definite object only," that being the framing of a constitution. A minority of the committee led by Andrew Hamilton and Colbert Coldwell disagreed, believing that "the social, political, and financial condition of the state is so peculiar and so embarrassing as to fully justify us in calling upon the military officer in command of this district, whose powers are believed to be plenary for the relief sought." Delegates sided with the minority report to protect debtors by a vote of forty-four to forty-one not cast upon factional lines. Delegates were also in earnest on the subject of homestead protection. Nathan Patten, a Republican originally from New York, proposed a declaration that was referred to the Committee on Public Lands, authorizing land donation to actual settlers up to 160 acres of the unsurveyed western public lands, conditioned upon the settler paying surveying costs, applying to the General Land Office for a patent, and paying all taxes when due.[45]

On July 29th, the Committee on Political and Legislative Department's proposal on the legislative article included a prohibition on the legislature authorizing by private or special law any sale or conveyance of public land. Meanwhile, when the Committee on Public Lands issued its report the first week in August, it proposed voiding land certificates issued after August of 1856 but not returned in accordance with an 1852 law setting a timeframe for filing surveys with the General Land Office, but it validated conveyances of lands authorized by any court having lawful jurisdiction, "excepting in cases of fraud." It also recommended that the legislature not grant lands in the future to any person or persons except "to actual settlers upon the same." And it provided that any land donated to railroad companies and not already sold to third parties would be forfeited to the state. Other than upholding the decades-long commitment to public schools, these Republicans were clearly interested in using public lands solely to settle the West with free yeoman farmers, not to subsidize railroads.[46]

In a further move to encourage and protect small farmers and mechanics, on August 18th the Committee on the Judiciary reported a section of the new constitution including the right for mechanics to have a lien upon "all articles of manufacture of every description made or repaired by them" and also granting them a right to retain possession of such property until the cost of repairing or fabricating was paid. On July 8th the Committee on General Provisions chaired by Andrew Hamilton made its report, which was amended and approved on August 21st.[47] Hamilton's committee proposed exempting married women's separate property from the debts of their husbands, providing homestead protection from taxation of up to a two-thousand-dollar value per family; a general prohibition on the state subsidizing any corporation, company, or association; and a constitutional provision guaranteeing the right to recover exemplary damages to the heirs of anyone killed by "a person, corporation, or company, through a willful act or omission." When the committee's proposal came up for action by the convention, two more sections were added, one entitling actual settlers to 160 acres of land if married and 80 acres of land if not, and the other guaranteeing the rights of mechanics and artisans to have the type of liens previously recommended by the Judiciary Committee.[48]

As finally adopted, the articles on general provisions and the legislative department (Articles XII and III, respectively) differed in important respects from the 1866 Constitution, and the addition of nine new sections in Article X on the general land office was a significant departure from the old articles on the subject, which aggregated only two sentences. The radical Constitution of 1869 for the first time created a constitutional mechanic's lien for skilled workers and adopted Hamilton's other proposal for a constitutional right to punitive damages against corporations and in favor of heirs of workers willfully injured. Both the 1866 and 1869 constitutions protected the separate property of wives and enshrined the doctrine of community property, but the newer constitution contained additional protections for women. Both constitutions contained provisions authorizing the legislature to protect homesteads from forced sales for debt, and while the maximum extent of homestead protection for rural land remained two hundred acres, the 1866 Constitution's maximum protection for urban lots of a total of a two-thousand-dollar value was increased to five thousand in 1869.[49] Whereas the 1866 Constitution's provisions regarding public lands were skeletal and relatively brief, the 1869 Constitution adopted a substantial separate article on public lands, which for the first time declared the policy in favor of donating homesteads of up to 160 acres to "actual settlers upon" the land, and against using this resource to fund economic development.[50]

The 1869 Constitution not only allowed the legislature to grant to actual settlers lots of not more than 160 acres, but it also required the issuance of genuine land certificates based on location and survey of any lands claimed by railroads under prior laws, so that there could be no misunderstanding about the extent of such holdings. It eliminated the prior schemes for railroad subsidy, whether land based or bond based, prohibited the legislature from extending the credit of the state to any corporations or owning any interest in their property, and instead made the simple provision that with respect to internal improvements, these would have to be funded by the legislature out of current expenses and only after a two-thirds vote.[51]

While the 1866 Constitution embodied the wishes of a probusiness elite anxious to use government to encourage economic development, the radical Constitution of 1869 reflected a desire to use the public lands to fund education and support the development of a farming middle class, while also encouraging the activities of mechanics and small businesses. Railroads and other enterprises could be subsidized, but only through current taxation, not by squandering the permanent assets of the state better used to fund education. Nevertheless, the Republicans of 1869 were certainly procapitalist and prodevelopment, as indicated by another unprecedented provision in the 1869 Constitution, this one absolutely prohibiting any laws against usury or otherwise restraining the freedom of contract. The constitution also included two unprecedented deletions, the omission of the decades-old constitutional prohibition on corporate banks and of the requirement of a two-thirds legislative vote to create other corporations. The Republicans strongly believed, however, that the public realty of the state should be reserved for the improvement of its human capital.[52]

The primary means by which the convention sought to improve the state's human resources and create a multiracial working class was free public education, but it also pursued other strategies. Delegates added an entirely new article creating an unprecedented "Bureau of Immigration." The legislature was authorized to pay immigrants' transport costs and to fund the bureau's activities, including "agencies in foreign seaports or seaports of the United States." The bureau's funding was restricted to the legislative appropriation of the "ordinary revenue of the State," its charge was to encourage Europeans to move to Texas, and it was to be headed by a Superintendent of Immigration appointed by the governor, with the senate's consent, to a term of four years. Appropriately, President Davis had appointed the German radical Edward Degener head of the convention's "Committee on Immigration," and his report, which was adopted with little change, explained the reasons for the broad Republican consensus on this issue. The North's economic superiority had, in the view of Degener's committee, resulted in part from its superior ability to attract cheap immigrant labor. The South was at a disadvantage because of the "abhorrence in which Slavery is held by Europeans, and the reluctance of a free laborer to enter into competition with a slave." Thus the large planters, shortsighted in their slave labor policy, were "now the loudest in clamoring for free white labor, and are willing, even by a special taxation for this purpose, to import laborers for their broad acres, to relieve themselves from the harsh contact with their former slaves whom they never can forgive—that from property they have become their equals at the ballot box."[53]

But that was not all. What Texas needed was "a hard working thrifty population . . . without nomadic propensities and of unquestionable *loyalty to the Government of the United States*" (emphasis in original). Without embarrassment, Degener confidently asserted that "it will not be denied, that the German and Scandinavian nationalities possess these qualifications in an eminent degree," and he urged a reduction of the residency requirement for citizenship and voting so that these new arrivals could be integrated as quickly as possible into the body politic. Republicans looked forward to augmenting their cadre of black and German loyalists with a new corps of northern Europeans who, in Texas at least, had traditionally voted antislave and prounion. It is unlikely that Degener's failure to mention Irish or Italian immigrants, historically part of the Democratic Party in the urban North, was an oversight.[54]

On July 31st, the Committee on Education reported a detailed proposal containing twenty-one sections and establishing a universal public school system for all "inhabitants in the state between the ages of six and eighteen years, without distinction on account of race, color, or previous condition." The proposal called for an appointed superintendent of public instruction to hold office for a term of eight years and a board of education composed of the comptroller and two members from each congressional district in the state to be elected and to serve terms of four years. Interestingly, this board of education was to "exercise full legislative powers in reference to the public free schools of the state, and its acts, when approved by the governor, or . . . by two-thirds of the Board in case of his disapproval, shall have the force and effect of law, unless repealed by two-thirds vote of the legislature." The proposal also provided that the alternate sections of land reserved by the state from railroad grants, together with all other public lands previously dedicated to public schools by the legislature, should form the "public free school fund." The legislature was instructed to "provide for levying a poll tax of one dollar on all male persons of over 21 years of age for educational purposes," and this fund was to be used "for the same purposes as the income which may be derived from the perpetual free school fund." Monies and lands previously appropriated for the support of one or more universities were confirmed to also constitute part of the public free school fund.[55]

This report was taken up and amended in some significant respects on August 27th. The Board of Education was dispensed with in favor of a single superintendent of public instruction to be appointed for four years by the governor, but afterward to be elected to four-year terms by the public. The legislature was authorized to "lay off the state into convenient school districts, and provide for the formation of a Board of School Directors in each district." It was also allowed to give such school districts legislative powers within their domains. Thus the convention, while it retained the other provisions of the original proposal dealing with the use of public lands, poll taxes, and other matters of school funding, opted for a decentralized system of public education reporting only to the statewide superintendent of public instruction, who would in turn report to the legislature as necessary.[56]

When the convention began considering the report section by section, the committee proposal for the "gratuitous instruction" of all residents of scholastic age "without distinction on account of race, color, or previous condition" was scaled back. James Flanagan's segregationist effort on August 27th to add language that the state's education laws "shall be equal and uniform, [but] . . . provision shall be made in said law to keep the races separate, to avoid prejudice that would otherwise arise" was defeated. Republican Julius Schuetze hearkened back to the 1866 Constitution by moving to insert language directing the board of education to establish "separate schools for white children and for colored children," but when it appeared this would not pass, he moved instead to merely strike the clause of the article guaranteeing racial equality, and the committee, on the defensive, accepted the amendment. The watered-down section then passed by a vote of forty-eight to twelve, but Livingston Lindsay, a US Army veteran from West Virginia, made one last attempt to offer a segregationist amendment. His proposal would have expressly authorized the board of education to establish separate schools, "but under no circumstances shall any children, of either color, be deprived of the benefits and advantages of the public free school system." This version of Flanagan's "separate but equal" proposal was also beaten back by the Republican majority.[57]

While the original proposal authorized the board of education to create school districts, the provision as enacted eliminated the board of education, leaving the legislature to map out districts. The wrangling over segregation produced a final provision without any mention of race, positive or negative.

The portion of the original proposal guaranteeing racial equality was stricken, while conservative attempts to add in provisions requiring segregation also failed. The best the radicals could do was add language to Section 9 of the ultimate article, making it "the imperative duty of the legislature to see to it, that all the children in the state, with the scholastic age, are, without delay, provided with ample means of education."[58]

Having assured only some level of education for black children, but leaving its quality to the local school districts and the legislature, the delegates achieved somewhat more progress on black suffrage and civil rights. To the Bill of Rights traditionally included in Article I of Texas state constitutions were added two provisions, the more important of which guaranteed "the equality of all persons before the law" and prohibited "any citizen ever being deprived of any right, privilege, or immunity . . . on account of race, color, or previous condition." This was an obvious borrowing from the Fourteenth Amendment and would provide blacks with a constitutional justification for demanding equal legal and social rights from the legislature and the courts. The other new provision, Section 22, outlawed the importation of "coolies" or the adoption of any other system of peonage amounting to "practical bondage," and the section also outlawed slavery and involuntary servitude except as punishment for crime.[59]

Most importantly for the Republicans, the race-based restrictions on citizenship and voting in the 1866 Constitution were abolished. The new Article III enfranchised every twenty-one-year-old male who was a citizen of the United States, or had "declared his intentions" to become one, and who had resided in the state for one year prior to the election. The only persons excepted were "Indians not taxed" and persons serving in the US Army or Navy. Article III's racial qualifications for holding office were eliminated. The rather draconian residency requirements for office-holding in the 1866 Constitution were scaled back from five years to two years for members of the House of Representatives and to three for members of the State Senate. The convention also added a requirement that no person was eligible for any office of any kind within the state if that person was not "a registered voter." The effect of these provisions was to place a premium on voter registration, which in the near term would be administered by the federal military. As long as federal occupation continued, this system would exclude large numbers of white ex-Confederate voters and guarantee blacks the right to vote.[60]

While they agreed to extend the vote and nominal equality before the law to African Texans, moderate Republicans allied with the Democrats to foil efforts in support of a key radical article of faith, disenfranchising as many ex-Confederates as possible. The radicals feared that, even augmented by an influx of German and Scandinavian immigrants, African American voters would not be enough to consolidate Republican hold on the state beyond the near term. That could only be accomplished by disempowering all but the most lukewarm of rebels (and hence white Democrats) for a generation. The radicals proved to be right in their calculation but unable to accomplish their objective. Pease's moderates, with the support of Democrats, simply enacted a universal adult male suffrage provision that excluded only those ex-rebels disenfranchised by the Fourteenth Amendment. Davis and the radicals had wanted significantly more. They wanted to add to the ranks of the disenfranchised anyone who ever preached or published in favor of Secession or joined a postwar "secret order hostile to the government of the United States," such as the Ku Klux Klan or Knights of the White Camellia.[61]

Regarding the structure of the new government, modest changes were made further strengthening the executive branch and rolling back some of O. M. Roberts's 1866 judiciary reforms. The first Reconstruction constitution had inaugurated four-year gubernatorial terms and the elected office of attorney general, adding them to the already existing offices of state comptroller and state treasurer. It also enacted a unique and important line-item veto for the governor. These features were retained, but the attorney general was not to be elected but appointed by the governor, and an elected commissioner of the General Land Office was added. Term limitations on the governor's office (no more than eight years in office for any twelve-year period) were removed. The Supreme Court was reduced from five members back down to three, appointed by the governor for nine-year terms instead of elected for ten. Roberts's 1866 reform of replacing justices of the peace, municipal courts, and a variety of other local magistrates with a unified system of constitutional county courts was entirely overthrown. The county courts were eliminated, district court jurisdiction was increased, and the new constitution granted to the governor one of his most powerful perquisites, the power to appoint all district judges for eight-year terms. Given the importance of the district courts and the elimination of elections to fill their benches, the 1869 Constitution stipulated a referendum in 1876 at which voters would determine which methods of judicial selection would obtain thenceforth. This debate would continue into the 1870s between Democrats who wanted a county courthouse-based grassroots political system and Republicans who favored a strong central government and a diffusion of less-powerful local officers.[62]

With much of its business tentatively settled, but little accomplished toward approving a final document, the convention recessed on August 31st. Although the stated reason for the recess was that all funds allocated by the military commander for convention expenses had been spent, commentators then and now thought otherwise. Historian Ernest Wallace has adduced strong evidence that the real reasons were political. If the convention completed its work and Texas was readmitted to the Union before the November national elections, Republicans feared the state would vote Democratic and cost them the White House. Radicals also feared that as things were going, the new constitution might be too lenient toward ex-Confederates, and these fears were exacerbated by the violence perpetrated with relative impunity against blacks and Republicans across the state. With the radicals in retreat over the outcome of the ab initio dispute and concerned over the results of the other summer deliberations, their focus in the intermission shifted to hoping for a mandate in the national elections and working to obtain their own state or states carved out of south and west Texas. As in 1866, debate over dividing the state continued to be connected with dealing with the public lands of the Indian frontier. Upon reconvening in December, the delegates became preoccupied with these issues.[63]

The convention had wrangled inconclusively over the western lands in the first session. Desultory proposals and counterproposals had continued until the convention opted to refer the matter to a special Committee on Division of the State to be appointed by Edmund J. Davis. Edward Degener was foremost among Davis's partisans in pushing for a new state in the West, while William Mills, a moderate Republican recently arrived from Indiana, led the move to sell West Texas, including El Paso, to the United States instead. The leading members of the committee appointed by Davis were Degener, the black leader George Ruby, and Armisted Munroe, its chairman. All supported Davis and division, and their faction held a slim majority in the committee. The federal Congress was simultaneously deliberating the same subject. Its most ballyhooed proposal was one authored by Michigan Congressman Fernando Beaman that would divide Texas into three states. The Texas committee endorsed the Beaman Bill, recommending only minor changes in its stipulated boundaries. The radicals in Congress and in the Texas convention wanted East Texas restricted to the area east of the Trinity River, concentrating the conservative Democrats in a small geographic region. The other two states would likely lean Republican, one in Central Texas roughly between the Trinity and Colorado Rivers and including Austin, Galveston, and Houston, and one in West Texas that essentially comprised the area south and west of the Colorado River and that included the vast majority of the state's land and its German and Hispanic populations. But a vote on the report was postponed repeatedly as a result of parliamentary maneuvering by the moderates. Ultimately they succeeded in combining with Democrats to pass a resolution by moderate Republican James W. Thomas that "no question relating to a division of the state . . . will hereafter be entertained, unless by authority of the Congress of the United States." Division appeared dead when the convention recessed for the summer.[64]

But when the delegates reassembled in December, radicals determined to resurrect the issue, encouraged by U. S. Grant's victory in the November 1868 national election and by continued congressional interest in dividing the state. For almost six weeks, the convention heard more proposals and counter-proposals, engaged in parliamentary maneuvering, filibustered, and accomplished nothing on the subject, with the two factions alternately cheered or excoriated by their respective press organs. Some delegates on each side began to vacillate. For example, moderate Colbert Coldwell finally conceded that the best compromise might be to finish the constitution and lay both it and the division question before the voters to decide, but this idea was narrowly defeated by extremists on both sides. With the latest of Texas' succession of military commandants, Gen. Edward Canby, having recently arrived on the scene, radicals finally succeeded on December 29th in repealing the summer session's Thomas resolution that had foreclosed action on division except at congressional invitation. A few days later, convention president Edmund J. Davis announced that he and six other prodivision delegates were already engaged in drafting a constitution for a new state in the Southwest. His cohorts were radicals J. P. Newcomb, Edward Degener, Morgan Hamilton, Jacob Kuechler of Fredericksburg, William Varnell of Victoria, and Dr. A. P. H. Jordan from the environs of Goliad.[65]

On January 6th, delegates found on their desks copies of a new "Constitution of the State of West Texas," drafted and printed by Davis and his radical hill country and South Texas friends. It purported to be the foundational document of a new state southwest of the Colorado River, north of the Rio Grande, and bordered on the west by a line from north of San Angelo down to the confluence of the Pecos River and the Rio Grande. This new state would dwarf most of the others in the Union and would include Austin, San Antonio, Victoria, the Rio Grande Valley, the hill country, and much of what is now West Texas. It departed from previous proposals like the Beaman

Bill by splitting Texas into two states, not three. This constitution had not required much drafting work. It was essentially the same as the document already agreed to in principle for the entire state, but with the most important of the rejected radical proposals reinserted. There was an entire new article on "Registration of Voters" that disenfranchised not only all the secessionist ministers and press editors the radicals previously tried to exclude but also anyone who "voluntarily aided or abetted the said rebellion in any manner." The ab initio doctrine was included by implication because Article VII's "General Provisions" provided that only Texas laws enacted before Secession were to continue in force in the new state, except for any law "for the purpose of protecting or sustaining the institution of slavery, or which recognize any distinction among human beings in regard to their civil or political privileges, rights and duties." These were declared null and void. Residency requirements for both voting and office holding were reduced to one year, with up to six months of residency elsewhere in Texas counting toward the total. And the article on education was strengthened, requiring free public schools for all with compulsory attendance for at least four months of every year.[66]

With the antidivision forces reeling, Newcomb and Degener rose and spoke in favor of the proposal, which was endorsed by a majority of Armisted Munroe's special committee. Degener sarcastically acknowledged the derisive sobriquets that conservatives had begun applying to the new state, "Coyote" or "Chaparral," but he argued that the Republicans in Congress wanted a loyal German buffer state along the Mexican border and that it would be economically self-sufficient. Andrew Hamilton replied for the moderates that the delegates were sent to Austin to frame a constitution for Texas and rejoin it to the Union, not to create another state. Press reaction was generally in his favor, but this did not deter the radicals. A week later, Munroe finally moved successfully for the convention to resolve itself into a committee of the whole to consider his committee's report on dividing the state. Davis then left the chair to propose a substitute proposal, which was to elect four "commissioners" to travel to Washington and report to Congress "all matters relating to the condition of the state and the wants of her loyal people as may require the consideration and action of Congress." All understood that the purpose was to lobby for a new state in West Texas. Davis's resolution gave as its rationale that "the extent of the territory of the State of Texas, the conflicting interest of the widely separated sections of the State, and the disorganization so largely prevalent, render a division of the State essential to . . . the re-establishment of law and order." Davis cited the reports of the convention's Committee on

Lawlessness and Violence, which had decried "war of races" by "whites against the blacks," including rampant murders of freedmen and white union men by ex-rebels.[67]

Davis's watered-down substitute proposal, likely the only one that had a chance of passing, was finally adopted by a vote of 39 to 31 on January 20th, and elections were held to fill the offices of commissioners two days later. At that time, delegates accepted radical Nathan Patten's suggestion that two at-large delegates be added to the original four, which Davis had suggested be geographically balanced. The six commissioners elected by the convention were Davis himself, James W. Flanagan, Morgan Hamilton, G. W. Whitmore, William M. Varnell, and James R. Burnett. About a week prior to this, on January 12th and almost as an afterthought, delegates had voted to form a committee to collate and redraft the various constitutional provisions already agreed to and report a final document. The committee reported almost all of what became the 1869 Texas Constitution on January 26th. The final version of the constitution was passed on February 5th and a heated convention adjourned the next day after a melee of insults, parliamentary moves and countermoves, and an exchange of correspondence between Davis and General Canby agreeing that the "records of the Convention will, when completed, be turned over to the custody of the assistant adjutant general of the district." This stratagem was made necessary by the parliamentary obstructionism of the moderate faction, arbitrary reprisals against them by Davis from the chair, and so much bad blood that many feared one more day of deliberations would scuttle the entire enterprise. Canby was forced to take control of the convention papers and appoint a small committee of scriveners to quickly produce the final document to be submitted to voters, since the convention called elections on ratification and for state offices on the first Monday in July 1869 "under the regulations to be prescribed by the Commanding General of this Military District."[68]

However, Congress intervened and delegated authority over Reconstruction elections in all the southern states to President Grant, who delayed the Texas election until November. In the interim, all the radicals' plans for state division unexpectedly fell on deaf ears in Congress, which was by then otherwise occupied. Texas would not be divided. Meanwhile, Gen. Joseph J. Reynolds, a radical Republican, replaced Canby as commandant of Texas and Louisiana. Reynolds's administration registered voters and held the election under the supervision of federal troops. Many Democrats were deemed ineligible to vote or stayed home. As a result of overwhelming support among

Germans, Hispanics, and the state's new black voters, Davis was elected governor in a tight race with fellow Republican Andrew "Colossal" Hamilton, who appealed to Democrats to join with the moderates within his own party. The election also granted Davis a Republican majority in the newly elected Twelfth Legislature. Congress approved the results of the election, and in 1870 Texas was readmitted to the Union. After almost a year of internecine fighting, the Republicans finally succeeded in establishing a liberal blueprint for Texas.[69]

The Collapse of Reconstruction: Of Semicolons and States Rights

Republican dominance, five years in the making, was destined to be short-lived. In January 1870, General Reynolds certified the election results, and he ordered the Twelfth Legislature to Austin in February, at which time they promptly ratified the Fourteenth and Fifteenth Amendments and elected Morgan Hamilton and James Flanagan, both Republicans, the state's US Senators. On March 30th President Grant signed the congressional act readmitting Texas to the Union. Army units remained in the state, but military rule was at an end. When Gov. Edmund J. Davis called the Twelfth Legislature into regular session in April of 1870, the Republican Party continued to pursue its liberal platform, but the seeds of its overthrow had already been sown. There would be no Canby or Reynolds to prevent racial intimidation, voter suppression, or election fraud—no one but the domestic public to turn to for legitimacy and protection. It would not take the Democrats long to reassert themselves.[70]

But between 1866 and 1873, a new dominant political ethos had undeniably emerged in Texas. The Twelfth Legislature passed major reforms in three areas, the state police, education, and the judiciary. Klan and Camellia violence and lynching were rampant, especially in North and East Texas, and the legislature succeeded in creating a new state police department and a reinvigorated state militia under an adjutant general appointed by, and responsible to, Davis. The recent elections had demonstrated the need for a strong force to replace the US Army in keeping order and protecting blacks at the polls. Several field commanders had encountered white vigilantes and local officials trying to intimidate or disenfranchise African American voters. In addition to chartering the state police, many of whom ended up being freedmen, the legislature increased the number of appointed district judges and expanded their powers to include directing police officers in maintaining order. And, in a provision that provoked bitter remonstrance from conservatives, Davis himself was granted authority to reinstitute martial law in any county where lawlessness ran rampant. His administration also succeeded in persuading the legislature to resurrect the old scheme of a board of public education to run the schools through local districts subordinated to the state board. Davis caused further controversy when his first nominee as superintendent of public schools was rejected by the legislature for refusing to endorse segregation.[71]

The Republican program required raising taxes, and this galvanized the old coalition of Hamiltonian moderates and Democrats to oppose Davis with renewed vigor. In congressional elections called for 1871, the new opposition coalition ejected all four Republican congressmen in favor of Democrats. The Democratic slogan to rally against Davis's administration was "Tyranny, Taxes, and Corruption," and these themes were amplified in the general election of 1872, where white Republican moderates continued to defect to the Democrats. In fact, the only real question became whether the hard-line old Democrats or their more moderate brethren reinforced by Hamiltonian Republicans would control the party. In 1872, the national Democrats endorsed the "Liberal Republican" Horace Greeley for president, who led a schismatic group of moderates unwilling to renominate President Grant. In the Texas Democratic Party convention, however, conservatives gained control. Lacking a credible alternative, they mollified moderates and Republican defectors by endorsing Greeley, but they nominated a full slate of conservative Democrats for the legislature. While Grant easily won reelection, the Democrats carried Texas, winning preemptive margins in both houses of what would become the Thirteenth Legislature.[72]

Hoping to complete their coup, the Democratic majority quickly repealed the state police law and scheduled the next general election, including for governor and all state offices, at the earliest possible date, December 2, 1873. The legislature also passed a constitutional amendment adding two justices to the Supreme Court with all five seats to come up for appointment by the next governor. Democrats in the House then proceeded to impeach twelve of the thirty-five judges appointed by Davis. In the party conventions of 1873, the Republicans renominated Governor Davis, and the Democrats nominated former judge Richard Coke to oppose him, a member of the Secession Convention and Confederate war hero. With the state Republican Party splintered and with white Democrats confidently electioneering and intimidating voters at the polls, many black voters did not turn out or their votes were not counted. Coke defeated Davis by a margin of two to one, and the Democrats

Richard Coke, governor of Texas after the disputed "semicolon election" of 1873 (Published with permission of the Tarlton Law Library, Jamail Center for Legal Research, University of Texas School of Law)

again swept the legislative elections. It appeared the brief interlude of Texas liberalism was over.[73]

But the radicals made one last stand. Although Davis initially conceded the election, other Republicans orchestrated a challenge in court. The sheriff of Harris County, one of the many Republicans ousted in the election, arrested one Joseph Rodriguez for allegedly voting twice. A. J. Hamilton, back in the Republican fold once the Democrats eschewed as unnecessary any further alliance with him and his fellow moderate Republicans, appeared as counsel for Rodriguez and agreed to a strategy with Davis's attorney general, William Alexander. Hamilton immediately filed a writ of habeas corpus with the Texas Supreme Court. He argued that Rodriguez could not be convicted if the entire election was invalid and that the election had been, in fact, unconstitutional. The duty of prosecution fell to Harris County District Attorney Frank M. Spencer, who moved to dismiss the writ on the grounds that the suit was fictitious, having been trumped up by the resentful sheriff, who was also alleged to be paying the fees of Rodriguez's attorneys. Spencer asked for leave to bring witnesses to prove these charges. When the lame-duck Republican Supreme Court refused, Spencer resigned in protest. He was replaced by the Travis County District Attorney when Rodriguez was transferred to the

Austin jail. At that point, the Austin Bar Association intervened and supplied the District Attorney with high-powered volunteer co-counsel, including Democrats George F. Moore, Charles S. West, and Alexander Terrell. Moore and West would soon sit on the Texas Supreme Court themselves, and Terrell would become its official reporter.[74]

The prosecution produced substantial evidence that the suit had been manufactured as a test case to attack the entire election. Hamilton's argument on behalf of Rodriguez was that the election was unconstitutional because the 1869 Constitution provided for all state elections to be held for four days, whereas the 1873 election law had specified only one day, December 2nd. The constitutional provision, Article III, Section 6, decreed that elections "shall be held at the county seats of the several counties, until otherwise provided by law; and the polls shall be opened for four days, from 8 o'clock, A. M., until 4 o'clock, P. M., of each day."

Hamilton's interpretation hung on a semicolon. Since the clause about the location of the polls with its dependent clause "until otherwise provided by law" was separated by a semicolon from the clause about the election's duration, the duration could not be shortened by the legislature "otherwise" providing "by law." Thus the 1873 election law violated the constitution. On January 6, 1874, the three Davis appointees on the Texas Supreme Court agreed. The one-day election held just five weeks before was illegal and would have to be held again.[75]

Democrats were livid. Coke caucused with his advisors to decide on a course of action. Davis, for his part, refused to leave office, feeling compelled to respect the ruling of the Supreme Court. Hamilton left for Washington to beg Grant and Congress for help in enforcing the decision and overturning the election. The Democrats ultimately decided to ignore what they soon came to call "the semicolon case." The legislature convened in Austin a few days after the semicolon decision as if nothing had happened, crowding into the capitol in the vanguard of a parade of armed supporters. They were able to climb into the second floor of the capitol over the protests of Davis and a few of his police and militia, some of whom were black, while the Davis supporters were able to maintain control of most of the first floor and most entrances to the building. When the Democrats threatened to immediately inaugurate Coke on January 11th, Davis anxiously cabled President Grant for US troops to maintain his position. Coke did take the oath of office on the second floor of the capitol, while Grant's reply, published in the *New York Times* two days later and confirmed on January 17th by US Attorney General George H.

Williams, was emphatically negative. "Would it not be prudent as well as right," Grant wrote, "to yield to the verdict of the people as expressed by their ballots[?]" Davis finally resigned, and the Texas House and Senate ratified the results of the election, including the state constitutional amendments that had passed. On January 24th, Governor Coke appointed five new justices of the Supreme Court, all Democrats, with O. M. Roberts as their chief. After a brief interlude, the liberal constitutional moment was over. The conservatives were firmly back in control, and Texans of African descent would have to wait another century for any semblance of equality before the law.[76]

5

The Constitution of 1876, the Turn Inward, and the Rise of the Judiciary

AFTER THE DEMOCRATIC TAKEOVER, THE PERIOD FROM 1875 TO 1890 left white Texans concerned with developing a modern economy and undoing the policies of Republican liberals. Secession and Reconstruction had demanded new constitutions. Now another new political reality called for another constitution equal to the task of what would come to be called "reform and redemption." Northerners continued to concern Texans, but as economic competitors, not politico-military threats. Except among Anglos of the sparsely populated areas of South Texas, Germans and Tejanos had receded into the cultural distance, never to have their own state. The Mexican government had long since accepted the border determined by the Mexican War, the unpacified Indian tribes had largely been ejected from the state, and domestic improvements and economic development soon came to dominate Texas politics. This is not to say that Indian incursions and Mexican bandits like Juan Cortina didn't continue to cause substantial trouble along the border, but Texas' last constitution, the Constitution of 1876, was the creature of "Redeemers" preoccupied with establishing a new progrowth identity. While resentment of Republicans and Reconstruction was still used to justify political action, the conservative elite's real challenge was to deal with a new class-based discontent among rural whites that began as Grange movements and ended as populism. Radical Republicans had tried to create a constituency of small farm and working-class whites that could, combined with black and immigrant voters, keep them in power, but this effort failed. Intervening events instead encouraged a form of race and class consciousness among these whites that caromed in unforeseen directions.

Redemption, inaugurated in Texas by the Democrats' 1873 electoral victory, grew out of the same causes seen throughout the South. Central were the withdrawal of federal troops and the decision of northern business elites to retreat from Reconstruction during the period from 1873 to 1877. Nell Irvin Painter summarized the economic and political situation by reference to economic fear and political weariness, explaining that "after the Panic of 1873 and the reorientation of political issues it entailed, northern Republicans were far less ready to support the fragile Republican regimes of the South." It is in this context that President Grant's refusal to come to the aid of Governor Edmund J. Davis after the 1873 "semicolon election" must be understood.[1]

And in the North, class had already emerged as an important line of political demarcation. As Arnold Paul argued in his book *Conservative Crisis and the Rule of Law*, working-class discontent began with the labor dislocations of the Reconstruction era, and soon spread to midwestern and southern farmers suffering through a decline in international farm prices exacerbated by the monopolization of the credit, transportation, and agricultural storage industries by banks, railroads, and grain elevators. As Paul concluded, "the social protests of the post Civil War era stemmed from the great pace of industrialization, and, more particularly, from the swift concentration of economic power in the large corporation."[2] A railroad strike in 1877 spread nationwide, reminding northern journalists and commentators of the 1871 Paris Commune General Strike that had become an icon of mob violence. Thus the late 1870s produced more northern political activity against the labor movement as "a genuine commune," than against the recalcitrant states' rights South.[3]

The same economic travails impelled farmers to organize much as labor had done. The Patrons of Husbandry was founded in Washington, DC, in 1867 as a farmers' guild that encouraged cooperative arrangements to protect farmers from exploitation by railroads and storage facilities. The Patrons, later known as "The Grange," found natural constituencies in the midwestern and prairie states whose legislatures began in the early 1870s to enact antimonopoly statutes and other regulations of common carriers and grain elevators. The movement spread quickly to the South, where a drop in cotton prices had caused hardship among small farmers. In 1873, a Texas Grange affiliate was organized in Dallas and by 1875 had acquired 50,000 members. Membership in the Grange was generally a private matter and the organization claimed to be apolitical and solely interested in economics, but in Texas, where the Grange became especially popular, some members had already begun agitating for constitutional reform in the early 1870s. For example, J. N. McFaddin presented an address to the Williamson County Grange particularly critical of "tax-gatherers and ... political judges" and urging a return to the old prewar ways of the Constitution of 1845, including a drastic reduction in government offices and the salaries paid their occupants. His sentiments were echoed by newspapers in rural areas that called for a return to the simpler, less intrusive government of 1845, and in general for "retrenchment and reform" to beat back the perceived evils of Reconstruction.[4]

With the North growing introspective and focused on economic development, the South was free to do the same without federal intervention. In Texas, this phenomenon is documented in the annals of its 1875 constitutional convention, which anticipated and sought to contain the conflict over agrarian reform that engulfed the state in the 1880s and 1890s. And the judicial branch that interpreted the convention's new constitution moved to the forefront of managing the class conflict that ensued. In 1874, Governor Coke appointed the old secessionist and soon-to-be governor O. M. Roberts chief justice of the state Supreme Court, and his tribunal would come to be known as the "court of the redeemers." Meanwhile one of the constitutional convention's principal tasks would be foiling attempts by the new Grange faction of the Democratic Party to reduce the size and reach of Roberts's judiciary. In fact, reforming the judiciary was high on the list of almost all the delegates at the 1875 constitutional convention, and the issue symbolized all that chafed about Reconstruction. The 1868–69 constitutional convention had already scheduled a plebescite for 1876 on how to select Texas' judges, and the "platform" ballyhooed for weeks prior to the 1875 constitutional convention by the Democrat editors of the Austin *State Gazette* began with demands for "the election of Supreme, District, and County Court Judges by the people ... [and] reduction in the number of District Judges, as well as their salaries." As two early-twentieth-century historians remarked, "the operation of the judiciary under the Constitution of 1869 had been especially disagreeable to the people. Specific changes were therefore made." Chief among the list of "disagreeable" operations was the semicolon decision, *Ex Parte Rodriguez*.[5]

Management of the public lands also preoccupied Texas politicians and the 1875 convention. Under the 1876 Constitution, some lands would be segregated by the legislature and appropriated to the support of a public school system, others to the support of land grant universities, and still others to other purposes. As he explained after the constitution's ratification and his election as governor in 1878, O. M. Roberts believed that the vast majority of these lands in the western part of the state were better adapted to stock raising than to farming. So he became an advocate of allowing "large tracts to be purchased by persons who had means to engage in that business in a dry country." He preferred to sell the lands to help pay the public debt, rather than "continue donating them to railroad companies." Others disagreed. Roberts's opposition notwithstanding, the practice of donating land to railroad companies as an incentive to have them build track was reauthorized by the 1876 Constitution and ran rampant in the 1879s and 1880s. Conditions were almost always placed upon such donations, and whether or not the conditions had been fulfilled would produce substantial litigation. Anticipating these fights over public lands, railroads, and education would occupy much of the constitutional convention of 1875.[6]

Other issues included the extent to which the state should continue to encourage immigration for the purpose of economic development, and the proper limitations to place on an executive branch that the Redeemers perceived as tyrannical and "black." In dealing with these issues as well, the conservative white majority had to learn to compromise with a faction of between thirty and forty Grange Democrats for the first time in a position to influence state politics. It is difficult to uniformly characterize these Grangers other than by membership in the Grange of the Patrons of Husbandry. All that otherwise can safely be said is that some delegates to the 1875 convention who were members of the Grange were less radical than others, but a large majority were poor farmers who more than anything wanted homestead protection, railroad regulation, and emasculation of the spendthrift Reconstruction government that had raised their taxes, worsened their lot, and diluted their political ability to protect themselves. So, at this early stage of the reform movement that would come to be known as populism, while many of the Grangers agreed with Republican protection of debtors and homesteaders, they also wanted much the same things the Democratic leadership wanted. In fact, what distinguished the Grange of the 1870s from the populism of the 1880s is simply that Grangers concentrated on cooperative economic activity at the local level in order to better their lot, but they eschewed political radicalism. Populism, on the other hand, was the creature of those former Grangers and others who decided that the old Grange had been too politically conservative and anemic.[7]

The tasks before the Democratic establishment would prove daunting. The Grangers, together with fourteen Republicans, five of whom were African American, constituted roughly 50 percent of the ninety delegates if they were ever to act in concert. During the convention, the Grange Democrats did show some solidarity but seldom agreed with the Republicans. Most of the Grangers saw freedmen and Reconstruction as the sources of their farm problems. They just wanted lower taxes and a weak state government, goals the Redeemers shared in the abstract. The result was a constitution that condemned Reconstruction and protected some of the interests of white laborers and small farmers at the expense of blacks. The one exception was a short-lived and ultimately unsuccessful alliance between some Grangers and moderate Democrats with Republicans to fight the poll tax as a method of disenfranchising blacks and other poor voters. Tellingly, the Grangers who opposed the poll tax did so because liberal voters posed no threat of changing election results in their home districts. As the sociologist Georg Simmel would predict a century later, those Grangers from counties with significant numbers of black or Republican voters did the opposite. They favored the poll tax and thereby sacrificed their egalitarian ideology in favor of blunting local black and Republican majorities in their home districts.[8]

The Convention of 1875 and Constitution of 1876

It is a mistake to characterize the 1876 Constitution as "populist," although this generalization is common among contemporary commentators. Strictly speaking, there were no populists at the 1875 convention. Seth Shepard McKay, an early-twentieth-century historian, collated and published the contemporary accounts of the convention printed in Austin's *Daily State Gazette* and a few other newspapers. This publication, supplemented by the official journal of the convention, is a valuable resource that lacks an analog for the previous five constitutional conventions. Another is McKay's 1924 book, *Making the Texas Constitution of 1876*. Later commentators have oversimplified McKay's claim that of the original ninety delegates, fifteen were Republicans and seventy-five were Democrats, of which "about one half of the delegates elected were Grangers." The specific evidence given by McKay was merely that of the forty-one farmers and twenty-nine lawyers elected as delegates, "many . . . were known to be members of the State Grange." Moreover, some have ignored McKay's own clarification that there were actually only fourteen Republican delegates that participated because one of the five African American Republicans resigned early in the convention.

He was replaced by a Democrat quickly elected from the same district to take his seat. There is some evidence that a few of the forty or so Grange members actually became radicals or populists in the 1880s or 1890s, but many Grangers were simply small farmers who were old-line Democrats that never became political radicals or outright populists. Contemporary accounts and later studies of the convention's delegates place the number of actual Grange members at thirty-eight or thirty-nine.[9]

Another factor casts the question of "Grangerism" at the convention in a different light than the accepted wisdom. The political stance of some of those delegates whom we now know to have been Grangers indicates that the situation was much more nuanced than commonly believed. The single most effective and influential member of the convention, the one most responsible for the content of its ultimate product, was a moderate Democrat ex-judge and congressman named John Henninger Reagan, and this John H. Reagan, traditional Democrat and successful railroad lawyer, was a member of the Grange. His outlook epitomized the Hegelian synthesis that would become the dominant political ethos of modern Texas. The Democratic Party he straddled possessed a more variegated spectrum of sentiment than might be supposed. In addition to business conservatives like railroad lawyers William Pitt Ballinger and Charles S. West from urban areas, the convention included Germans and other Democrats from heavily Hispanic and sparsely populated South and West Texas who defied easy characterization other than as mavericks, men like Texas Ranger John S. "Rip" Ford of Brownsville, Irish rancher J. B. Murphy of Corpus Christi, and the Germans Dr. Cayton Erhard of Bastrop and Jacob Waelder of San Antonio.[10]

John H. Reagan was no maverick or populist. He made his political reputation in East Texas as a lawyer and judge who effectively campaigned for the Democratic establishment against Know-Nothings and other whigs. In 1857, his Democratic constituents rewarded his fidelity by electing him to Congress. As a precursor to his flexible and pragmatic views, he handily won reelection in 1859 on a conservative prounion platform while still endorsing secessionist Governor Hardin Runnels, the official Democratic nominee, against Sam Houston's successful unionist campaign. Reagan was, if anything, a compromiser, a trimmer in matters of ideology, and a staunch party man. As evidence of his political deftness, he managed to quickly shed any unionist taint in 1860 and was elected a delegate to the Secession Convention and then as one of the seven delegates to the Confederate Convention in Montgomery, Alabama. This led to his being made postmaster general of

Prominent railroad lawyers **William Pitt Ballinger** (right) and **Charles West** (below). West would become a member of the Texas Supreme Court (Published with permission of the Tarlton Law Library, Jamail Center for Legal Research, University of Texas School of Law)

the Confederacy and by the end of the war, head of its treasury. Although a prominent Confederate official, after defeat in the war, like other moderate Democrats, Reagan advised Texas to accept the federal demands necessary for readmission to the Union, not out of ideology, but as a matter of economic and political expediency. The failure of Presidential Reconstruction and the resentment among white Texans produced by Congressional Reconstruction made Reagan's pragmatic counsel appear uncannily prophetic. When the Democrats regained full control in the state elections of 1873, Reagan was prominent among the Redeemers, and he regained his seat in Congress by a wide electoral margin in 1874. A successful railroad lawyer after the Civil War, he frequently had to fight off opponents to his left who accused him of being too close to the industry, and he spent much of his political energy convincing Greenbackers and populists that third parties were unnecessary because the Democratic Party could be trusted to provide a modicum of economic regulation. Although a card-carrying member of the Grange, this man was no "Grange radical." He was a remarkably nimble and accurate weathervane of political sentiment among Democrats, often a few years but not too far ahead of his time.[11]

The most important and contentious debates in the 1875 convention surrounded the issues of fiscal responsibility and taxation, public lands, public education, immigration policy, the judiciary, railroads, and the poll tax. The Republicans and business Democrats generally agreed on the questions of immigration and economic development, including some aspects of education, railroads, and public lands. The Grangers and business Democrats were allies on the questions of weakening government, cutting spending, and segregating education. And the Republicans and some Grangers agreed in opposing the use of a poll tax to restrict voting, but they were joined in this by many mainstream Democrats still stinging from the voter registration tactics of the Reconstruction Republicans. Ultimately, the resolution of each of these questions involved compromises sufficient to carry a majority of the delegates, a different majority coalition in each case. And perusing the records of this convention, one finds that the leading broker of the necessary compromises was often "Judge" John H. Reagan. Indeed, the editor of the *Debates* of the convention opined that "Judge Reagan was probably the most highly respected of all the delegates."[12]

The framework the convention produced, although it did not resolve all disputes between the Democratic establishment and the Grangers, did provide an agreeable structure and mechanism for arbitrating any lingering

The Constitution of 1876, the Turn Inward, and the Rise of the Judiciary   135

disputes in the future. For the entire Democratic spectrum, this was preferable to any alternative that would have continued the strong Reconstruction government of the 1869 Constitution or allowed the Republicans any chance of regaining power.

That 1869 Constitution was a detested symbol of radicalism and Reconstruction. Even before the 1874 Democratic takeover of the government, some had been agitating for constitutional reform. Prominent within the successful Democratic platform of 1872 was a condemnation of the "obnoxious acts" of the Republican Twelfth Legislature. After winning the 1872 election, Democrats in the legislature passed a law requiring another election just a few months after they took office in 1873, and that law would become the lynchpin of the Supreme Court's decision in the "semicolon case." At the Democratic convention that nominated candidates for the 1873 election, delegates approved a platform plank calling for a constitutional convention to repeal the Constitution of 1869, and several measures were introduced in the ensuing Thirteenth Legislature suggesting various methods of revision. Governor Coke and many legislators initially supported appointing a commission to prepare amendments for voter approval, but the result was instead the formation of a joint legislative committee to do so. This "Camp-Sayers Committee" recommended several amendments, including popular election of the Supreme Court and attorney general, some reduction in state officials' salaries, local option elections on the prohibition of alcohol, and a constitutional poll tax of one dollar that the legislature could make a prerequisite to voting if it wished. This report, which did not produce any definite action, did nothing to abate the calls in the Democratic press and at local party meetings for a full-blown convention. Partisans demanded more far-reaching measures, such as the election of all judges and state officers, more drastic reductions in taxes and spending, and only biennial sessions of the legislature. In 1875, in response to this growing public pressure, Governor Coke and the legislature finally agreed that a convention was desirable. A joint resolution passed both houses and was signed by the governor calling an election of delegates in August and a constitutional convention for September of that year. The obvious political revolution that occurred in Texas in 1873–74 required a new foundational document.[13]

The convention met in Austin on September 6, 1875, and E. B. Pickett, an uncontroversial and experienced ex-Confederate Democrat, was elected chairman.[14] Everyone knew the most contentious issue would be the poll tax. Suspicion immediately arose among the Democratic press that the convention was under the sway of an insidious cabal of Grangers bent on defeating this form of voter suppression. While the San Antonio *Daily Herald*, on the day before the convention, extolled the delegates as "men, the majority of whom have been chosen for their ability and sterling worth," just two days later the same paper sounded an entirely different note, reporting that "the convention has relatively but a few able men in its composition" and warning that instead there might exist "a secret political organization, which may have combined to bring under its control the whole machinery of State Government for their own peculiar ends and objects. . . . The times are out of joint; our rights are insecure." A few weeks later, the *Daily Herald* would follow up these ominous reports with the hysterical claim that 80 percent of the delegates were Grangers.[15]

And it would not be alone in making such accusations as the convention wore on. By the convention's midway point, the Democratic Austin *Statesman* was claiming that a "holy alliance" between Grangers and Republicans had defeated mainstream Democrats' attempts to suppress black voting via a constitutional poll tax. In its editions of October 8th, 9th, and 10th, the *Statesman* charged that the "holy alliance" was composed of the fourteen Republican delegates and thirty-three of the forty-two Democrats who were allegedly members of the Grange, thus making an anti-poll-tax majority of forty-seven. However, the *Statesman* garbled the facts. Repeated votes taken on various parliamentary maneuvers making the poll tax a prerequisite for voting were rejected by votes of fifty-two to twenty-eight, a slightly larger margin than its figures would suggest.[16]

When the *Statesman* launched its conspiracy theory in the October 8th edition, the opening of that day's convention session became heated. One of the Democrats implicated, Gen. John W. Whitfield, a member of the state Democratic Executive Committee years before any Texas Grange existed, rose immediately on a question of privilege and "protested against the remarks of the *Austin Statesman* of that morning." He admitted Grange membership but condemned the charges of a conspiracy with Republicans as groundless. He was followed to the podium by another Granger who expressed similar outrage, Francis J. Lynch, an antebellum politician and plantation owner from DeWitt County. Meanwhile, the troublesome John H. Johnson, a radical Granger from Collin County, also took the floor not to deny the charges but to reply to the press that Grangers had been propping up "this description of gents—officeholders—from the foundation of the world," that the Grange was accustomed to this sort of attack, and that "the more they attacked him the stronger would be his conviction that he was right." But these remarks, if anything, only egged the *Statesman* on. Johnson's contributions to the discourse for the rest of the convention were often equally sarcastic and almost uniformly radical. He would become a lightning rod for conservative press criticism of the Grange and the convention.[17]

The *Statesman* made more specific charges the next day. Its October 9th edition claimed that Johnson himself was the prime conspirator along with Republican S. H. Russell of Harrison County. This produced another spate of denials from the floor of the convention. Whitfield, Reagan, Frances Marion Martin, Edward Chambers, G. B. Cooke, H. W. Wade, Thomas L. Nugent, W. W. Dillard, and Elijah S. C. Robertson either admitted Grange membership outright or implied sympathy with it by their remarks, but they emphatically denied any conspiracy. Ebenezer Dohoney denied Grange membership but admitted that as editor of the *North Texan*, he "had advocated the principals [sic] they did before there was a lodge of the order in the State." Of those who remained prominent in politics, Martin and Dohoney were soon to become radical populist reformers who argued for railroad regulation and prohibition; Nugent, later a socialist, would become the third-party People's (Populist) Party candidate for governor in 1892; Chambers was a former Whig turned moderate Democrat; and Reagan and Whitfield were old-line ex-Confederate party men, as already described, as was Robertson. As such, these men represented a good cross-section of Granger delegates, and they demonstrated that such affiliation hardly determined either their votes or their politics. Reagan, Whitfield, Robertson, Lynch, and even the radical Nugent, for example, had all argued *for* a poll tax, yet all later confessed to membership in or sympathy with the Grange. Nonetheless, an outraged Martin moved for an immediate investigation of the *Statesman's* charges. The flummoxed delegates initially tabled the motion on voice vote and then reconsidered and passed it moments later. A committee was appointed composed of delegates who could aver they were not Grangers. One of the convention's last acts was to receive the report of that committee, which pronounced that it had obtained several affidavits from those mentioned by the *Statesman* (excepting the most important ones, the alleged "bargainers" Johnson and Russell) and that it lacked the "the time, if it had had the disposition, to make any further investigation." On motion of Russell, the alleged Republican ringleader, the entire matter was then permanently "laid on the table."[18]

Though it resulted in little but annoyance for the delegates, the accusations that arose from the debate over the poll tax signified much about the fears of the Democratic establishment and its press. The direst threat posed by the convention was that white agrarian reformers would form an alliance, holy or not, with Republicans and blacks. The debate echoed those fears, which were later trumpeted by those who would oppose ratification of the convention's work. Indeed the strongest argument made against the Constitution of 1876 during the campaign for its ratification was the claim of the conservative Democratic *Galveston News*, the most widely read newspaper in the state, that with an elected local judiciary and without a poll tax as an instrument of voter suppression, the Grangers had ceded to the Republicans electoral control of fifteen to eighteen counties along the Gulf coast as a "Senegambia" subject to inevitable black (and Republican) rule.[19]

And within the convention itself, racial politics was not euphemized. It was overt. Republican Webster Flanagan, in the October 9th debate over the *Statesman*'s conspiracy charges, denied not a "holy alliance," but a "supposed contract that was said to exist between the Grangers and the so-called negro or radical party of the Convention." Frances M. Martin's very resolution to investigate the charges described them as allegations that Grangers had "formed an alliance with the negroes and radicals of this Convention." Republican R. B. Rentfro, in connection with Martin's demand for an investigation, "protested against the language used by individual members [and] hurled at Republicans that were unnecessary and unkind. They had been spoken of as 'radicals, negroes, etc.' [and] designated... as 'n****rs and radicals.'" Fletcher S. Stockdale, a prominent conservative member of the convention who had served as lieutenant governor during the Civil War and as president of the Indianola Railroad, diplomatically suggested an amendment to Martin's resolution substituting "Republicans" for the words "negroes and radicals," and this was adopted. Yet, toward the end of the convention, the irascible Johnson still felt it necessary to rise and defend himself again from charges of consorting with black Republicans. Complaining that someone had sent a report to his home newspaper that he had "chosen to sit among the negroes of the convention," he replied that "he had had to take the seat he had drawn, though he would have preferred to be somewhere else." He continued that he "had carried every point he had started out with when he left his county.... There were thirty-six lawyers in that body, but [he] ... had beaten the talent of the Convention all along the line." The limit circumscribed by the establishment and its press was clearly marked: the more radical the Granger, the more easily he might be dismissed as beyond the pale, a friend of "negroes."[20]

The *Statesman* had indeed overheard a conversation between the radical Granger Johnson and the Republican Russell mentioning a Grange-GOP vote trade on poll taxes in the presence of other delegates. But both Johnson and those who overheard the conversation, including Reagan and Ballinger, claimed that whatever he said to Russell was boasting or a joke made in bad taste (which made sense given Johnson's acerbic personality). Nonetheless, the rumor of a conspiracy could not be defused. The *Statesman* was suspicious of the solidarity shown by repeated anti-poll-tax votes by the same margin. Originally, the Committee on Suffrage of the convention chaired by Dohoney (who would soon be a radical populist) had reported an article on September 30th mandating payment of all levied poll taxes as a prerequisite to voting. The proposal also required twelve months' residency in Texas for voters who were US citizens, and it required the same twelve months plus a "declaration of intent to become naturalized" from foreign immigrants. Evidently, the committee was equally concerned about an influx of Mexican or European immigrants and about northern carpetbag voters. Republican R. B. Rentfro submitted a minority report condemning any poll tax as operating "most severely against the interests of the working classes of this State." In accordance with parliamentary routine, copies of the reports were printed and distributed to come up for consideration in due course.[21]

They did come up as "unfinished business" on October 6th, when Edward Chambers moved to strike the poll tax portion of the proposed article on suffrage. Republican John S. Mills rose in support and condemned the poll tax as "a thrust against the colored man." John H. Reagan then spoke against any such interpretation, acknowledging that if true it would mean the state intended to violate the Fourteenth and Fifteenth Amendments. He suggested a compromise leaving in the poll tax requirement, but only as to payment of the most recent poll tax before any given election. H. W. Wade attempted another compromise by limiting the amount of any poll tax to no more than two dollars. Tellingly, Democrat John Henry Brown, the aging ex-Confederate editor and historian, compared the poll tax to the "registration law . . . and infamous police bill under Governor Davis." Why, he asked, "when they had gotten rid of the registration act, should they pass a law similar in effect, forcing every man to carry his pass in his hand?" His contemporary, the old ranger Rip Ford, shared the same view. "If the Government had a right to levy $1 as a qualification for voting, it could levy any amount," Ford argued. In an effort to lure away conservatives, mavericks, and others opposed to any form of voter registration on principle, Democrat Littleton W. Moore proposed leaving in the poll tax but prohibiting the presentation of a payment receipt in order to vote. Dohoney then tried limiting poll taxes to those enacted subsequent to adoption of the new constitution. None of these tactics could budge the vote count, which coincidentally remained fifty-two to twenty-eight against, although a few members moved in and out of the majority depending on the question at hand. Finally, W. D. S. Cook made one last stab at voter suppression by offering a substitute that would only *authorize* the legislature to make a poll tax a prerequisite to voting but not *require* one. Even this measure was defeated, but by the closer margin of forty-four to twenty-eight. The conclusion is inescapable that mainstream Democratic rejection of any form of voter registration was just as important to the initial defeat of the poll tax as the opposition of Republicans and some of the Grangers.[22]

The suffrage article was passed in its final form on October 8th after an amendment by Democrat newspaper editor and Granger Charles DeMorse passed by a vote of fifty-seven to nineteen and after another amendment by Whitfield passed by forty-five to thirty-two. DeMorse's amendment added a provision restricting voters on municipal bond elections to those paying property taxes in the city. Whitfield's required that all voters cast their votes in their home precincts. "Precinct voting" was seen as a particular necessity in response to what Democrats believed had been voter manipulation during Reconstruction, since the 1869 Constitution had mandated that every voter be allowed to vote "anywhere in the State for State officers." After this bitter fight, some of the conservatives and Grangers who allied with the Republicans would ultimately, in the interest of fiscal frugality, accept a poll tax, but without constitutionally requiring or prohibiting its use as a prerequisite for voting. In a compromise suggested by Reagan on the very contentious subject of public education, the convention adopted a poll tax of one dollar to help fund the public schools, but not as a constitutional prerequisite to voting.[23]

And the debate over education similarly pitted a number of factions against each other. One faction led by Conservative Democrats Elijah Robertson, Stockdale, Richard Sansom, and G. B. Cooke believed the government had no business educating children other than orphans. They claimed education was a parent's job with church help, and that tax-funded compulsory public education was an invasion of parental rights. In an allusion to the fiscal irresponsibility of the Davis administration, Stockdale described public education as "putting the hand into one man's pocket to obtain money with which to educate the children of another man." Robertson decried that the institution was "absolutely subversive of civil and religious liberty." Sansom, in authoring a dissent from the initial committee report in favor of public schools, said that, excepting orphans, public schooling endangered religious liberty, which implied "not only the right of the parent to worship God according to the dictates of his own conscience, but . . . his right to direct the religious instruction of his children."[24]

The strongest supporters of well-funded public education were the Republicans and the Democrats one might categorize as among the professional class and in favor of economic development whether Grangers or not, including Reagan, Ballinger, Whitfield, Flournoy, Chambers, DeMorse, and George McCormick, who would serve as attorney general under both Richard Coke and O. M. Roberts. They were joined by old whigs and others from frontier areas, such as the Germans Waelder and Erhard, and Rip Ford, as well as Grangers and radicals who saw public education as a means to check the power of wealth and privilege. Among these were Johnson, Lynch, Dohoney, and Nugent. This amorphous proeducation coalition would, after much debate and maneuvering, have its way. The provision ultimately agreed upon was anathema to the social and fiscal conservatives who opposed it, including many Grangers, but it was modest in comparison to the Reconstruction educational regime. The article on public education in the new constitution eliminated the entire state education bureaucracy universally disliked by Democrats, replacing it with a State Board of Education composed of the governor, comptroller, and secretary of state. But their primary duty was fiscal management of the school fund created by the Constitution of 1866 and augmented by the Constitution of 1869. All other matters rested with local school officials. The article enacted the following features without substantive change from that originally proposed by the committee: (1) explicitly separate schools for whites and "colored children, and impartial provision . . . for both"; (2) a permanent public school fund, the principal of which was comprised of all lands previously so dedicated, plus all alternate sections of land reserved by the state from donations to railroads and corporations, plus "one half of the public domain of the State"; (3) an available school fund for current expenses of the public schools comprised of the income off the permanent fund; (4) affirmation of the previous allocations of public land to counties for education, and to the state "Lunatic, Blind, Deaf and Dumb, and Orphan Asylums"; and (5) a system for the state to periodically allocate money from the available school fund to counties for expenditure on public schools to be maintained in such counties.[25]

The original proposal, in addition to the available fund, allowed the expenditure for schools of no more than 10 percent of the state's annual tax revenue plus "such poll tax as may by law be levied." After debate, the cap was raised to 25 percent and the poll tax was capped at one dollar upon Reagan's suggestion. It was in this way that the poll tax initially rejected after a heated debate quietly made its way back into the constitution, but not as a prerequisite to voting. The convention also added similar "permanent" and "available" university funds for higher education, including for the establishment of "a university of the first class . . . styled 'The University of Texas'" with the Agricultural and Mechanical College already founded by the legislature in 1871 to be made "a branch of The University of Texas." The permanent university fund contained those lands already pledged by the legislature to establish the university, except for the one-tenth of alternate railroad sections previously allocated to the university by the 1868 statute initially authorizing its creation. Added to this was an additional "one million acres of the unappropriated public domain of the State, to be designated and surveyed as may be provided by law." Continual government subsidies of this kind on the assumption that there existed an almost inexhaustible supply of land would soon become problematic and have to be sorted out by the courts.[26]

Fiscal issues also occupied the convention as indicated by its first several sessions, which were taken up with arguing over whether to spend the money necessary to hire a stenographer to report the proceedings. Party regulars and lawyers like Stockdale, Reagan, Flournoy, Ballinger, Charles S. West, and William L. Crawford supported the idea, which was repeatedly defeated by fiscal conservatives after several days of motions, amendments, and reconsiderations. There were prominent Grangers on either side of the issue. Fiscal conservatism and limited government were the watchwords of a consensus of members, the only significant exception being among Republicans, or depending upon the issue, business development Democrats. One thing a vast majority agreed upon was emasculating the perceived omnipresence of state authority under Reconstruction. When Ballinger reported for his "committee on the executive" a proposed article leaving executive officers in place, but reducing all of their terms of office of all from four years to two years, this drew immediate criticism as not going far enough. Ballinger's report also recommended that all executive officers other than the secretary of state be elected. What the convention added in order to assure a less powerful executive was to abolish the detested office of state superintendent of public instruction and to drastically reduce all officers' salaries. When the legislative article was debated, it was also decided to reduce legislative salaries and to authorize the legislature to meet only once every two years in the absence of an emergency declared by the governor. The Texas Legislature still operates on this "biennial" basis.[27]

Arguments over railroads, public lands, and immigration broke more clearly along ideological lines. Grangers and fiscal conservatives wanted less government subsidy of railroad building either for reasons of austerity, or more commonly, out of outright mistrust of corporations, especially railroads. Business Democrats like Reagan, Ballinger, and West joined Republicans to support subsidization of railroads by donations of public land. But these men saw that in order to protect nascent industrialization, compromises had to be made that would satisfy Granger demands for regulation. As Reagan complained at one point in the debate over railroad subsidies, "with a large proportion of the people of the State, which feeling was represented in part by the Convention, . . . [their] hair turned the wrong way when 'railroad' was mentioned, but prejudice ought not to prevail against a policy which had conferred such great benefits upon the State."[28]

The Constitution of 1866 had approved a policy of government subsidization of railroad building, while the 1869 Constitution had made certain amendments. Although the policy of land subsidy to railroads had begun with state statutes passed in the 1850s, the 1866 Constitution had added to this an authorization for the state to guarantee railroad bonds. The 1869 Constitution had instead provided for monetary expenditures for internal improvements and forfeited any land subsidies back to the state if the railroads had not yet sold them. No new land subsidies were allowed. The Democrats had become critical of the strain that Reconstruction bond subsidies and cash stipends placed on the state treasury. So, when the committee on the legislative branch reported its proposed article on the legislative department, it prohibited government appropriations of money "to any individual, association of individuals, municipal corporation or other corporation whatsoever." Meanwhile, the committee on public lands recommended continuing the 1869 policy of also prohibiting land subsidies to railroads. The land donation scheme, extending back to the 1850s, involved donating sections of land to railroads beyond those used for rights of way. The extra land constituted a reward for building track. Reagan defended land subsidies and, joined by Rip Ford, Stockdale, and the Granger Lynch, argued that while it might be wise to prohibit direct funding of railroads, the land subsidy system had worked to bring development to the eastern and northern sections of the state and it would be unfair to deprive the west of "similar advantages." Their opponents argued chiefly that the public lands should be used only to fund education, an extreme position consonant with the spirit of 1869 that was ultimately rejected. After long bouts of parliamentary maneuvering over both committee reports, the moderate position argued by Reagan prevailed. The legislature would not have the authority to subsidize railroads in cash, but the land subsidy program would be reinstated.[29]

The article proposed by the committee on public lands continued the Reconstruction policy of encouraging small-family farm settlement of the public domain, and the committee on special provisions recommended continuing the protection of homesteads from creditors. These recommendations were adopted. Article XIV, Section 6, of the Constitution of 1876 continued the guarantee in the Reconstruction constitutions of 160 acres of land to every head of a family as long as the head of household occupied the land for three years and paid a slight fee, and it made similar donations of 80 acres to all single men. But the 1876 Constitution added further protections for farmers and laborers. Section 28 of Article XVI outlawed garnishment of current wages for payment of debt, and further enacted a new usury law capping all interest charges at no more than 12 percent per annum. Both were significant departures from the free market business policies of radical Reconstruction.[30]

The debate over state subsidization of immigration was another bellwether of factional strength on economic development issues. The same coalition of business Democrats, Republicans, and some westerners and Germans like Waelder and Erhard supported a continuation of the Reconstruction policy of a state immigration bureau that advertised for immigrants and paid their transportation to Texas. At this convention, however, they were overwhelmed by Democrat and Granger sentiment for thrift and small government. The committee charged with reporting an article on the subject set the tone that was ultimately approved by the convention: "The people ought not to be taxed for any such purpose."[31]

John Reagan's influence within the convention was nowhere more evident than in the contentious debate on the judicial branch. Reagan had been appointed chair of the committee on the judiciary, but a slim majority led by William Pitt Ballinger submitted the committee's majority report, with which Reagan disagreed. The radical Reconstruction constitution had eliminated county courts and instead provided five elected justices of the peace to try small claims and misdemeanors in each county. It had also increased the number of district judges to thirty-five and made them appointed by the governor for eight-year terms, and the three members of the Supreme Court were also appointed by the governor for terms of nine years. Recent constitutional amendments had given Governor Coke appointment of a new five-member court, and Ballinger now proposed leaving the number of justices at five, but making each seat elective by single-member district. The court would be required to convene each October until the end of June, and to sit "at the seat of government and at not more than two other places in the State." District judges and other judicial officers were all to be locally elected. Because of the growing backlog of cases in the Supreme Court, the legislature was authorized to create a Commission of Appeals that could hear and decide cases by assignment from an overburdened court. For the same reasons, appeal of any misdemeanor case was outlawed unless authorized and specifically endorsed by the local district judge. Roberts's old system from 1866 of elected county judges and county commissioners, still in effect in the twenty-first century, was also part of the plan, and to speed trials in all civil and non-felony criminal cases, Ballinger suggested that a vote of only nine of twelve jurors be sufficient for a verdict.[32]

Reagan's minority report acknowledged the importance of reform, claiming that "objections to the present judicial system, more probably than those to any other part of the present constitution, induced the people . . . to vote for . . . a Constitutional Convention." His primary objection to the majority report, though, was that it would not go far enough to relieve the fiscal and administrative strain of the current system. He pointed out that although county courts were proposed for reinstatement, their concurrent jurisdiction with district courts and Ballinger's proposal that county court judgments could be appealed to district court and retried de novo would only multiply backlogs, not decrease them. Reagan's plan allowed these appeals but only on the record and without retrial. Reagan also urged return to Roberts's 1866 plan limiting district court jurisdiction to felonies, serious misdemeanors, and civil cases with more than $500 at stake, while county courts and justices of the peace would handle smaller cases. He thus created a hierarchy of separate trial courts based on the significance of the controversy or crime. The Supreme Court would only hear appeals from district courts (i.e., of the most significant civil and criminal cases). These majority and minority proposals generated much debate and amendment. The convention chose to proceed with Reagan's proposal as a starting point, rather than Ballinger's. Both reports envisioned district judges to serve six-year terms for a salary of $3,000 and Supreme Court judges to serve for eight-year terms at salaries of $4,000. John Lane Henry and Sul Ross spoke against the lower judicial salaries as promoting a cheap but inefficient judiciary, while a majority of the convention nonetheless voted to reduce salaries to $3,550 for the high court and $2,500 for district judges and to reduce the number of Supreme Court justices to three. Jacob Waelder proposed adding a "Court of Appeal" that would relieve the Supreme Court of hearing appeals in criminal cases, and this notion of a "dual supreme court" was ultimately approved. The upshot was a new judiciary along the lines suggested by Reagan, but with lower salaries, shorter terms of office, and a new criminal appellate court. All judges would be elected, and the Constitution of 1876 continued the guarantee of tort remedies for wrongful death contained in the 1869 Constitution.[33]

In addition to reducing state government and its judiciary and scaling back public education, the 1876 Constitution made other changes indicative of the new mood of the state. The mirage of vast public lands was relied upon to fund almost everything in an effort to avoid taxation while still promoting public education and economic development. The yeoman farmer-homestead ideal of Radical Reconstruction was continued, but the program of unrestrained commercial development Republicans had enacted was rolled back with new usury and worker protection laws and discouragement of any subsidization of business other than land donations to railroads that laid more track.

Moreover, while the 1869 Constitution had done away with the decades-old prohibition on corporate banks and the requirement of two-thirds legislative vote to create other corporations, the new Redeemers' constitution now provided for the regulation of these recently liberated business enterprises. For the first time, the Texas constitution contained separate articles entitled "Private Corporations" (Article XII) and "Railroads" (Article X). The only limitations on corporate activity in the 1869 document were the continuation of the prohibition on monopolies and perpetuities contained in all previous Texas constitutions, and Article III, Section 6's requirement of a two-thirds vote for the legislature to spend any money on "private purposes" or "internal improvement." The 1876 Constitution renewed the old prohibition on corporate banking and envisioned a new regulatory bureaucracy to control the excesses of railroads and other corporations. The legislature was specifically mandated to provide "a mode of procedure by the attorney general and district or county attorneys, in the name and behalf of the State, to prevent and punish the demanding and receiving or collection of any and all charges, as freight, wharfage, fares, or tolls, for the use of property devoted by the public, unless the same shall have been specially authorized by law." And the legislature would "regulate freights, tolls, wharfage or fares levied and collected or proposed to be levied and collected by individuals, companies or corporations, for the use of highways, landings, wharves, bridges and ferries, devoted to public use." Likewise, the new Railroad Article provided:

> Railroads heretofore constructed, or that may hereafter be constructed in this State, are hereby declared public highways, and railroad companies common carriers. The Legislature shall pass laws to correct abuses and prevent unjust discrimination and extortion in the rates of freight and passenger tariffs on the different railroads in this State; and shall from time to time pass laws establishing reasonable maximum rates of charges for the transportation of passengers and freight on said railroads, and enforce all such laws by adequate penalties.[34]

In this way, "Granger laws" became part of Texas' constitution. But it is an exaggeration to dub the new constitution a creature of either Grangers or populists. Rather, it represented a new ideology synthesizing ex-Confederate Redeemerism with the concerns of unhappy white small farmers and those of lawyers and businessmen who saw the need for economic development. These groups each achieved a modicum of success by avoiding the demands of the most radical white reformers while freezing out blacks and Republicans, and the primary tool for accomplishing this feat was racism. Maverick white politicians that went too far quickly drew accusations of being in league with Republicans and blacks.

The new constitution was ratified in the general election of February of 1876 by a margin of almost three to one, roughly the same margin by which Governor Coke won reelection over Republican nominee William Chambers. Compared to the 1873 election, 65,000 more Democratic votes were cast in 1876, returning a preemptive Democratic majority to both houses of the Fifteenth Legislature. Republicans showed only pockets of support in heavily black counties in North and East Texas and in the Hispanic and German strongholds in Southwest Texas around San Antonio and the hill country. The new white Democratic machine seemed formidable, but cooption of the Grange would not last. Soon populism would shake the very foundations of this Democratic edifice.[35]

Post-Redemption Texas: National and State Populism in the 1880s

Although the period from Reconstruction to 1890 was characterized by geographical expansion, industrialization, and conservatism in America, populist reaction to this dominant ethos profoundly affected the politics of the 1880s, especially in Texas and a few other parts of the South.[36] The accommodation reached in 1876 between the Democratic establishment and the Grange proved temporary. While Frederick Jackson Turner's contemporaneous theory of populism was that farm radicalism occurred because of the closing of the frontier, this is only a superficial explanation. Once free land was exhausted, people did tend to demand government action as a substitute for the free land that had vanished. However, this does not explain why populism was such a southern and western phenomenon and why it arose in three compact southern and western locations. These were all rural, and all dominated by a product whose price had declined precipitously: the South and cotton, the northern plains and wheat, and the mountain states and silver.[37] But, even among these areas, the primary hotbed of populism was Texas, where it represented an effort among a few segments of a highly varied capitalist agriculture to, as Richard Hofstadter has demonstrated, "restore profits in the face of much exploitation and under unfavorable market and price conditions." Populism was a product of price deflation combined with an ideological feeling of entitlement based upon the agrarian myth of the indispensable place of the yeoman farmer in southern and western democracy.[38]

The dominant themes of populist ideology were (1) the idea of a Golden Age, (2) the concept of natural harmony, (3) a dualist version of social struggles, (4) the conspiracy theory of history, and (5) the doctrine of the primacy of money. Since the commonly accepted agrarian myth held that the yeoman farmer kept the government strong, it was unavoidable that populists believed that the shrinkage of the agricultural community would corrupt the state. Natural harmony was the theory that agrarian life was best and that industrialization upset the very balance of nature. The theory of social struggle was a simple duality posited between the haves and the have-nots. A conspiracy theory of history was self-evident. Ignatius Donelly's book *Caesar's Column* was an example of both the duality of conflict and the conspiracy theory of history. Donelly, who would soon become a prominent figure in the national Populist Party, imagined a future where "the council of governing plutocrats" and the "brotherhood of destruction" are secret organizations vying to take over society. His notion of a conspiracy among the "moneyed power" echoed a theme as old as the fight over the national bank in the Jackson administration. Populists believed that the contraction of currency was a conspiracy to increase the price of gold for those who held it. This in turn created distrust and hatred of bankers, and in particular Jewish bankers. Here the racial overtones within the populist impulse began to appear. Populists like Donnelly were looking for a magic solution to economic malaise and political inequality, and they were often both strongly nationalistic and racist.[39]

By the 1880s, many Americans, especially those in the South and West, held the view that the nation was already fixed in geographical limit. And as Turner originally theorized, many people did come to believe that the nation should be redefined and recreated economically and politically, since the frontiers were closed. Robert H. Wiebe's conclusion, more recent and nuanced than Turner's, was that this "offered a particularly inviting field for coarse leadership and crudely exercised power," and that "as the network of relations affecting men's lives each year became more tangled and more distended, Americans in a basic sense no longer knew who or where they were. The setting had altered beyond their power to understand it, and within an alien context they had lost themselves." Rural Americans came to believe that they were "besieged by giant forces abroad and beset by subversion at home." They were victims of circumstances they did not understand. Much of this translated into a belief that large corporations were stifling opportunity. Both small owners and labor were being alienated by the quickened pace of industrialization. This involved not only the commoditization of time and labor, but also the mere incomprehensibility of an increasingly complex economy. Small business owners also began to feel a loss of control.[40]

Meanwhile, it was these small farmers and townsmen in the relatively poor lands of the southern and western frontiers who came together in local Granges, some of which would ultimately spawn populism. While populism and the northern labor movement shared a critique of the emerging capitalist order, populism was a uniquely southern and western phenomenon imbued with an anti-immigrant and racist perspective because one characteristic shared by agrarian reformers was a desire for community self-determination. This xenophobia was a fundamental part of what Wiebe called the "community crisis" of the 1880s. Southern Grangers felt a profound sense of injustice at being among those punished for a rebellion that seemed to only have been for the protection of wealthy planters. Another impulse within the Grange was a preoccupation with purity and unity epitomized by temperance movements and the development of institutionalized segregation, both features found in the Texas Constitution of 1876. The reform impulse also produced such disparate notions as Christian socialism, the Knights of Labor, and Protestant Fundamentalism. What all these apparently unrelated movements shared was a belief that the purification of society was necessary in order to bring back idyllic Jeffersonian democracy. Postbellum southern Republicanism and northern labor movements shared populism's egalitarian impulse, but Texas populists could not abide alliance with these factions because of race. In the long run, yeoman farmers and tenant farmers became equally suspicious of freed blacks, Republicans, northern capitalists, local storekeepers and landlords, and an array of other rich white folk.[41]

Texas populism grew out of Texas Grangerism after the adoption of the Constitution of 1876. It started with the founding of the Farmers' Alliance the following year by farmers dissatisfied with the apolitical tactics of the Granges. Chronologically, this agrarian revolt started on the Texas frontier and swept eastward across the state. It then bled into the South and circled back in a northwesterly direction into the Western Plains. Economic distress caused by a crop lien credit system was exacerbated by the drop in cotton prices and produced a mass radicalization of farmers. As Lawrence Goodwyn put the matter, "every year more and more of them lost their land to their furnishing merchant and became his tenants." A common response to this subservience was for Texas tenant farmers to move ever westward in search of new land. But ultimately they reached the Edwards Plateau or the Staked Plains, at which time they ran out of room in the face of impinging cattle barons, harsh weather, and the fact that the Texas and Pacific Railroad owned much of the land already by subsidy. It was no accident that Lampasas County in the foothills of the Edwards Plateau was where these poor Texas farmers organized the first Farmers' Alliance in 1877, and in 1878, surrounding counties formed a Grand State Farmers' Alliance. This initial movement was not strong enough to last and failed in 1880.[42]

In 1884, farmers founded a new statewide Alliance organization and the Lampasas group reconstituted itself as a local chapter. Farm radicals organized most effectively in places where times were particularly tough, and where they were fairly well removed from the beaten track. This happened first in what was then western Texas and was duplicated in southern Kansas and the Georgia piedmont. W. L. Garwin was the first Texas Alliance president, and he appointed S. O. Daws as a "traveling lecturer." Daws preached up and down the state and created fifty suballiances, duplicating the organizational scheme at the local level in these new clubs. One of the lecturers he recruited was William Lamb, a radical who saw the benefits of allying with the Knights of Labor that was just beginning to organize railroad workers. Lamb promoted grain and produce cooperative arrangements, and he also began to speak out politically against big business. In 1885, the Alliance state convention passed a resolution, probably introduced by Lamb, for unity of action between the Farmers' Alliance and the Knights of Labor.[43]

In growing, the Alliance had to assimilate the Grange, which had begun in disjointed local organizations in the early 1870s. One of the Alliance's political advantages was the attractiveness to farmers of its cooperative crop marketing plan in comparison to the Grange's methods of cash-only cooperative stores, which most farmers could not afford to participate in. Moreover, the Grange, earlier, more loosely organized, and more geographically dispersed, was simply more conservative and less willing to deal in politics than the populist Alliance. It ultimately faded away.[44]

The populist identity, first in Texas and then nationally, was determined in the mid-1880s, both in method and ideology. The basic strategy was to free farmers from the credit system, and Alliance populists learned a tactical lesson from a new labor strike, the Great Southwest Strike of 1886. This taught them that they could be successful through mass organization of farmers, and through allying with local unions and other labor organizations. Already having decided to join forces with industrial labor, the Farmer's Alliance still had to decide whether or not it would involve itself in politics. Deciding that the group would be politically active was what finally distinguished the Alliance from the Grangers and surpassed their organization as increasingly irrelevant. Alliance populism became overtly radical when William Lamb issued an 1886 proclamation in support of the Knights of Labor and their participation in the Great Southwestern Strike. Meanwhile, in the same year, S. O. Daws, the father of the Alliance movement, lent his substantial influence to the notion of Alliance political action by distinguishing proper political involvement from the old political machines. Daws's suggestion was to avoid party politics, but to use local suballiances as nominating conventions for candidates (whether Democrats or not) who were antimonopoly. These came to be called "anti-monopoly leagues."[45]

In 1886, the Texas Alliance held a state convention in Cleburne. It adopted a platform that demanded recognition of trade unions, establishment of cooperative stores, the abolition of state convict leasing to private employers, an interstate commerce law to regulate railroad rates, a federally administered banking system embracing a flexible currency (bimetallism and greenback-ism), high taxation of land held for speculative purposes, and reversion of unused railroad lands to the state for immediate settlement. This statement of demands was issued in August of 1886, the same month in which Dr. Charles W. Macune began his populist political career. At the

1886 convention, he was elected chairman of the executive committee. He adopted a moderate position between the right-wing (nonpolitical) faction led by former president Andrew Dunlap and the radical political faction of Evan Jones. Eventually Macune would lead the moderate wing of the Alliance when the whole movement veered to the left and toward partisan electoral politics. After the 1886 convention, lecturers swept the state with increasing frequency, and by 1887 the Alliance claimed to have 200,000 to 300,000 members in over 3,000 suballiances. Under Macune's leadership, populism engulfed Texas over the remaining decade.[46]

Not surprisingly, the Texas politician best able to benefit from and yet control this groundswell was John H. Reagan. In 1887, with over a decade of seniority in the post-Reconstruction Congress controlled by Democrats since 1884, Reagan served as chairman of the powerful House Commerce Committee. He had been tinkering for years on a railroad bill that would pass muster among reformers and railroad barons alike. His efforts culminated in passage of the 1887 federal Interstate Commerce Act that created the first Interstate Commerce Commission, icon of federal commercial regulation. This legislation, seminal as it was, demanded the praise of reformers while it also quietly garnered the support of railroad men and other industrialists who believed it would increase their profits by reducing competition through the stabilization of freight rates. Reagan's growing popularity was such that later the same year, the Texas Legislature elected him to the US Senate.[47]

But as distinguished from its trajectory in Texas, the political radicalization of populism developed unevenly across the rest of the West. Milton George, owner of a Chicago-based farm magazine called *The Western World*, attempted to hold national meetings of Alliance men in 1886 and 1887, but not much came of it. Things were disorganized because while Texan Charles Macune was heading the national Alliance, rival groups were also springing up, including an Arkansas-based group called the Agricultural Wheel and another group called the Farmer's Mutual Benefit Association. Meanwhile, the Northwestern Alliance, representing what was left of western radicalism, had fewer than ten thousand members. There was a joint meeting in St. Louis in 1889 between the National Alliance and Northwestern Alliance leadership, but the attempt to meld the two organizations failed. The Northwesterners had three preconditions: (1) a change in name, (2) the elimination of the "white clause" for eligibility for membership, and (3) the elimination of secrecy. The Southerners agreed to the first two, but could not negotiate the third because confidentiality was essential to a number of cooperative decisions, including choosing among competing bids of trade stores. Instead, at the St. Louis meeting Macune revealed his new Sub-Treasury Plan, a method by which farmers would cooperatively store crops until prices were right, financed by loans in the meantime. It became obvious that such a system, in order to work, would have to be supported by legislation because farmers lacked the capital to make large-scale cooperatives really workable, and they needed the ability to essentially print money.[48]

These radical political implications of the Sub-Treasury Plan made many Alliance men think more and more in third-party political terms. There was a basic division of ideology. The more conservative group led by Macune thought that all that was necessary was to elect good men to public office. The radicals believed that both political parties had become captives of corporate America and could not be trusted, certainly not to establish and support the Sub-Treasury Plan. Local alliances tended to support "farm-labor" leaning Democrats in the late 1880s, but these officeholders proved unable to get much accomplished. Real political success would have to wait until the 1890s, but throughout the 1880s, Texas populists within the Democratic Party continued to lead the national movement and, as they had in the 1875 convention, to discomfit the Democratic Party establishment.[49]

The Establishment Response: New Judges and New Jurisprudence

Meanwhile, in 1881, with the first Lampasas Alliance dead and the second not yet born, the Texas political establishment continued about the business of fostering internal economic development and redeeming the state from federal influence. One November day in that year, while Congressman John H. Reagan was busy developing a federal regulatory plan to sublimate the populist impulse in a way acceptable to industry, prominent state officials in Austin including Governor O. M. Roberts watched in stunned amazement as the state capitol shot flames and cinders into the crisp autumn air. Governor Coke had resigned in 1877 to accept the US Senate seat offered him by the Texas Legislature, and Roberts was elected in 1878 over Coke's more obscure appointed successor, Richard B. Hubbard, formerly Coke's lieutenant governor. Reelected in 1880, Governor Roberts was midway through his second term. Ironically, only minutes before, he and his entourage composed of a "Capitol Board" and the construction commissioners it had appointed were inside the building poring over plans for a proposed new capitol that was intended to symbolize the new modern Texas. Those drawings, submitted by architect E. E. Myers of Detroit, called for a much larger capitol to be built on a site one block north of the existing structure now ablaze. The old 1853 capitol,

The Supreme Court in 1881: Chief Justice **Robert S. Gould** (above) and Associate Justices **Micajah Bonner** (above right) and **Robert W. Stayton** (right) (Published with permission of the Tarlton Law Library, Jamail Center for Legal Research, University of Texas School of Law)

while small and inelegant, was serviceable, and Roberts and his commission foresaw no problem continuing to run the government from within its walls while construction proceeded, but even the best-laid plans often go awry. As the governor and his commissioners discussed these plans in a room of the old capitol, according to a local newspaper, it "was being set on fire a few feet from them through the carelessness of a department clerk, and the ignorance of a mechanic who run [sic] a stovepipe against the paper and plank sides of a room full of books, instead of into a flue, as he supposed he was doing."[50]

Although the mechanic provided the source of ignition, the clerk, who smelled smoke coming from the book-filled closet, fanned the smoldering paper and planks into a full conflagration by throwing open the door. While many of the state's luminaries stood waiting for the Austin volunteer fire brigade or someone else to appear and take action, an African American man charged into the building in an attempt to save something of the state's records storehouse, now serving as fuel for the growing inferno. He managed to retrieve only a desk and a few bundles of papers which were promptly scattered by the strong north wind fanning the flames. The man gave up and the old capitol, which some contemporary newspaper accounts described as an eyesore anyway, burned on.[51]

While other buildings near the capitol were damaged, the Texas Supreme Court building one hundred yards or so to the northeast was never in danger. The same northerly wind that fed the flames at the capitol deflected them away from the courthouse. Fortunately, the Supreme Court was not in residence at that time. Reduced in size from five justices to three by the 1876 Constitution, its members, Chief Justice Robert Simonton Gould and Associate Justices Micajah Bonner and John W. Stayton, were two hundred miles away holding session in Tyler, one of the 1876 Constitution's "two other places" provided by law. Within ten years Tyler would host no more such sessions, and the entire judicial branch of government would be expanded by a set of 1891 constitutional amendments well beyond the limits circumscribed by the Constitution of 1876. A new modern state needed a new and vigorous judicial branch that would ameliorate some of the 1876 Constitution's impediments to progress.

The process of judicial reform in Texas which began in the 1880s was part of a national movement for judicial activism in response to populist agitation and legislation, but it was also unique in the precise nature of its judicial response. The penchants and personalities of the newly trained cadre of professional judges that would occupy the Texas bench would mean much. Unlike the decades before 1876, Texas' constitutional identity at the end of the century would be heavily influenced by the judiciary and its burgeoning civil dockets.

When word of the loss of the thirty-year-old state building reached them, the reactions of the members of Texas' highest court were bound to have been somewhat diverse. The new chief justice, Robert Simonton Gould, was doubtless relieved at the narrow escape of Governor O. M. Roberts, his close friend and political mentor. Only nine days before the fire, it was Roberts who had elevated Gould from associate justice to chief. In 1881, newly appointed Chief Justice Gould may well have wondered how the fallout from the fire and confusion in Austin might affect his run for reelection the following year. While the general election was a full twelve months off, Gould knew that a serious challenger might surface at the Democratic Party nominating convention in the summer. Gould had reason for concern. No one had opposed him in his first election to retain his associate justiceship in 1876. Now, with his imposing sponsor Roberts retiring after four years in office, and with another convention and election looming, things might well be different, and Gould was at best a reluctant campaigner.[52]

Like Roberts, Gould was, as one close associate described him, "an ardent Southern man." However, as former colleague R. L. Batts put it, the two friends "had little in common save a common patriotism." While Roberts was "an astute politician," Batts thought, Gould "was in all relations of life frank and ingenuous." He was the classic ex-Confederate conservative and as another colleague put it, that conservatism was "displayed in all his work ... based upon an abiding respect for allegiance to constituted authority. He most earnestly believed that legislation was not the province of the judiciary." Gould was a reasonably successful lawyer and judge, modest and unassuming. His final campaign would be one of a respected old soldier-scholar who felt deserving of public confidence. But in the new Texas of the 1880s, it was no longer sufficient recommendation to have served as an officer in the Confederate Army or comported oneself as a gentleman. Texas was quickly moving beyond the Redemption mindset toward the class conflict of the 1880s and 1890s over emerging modernity. New men, or very flexible old men like John H. Reagan, were needed. Being a Redeemer was no longer good enough. Gould would soon discover that other more energetic candidates wanted his job. While the disastrous fire of 1881 had left him unscathed, the election of 1882 was not so kind. Within a year, Gould would lose his bid for reelection.[53]

Associate Justice Micajah H. Bonner would also leave the court soon. He had been appointed in 1878 by departing Governor R. B. Hubbard. Like

Gould, he was a Confederate veteran, and before the war he had practiced law in East Texas in partnership with J. Pinckney Henderson, the firebrand secessionist US Senator elected by the legislature in 1857 as an affront to Sam Houston. Before he was elevated to the high court, Bonner served as the district judge in Tyler for five years. Months after the fire, he retired and Governor Roberts replaced him with Charles S. West, a member of the 1875 convention and a candidate symbolic of the transition from Old South to New Southwest. While Judge West was another ex-Confederate lawyer and statesman, he had a somewhat more distinguished legal practice, and he represented, among others, the economic hegemon that would come to replace the Confederacy as the source of conservative political respectability, the railroad industry.[54]

The youngest justice, John W. Stayton, also a member of the 1875 convention, differed from Gould and Bonner. He had been appointed by Governor Roberts to one of the two associate justice positions on the court only a week before. Nonetheless, as his new judicial career stretched before his imagination, he must have wondered at its inauspicious and fiery beginning. If he harbored much in the way of such fears, he worried needlessly. As the capitol fire burned and Stayton began learning the court's daily routine in Tyler, he could not have foreseen that his career would span thirteen years on the court, half of them as its chief, and that his scholarship would become legendary. Having practiced law in Pleasanton south of San Antonio and then in Victoria near the Gulf Coast, Stayton was said to have read forty pages of law every day of his adult life, excepting only Sundays. His grandson, Robert W. Stayton, became a distinguished law professor at the University of Texas, served on the Commission of Appeals, and authored a definitive treatise and formbook for use by Texas lawyers in the early twentieth century. It was the elder Stayton's reputation as a calm and scholarly small-town lawyer that resulted in his appointment to the high court by Governor Roberts, even in the absence of prior judicial experience or significant political involvement.[55]

It was fortuitous that five years earlier the Redeemers' constitution had allocated three million acres of land to fund the construction of a new capitol building, and that in 1879 the legislature had possessed the foresight to pass two laws providing for its erection. One of these acts provides an example of the procedure for legislative appropriation of public lands that would fund so many public improvements and produce so much litigation in the latter part of the nineteenth century. It provided that certain state-owned lands in West Texas should be surveyed and then sold to private parties at a minimum price of fifty cents per acre. The survey itself would be rather expensive, the lands being so vast, and it would be paid for in the same way, by sale of some of the land surveyed.[56] The second act provided for a Capitol Board authorized to contract for the erection of the building itself. This board was composed of the governor, attorney general, comptroller, state treasurer, and land commissioner.[57] It was this board and the building commissioners and superintendent it had appointed to help plan and execute the new structure who stood with Governor Roberts in November 1881 watching the capitol burn.

Back in Austin, temporary quarters had to be found for many state offices, and the Supreme Court building, while spared by fire, had to be torn down when construction of the new capitol complex began. The court was relocated by an April 1882 act of the legislature authorizing part of the Brueggerhoff Building to be rented for three months at a time.[58] By early 1883, Chief Justice Gould had been replaced on the court by his successful opponent at the 1882 Democratic convention, Asa Hoxie Willie, and the cascade of moving offices caused the court to leave the Brueggerhoff Building in favor of a temporary capitol quickly constructed on the west side of Congress Avenue on Eleventh Street, pursuant to another emergency law passed by a special session of the legislature in May of 1882. Willie's Supreme Court had to wait sometime before moving in, however. To compound the court's toils and troubles in the early eighties, it was only four more months before a rainstorm caused this temporary capitol to collapse while still under construction. The building was finally completed just in time for Chief Justice Willie's inauguration in early 1883, although the Austin *Statesman* lamented that "it will never be more than a very cheap affair."[59] The Willie Court would occupy it from that point until the completion of the permanent capitol in May 1888, after substantial delays, cost overruns, and labor difficulties characteristic of the 1880s.[60]

All of this was perhaps more frustrating than Willie had anticipated when maneuvering in 1882 for the party's nomination for chief justice. This was the same year that saw "Oxcart" John Ireland succeed O. M. Roberts as governor. The well-known and politically long-lived Roberts, the Texas Supreme Court's chief justice for four years, had been easily elected governor in 1878 and again in 1880. Ireland, on the other hand, was the first of a series of quasi-anti-business politicians of the 1880s who used populist rhetoric to get elected, supported public education and close control over the sale of public lands to railroads and speculators, but who never seriously considered the Farm Alliance's subtreasury plan or dismantling the influence of railroad money on the state government.[61]

Governor "Oxcart" **John Ireland** (right) and Supreme Court Justice **Asa Hoxie Willie** (below) (Published with permission of the Tarlton Law Library, Jamail Center for Legal Research, University of Texas School of Law)

An ex-Confederate, Asa Willie had previously been elected to the Supreme Court in 1866, but had been removed by federal authorities in September 1867 as an impediment to Reconstruction. Thus he had what one legal historian described as "something of a sentimental claim on the office." He also had more than sufficient political backing, and most importantly, he aggressively worked the Democratic convention and its delegates. Judge Gould, as his grandson later wrote, "had neither taste nor talent for politics and . . . he was at a severe disadvantage against a candidate who campaigned aggressively." The retiring chief justice, however, held the view for the rest of his life that an altogether different factor accounted for his loss to Willie. The convention occurred during a time when eastern railroad tycoon Jay Gould was the new bogeyman of the Democratic Party, especially in the agrarian states of the South and West. Judge Gould came to believe himself the unfortunate victim of an inauspicious surname. Eastern and northern industrialists were despised in post-Reconstruction Texas. Given this fact, Gould's self-justification is altogether plausible. But it is just as likely that his taciturn temperament both ensured his defeat and led him to an explanation consistent with his disdain for the rough and tumble of electoral politics.[62]

His victorious rival, Asa Willie, was a transitional figure who came from an old Democratic Texas family. His elder brother James, with whom Asa practiced in Brenham from 1848 to 1857, was elected attorney general in the 1857 election that swept conservative Democrats into state offices at the expense of Sam Houston's party of independent unionists. Asa joined his brother in Austin as an assistant attorney general. After his brief and disappointing service on the 1866–67 Court, he moved to Galveston and was elected to Congress in 1872, returning to Galveston after just one term "to devote himself to the law." Willie's political popularity is demonstrated by the fact that his 1882 vote total was the highest in Texas history to that date. He worked hard under adverse circumstances to alleviate the court's burgeoning backlog caused by the spate of litigation generated by industrialization and the closing of the West, but he did so to little avail. His public career, while full of promise, seemed always to place him at the wrong place at the wrong time. In fact, after serving only one term, and with his repeated pleas for legislative relief of the court's workload rebuffed, in 1888 Chief Justice Willie retired to a lucrative private practice as a distinguished ex-judge.[63]

Associate Justice Stayton's service on the court also enhanced his reputation as a lawyer's lawyer, but he never succumbed to the temptation to return to private practice. And when the Democrats of South Texas nominated him in 1884 to run for Congress, he declined, acceding to unprecedented and urgent requests from the newly established state bar association that he not leave the Supreme Court. When Asa Willie resigned his bench on the eve of the dedication of the new capitol in 1888, it was Stayton that Governor Lawrence Sullivan "Sul" Ross promoted to chief justice. Stayton's opinions laid the groundwork for much of modern Texas law. He would come to symbolize the professionalization of the bar and growth of the bench that began in the 1880s. He witnessed the establishment of not only the University of Texas School of Law (1883) but the Texas Bar Association (1882) as well. These two institutions symbolized the new class of professionally trained lawyers and judges that would change the nature of the Texas judiciary.[64]

Most of the founders of this Texas Bar Association were judges, including past, present, or future Supreme Court Justices Roberts, Gould, Stayton, Bonner, and West, as well as the court's longtime official reporter, A. W. Terrell. Also in attendance at the organizational meeting in Galveston on July 15, 1882, was the man who had just received the Democratic Party's endorsement to replace Gould as Chief Justice of the Court, Asa Hoxie Willie. Each of these dignitaries had signed the "Call" for the first bar convention in Galveston, one of the avowed purposes of which was "to promote reforms in the law," and of course Roberts had drafted the first "Call" for a secession convention twenty-two years before.[65] At the association's first regular meeting scheduled for December 12, 1882, it planned to take up the resolution offered by W. S. Robson of La Grange that the association publish weekly the opinions of the "Supreme and Appellate Courts," which were, until then, published only annually by the courts' official reporters, usually lawyers commissioned and contracted part-time for that purpose.[66]

Before the meeting in December could turn to these previously scheduled agenda items, three separate resolutions were extemporaneously offered from the floor demanding constitutional amendments overhauling the Texas judiciary. W. L. Davidson's motion captured the spirit of the bench and bar: "Owing to the increased business before our courts and the fact that our Supreme Court, as now organized, is unable to dispose of the business before it, a change in our judicial system is imperatively demanded." The resolution ultimately adopted was one proposed by Judge X. B. Saunders that authorized the Bar president to appoint a blue ribbon committee to propose appropriate amendments for association approval at a special meeting scheduled the following year.[67]

The blue ribbon committee was headed by newly elected Chief Justice Asa Willie's friend, William Pitt Ballinger of Galveston, the state's premier railroad lawyer, member of the 1875 convention, and the same fellow who had escorted the ill-fated abolitionist Lorenzo Sherwood off Galveston Island in 1855 on pain of death. This committee proposed reforms in court organization, but they were rejected by the legislature. Similar but less well-organized efforts by judges and lawyers had already been rebuffed by the electorate in a constitutional referendum of 1880. These unhappy results were reported to the 1884 annual bar meeting by A. W. Terrell, who was both the Supreme Court's official reporter and chairman of the association's standing committee on judicial administration and remedial procedure. He added the pessimistic prediction that there was "little hope of early relief from legislative action, nor do we believe that any important reforms, which a speedy administration of justice demands, will ever be made until a deeper interest is felt, and more concert of action shown by the Bar of the State. Former failures are chargeable to the disagreement and apathy of the lawyers themselves."[68]

Terrell described the biggest problem as the Supreme Court's backlog, still unresolved even after an experimental "Commission of Appeals" was created by the legislature in 1879 to hear Supreme Court cases whenever all parties to the suit agreed, which was seldom.

In the spring of 1888, Asa Willie submitted his letter of resignation to Gov. Sul Ross, "Oxcart" John Ireland's successor, to be effective on the date of the new capitol's opening, May 16, 1888. State offices officially began occupying the premises on May 14th, and a huge celebration was held that entire week in honor of the dedication of the building. There was a parade and a tremendous turnout from across the state, but Willie had already taken the road home to Galveston, soon to become one of the most prestigious and wealthy private lawyers in the state.[69] Not long after his departure, the court reforms sought by him and his colleagues in the bar would be adopted. In the early 1890s, in response to organized nationwide pressure from lawyers and judges, the federal Congress and many state legislatures would significantly alter the appellate court structure in each respective jurisdiction.

The Reach of the New Legal System, 1880–1890: Judges, Farmers, and Railroads

As a result of population growth, industrialization, and the development of a professional culture among judges and lawyers, the judicial branch was called upon to answer important questions raised by the Texas spirit of 1876. By the early 1880s, the court's docket was fuller than it had ever been. For example, throughout 1882, with Gould as chief justice and Stayton and Bonner serving as associate justices, Gould wrote forty-two opinions including three on motions. Of these, twenty were reversals, usually on technical grounds such as lack of standing or deficient pleading. These were most often in trespass to try title or other real estate cases. Bonner wrote fifty-two opinions, of which more than 50 percent (twenty-eight) were reversals. He showed a heightened suspicion of any kind of large jury verdict, particularly but not exclusively in railroad tort cases like *Houston & Tex. Ry Co. v. Fowler*.[70] His dissent in *T. & P. Ry. Co. v. O'Donell*[71] was emblematic in that he wanted to reverse a jury verdict of substantial damages for the death of a child hit on a track on the grounds that the railroad owed no duty of care to children trespassing on the track. He was particularly miffed that the plaintiff, the child's mother, was nearby and should have known of the danger. He also reversed large damage awards in *P. J. Willis Bros. v. McNeil*[72] because evidence of the plaintiff's circumstances in life "inflamed the passions of the jury," and similarly in *Glasscock v. Shell*,[73] a breach of promise case incident to a divorce.

Stayton, on the other hand, the newest member of the court, was most likely to affirm jury verdicts. Out of sixty opinions, including two on motions, he only reversed the lower courts fifteen times. He clashed with Bonner five times, where either he dissented from Bonner's opinion reversing a verdict or Bonner dissented from Stayton's affirmance of a verdict below. In these cases, Gould was the deciding vote. Some of these were real estate cases that Bonner seems to have wanted to be decided on a more formalistic or legal basis than Stayton. The primary cases handled by the court were real-estate disputes generated by increased population density and the closing of the frontier (trespass to try title, homestead claims, etc.), contract matters (commercial transactions, bonds, suretyship, etc.), and railroad personal injuries.

In 1883 both the composition and the output of the court changed dramatically. Gould, after his defeat in 1882, was offered a position joining his old friend and colleague O. M. Roberts on the founding faculty of the University of Texas School of Law. Meanwhile, when Bonner retired in the same year, he was replaced by railroad lawyer Charles West. For most of its tenure, the itinerant Willie Court of the 1880s was composed of Willie, Stayton, and West. Each justice authored between eighty and ninety opinions. This was an increase in output of around 50 percent in one year, even by the standards of the court's previous workhorse, Stayton. The largest single category by far was again real estate cases, including land titles, deeds, mortgages, and homestead rights. In addition, commercial sales and common carrier cases were on the rise, an indication of increased economic activity and a growing transportation industry.

After 1883, the number of opinions generated by justices remained relatively constant until the 1890s, increasing by only about 10 percent over that seven-year period. In 1882 and 1883, only 10 to 13 percent of the opinions dealt with railroads or telegraph operators, whereas approximately 40 percent of all opinions dealt with real estate cases of one sort or another, including the interpretation of homesteads, deeds, mortgages, liens, and landlord/tenant relations. For example, in 1883, only 13 percent of all opinions dealt with railroads or telegraphs. These were disproportionately written by Justice Stayton, who wrote twenty of the thirty-three such opinions. As to real estate cases, the load was distributed more evenly, with Stayton, Willie, and West writing thirty-four, thirty-three, and thirty such opinions respectively. In addition to Stayton's acknowledged expertise, the bar saw Willie and West as equally proficient in this area of law.[74] Overall, however, Stayton and Willie far outpaced the elder West in output. Stayton wrote ninety-one opinions, and Willie eighty-seven, while West authored only sixty-seven.

Tellingly, in 1884, the number of cases involving railroad and telegraph companies mushroomed to about 20 percent, and it stayed at that level throughout the 1880s and 1890s until it reached 25 percent in 1895. Railroad and telegraph cases continued to comprise about 25 percent of the court's docket for the remainder of the nineteenth century. The new transportation and communication technologies produced a steady stream of conflicts. The boom in railroad building affected much more than just the public domain. The rapid development of tort law in the latter part of the nineteenth century was due in large part to the proliferation of railroads. While earlier courts were extremely cautious in extending tort remedies to victims of railroad activity, with Justice Stayton's appointment to the bench in the 1880s, the Supreme Court adopted a somewhat more liberal attitude that would accelerate and mature in the 1890s. A more receptive system of jury compensation for railroad-caused injuries and property damages operated to sap some of the working-class energy that might otherwise have been expended pursuing legislative or regulatory reforms.[75]

For example, in 1883 the court adopted the doctrine of attractive nuisance in the case of *Houston & Texas Central Railway Company v. Simpson*. This doctrine holds that while adult trespassers are not allowed to recover damages under any circumstances, an "attractive nuisance" constitutes an exception in the case of children, "for it is the duty of every person to use due care to prevent injury to *such person*, even from dangerous machinery upon the premises of the owner, if its character be such as to attract children to it for amusement."[76] The case represents, in a sense, the beginning of modern tort law in Texas, the kind of tort law that takes cognizance of modern technological and psychological reality. In the 1880s, the Texas Supreme Court first began exalting this type of realism over legal formalism in adjusting the rights of parties to an accidental injury. While young Simpson was technically a trespasser on the railroad company's land, and while landowners generally owe trespassers no duty of care, courts in other states had begun making exceptions for minors, and in this case Justice Stayton, speaking for Chief Justice Willie and Associate Justice West, also rejected formalism in light of what they considered to be the realities of the situation.

Railroads and railroad yards were becoming ubiquitous in urban Texas, and the development of public schools and economic prosperity had begun to create a new social reality, the conception of children as only quasicompetent innocents who deserved protection. Earlier in the nineteenth century, children were viewed legally and culturally as little different from small adults. They therefore worked, earned, owned, and soldiered as their ability allowed or need required, and they did so without any particular legal exception or protection. In the Victorian era, however, the idea of the vulnerable child developed alongside notions of affective motherhood and female domesticity. By the Civil War, this cultural shift had wrought significant changes in American law. By the 1880s, matters had reached a point in Texas where the Supreme Court would excuse minors from conduct that would have left them without remedy if they had been adults.[77]

Here was jurisprudential innovation that ingratiated the court with populists but was in reality modern, paternalistic, and hence "progressive," as that term would come to be understood. The judicial system wrestled with the Hegelian dialectic between underdog populism and the imperative of economic development. In anticipation of changes in the other two branches of government and the public at large, the courts developed a synthesis that could be termed "capitalist progressive." By the early twentieth century the new dialectic would be between progressivism and radical social Darwinism, as reflected politically in the presidencies of Theodore Roosevelt, William Howard Taft, and Woodrow Wilson and jurisprudentially in *Lochner v. New York*, the 1905 US Supreme Court case that constitutionalized laisse-faire capitalism, hamstringing regulation of business until well into the New Deal.

When Stayton became chief justice in 1888, his associate justice seat was filled by A. S. Walker, who then was quickly succeeded by railroad lawyer John Lane Henry.[78] In 1886, the other associate justice position was filled by Reuben Reid Gaines, a man of the new South. Gaines had first been elected to the bench in 1876 as judge of the sixth judicial district. He served for eight years and then returned to private practice in East Texas. His respite from public office was cut short in 1886 when Governor Ireland appointed him to the Supreme Court, and he served for an exceptionally long time. When Judge Stayton died suddenly while visiting his daughter on the day after the fourth of July 1894, Gaines was the logical choice to succeed to the chief justiceship in his stead. By the time of his retirement in 1911, Gaines served a total of twenty-five years on the court, eight as associate justice and seventeen as chief, the longest tenure on the high court up until that time and for six decades thereafter.[79]

While the Stayton/Gaines court of the 1880s and 1890s demonstrated its receptivity to liberalizing *liability standards* to account for the realities of modern life, it continued the prior court's vigilance in guarding against liberal *damage awards*. In 1883, twin cases of the same name, *Gulf, Central, & Santa Fe Railway Co. v. Levy*,[80] wonderfully illustrated the way this court, early on, charted a moderating course between the Scylla of denying any redress to the injured on the one hand, and the Charybdis of runaway jury awards against businesses on the other. They initiated two interconnected discourses within Texas law that remain confused and controversial: what to make of torts that arise between parties to a contract (now often known as "con-torts") and how to understand mental anguish and other "intangible" damages.

These cases represented the first announcement by the Texas Supreme Court that damages for mental anguish might sometimes be recovered in the absence of physical injury. However, the *Levy* cases actually reined in developing Texas law, which was evolving to allow recovery of mental anguish in such situations. Just two years earlier the Commission of Appeals had allowed a similar claim in *So Relle v. Western Union Tel Co.* on the simple theory that since it was eminently foreseeable to the telegraph company that intense mental distress would be caused by its neglect to use ordinary care in delivering emergency messages, any damage of that sort sustained by the addressee was recoverable as actual damages.[81] Four years later, *Stuart v. Western Union Telegraph Company*[82] affirmed the liberal *So Relle* rule but limited its application to suits by paying customers. For the remainder of the century, a newly invigorated judicial branch would continue to modify common law rules to new circumstances.[83]

Turning Inward: Public Lands

The courts would also decide disputes arising from demands on Texas' public lands caused by population growth in the 1880s. O. M. Roberts recited some impressive statistics at the time of his last gubernatorial message to the legislature in early 1883. He claimed that during his four years in office, property tax rates were reduced by 40 percent, and yet the state was still able to reduce its deficit by about 25 percent. This resulted from an increase in the value of the real estate tax base from 280 million dollars in 1877 to 410 million dollars in 1882. More people were rapidly settling and improving more and more land, and the state's supply of uninhabited western land was dwindling.[84]

Roberts's successor, Gov. John Ireland, recounted in his 1883 inaugural address that as late as 1870, the total population of the state was substantially less than one million persons and that "up to near that period we had no disturbing questions about public land . . . [and] the principal duty of the executive was to sign patents and to look to the frontier." By 1883, the population of the state had more than doubled to over two million inhabitants, and "the public lands are exciting that energy and calling forth that same spirit of gain that the gold fields of Australia and those of California did." Ireland was adamant that "prominent among the subjects that will challenge the attention of the administration is the preservation of our common school fund, including the lands set apart for that purpose."[85]

Ireland set before the legislature specific proposals for protecting uninhabited public lands. He suggested that minimum prices be fixed for the sale of such land, as well as maximum sizes for plots to be sold. Speculators had been buying up patents to the lands and held them expecting an increase in value over time, and this undercut the state's policy of using the lands to encourage further settlement. It was important to Ireland that the law should "provide that the lands shall be sold in quantities so as to place them within reach of all."[86] In this, "Oxcart" John Ireland indicated a policy more antagonistic to business investors and speculators than that of his predecessor, O. M. Roberts. Roberts was interested in quickly raising money from land sales to fund tax and deficit reductions, while simultaneously financing his brainchild, the University of Texas. Ireland, on the other hand, was enamored of the Jeffersonian ideal of the small-scale yeoman farmer/rancher. Here, in microcosm, was the tension between the new populist ideology and the old ex-Confederate Redeemer paradigm of internal improvement.

After the 1876 Constitution's mandate to set aside public lands for the school fund, Redeemer Governor Roberts was successful in convincing the legislature to pass a law in 1879 to allow sales of the unoccupied western lands "without limit as to quantity to the purchaser." He later saw to it that an act was passed granting to disabled Confederate veterans 1,280 acres of land apiece. This constituted a variance from the more homestead-oriented land policies of the administrations before and after his. Roberts was cognizant of the criticism his policies engendered, particularly among small farmers that would become the Populist Party's political base. In response, he could only argue that "the experience of our past history in the land business was that, however careful the government had been to prevent them, frauds would continually be perpetrated in its management, which [only] conclusively demonstrated the impropriety of the government's undertaking to handle such property permanently." Roberts's argument was that selling the lands in large blocks to private investors was preferable to allowing the government to keep fiddling with them. For him, the state's fiscal burdens and woes were sufficient to override any Jeffersonian mythology about building a state of small-holding farmers and ranchers.[87]

Conflicts between the more pro-business policies of Roberts and the subsequent agrarian policies of Ireland generated ever more land disputes. Many of these would ultimately be determined by the Texas Supreme Court. At annexation in 1845, Texas' public lands were estimated to aggregate in excess of 170 million acres.[88] The Texas Constitution of 1876 reflected the Jeffersonian yeoman model for land policy. The paradigm was to use the land to encourage settlement by independent heads of families. The legislature, after 1876, continued to face political pressure from speculators who wanted to monopolize large amounts of public land for their private use, just as Roberts had predicted in 1879, but in 1878 the Supreme Court announced the rule, ironically prefigured in the Reconstruction Constitution of 1869, that "actual settlers are favored by the law."[89]

Thus, prior to the financial pinch suffered by the Roberts administration, Texas courts had favored homesteaders and the Jeffersonian model of land policy as against the land speculators. The court created what Paul Kens has described as "a presumption in favor of those who settled on plots of land and made improvements with the intention of making it their homestead."[90]

Occupiers were favored over adverse possessors, adverse claimants, or persons who had filed for a homestead right but had never actually occupied the land. The basic doctrine utilized to vindicate and protect titular claims of homestead occupiers was that occupation with an intent to claim the homestead right resulted in a presumption of legal ownership, and in an equitable right to title to the land enforceable in court.[91]

Just because the court indulged a presumption in favor of homesteaders in possession, this did not mean that it would look kindly upon those who saw an opportunity to *momentarily* "squat" on land and thereby obtain it as a free homestead. The statutory scheme for homestead appropriation of unoccupied lands was that the homesteader could only earn the constitutional "gift" of 160 acres by continuously occupying the land for three years and devoting it to some form of productive agricultural use. When it became apparent that the court favored Ireland's yeoman model of land use over the fiscal model of Governor Roberts, enterprising citizens sometimes attempted to benefit from that presumption. They were often frustrated by the Supreme Court.[92]

Nevertheless, this type of case began to multiply. The reason was simple. The public lands of the state existed, but no one knew exactly where they were. The legislature had provided for the establishment of several counties out of the unsurveyed land in West Texas, but no one knew the precise character of the land within them. The General Land Office, because of this uncertainty, and because of constantly conflicting claims, was never certain exactly how much land remained unoccupied. The problem was further complicated by the difference between the types of land claims asserted. On the one hand, a settler could obtain essentially free land if he could locate unoccupied land that had not been surveyed and patented to another owner, and if he built a residence, moved his family onto the land, and occupied it for three years and put it to agricultural use. On the other hand, large landowners and land speculators could apply to the Land Office, under laws passed from time to time by the legislature (such as the one passed during the Roberts administration), to buy land in bulk by applying for a land certificate contingent upon the completion of a satisfactory survey proving the acreage was public land. Thus it often happened that settlers squatted upon the land and made application for the 160-acre gift, while a purchaser might simultaneously be in the process of purchasing that land as part of a larger block. Toward the end of the century, the upshot of this unfortunate situation was that the governor, the legislature, and the courts began to realize that the mythical unoccupied lands were not an inexhaustible resource. Ultimately, in 1898, the Supreme

Court was forced to expressly declare that no more unoccupied public lands remained to be had.[93]

The Stayton/Gaines court understood that unidentified public lands were intended to serve the people at large, and that homesteaders should be given the benefit of the doubt. Nonetheless, such lands, once appropriated by the legislature, also had to be zealously guarded from squatting and pilferage. It was well known to the court that the public lands had often been squandered by unwise actions of the legislative and executive branches, and that powerful economic interests had essentially appropriated the land to themselves without paying for it. For example, railroads were constantly threatening the School Fund, the Permanent University Fund, and the other programs to be financed by the state's vast holdings in West Texas. The Constitution of 1876 allowed the legislature to grant public lands to railroads, but only to the extent of sixteen sections per mile of track laid. While the legislature was originally quite free in using this constitutional provision to encourage the building of railroads, in 1882 it repealed the existing railroad law, effectively removing its authority to grant land to railroads. This, however, did not stop railroads from claiming lands under the law as it existed prior to 1882.[94]

As Governor Roberts had reported to the legislature, much land had been given to railroads prior to 1882, and much track had been laid in return, all to great effect. He proudly took credit for all this railroad expansion, even though he claimed to prefer selling to large ranchers instead. In 1882, he boasted that

> population and capital have flowed into the country far beyond any previous period. Enterprise in all of the useful industries has been quickened and enlarged. Railroads have been pushed into the heretofore unsettled territory of the state, until now we have almost no frontier as it was formerly known. Two branches of the Pacific Railroad have been completed and now pass through the state, one through the northern and the other through the southern portion of Texas, and a third one (the International) will soon have its connections by other roads through Mexico to the Pacific Ocean.... This result is due to the action of the legislature, the executive, and the judicial officers and employees of the government generally.[95]

On the other hand, when a less sanguine Governor John Ireland took over from Roberts in 1883, it was already clear that the public lands had been squandered. As he told the legislature, he was sure that posterity would judge the Roberts administration harshly: "No more public lands; no more cheap homes; poverty and squalid want gathering fast and thick around the inhabitants. . . . I see them turn with deep mutterings from the wicked folly that crazed our people from 1865 to 1882."[96] From Ireland's perspective, the repeal of the railroad land subsidy law in 1882 had been too little, too late. He had a point. Railroad land claims continued to clog the courts under the pre-1882 law for many years.[97]

The state judiciary struggled to conserve the public's resources, not by creating any new law, but by tailoring existing principles to meet policy goals. In the 1880s, the judicial branch, described by Alexander Hamilton as "the least dangerous" branch of any government, mediated and tried to defuse the growing dissonance between economic modernization and the yeoman agrarian myth.[98] The new conflict after Reconstruction was between industrialization and the domestic populist ideology. Like the 1875 constitutional convention, the Supreme Court upheld the rights of homesteaders but also effectively guaranteed continued railroad building by its decisions. In the 1880s, the Texas Supreme Court became the arbiter of the compromises reflected, often inartfully, in the Redeemers' constitution. The year 1876 saw Texas' final written constitution, one that, although frequently amended, continues in force today. In the 1880s, a new professional class of judges began to refine the constitutional identity thereby created, an identity that would survive well into the twentieth century.

6

The Birth of Conservative Modern Texas, 1891–1902

THE NATIONAL DEBATE OVER POPULISM AND PROGRESS CLIMAXED IN the 1890s, and Texas was its crucible. Candidates of the protopopulist "Greenback Party" had already far outpolled Republicans in the statewide elections of 1886 and 1888. Texas Republicans, connected in the popular imagination with Reconstruction and defeat in the recent Civil War, had little influence in the decades after Redemption. In 1890, Attorney General James Stephen Hogg was nominated for governor by the Democratic Party and easily won the election with widespread support from farmers, reformers, and party regulars. Hogg, a close associate of John H. Reagan, was the central figure in 1890s Texas politics, serving two terms as governor after making a reputation for himself as a trust-busting attorney general in the late 1880s. His efforts as governor to moderate and contain populism within the Democratic Party were opposed by radical former Democrats and erstwhile Grangers and Greenbackers who united to form a populist "People's Party," which reached the height of its power in the mid-1890s. But by the end of the decade a judicial branch reorganized by constitutional amendment, and a new regulatory bureaucracy founded by Hogg and headed by Reagan, would usher in a regime that coopted populism and transformed it into progressivism. That regime, which can be viewed as a new constitutional moment, a seventh constitution over Texas, ended the third-party threat with the help of the skillful maneuverings of one of Texas' first "political consultants."

That consultant was Hogg's ingenious political manager, Col. Edward Mandell House, who adroitly turned back the electoral attacks of those to the left and right in Hogg's 1892 reelection campaign. Thereafter, House selected and managed a series of moderately progressive Democratic office seekers built in the Reagan-Hogg mold in an attempt to frustrate the People's Party, but even the masterful colonel could not eliminate such a substantial threat by electoral means alone. A different strategy, one that also involved the constitution and an invigorated judiciary, would be needed to accomplish that.[1]

The "People's Party" of the 1890s advocated a program of labor organization and extensive regulation of railroads and other big businesses. This relatively simple platform was based on the Farmer's Alliance of the 1880s, and it attracted increasing electoral support. People's Party candidates polled a respectable 25 percent of the vote in the gubernatorial election of 1892 when the Democrats were split between the incumbent Hogg and a conservative coalition of ex-Redeemers and hard-money businessmen who followed the national party under Grover Cleveland. Using grassroots organization and the old party *padron* system to deliver blocs of poor voters, especially Hispanics, House was able to keep Hogg in office with the support of moderate Democrats, moderate populists, and conservatives, especially in South Texas, where they valued patronage and party cohesion more than ideology. By 1900, this formula would eventually forge a new progrowth progressive Democratic consensus and, with rapid urbanization, make populism irrelevant. Yet, until then, things only got worse for the Democrats after Hogg's retirement in 1894 and the reunification of the state party behind less flamboyant politicians. One of these was Hogg's attorney general Charles Culberson, who with the help of his national party connections and his manager Colonel House, kept peace between the party's left and right wings. House's milquetoast strategy, however, lost ground compared to Hogg's vote totals instead of producing a broader majority. The populist People's Party garnered a full 36 percent of the vote in the gubernatorial election of 1894, but the zenith of the movement was yet to come. In 1896, Texas populists agreed to the "fusion" (joint Democratic and People's Party) national ticket led by William Jennings Bryan, but were so suspicious of business interests within the Democratic Party that they refused to endorse a fusion ticket for statewide office or even for vice-president. They ran their own People's Party candidates in those races. The Texas Populists' belief that they could compete effectively against the Democrats was validated when their 1896 gubernatorial nominee, Jerome C. Kearby, garnered a dangerous 44 percent of the vote against Culberson, the incumbent.[2]

The rapid growth of populism within and outside the Democratic Party fueled political controversy over the relationship between private property and government regulation. Populists of varying stripes and party affiliations were elected to state legislatures across the South and West, and they quickly introduced new regulatory measures. In Texas, one reaction to this surge of activism was growth in the size and power of the judicial branch of state government. In 1891, the 1876 constitution was amended to strengthen the judiciary's role as political ballast against radical reform, and this was consistent with developments throughout the nation. An intimidating corps of newly trained and professionalized judges and lawyers began to arbitrate just how much reform would be tolerated (i.e., found to be constitutional). Their authority was based on the supposition that law was a systematic science that could only be divined by trained votaries, not by popularly elected politicians. In the early 1800s, Federalist judges like John Marshall and James Kent had promoted these notions of law as a brooding omnipresence beyond the ken of democratic legislatures, but this ideology would not come to fruition until the late nineteenth century. Conservative business interests accepted some minor reforms like a modest expansion of tort remedies for those victimized by economic progress, but they judged the defeat of broader regulatory initiatives well worth it. When conservatives realized the extent to which a powerful and apparently neutral court system could stand against political radicalism, their opposition to the very series of expansionistic judicial reforms sought by lawyers and judges just a few years before evaporated.[3]

With judicial help, populism would dwindle as the twentieth century dawned. Although it marked the height of populism in Texas, the election of 1896 also augured the doom of the People's Party by skimming off to the Democrats and the popular William Jennings Bryan much of the populists' platform and electoral support. This soon filtered down to the southern and western grassroots of the party. By 1900, only four years after their high watermark in Texas, the Populists only polled 6 percent of the gubernatorial vote, and by 1902, the state was, for all practical purposes, again a one-party state controlled by nominally progressive but equally pro-business Democrats. Business "progressives" like Reagan, Hogg, House, and his friend President Woodrow Wilson eventually supplanted and co-opted the old agrarian populists swamped by urbanization and technological change. What has been overlooked by historians is the role played by 1891 constitutional amendments and a strengthened judiciary in bringing about the rise of paternalistic and probusiness progressivism as a new synthesis that would bolster capitalism while simultaneously rendering populism obsolete.[4]

The political divisions and realignments of the 1890s were, in a broad sense, products of changes in the entire South. From an economic point of view, the Civil War represented the victory of industrialization and urbanization over agrarianism and rural living. As James L. Roark has said, in both North and South, "most urban populations grew rapidly as whites and blacks converged to work in war industries, hospitals, and supply depots."[5] It was the common wisdom that railroads and manufacturing plants were indispensable to the North's victory in the war, and as seen in the previous chapter, the Redeemers soon adopted this prescription in the South to improve their own lot. Economic development was their primary goal (i.e., the creation of more wealth through capitalism). This is why the conservatives and the Republicans at the 1875 convention had agreed on continuing state aid to immigration of new workers into Texas, only to be defeated by a coalition led by Granger Democrats. It was also why they were bent on crafting compromises that would settle public lands, build railroads, and continue public education and a university system. And during the 1870s and 1880s, these same leaders spent considerable effort attracting northern capital and immigrants to grow their new cities.[6]

This rapid growth in American industry, as well as massive immigration of both blacks and whites into cities, helped create the economic and social uncertainty of the 1870s and 1880s, but an economic panic in 1893 exacerbated these dislocations. Rapid industrialization and speculation in railroads, banks, and other booming new industries culminated in a collapse caused by financiers trying to take profits before the unsound nature of their investments was revealed. A three-year depression ensued from 1893 to 1896 marked by violent labor strikes and an unemployment rate in excess of 15 percent. Deflation in farm prices was particularly acute, and Texas, increasingly urban but still an agrarian state, was particularly hard hit by the depression of the mid-1890s. This economic distress combined with the Cleveland administration's unpopular 1893 repeal of the Sherman Silver Purchase Act to make populist radicalism effloresce, as witnessed in the elections of 1894 and 1896.[7]

In 1890, the separate Sherman Antitrust Act had symbolized popular dissatisfaction with industrialization and economic uncertainty at the national level. That same year the Texas Constitution was amended to authorize the legislature to "provide and establish all requisite means and agencies invested with such powers as may be deemed adequate and advisable (to regulate Railroads)." Texas populists' agitation for regulation came to fruition when in 1891 the legislature created the Texas Railroad Commission to regulate the rates and operations of railroads, terminals, wharves, and express companies. The credibility of this regulatory measure was deemed so critical by Governor Hogg that he appointed the venerable John H. Reagan its first chairman, who agreed to resign his seat in the US Senate in order to take the post. Like the federal Interstate Commerce Act, the Texas Railroad Commission met with approval from many business and railroad interests in the state, but it still evidenced the Democratic administration's commitment to reform. The central plank of the populist reform program was coopted by the Democrats, who would argue forcefully for the remainder of the decade that no third party was needed to protect the poor farmer.[8]

But the populist movement's growing power to influence state and federal legislatures also produced a counterrevolution within the most conservative branch of government, the bench, and its adjunct, the bar. Nationally, the parameters of this counterrevolution were circumscribed by two US Supreme Court decisions. *Munn v. Illinois* (1876) approved the kind of state economic regulation championed by the Grange, but only three decades later a changed court decided *Lochner v. New York* (1905), which announced the doctrine of substantive due process, a judge-made innovation protecting business from precisely that kind of regulation. *Lochner* was a result of the appointment of new justices trained in, and molded by, the law schools and bar associations established in the 1880s, schools and clubs populated with young students and old lawyers in favor of economic development. For example, at the 1892 meeting of the American Bar Association, three speeches, including the presidential keynote address of John F. Dillon, warned delegates of the dangers of overly democratic government with respect to the legislative expropriation of private property.[9] In an 1893 speech to the New York Bar Association, newly appointed Supreme Court Justice David Brewer, nephew and ideological ally of Justice Steven J. Field, who was one of two dissenting voices in the proregulation *Munn* case, made his antipopulist views known. Simply put, Brewer believed that it was the job of a strong judiciary "to restrain the greedy hand of the many from filching from the few that which they have honestly acquired."[10] Indeed, "the paternal theory of government is, to me, odious," he wrote. "The utmost possible liberty to the individual, and the fullest possible protection to him and his property, is both the limitation and duty of government." In 1905, a new majority of his brethren on the US Supreme Court would agree with him in *Lochner*.[11]

Meanwhile in Texas, while the Railroad Commission helped pacify reformers, the courts and the constitution were also used to thwart or defuse the populists. But in Texas, the radicals were stronger and the situation more precarious, so the response was more subtle. Texas judges did not risk their institutional credibility by declaring legislative measures like the Railroad Commission unconstitutional. Rather, they adopted a strategy of mollification by minor repairs. They tinkered with liberalizing common law rules in favor of workers and other industrial victims, thereby protecting the existing order of business development from greater reform by legislative action.

The judicial branch crafted a new strategy for sublimating cultural conflict, and this conflict, even within the organized bar, was pronounced. While in the 1890s the eastern state bar associations, the ABA, and corporate and railroad lawyers' contributions to national law reviews were combining to launch the judicial counterattack against legislative regulation that would culminate in *Lochner*, the effort met serious opposition within the bars of the agrarian southern and western states. For example, at the 1896 Meeting of the Texas Bar Association, Seymour D. Thompson railed against "government by lawyers" and warned that the entire rule of law was in danger of collapse unless the bar stopped undermining public confidence in the system by merely serving as the tool of monied interests against ordinary people.[12] The judicial battlegrounds for this political war were civil cases seeking compensation for victims of new industries and constitutional cases challenging government regulation of big business. Because of the unique position of the judiciary and the continuing mystification of the professions generally and of the legal profession in particular, doctrinal innovations could be subtly engrafted upon the common law via the decision of individual cases. While the most attuned or most radical elements in society might continue to rail that law still only preserved the existing order, more lukewarm reformers could easily be convinced that progress was being served. The judiciary played an important role in marginalizing radicalism and replacing it with more business-friendly "progress."

The Texas courts, strengthened by a new constitutional regime adopted in 1891, would demonstrate that the law was flexible enough to deal with new economic realities, but not so flexible as to change the foundations upon which it was based. Above all else, the institutional credibility of the judiciary had to be maintained, and to do so required walking this fine line.

The methods for accomplishing the task included employing the doctrine of judicial restraint to deflect political criticism to the legislature and selectively adjusting common law precepts to provide remedies for farmers and workers hurt by a newly urban and industrial society. In Texas, populism died not with a bang but with a whimper. It was marginalized by coopting its least controversial elements into a new ideological synthesis: business progressivism.

The Texas Supreme Court and the Constitutional Amendments of the 1890s

When Governor Hogg took office in 1891, one of the first orders of legislative business was the introduction of a series of constitutional amendments along the lines bar leaders had been urging since the 1880s. In part, this reassertion of judicial reform resulted from national momentum for similar changes. But a second reason was that in the 1890s the Texas political establishment recognized that a stronger judiciary was needed to conserve the existing distribution of wealth and power. By 1887, US Supreme Court Chief Justice Morrison R. Waite was demanding congressional action to relieve the increasing caseload of the federal judiciary, particularly the appellate caseload of the Supreme Court.[13] In response, Congress enacted the 1891 writ of certiorari statute relieving some of the Supreme Court's burden by allowing it latitude in refusing to even consider some appeals from lower circuit courts.[14] The same session of Congress also abolished the old circuit court system, which involved an ad hoc amalgam of circuit-riding Supreme Court justices with federal district judges. It enacted the current system of circuit courts of appeal, thus expanding drastically the capacity of lower federal courts to reduce the Supreme Court's appellate workload. Business lawyers' resort to the courts for relief from economic regulation, increased urbanization and industrialization, and the rapid expansion of criminal laws and law enforcement are the factors that caused this mushrooming judicial caseload.[15]

In Texas, the situation was much the same. For example in 1879, as authorized by the 1876 Constitution, the Texas Legislature had created a "Commission of Arbitration and Award." Parties to an appeal from a Texas trial court could, by agreement, have their appeals heard by the Commission and avoid the Supreme Court or the criminal court of last resort, then known as the Court of Appeals. Texas is one of very few states to have a bifurcated structure of courts of last resort.[16]

Since the Civil War, California had also been struggling with rapidly growing caseloads due to an expanding population. In 1879, the California

Supreme Court was increased in size from five judges to seven, and the court was also authorized to divide into three judge panels to hear cases separately. Illinois created its first intermediate appellate court in 1877 for the purpose of relieving Supreme Court caseloads. This had only a temporary effect. The Illinois Supreme Court's docket fell to an average of 240 opinions in 1880 and 1885, but by 1900 and 1905, as population grew, the caseload had climbed back to an average of 475 opinions per year. This was still better than the 600 cases a year heard in 1876, but not as much of an improvement as the legislature had hoped.[17] In 1885, the California legislature adopted the same type of "commissioner" system started in Texas in 1879, and this did provide temporary relief by cutting the number of opinions actually handed down by the California Supreme Court (as opposed to those written by commissioners and merely rubber-stamped) by 40 percent.[18]

It is logical to assume that the use of the writ of certiorari and the availability of new circuit courts of appeal reduced the US Supreme Court's caseload substantially. With respect to Texas, however, the situation is more muddled. In 1881, the Texas Legislature amended the original enabling statute to rename the Commission of Arbitration and Award the "Commission of Appeals." It further authorized the Supreme Court and the Court of Appeals to refer cases to the Commission of Appeals without the parties having to agree. While this was of some help, in 1891 the Texas Legislature finally acceded to the bench and bar and acknowledged that the whole system was being overwhelmed by lawsuits generated by new technology and the injuries and damages it caused. It is remarkable that this occurred so soon after the mistrust of the judiciary manifested in the 1875 constitutional convention. The amendments proposed by the legislature for public vote continued to limit the Supreme Court's appellate jurisdiction to civil cases only and stripped the Court of Appeals of all civil jurisdiction, renaming it the Court of Criminal Appeals. Most significantly, the 1891 amendments also created subsidiary Courts of Civil Appeals. Each had final appellate jurisdiction within its geographical region in all cases in which its opinion was unanimous and did not conflict with holdings of other Courts of Civil Appeals on the same question of law. The proposed amendments were ratified by the public by only a narrow margin, 51 percent for and 49 percent against. From a political standpoint, this illustrates two of the arguments made in this book. First, amending constitutions is a laborious process, so constitutions tend to be more reliable and enduring reflections of political, ideological, and cultural settlements and accommodations than ordinances or statutes. Second, a close constitutional election indicates a hinge point in fundamental disputes over political ideology. By this reasoning, the biggest danger to the Texas political establishment from populism was the 1896 elections, but an ideological corner had already been turned in 1891, at least among the smaller and presumably better-informed electorate that voted in that year's special constitutional referendum.[19]

A statute passed in 1892 to effectuate the 1891 constitutional amendments stipulated the simultaneous phasing out of the Commission of Appeals system by 1893. By its provisions, all civil cases pending in the Supreme Court and Court of Appeals were transferred to the Courts of Civil Appeals. There were approximately twelve hundred cases transferred from the Supreme Court and three hundred from the Court of Appeals. All of these changes occurred during John W. Stayton's tenure as chief justice. He led the Supreme Court into the promised land of smaller dockets that his predecessors had only glimpsed from the wilderness.[20]

The impact of the 1891–92 changes in the Texas appellate court structure was rapid. The transitional year was 1892, the last year under which pending civil appeals (other than from probate and county court) were resolved only by the Supreme Court and the Commission of Appeals. By 1893, the newly created Courts of Civil Appeals had substantial dockets. The effect of these changes can be seen by comparison of the Supreme Court's opinion docket during representative years. Before the 1891–92 changes, the commission structure was of only sporadic help in relieving Supreme Court dockets. Even after the 1881 legislative changes that allowed the high court to refer cases to the Commission of Appeals without litigant consent, the Commission resolved remarkably few cases, perhaps because the Supreme Court was hesitant to use its new power of referral. For example, in 1887, the Supreme Court issued 334 published opinions in civil cases, while the Commission of Appeals issued only 50 opinions approved by the Supreme Court. In 1888, the Supreme Court issued a staggering 471 published opinions, to only 21 by the Commission. In 1889 the trend reversed direction again, with 331 Supreme Court opinions and 142 by the Commission.[21]

Leaving aside the transitional years around 1891–92, later court records show the more profound impact of creating the new Courts of Civil Appeals. In the late 1890s, the Supreme Court's docket of published opinions had dwindled by 60 percent to 75 percent compared with the 1880s. In 1897, the Court issued only 118 opinions. In 1898, it issued 150 opinions, and in 1899 only 111. Clearly, the judicial reorganization of 1891 allowed the Supreme Court to render speedy decisions for at least the rest of the century. This undoubtedly contributed to the collegial and relaxed style of the post-1891 Stayton/Gaines court where dissents were almost unknown. In contrast, the Willie court from 1882 to 1888, like many other courts nationwide, was chronically behind in its docket and seriously overworked. By the early twentieth century that unfortunate situation would return. The continued rise in the state's population, in urbanization, and in business activity would gradually increase civil litigation to the point that it outstripped the late nineteenth-century efficiency gains, and the question of appellate backlog would again have to be addressed.[22]

Temporarily though, the Courts of Civil Appeals were far more effective in relieving Supreme Court congestion than either the voluntary or discretionary Commission system had been. The key was removing the Supreme Court and the litigants from any consideration of which cases the high court would take and which it would refer elsewhere. Legislative action circumscribing the Supreme Court's power and mandating that most appeals would reach no further than the intermediate appellate courts relieved the backlog. Evidently, even courts that complain of crowded dockets have a hard time *voluntarily* relinquishing discretionary decision-making power, even when provided by legislatures with tools with which to do so. Mandatory legislative curtailments of jurisdiction are required to wean judicial authorities onto a diet of fewer cases to decide.

These jurisdictional and organizational changes were mirrored by contemporaneous improvements in the high court's facilities and clerical logistics. Alexander Terrell remained reporter of the court until 1884, when he was not reappointed. As early as 1882, Terrell could see the writing on the wall. William Pitt Ballinger, then abed in Galveston with a terrible urinary tract infection, described a visit from Terrell where "Judge Terrell . . . brought me 56th Texas—Decidedly interested in keeping his place—Thinks Willie not favorable to him." Terrell was evidently right.[23] Terrell's replacement as reporter, A. S. Walker, served until 1896, when he was replaced by Alfred E. Wilkinson. While the reporter of the court continued in his statutory responsibility to publish the Texas Reports at state expense, West Publishing Company, founded by John B. West in 1872, began also publishing Texas decisions in its new *South Western Reporter* in 1882.[24]

The Supreme Court continued to sit in Tyler, Galveston, and Austin only until one of the constitutional amendments of 1891 required the court to sit only at Austin, instead of "at the seat of government and not more than two other places."[25] This amendment also required consolidation of the office of court clerk. In 1892, the terms of the Galveston clerk, Daniel Atcheson, and the Tyler clerk, S. J. Reeves, expired and they were not reappointed or replaced. Charles S. Morse, the Austin clerk, remained with the new "Capitol Court" until 1902.[26]

In addition to institutional reform, constitutional change, and improvement of physical facilities, the years from 1888 to 1891 represented a significant transition in membership of the state's highest civil court. The new chief justice, John W. Stayton, would lead a court that would issue its opinions from within the halls of the impressive new granite edifice denied to Asa Willie and his colleagues. The opinions of that court, even after Stayton died in office in 1894 and the chief justice's chair transferred to Reuben Gaines, would not vary in judicial philosophy from those of the justices profiled in the previous chapter, but they did go further in providing limited remedies to the victims of industrialization. In the midst of all manner of external change, the internal springs of judicial restraint and *stare decisis* would continue to drive the judicial department as it navigated the swirling currents of social conflict generated by new technology and a new urban landscape. The judiciary provided a subtle but necessary inertia. Whether dealing with the long-standing issue of the appropriate disposition of public lands; or the growing imposition upon farmers, landowners, and accident victims of the railroads; or the growing presence of insurance in people's lives, the Supreme Court would chart a steady course, but it would innovate when necessary, adapting old traditions to new economic, political, and technological realities.

The man who was appointed to replace Gaines as associate justice when he was elevated by Governor Hogg to chief justice in 1894 was Leroy G. Denman of San Antonio. Dissents were extremely rare among the opinions of the Stayton/Gaines court of the 1890s, and Denman was no more likely to write one than the next associate justice, even though he was one of only two justices appointed by James Hogg. This, together with the fact that Denman was younger than his colleagues and had played no role in the rebellion against the North, caused him to undergo more partisan scrutiny and controversy than some of his more politically orthodox fellow justices.[27]

But even more controversial was the other Hogg appointee, Thomas Jefferson Brown, who, according to a contemporary, "was among the ablest and most efficient of those leading citizens of Texas who succeeded in curbing railroad aggression in several directions. . . . Several persons connected with corporations in Texas . . . did not welcome the appointment of Justice Brown." Governor Hogg must have savored the poetic irony of Brown's appointment in 1893 to succeed the conservative railroad lawyer John Lane Henry. Brown had been a champion of the movement epitomized by the Grange and the Farmer's Alliance, and in 1888 was elected to the state legislature as an antibusiness Democrat from McKinney near Dallas, a center of farm-populist radicalism in north Texas. Before his appointment to the court, he argued strenuously in favor of the creation of the Railroad Commission.[28]

Gaines, on the other hand, was remembered fondly as an affable storyteller with a wonderful sense of humor, given to telling jokes, a gentleman of the old school. He had the habit of each morning calling to the court porter, Alec Phillips, to bring his carpet slippers, which he wore while working, and then replacing them with his shoes at precisely five o'clock every evening. When departing the capitol at this appointed hour, he would sometimes say to the justices and clerks, "There will be lots of cases pending before the court when I am dead and gone, so why worry." He was so popular among members of the bar that even when caught napping during oral argument, he was excused by counsel as having "more legal sense while asleep than most judges had while awake."[29]

Justice Thomas Jefferson Brown was not cut from the same cloth, and the courthouse folklore surrounding him was correspondingly different. He kept up with all the politics of his day, and as late as Woodrow Wilson's administration would still write long weekly letters of advice to his friend Colonel E. M. House, soon to be Wilson's closest advisor in Washington and already the manager of every successful campaign for Texas governor since Hogg. Due to failing eyesight, writing became a bit of a chore for Brown, although he continued doing it. In addition, he became notoriously hard of hearing, which made for some rather unusual court conferences. He was a strong opponent of hard liquor and an accomplished Sunday school teacher, which in those days was not at all inconsistent with his rather radical economic views. He arose at dawn each day to a cold bath, followed by a long morning walk. Despite his appearance and personal habits, he was not a stern person. The only time he is known to have taken a drink was on a camping trip with Gaines and some clerks from the court's staff. When a norther blew through and began to soak the expedition (which had neglected to bring tents) with freezing rain, Brown was prevailed upon to take a shot of whiskey and, under the circumstances, finally did. When asked to explain, he remarked "circumstances alter cases."[30]

The division between those members of the court who drank spirits and those who politely declined was indicative of one of the issues that would come to divide Texas politically in the early twentieth century. Prohibition was just one of the "new issues" that had arisen in the "new South." Others

(Left and below) Governor **James S. Hogg**, Chief Justice **Reuben R. Gaines**, (facing above and below) Justice **Leroy Denman**, and Justice **Thomas Jefferson Brown** (Published with permission of the Tarlton Law Library, Jamail Center for Legal Research, University of Texas School of Law)

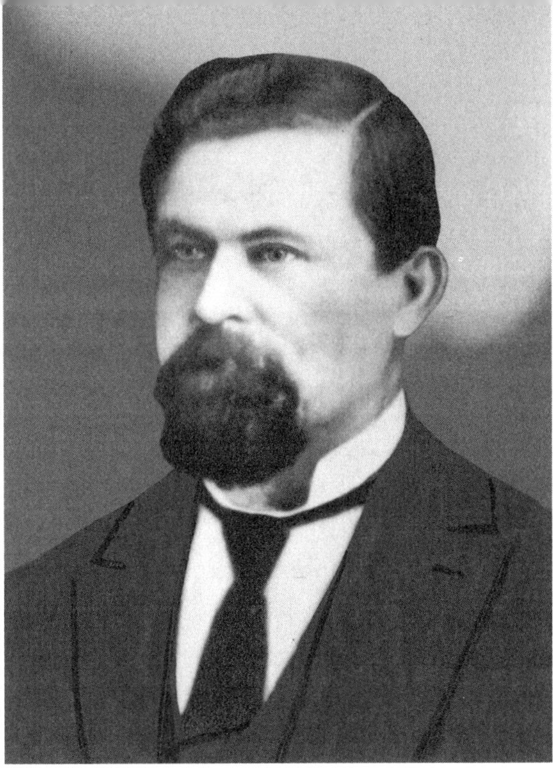

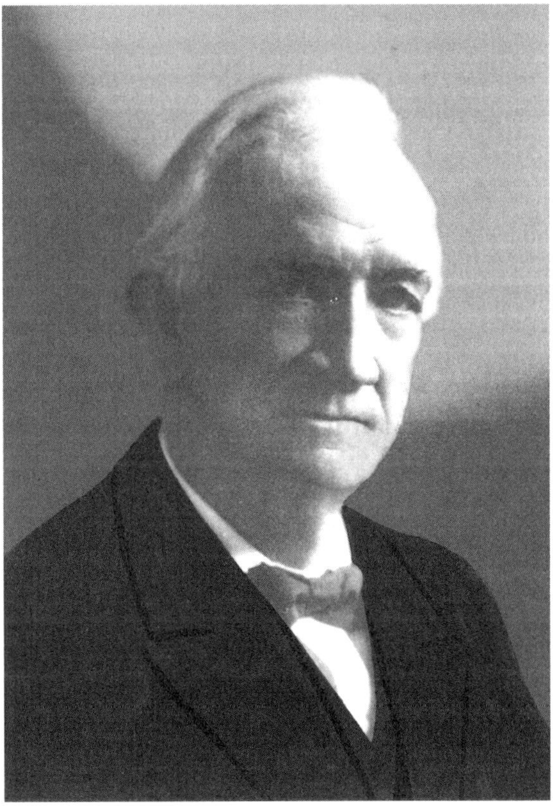

included women's rights, workers' rights, railroad regulation, insurance, and monetary policy. Gaines, Brown, and Denman, from the collegial and undisturbed confines of the court's chambers, had witnessed incredible change in the latter part of the nineteenth century, political, social, economic, and legal. Yet the three of them, together with the late Judge Stayton, calmly accounted for more than 70 percent of the court's opinions from 1882 to 1900, and dissents in these cases, or rehearings of them, were almost unknown. Adding to them the work of Stayton's predecessor, Asa Hoxie Willie, chief justice from 1882 to 1888, yields a total of approximately 80 percent of the court's work over the same eighteen-year period. The long tenures of these five judges—Willie, Stayton, Gaines, Denman, and Brown—provided remarkable stability in the state's highest court at a time when social and economic change demanded adaptation of the state's laws to new circumstances. Brown himself, on the occasion of Gaines's memorial in the Supreme Court chambers in 1914, would remark that their "service came at a time when the state was in an era of development and change which brought to the court new questions that required the ability to discern the issue, as well as learning to apply the law to the new conditions out of which the litigation arose."[31]

These five justices were all conservatives by modern standards. All were segregationist southern Democrats, and all but Denman served in the Confederate Army, but they were also respected lawyers, although Willie and Brown were substantially more politically active than the other three.[32] Stayton was the most reticent of the group. When Governor Roberts appointed him associate justice in 1881, for example, few lawyers had ever heard of him because Stayton was essentially a lawyer, not a politician. So when someone inquired, "Who is he?," the governor replied, "You do not know him now, but when he serves on the court a while, you will know him without the necessity of an introduction."[33] Moreover, although all were typical southern Democrats, Willie's opinions were generally professional and well-reasoned. Gaines was an apolitical moderate who never drew an electoral opponent. Denman raised some suspicions among railroad and business interests, and Brown raised even more. In fact, one of the symptoms of the rapid change of the late nineteenth century that manifested itself politically was a renewed partisan interest in the judiciary sparked by Governor Hogg's appointment of Denman and Brown in the 1890s.

Yet somehow, within its chambers, the court insulated itself from the storms thundering about it. For example, unlike in 1882 when Justices Stayton and Bonner disagreed occasionally, after 1883 and until 1900 there were no dissents or concurring opinions whatever for the entire period. During the 1890s, the variety of the court's caseload, outside the railroad docket, increased as a result of a growing population and new urban and industrial life. An electric power plant was built in Austin in the 1890s, and there were already telephone lines in place by 1886. Electric streetcars ran in downtown Austin from 1891 to 1940.[34] Instead of a steady diet of property disputes, the court began handling a smaller but more diverse load of cases, including suits involving licensed professionals like physicians, limits on local and municipal government power, commercial sales, and strictly procedural matters such as jurisdiction, pleading, and interpretation of the new rules of appellate procedure necessitated by the 1891 changes.

Thus one factor in the high court's collegiality during this period was that after the constitutional changes of 1891, the court's output was significantly reduced as the result of the transfer of several cases to the new courts of civil appeals in 1892. Whereas the more productive justices of the 1880s authored nearly one hundred opinions a year, that number fell to less than fifty per judge per year during the period from 1895 to 1898 when the court's composition was static, composed of Gaines, Denman, and Brown. For example, by 1898 the 1891 constitutional changes had certainly become standard routine. In that year, Chief Justice Gaines wrote only forty-eight opinions, fully thirteen of which involved railroads, including short dismissals of motions for rehearing or to dismiss for want of jurisdiction. Justice Brown wrote forty-nine, eleven of which were in railroad cases, and Justice Denman only forty-five, eight of which involved railroads.

The calm within the court contrasted starkly with the multifarious social change and political controversy of the era. Sometimes these controversies threatened to intrude into the court itself. Brown and Denman both had to weather political challenges to their respective nominations for reelection at the Democratic convention of 1894. Hogg, the immensely popular "common man's governor," was retiring after the customary two terms in office. He had made a reputation for himself as a progressive attorney general by suing railroad companies. As governor, he supported the legislature's creation of the Railroad Commission, but he had moderated in office, causing equal dissatisfaction among conservative "sound money" Democrats and his farm populist base. Two years earlier, in the campaign of 1892, the Democratic Party had split, with disaffected conservatives bolting to hold their own rump convention and running their own candidate for governor. At the 1894 Democratic convention, the conservatives, who returned to the party and influenced the selection of Hogg's successor, Charles Culberson, decided to make trouble for his recent appointees to the high court, Denman and Brown.[35]

As was the custom, judicial nominations were perfunctorily placed before exhausted delegates at the end of the convention, after the platform and major political offices had been debated and decided, but this time a surprise was lurking. As O. M. Roberts would later report, "the nomination of judges for the Supreme Court and Court of Criminal Appeals provoked a scene so disorderly as to be disgraceful, and called forth a resolution (which did not pass) to hereafter have these judicial officers named in separate conventions." While Chief Justice Gaines was nominated to succeed himself without opposition, several candidates were named to run for the associate justiceships held by Denman and Brown. These included conservative attorney John C. Townes, who would later become dean of the University of Texas Law School, and Nathan A. Stedman, a district judge who later became general counsel for the International-Great Northern Railroad Company in Palestine. While the plot was unsuccessful, for veterans like Roberts, it represented a marked politicization of an informal nominating system that had theretofore been based solely on the opinions of prominent attorneys throughout the state.[36]

Nevertheless, Stayton and then Gaines were able to craft a consensus within the Texas Supreme Court that would demonstrate that the law was flexible enough to deal with new economic realities, but not so flexible as to change the conservative foundations upon which it was based. In this sense, the judicial branch invigorated by the 1891 amendments represented a new seventh constitutional regime, the final regime upon which would rest Texas' political identity that endured well into the twentieth century.

Public Lands and the Closing of the West

By 1895, the Gaines court knew that homesteaders and purchasers were not only fighting over resources that the legislature had already exhausted, but that the legislature had probably sold or appropriated more land than had existed to begin with. To compound the problem, even the General Land Office had no definite knowledge of how much land had been appropriated because it never implemented a system of accounting to keep track.[37]

These problems and the pressure from railroads to use more land and lay more track required some level of retreat from the court's prior partiality to farm homesteaders. The method adopted by the court to accomplish this was closer enforcement of the "actual occupation" requirement of homestead title. In the 1893 case of *Busk v. Lowrie*,[38] the court issued a strong statement designed to deter "fictitious" homesteading. In that case, Lowrie was a tenant sharecropper of a man named Starkweather. Starkweather sold some land to Busk, including portions of the acreage that Lowrie was working. Soon thereafter, all the parties discovered that some of the land was actually unsurveyed public land which Starkweather had simply fenced off, but to which he had no patent, and for which he could trace no chain of title back to a patent or other sovereign land grant. At that point, both the tenant Lowrie and the purchaser Busk began looking for ways to establish title to the disputed portion of the land that was public. Busk eventually figured out that the only way to get a clear title was to apply to the General Land Office to purchase the land under the "scrap law" passed by the legislature in 1887 to deal with just such cases. He had the land surveyed and paid the required purchase price to the state.

Prior to Busk's having made this application, Lowrie went on the land and "smoothed off the ground and made rock pillars for a house in which he intended to live." However, he did not occupy the property until *after* Busk made his application under the scrap law. Tellingly, Lowrie also brought with him a friend named Cornelius, and either connived or agreed with him to have Cornelius perform similar acts on the remaining 74 acres that comprised the public "scrap" land. Since Lowrie could only obtain 160 acres by donation, and since the entire "scrap" comprised 234 acres, this latter tactic was necessary for Lowrie to deprive Busk of the entire tract. It is unknown whether he intended to buy the additional 74 acres from Cornelius, or whether the two were friends and merely agreed to be neighbors. Whether innocent and well-intended or not, their apparent collusion did not escape the notice of the court.[39]

Of particular note from a political standpoint was the fact that Justice T. J. Brown wrote the unanimous opinion rejecting Lowrie and Cornelius' homestead claims. His opinion makes clear that his Protestant ethics outweighed his well-known affection for small farmers and populist politics. Brown began his opinion by carefully acknowledging that the court continued to believe that homesteaders should not be deprived of free land, and the state should not be deprived of a growing class of yeoman farmers, merely as a result of technicalities. For example, Brown repeated that the court had refused to disenfranchise such claimants merely because they had been late in filing paperwork, or in obtaining surveys, or in following other procedural requirements. This did not mean, however, that the court had abdicated its responsibility to enforce the law as written. For Brown, the gist of the matter was that "the only condition which the law imposes is that of settlement and improvement on vacant land ... but the actual settler intended by the statute must reside on the land, or occupy preparatory to and with the bona fide intention of residing thereon." The old tee-totaling populist went on to emphasize the use by the statute of the word "actually" as an adverb modifying the verb settlement. "The word actually is used in the sense of being a *real*, and not a *constructive or virtual settlement*."[40]

Because Lowrie and Cornelius had not returned to the land and actually settled there with their families until *after* Busk made his proper and legal application to the General Land Office to purchase the land, Busk already owned the land and it was no longer public when Lowrie and Cornelius tried to claim it. Thus the settlers lost. For Brown, it was one thing to favor government policies that would empower the yeoman farmer idolized by Jefferson, but it was quite another to ask judges to wink at attempts to grab depleting state resources out from under legitimate purchasers who had observed all the formalities and properly paid the state treasury.

Three years after the *Busk* decision, the Galveston, Harrisburg and San Antonio Railway Company, like many others, sought even more state land than it already had. The Galveston-Harrisburg was corporate successor to the Buffalo Bayou, Brazos and Colorado Railway Company. The Buffalo Bayou line had become insolvent by 1870, so it was bought out by the Galveston-Harrisburg. The legislature passed a special act in that year recognizing the Galveston-Harrisburg as the successor, for all purposes, of the Buffalo Bayou line. However, in 1870, when the Galveston-Harrisburg acceded to all of the Buffalo Bayou's rights, the Reconstruction Constitution of 1869 prohibited legislative grants of land to railroad companies, or to any person whatsoever "except to actual settlers upon the same."[41]

The original 1854 act chartering the Buffalo Bayou company only authorized it to lay track from Buffalo Bayou (the environs of Houston) to Austin, and the railroad had already been compensated in land by "alternate sections" for having laid that track. After 1870, the Galveston-Harrisburg, its successor, had constructed track from San Antonio toward El Paso, for which the state refused to pay with land. This track had been laid pursuant to the 1876 law providing for alternate sections to be gifted to railroads who constructed track. However, since that law was repealed in 1882, Governor Roberts had refused to issue the land certificates. In his opinion against the railroad for a unanimous court, Justice Gaines held that the railroad was not entitled to the land because it had no rights beyond those of its corporate predecessor. While the 1876 law allowed railroad companies to "earn" acreage for every mile of track laid, this did not expand the original 1854 grant of authority from the legislature to the Buffalo Bayou line to construct its track *only* from Buffalo Bayou to Austin. Thus the Galveston-Harrisburg railway had constructed the new track in violation of the limitations of its predecessor's original charter. Here the Court again protected the public domain from schemes to appropriate it for private purposes.

The most likely explanation for this judicial attitude is the obvious one that it was common knowledge throughout the government that there were more legislative appropriations of land and claims against the public domain than public lands to satisfy them. As the years of the nineteenth century rolled by, this fact became more and more obvious, the pressure on mythical public lands became stronger, and the Court's attempts to preserve it intensified, against the claims of both homesteaders and railroads.

The similar 1896 case of *Thompson v. Baker*[42] demonstrated the court's increasing reluctance to allow railroad claims against public lands. The case involved the same 1882 provision repealing the prior law that allowed earning land by laying track. After 1876, but prior to 1882, the Tyler Tap Railroad constructed 54 miles of track and claimed entitlement to 872 sections of land. However, the Commissioner of the General Land Office, after passage of the repeal, predictably refused to issue title certificates to the railroad. The railroad's receiver, Thompson, sought a writ of mandamus from the Texas Supreme Court commanding delivery of the certificates. While the US Constitution prohibits states from impairing their contracts with private parties, Chief Justice Gaines nonetheless found a way to refuse the railroad's claim. He disclaimed any desire to decide the merits of whether or not the state had breached a contract with the Tyler Tap allowing it to earn the lands. Instead he simply held that the Repeal Act of 1882 was intended to not only prohibit the *acquisition* of future lands by railroads, but also to prohibit the Land Commissioner from *issuing* certificates for past or future construction. There was no judicial remedy provided by the 1876 prior law if the Land Commissioner failed to issue earned certificates, so the 1882 law prohibiting him from doing so had taken away no right vested in the railroad. Thus it was not unconstitutional. Moreover, under the current statute, the Supreme Court was without legislative authority to command the Commissioner to convey the land. The matter was one for legislative, not judicial, action. The old doctrine of judicial restraint was pressed into service defending the public domain.

In *Houston & Texas Central Railway Company v. State*,[43] the Attorney General sued the railroad company to recover sixteen sections of land it previously acquired. Houston & Texas had obtained the land by building a railroad from Brenham to Austin. However, that line was only authorized by an amendment to its charter passed by the legislature in 1870. Its original charter had authorized no such line. As already noted, legislatures governed by the Constitution of 1869 could not allow railroad companies to earn land by constructing a track. Therefore, it was an easy matter for Justice T. J. Brown to uphold the trial court's disgorgement of the land from the railroad company back to the state. The only legislative grant of authority to build the track could not have constitutionally allowed the railroad to earn land in compensation for doing so.

Brown was following precedent from an 1896 case involving the same railroad, *Quinlan v. Houston & Texas Central Railway Company*.[44] This was a case where Jim Hogg's Attorney General (and gubernatorial successor), Charles Culberson, had instituted suit to void land certificates issued to a railroad and recover the land for the state. It took approximately four years for the case to make its way to the Supreme Court. By that time, Culberson had succeeded Hogg as governor. Chief Justice Gaines made essentially the same ruling that Brown made in the later *Houston & Texas Central* case. Again the Court was confronted with a company authorized to construct track by a law passed prior to the Civil War, but who did not actually construct the track until after the Constitution of 1869 prohibited public land grants to railroads. In this case, however, the crucial fact question was whether the railroad company had organized itself pursuant to legislative charter prior to the time the Constitution of 1869 was passed. If so, it could claim the track. If not, it had no pre-1869 rights upon which to base such a claim.

The court held that this was a question of fact and remanded the case to the trial court for the determination of it. The trial court had decided the case in favor of Quinlan and against the railroad. The effect of the Supreme Court's opinion was to generally side with Quinlan on the law, but to sidestep the actual resolution of the matter by remanding the case to the trial court for a jury verdict on the undetermined issue of fact. However, Gaines made clear what he thought that resolution should be "at the time [1869] . . . the railroad company had never been organized," so the railroad should lose.[45] The frontier was closed. There was no more free land. Both liberal homesteading policies and the subsidization of railroads had to be dialed back while

The Birth of Conservative Modern Texas, 1891–1902

not obstructing industrialization. Otherwise chaos would ensue that might threaten the land titles upon which the entire capitalist edifice was built.

Railroads and Tort Law

The 1895 Supreme Court case of *Texas & Pacific Railway Company v. Gay*[46] continued the Texas judiciary's solicitude toward victims of railroad accidents, this time adult victims. The case produced two appellate decisions, the first authored by Chief Justice Stayton (one of his last opinions), and the latter by Justice Denman soon after his appointment to the bench. Both opinions dealt with the same defenses raised by the railroad: jurisdiction and limitations. John M. Gay, a fireman for the TexPac Railroad, was killed by a defective coupling apparatus, which allowed the engine and its tender car to separate, throwing him down between them where he was killed. A suit for wrongful death was filed by his wife for herself and their minor daughter. Shortly before the accident, the railroad had been placed in receivership by a federal court in Louisiana. Therefore the suit was originally brought against the receiver, a Mr. Brown. More than a year later, a supplemental petition was filed adding the railroad itself to the suit, although it was still in receivership under the supervision of the Louisiana federal court.

The problem for the Gays was twofold. First, the Texas Wrongful Death Statute, passed in 1860 and always strictly construed, did not at that time authorize suits against receivers, but only against "persons, partnerships, and corporations." Since a tort remedy for wrongful death was unknown in the common law and solely a creature of statute, there was no valid claim against a receiver for wrongful death at the time the Gays filed their suit. Soon afterward, the statute was amended to include receivers among possible defendants, but this did not help the Gays. Second, the statute of limitations for wrongful death was one year from the time of the death. As part of Texas' progressive policy of solicitude towards minors, the statute did not begin to run against a minor's claims until he or she turned twenty-one. However, the widow's claim could not be similarly rehabilitated, and the railroad claimed that Mrs. Gay's suit was untimely because the receiver could not be sued at all, and as to the railroad itself, it had not been joined in the action until more than a year after the accident.

The trial court initially dismissed the case on these and a number of other grounds. The matter reached the Supreme Court where Chief Justice Stayton, in an uncharacteristically long opinion, meticulously explained why there were fact issues that required determination by a jury. Therefore dismissal had been improper. The rationale for the decision boiled down to the fact that Gay's attorneys had alleged that the railroad had placed itself into receivership through collusive litigation filed in the Louisiana federal court. In other words, no one had forced the railroad into receivership, but rather the railroad had sought to place itself in receivership under the authority of the federal court because it knew this would shield it from a number of pending state claims. Under these circumstances, Stayton reasoned, the plaintiff should be allowed to avail herself of the doctrine of fraudulent concealment. By analogy to the public lands cases, the Court reiterated the rule that in Texas, a plaintiff would be excused from tardiness in filing suit if that tardiness had been produced by the defendant fraudulently concealing the existence of a claim. Fraudulent receivership was a form of fraudulent concealment because it had led the plaintiffs to believe they should sue the receiver (an ultimately futile gesture) rather than the railroad itself, and this misrepresentation by the railroad was fraudulent because it knew there was no real need for a receivership. Therefore, the case was allowed to proceed to trial where the plaintiffs could try and prove that the receivership was in fact fraudulent and collusive, which would relieve them of the necessity of having filed suit sooner.

Ironically, when the trial ensued in Travis County District Court, the railroad declined to even raise the issue. It requested no instruction or question to the jury as to whether or not limitations had expired. This was undoubtedly because the railroad did not want the jury to be further inflamed against it by evidence of its effort to avoid liability for the death by tricky lawyering. It was bad enough that the jury did hear evidence from the railroad's own employees that the reason the coupling pin had "worked up so as to let the bar connecting the engine and tender slip out" was because the coupling pin "did not have a slot and key in the lower end of it to prevent its working up." The railroad's own managerial employees admitted that after Gay's death "we used slots and keys now on all engines." In other words, the railroad knew of the danger but only had an after-the-fact safety program.

The Gays won the suit and were awarded substantial damages. When the case returned to the Supreme Court on appeal of the verdict, Justice Denman affirmed the verdict with no trouble, given the state of the evidence and the defendant's failure to pursue the issue of limitations below. In fact, according to Denman, "there is nothing in the record to show that such defense was urged or called to the attention of the court or jury on the trial."[47] The Court's increasing concern over the callous corporate conduct that was producing more and more injuries is reflected in another passage of Denman's opinion. In discussing the damning testimony of the railroad's own employees on the subject of post-accident modifications to their safety procedures, the Court held that the railroad had waived any objection to the admissibility of that testimony. It should be noted that in today's Texas courts, such testimony is usually not admissible by virtue of rules of evidence codified in the twentieth century. Yet here, in 1895, Denman made sure that lawyers and lower courts did not misunderstand his opinion as relying solely upon technical grounds. Even though this type of evidence would come to be excluded in Texas in the coming decades, and even though it was similarly treated by other states in Denman's own time, he went out of his way to say, "We do not wish to be understood as holding that such evidence was not admissible, as each member of this court is strongly inclined to the opinion that the cases excluding such testimony (in other jurisdictions) are not founded upon sound reasoning."[48]

In cases involving industries other than railroads, the Court sought to provide remedies to workers and consumers but also to control the economic consequences to the business of adapting traditional tort formulas to provide such relief. In *Joske v. Irvine*,[49] the court reversed a $250 false arrest verdict against Alexander Joske, the famous department store owner, and did so by adoption of a procedural rule designed to circumscribe jury discretion in compensating individuals aggrieved by corporate action. Irvine worked as a deliveryman for Joske. One evening upon returning from work, a dispute arose between him and Joske over some missing merchandise from his truck. Joske, unsatisfied by Irvine's explanations, fired him and called in the police to investigate. Irvine, in turn, withheld from Joske three dollars of his receipts for the day, claiming that Joske owed him this much in back pay. When the police arrived, Irvine explained the situation and offered to take an officer to his apartment where he had sufficient funds with which to repay Joske. The officer told Irvine that he would arrest him if he did not do so. Irvine's trial testimony was to the effect that he saw Joske intensely discussing matters with the police officer before they departed. On the way to the apartment, Irvine ducked into a bar, spoke to a friend, emerged with the three dollars, and offered to return with the officer to pay Joske. The officer then told Irvine that he still wanted to go to his apartment, presumably because he suspected that the missing goods were there. Irvine, perhaps for the same reason, refused to take the officer there, at which point he was arrested.

The arrest was without a warrant, and the Supreme Court, through Justice Denman, acknowledged that under these circumstances, the officer's actions were unlawful. However, in reversing the judgment, Denman focused on another part of the record he considered more problematic. While the jury had believed Irvine's testimony and found that Joske directed Irvine's arrest, Justice Denman was not so sure. Since Irvine had not actually overheard Joske give such an order, the jury must have inferred only from the surrounding facts and circumstances that such an order had been given. In aid of his ultimate disposition of the case, Denman relied upon authority from several other states in support of a new "mere scintilla" rule, but first he had to acknowledge the old maxim of Texas law: "Whether there be any evidence is a question for the judge. Whether sufficient evidence, is for the jury."[50]

While acknowledging this to be the rule, Denman regarded it as "much quoted and often misunderstood."[51] He reasoned that the justification for the rule was that the court should take the case from the jury's discretion when "there is no room for ordinary minds to differ as to the conclusion to be drawn from (the evidence)."[52] Since statements like this in a number of cases had to assume that there was "some" evidence for the court to evaluate, Denman reasoned that the court's "no evidence" responsibility was not limited solely to cases where there was really "no" evidence on a material issue of fact. Rather, the important question was whether the evidence, viewed as a whole, was such that a rational person could conclude that such an ultimate fact had occurred—in this case whether Joske had directed the arrest. Thus Denman reformulated the "no evidence rule" to expand the ability of judges to overrule jury verdicts for lack of evidence. Even if there were some evidence from which a jury might conclude that something had happened, if it were a "mere scintilla," Denman reasoned, that was the same as no evidence at all because no reasonable mind could reach a logical conclusion from it.

With respect to the media, the Court continued until the end of the century to refuse to protect publishers from libel verdicts obtained by prominent citizens. In *A. H. Belo & Company v. Smith*,[53] Chief Justice Gaines affirmed a $1,000 verdict for Smith, a prominent cattleman, against the *Dallas News* and the *Galveston News*, both owned by the Belo Corporation. They both published an article to the effect that Smith had been arrested in Kansas City on a warrant sworn out by a local bank to recover almost $15,000 allegedly advanced to him several years ago but never repaid. The newspapers argued that the article could not be construed as accusing Smith of any nefarious or criminal conduct, since merely owing money was no shame, nor was it a crime under Texas or Missouri law. While Gaines saw the logic of the argument, he nonetheless believed that "the whole writing is calculated to produce the impression that in the transaction there was some criminal conduct." The trial court had left the meaning and implications of the articles to be determined by the jury, and the jury had found in favor of Smith. The Supreme Court approved. The newspapers lost.

One other area in which the court was progressive and sympathetic to plaintiffs was in the area of family law and the protection of women. Of course, this can only be judged by the standards of the time. Family law in Texas had always been a blend of English common law and Spanish civil and community property law. The general rule was that spouses were immune from suits against each other. That rule was a vestige of the English common law belief in the "entire unity" of the married couple. In *Nickerson v. Nickerson*,[54] Mrs. Nickerson was falsely imprisoned by her estranged husband and a co-conspirator in order to get possession of her two sons, upon whose services she relied for support. The Nickersons had been separated for several years, but this incident prompted Mrs. Nickerson to sue for and obtain a divorce. After obtaining the divorce, she filed suit against Nickerson and his co-conspirator, one Matson.

Bound by precedent, the court was required to affirm the dismissal of the case as against Mr. Nickerson because even though the suit was not filed until after divorce, the wrongful conduct upon which it was based occurred during the marriage and could thus produce no liability from one spouse to the other. However, the court affirmed the jury's award of two hundred dollars against Matson, and in so doing made a minor exception to another established common law rule. Matson had argued that since the tort occurred during the marriage, Mr. Nickerson was a necessary coplaintiff and had to authorize and join with his wife's suit. The court, while acknowledging that this was the general rule, carved out an exception under circumstances like these, where the wife was justifiably separated from her husband, although still married, at the time the cause of action arose. While it was not much in the way of service to battered women, it was an improvement on the then-existing state of affairs.

Similarly, in *McMurray v. McMurray*,[55] the court showed an increased understanding of the precarious position of many contemporary women. In that case, Mr. McMurray had filed for divorce after encouraging his wife to visit her mother out of state. He then fraudulently concealed from his wife and from the court the true extent of their community property, and actually testified falsely to the court as to this and a number of other facts. Once she became aware of the fraud and the divorce, Mrs. McMurray moved the court to set aside its previous decree. Her husband argued in favor of the general finality of the judgments of all the courts of this state. While there was no authority directly on point, Justice Stayton ruled that a court has the power to set aside even final divorce decrees, if obtained by false testimony "introduced through the procurement or connivance of the party to be benefited by it." The case was remanded to the trial court with instructions to conduct "a reexamination of the question of community property."

The odd case of *Wright v. Tipton*[56] is an illustration of the simultaneous conservatism, paternalism, and increased solicitude toward women of the late-nineteenth-century court. In 1887, in the throes of the debate over temperance, the legislature passed a law allowing women to prevent liquor sales to their husbands. In this case, Mrs. Tipton had sued Wright, a saloon keeper, upon his statutorily required "liquor dealer's bond," alleging that he had breached the bond by selling liquor to her husband after she had given written notice that he should not do so. Wright, following *Nickerson v. Nickerson*, argued that Mr. and Mrs. Tipton were not separated, and thus that the general rule required that Mr. Tipton join her in asking that his bond be forfeited. Mr. Tipton, the drinker, of course declined to do so. Justice T. J. Brown, the teetotaler, had no problem disposing of that argument. Referring to the *Nickerson* case, he curtly pointed out that it "was decided in the early part of 1886, and the law under which this suit is brought was enacted in 1887," Brown then recited the well-worn adage that the legislature is always presumed to know the existing law. The legislature must have known the new statute would be pointless unless it created an exception allowing wives to sue without their husbands' permission. Thus the new statute "was intended to do just what the language expresses, that is, to give the wife the right to sue in her own name."[57] It is an instructive case indeed that brings together the social and political currents of women's rights, temperance, prohibition, and judicial paternalism in an opinion of less than two pages.

Segregation

Both by legislative enactment and constitutional tradition, segregation was enshrined in Texas law. The 1866 Constitution, while requiring the legislature to "encourage colored schools," also required that they be separately run from white ones. Later that year, the legislature passed a statute that required that "all railroad companies shall attach one passenger car for the special accommodation of freedmen," a provision unnecessary under the regime of slavery where social segregation was easily and more informally enforced.

The Birth of Conservative Modern Texas, 1891–1902

Other laws also forbade racial intermingling in other public accommodations. The 1876 Constitution required racial segregation in all public schools. In 1879, the legislature thought it prudent to update the miscegenation statute passed in 1858, and with the proliferation of railroads, a new statute was passed in 1889 requiring railroad companies to maintain separate cars for white and black passengers, "equal in comfort." In 1891, with respect to public transportation, and in 1893, with respect to education, this was supplemented with more specific requirements designed to satisfy, on the law's face, the "separate but equal" doctrine approved by the US Supreme Court five years later in *Plessy v. Ferguson*. And, for decades, Hispanics had been treated similarly by local practice and application of law. While segregation ensured separation, the "equality" supposedly provided to Hispanics and African Americans left much to be desired.[58]

These late nineteenth-century laws and customs were seldom challenged in Texas, as there appear only a few reported opinions on the subject of race until the 1897 case of *Pullman-Palace-Car Co. v. Cain* and the 1913 case of *Gulf C.& S. F. Ry. Co. v. Sharman*, but those two cases are certainly illustrative of the dominant ethos of the era. Cain was an African American minister traveling to Texas from Missouri, and when his train reached Texas, he was removed from the Pullman berth he paid for, and he was segregated with the other black passengers. He sued and won a verdict for $100. Over a stinging dissent by Justice Henry Clay Pleasants, a majority of the Texas intermediate Court of Civil Appeals in Galveston upheld the verdict, not because Cain had been forcibly segregated, but because the Pullman sleeping car Cain had paid to occupy had not been fitted with a wall so that he could remain in it segregated from white passengers. If the railroad was going to sell Cain a Pullman car ticket, the law required it to protect him from having to mingle with whites, the court reasoned.[59]

In the *Sharman* case, Sharman, who was the sheriff of Liberty County, boarded a Gulf C. & S. F. train with a prisoner he was charged with escorting to Beaumont. The prisoner was an African American charged with murder. When Sharman boarded the train with the prisoner, the conductor compelled both men into the "negro coach" because he thought it his duty under law "to prevent said negro from riding in the car with whites," and as the sheriff was compelled by his duty to accompany the prisoner, he would have to go, too. Sharman did so under protest and then filed suit against the railroad seeking damages because as a result of the conductor's actions in forcing him "to ride in said negro coach . . . he was greatly humiliated and mortified."

Sheriff Sharman also claimed that "there were a number of negro men in the coach and that he was afraid his prisoner would be rescued by them." The local jury agreed and awarded the outraged Sharman five hundred dollars, a considerable sum by the measure of that day. The Austin Court of Civil Appeals reversed and rendered judgment that Sharman take nothing, but perhaps not on the grounds a modern observer might assume.[60]

The court acknowledged the statutes[61] requiring railroads to furnish separate coaches for white and black passengers and prohibiting "either race from riding in the car provided for the other race." Since neither party had challenged anything about the segregation statute, the court was not called upon to examine its validity, although it seems clear from the context that this court, like others in the South, approved. In a candor rare among government officials pretending that separate was equal, Justice Jenkins wrote for the Court of Civil Appeals that "while the statute, in terms, equally protects whites from the presence of negroes, and negroes from the presence of whites in their respective coaches, *yet it is well known that the leading purpose* of the statute was to protect the white race from the presence of negroes while traveling" (italics added). Under these circumstances, the court approved the conductor's exercising his discretion to compel the sheriff into the Negro car, rather than to allow the black prisoner into the white car, since the sheriff's right to custody of his prisoner would necessarily require one or the other result. A "rule of reason" ought to obtain, held Justice Jenkins. Moreover, said the court, it could not allow a sheriff to claim damages in these circumstances. "We can see no reason why a sheriff should feel humiliated by being compelled to ride in the negro coach with his prisoner," wrote Jenkins. "There are many places in which a man who claims to be respectable would feel mortified and humiliated, if found therein, except in the discharge of his duty, and yet no sheriff would hesitate to enter such places when necessary to discharge his duties."[62]

Meanwhile, it would take forty years for a unanimous US Supreme Court, in *Brown v. Board of Education*, to affirm and declare what white Texans and their judges took for granted as true, that the mere act of segregation by a white government implied inferiority among blacks, and that to separate them from others "solely because of their race generates a feeling of inferiority as to their status in the community that may affect their hearts and minds in a way unlikely ever to be undone." What Justice Jenkins added in a moment of clarity was that segregation implied more than just a power relationship; it was a result of fear, the fear that would require a law to "protect the white race from the presence of negroes." Segregation not only made "respectable" white travelers feel secure; it also helped prevent any political or social solidarity among blacks and poor or radical whites. The new progressive Democrat in the style of Chief Justice Gaines, Governor James Hogg, and John H. Reagan, concerned with issues of urbanization, industrialization, and transportation, was exclusively white.[63]

Municipalities, Trusts, and Insurance

As a result of urbanization and industrialization, the Texas Supreme Court was also faced with other questions of corporate power, public and private. Municipal corporations, chartered and authorized by specific legislation, were just beginning to come into their own as a result of the rapid economic expansion and urbanization occurring in this period. Simultaneously, the controversies over railroads, public lands, and farmers' rights gave rise to populist demands for actions against predatory corporate practices of combination and monopoly. As society and technology continued to advance, a new form of corporation would come to dominate litigation to an event greater extent than the railroads, the insurance company.

At this time, Texas had a general municipal and corporate statute, but most significant municipalities were established by a special act of the legislature describing their boundaries and the methods by which they might grow. The city of Oak Cliff near Dallas was established under the general statute, and the court was called upon to determine the limits of a city's power under that statute to expand its borders, and thus its tax base. Oak Cliff held an election to increase its surface area by 500 percent by annexing surrounding rural acreage. Since that area was sparsely populated, an election conducted over the entire region was easily carried out by those actually living in the city. The county attorney of Dallas County, undoubtedly spurred to do so by the established and growing city of Dallas or by his rural constituents, sued to have the election set aside. Justice Gaines had no choice but to fashion a judicial remedy for this kind of municipal conduct. Because of the generality of the incorporation statute, the best he could do was to state the general rule that cities were empowered by the general incorporation statute to incorporate "themselves, and not also such portions of the adjacent territory as their inhabitants may be pleased to embrace within the limits of the corporation." The only guidance he could give courts in making such a determination was that "a city does not extend beyond the area occupied by its houses and inhabitants.... The fact that much of the territory lying beyond the actual city has been laid off into blocks and lots as prospective additions does not aid . . . [the] case."[64] For some time, litigation on this issue would have to proceed by case-by-case factual evaluations of urban geography.

In 1895, the court evidenced a similar suspicion of growing municipal power in *Higgins v. Bordages*.[65] In that case, the city of Beaumont attempted to foreclose on Higgins's homestead to pay assessments for local improvements. This case would overrule the court's decision in *Lufkin v. City of Galveston*[66] just twelve years before, which had included such assessments within the provision of the 1876 Constitution providing that homesteads, while normally exempt from any forced sale, could be executed upon for "taxes."[67] In deciding that assessments would no longer be considered "taxes," Justice Brown reasoned that a tax, under the constitution, "must be uniform and equal." Since numerous Texas decisions had exempted assessments from this requirement of equal treatment, Brown had no trouble determining that an assessment was not a tax "when it has none of the characteristics of a tax in any sense in which it is used in the constitution."[68] That the court reversed itself in such a short time is an indication both of the influence of its newest members, Denman and Brown, and of the court's growing concern with the expansion of municipal authority in an ever more urban state.

While the extent of municipal power might be of some interest to legislators and civic boosters, the public at large was much more interested in reining in the predatory practices of private corporations. In 1889, the legislature enacted Texas' first antitrust law as a result of public agitation and the efforts of Attorney General Jim Hogg. In fact, one contemporary commentator explained that "the formation of gigantic combinations for these purposes (of monopolization) in late years has created alarm and excited the liveliest interest in the public mind. The amount of discussion which it has invoked, considering the time during which it has progressed, is probably without parallel."[69] As the Supreme Court would later acknowledge, "in the year 1888 the discussion seems to have become general, and in 1889 many legislatures, including our own, made laws for the purpose of punishing and repressing such conspiracies."[70]

The 1889 antitrust law was challenged in *Houck and Dieter v. Anheuser-Busch Brewing Association*.[71] In that case, Busch sued Houck and Dieter, distributors, for money owed for beer sold to them. The distributors responded by counterclaim that they had been damaged in excess of the amount owed because Anheuser-Busch refused to abide by the terms of a written agreement between the parties appointing Houck and Dieter as *exclusive* Budweiser distributors in El Paso County. Busch's rejoinder was that it had not abided by that contractual provision because of the passage of the antitrust law, which made it illegal. This required Houck and Dieter to claim that the antitrust law was, itself, unconstitutional. Chief Justice Gaines made short work of that argument. He simply agreed with the lower court of appeals, for the reasons given in its opinion, that the act was fine.

However, while Gaines had no intention of exhibiting the judicial activism required to strike the act down as unconstitutional, he was not averse to limiting its application so as to ameliorate its effects upon certain classes of business. In *Queen Insurance Company v. State*, Gaines, while still associate justice, required an uncharacteristically long opinion to explain why the 1889 antitrust statute in no way limited or affected the activities of the growing insurance industry. The antitrust law defined trusts as "combinations of capital ... to create or carry out restrictions of trade." Gaines argued that the act was not intended to apply to combinations to fix insurance premiums or commissions of agents. Even though Gaines had to admit that "a combination between two or more insurance companies to increase their rates or to diminish the rates to be paid to their agents, is in a general sense a combination in restraint of trade," he nonetheless argued that the statutory phrase "restrictions of trade" was "not intended to receive that construction in the statute under consideration."[72]

Gaines painstakingly documented his understanding of the public outcry that generated the antitrust law, and he came to the conclusion that the law was motivated by a desire to control combinations "organized for the purpose of affecting the prices of articles of prime importance in commerce or the rates of transportation and intercommunication." In other words, for Gaines, the term "trusts" was not to be understood in either a technical, economic, or legal sense, but only, by "very recent commercial usage," to comprehend "combinations of corporations or capitalists for the purpose of controlling the price of articles of prime necessity, or the charges of transportation for the public." This, indeed, was an odd form of judicial conservatism. Rather than interpreting the words of the statute by their literal meaning, Gaines was careful to restrict their application to only those cases known to the public and complained of at the time of the adoption of the law. The court might stand aside as the legislature bowed to popular pressure, but it would construe the legislature's enactments as narrowly as possible, requiring that every attempt to circumscribe private corporate power be specifically enumerated so as to leave no doubt of the intention of the legislature and the public.[73]

The rise of insurance also required that the court educate itself on the theory of risk allocation and begin to craft a jurisprudence designed to prevent this modern industry from degenerating into mere gambling conducted on a massive scale. For example, in *Price v. Supreme Lodge of the Knights of Honor*,[74] Chief Justice Willie struck down so-called "graveyard insurance" as bogus. Price sued the Supreme Lodge for amounts allegedly payable on a policy issued on the life of his fellow knight, Thomas C. Harper. The Supreme Lodge was a sort of mutual benefit association that agreed, in exchange for membership dues, to insure the lives of its members. Harper's original beneficiaries were his wife and children, but he got behind in his dues and agreed with Price to make Price his beneficiary if Price would pay his arrearages. Price paid the dues, and he was recognized as the owner of the policy by the Lodge.

The problem for Price was the English common law doctrine of "insurable interest." Early on, the English courts, followed by the US Supreme Court, had determined that while a policyholder in arrears might pledge his insurance to a creditor as a means of repaying his debt, that creditor would not be allowed to essentially buy the policy. In other words, in order to become a beneficiary of a life insurance policy, the common law required that one have an "insurable interest" in the life of the insured—that is, stand in relation to the insured such that his death would cause financial hardship. Otherwise, anyone could gamble on the death of anyone else. Thus business partners, widows, orphaned children, parents, and other close relatives were automatically assumed to have insurable interests. With respect to strangers, their status as a beneficiary of a life-insurance policy was presumed to be suspect. In *Price v. Supreme Lodge*, the Supreme Court adopted this doctrine of insurable interest to deprive Price of the benefits of his bargain. To hold otherwise would be to allow strangers to place themselves in a position where the "early death" of the insured will "bring him pecuniary advantage. The temptation to bring about this death presents itself as strongly to him as to a party who originally affects insurance for his own benefit upon the life of another. Public policy removes the temptation to take human life, and it cannot matter how that temptation is brought about."[75]

A few years after the Supreme Court's foray into the realms of torts and insurance, the Texas legislature succumbed to populist-progressive pleas for insurance regulation and protection. As early as 1897, Governor Culberson had harangued the 25th Legislature about insurance companies collecting inflated premiums from Texas policyholders and investing massive profits out of state. In 1907, the legislature passed the Robertson Insurance Law, which required all life insurers doing business in Texas to submit to financial regulation. The primary feature of that regulation was to require 75 percent of company funds to be invested within Texas. As with Hogg's and Reagan's initial foray into railroad regulation over a decade before, this reform was as much a matter of protecting Texas insurers from big out-of-state competition as it was a consumer protection measure. But in 1909 and 1910, the legislature passed additional statutes regulating the fire insurance industry, including government control of premium rates. Then in 1913, the legislature established the Industrial Accident Board, taking the first step to inaugurate a system of state insurance for on-the-job injuries that continues to this day.[76]

By the early twentieth century, all three branches of government were working together in the service of progressive conservatism. The Texas brand of that new ideology had synthesized and for generations would blunt efforts to overturn the Democratic business establishment or to threaten one-party rule.

Epilogue

Looking Backward

ON THE THRESHOLD OF THE TWENTIETH CENTURY, THE TEXAS SUPREME Court supported the Hogg-Reagan-House establishment, compromising between hidebound adherence to tradition and freewheeling judicial activism. Pragmatism reigned, the kind of outlook epitomized by Chief Justice Gaines and practiced by the Hogg-Reagan-House majority within the Democratic Party. Although changes in court personnel occasionally made a difference in particular cases, a fundamental consensus in judicial philosophy remained, and the unanimity exhibited within this branch of government was as remarkable as it was effective. Throughout this period, especially after the constitutional regime was modernized by the amendments of 1891, the Supreme Court consistently faced the same task: adapting existing law to rapidly changing social and economic reality without undermining the institutional credibility that was its very foundation. This was not always easy when faced with an often churlish, shortsighted, and unresponsive legislature on the one hand and serious grassroots agitation for radical reform on the other.

The modern Texas Court of the 1880s and 1890s could have struck down the state's antitrust law or railroad regulations, or used antiquated common law rules to stifle attempts to help children, widows, workers, and other victims of growing industrialization. Other courts had done so. The Texas Court chose not to. Yet it also shielded itself from any serious conservative criticism by carefully circumscribing how far a jury, the ultimate democratic institution, could go. The Court, by mechanically following precedent, could have turned a deaf ear to the plight of injured workers, battered women, or abused spouses, yet it did not do so. It may not have done much by modern metrics, but what it did do was moderately progressive by contemporaneous standards.

On the other hand, while the Court occasionally innovated, it was no pathfinder. In the tradition of common law jurisprudence, which is to say the English tradition of judge-made case law, the Court did its innovating only "interstitially." As Benjamin Cardozo said in 1921, a judge's room for policy maneuvering is narrow: "He legislates only between gaps. He fills the open spaces in the law, [yet] how far he can go without traveling beyond the walls of the interstices cannot be staked out for him on a chart."[1] More than one hundred years earlier, Sir William Blackstone would claim that even in such instances, judges do not "make new law, but . . . vindicate the old one from misrepresentation. For if it be found that the former decision is manifestly absurd or unjust, it is declared, not that such a sentence was *bad law*, but that it was *not law*; that is, that it is not the established custom of the realm."[2]

The late-nineteenth-century Texas Supreme Court took Blackstone and the tradition he embodied seriously. It lived up to Alexander Hamilton's prediction that of the three branches of government, "the judiciary, from the nature of its functions, will always be the least dangerous. . . . It may truly be said to have neither force nor will, but merely judgment."[3] This also meant that the function of the Court was essentially conservative, not to change things, but to adapt legal rules only so far as necessary to conserve the existing rule of law, the predominant sociopolitical arrangements.

The activities of that judicial branch dovetailed with the more overtly political work of John H. Reagan, James Stephen Hogg, and Colonel Edward House. The two more political branches of government eventually coopted the populist third-party movement by institutionalizing and making acceptable to business the most iconic features of its program, and by adopting public personae designed to blur the distinction between them and their radical competitors. What these men accomplished was to appropriate much of the political content of populism, thereby marginalizing the radicals and establishing a new dominant ideology. As the twentieth century dawned, the work of all three branches of Texas government combined to produce a consensus, a new ideological identity, the modern white progressive interested in economic development, family values, public safety, and technological progress, but not in the redistribution of wealth or power. The progressive was ironically progrowth but antitrust. The poor farm agitator was lured back to the Democratic Party, reassured by segregation, and soon dwarfed in any event by the political power of a middle class expanded by urbanization, public education, and economic development. Order was maintained. The extreme underclass of blacks and Hispanics continued to be subordinated.[4]

From the 1830s to 1900, the contests over political identity in Texas were most fundamentally about the desire of Anglo Texans to gain wealth by developing cheap land through exploitive agriculture and immigration-driven speculation. Whether one accepts that the Texas War of Independence was caused by the curtailment of white immigration by Mexican authorities or by their contemporaneous efforts to abolish slavery is really a choice between two sides of the same coin. The land speculator Bowie and the empresario Austin had the same goals. They wanted continued immigration of Anglo settlers to increase the demand for land and hence its value, *and* they wanted the protection of the system of slavery that made large-scale exploitation of that land by agricultural means profitable. Similarly, both the Houston party and Lamar's hotheads wanted to eliminate Mexican and Indian threats to the peaceful development of more and more land by greater numbers of white owners, black slaves, and Hispanic farm workers. What they disagreed on were tactics. Houston wanted peaceful coexistence with, and containment of, Indian tribes; Lamar wanted them exterminated. Houston wanted American help to secure the border from Mexican incursion. Lamar thought his rangers and militia not only up to the task, but capable of expanding Texas' borders further westward.

The Civil War, Reconstruction, and the drastic political, social, and technological changes they produced overthrew the existing order but did not alter the fundamental motivation of, or prevent the return to power of, the Anglo elite. After the Civil War, that elite faced new challenges: maintaining wealth and hegemony in a world without African slave labor, and overcoming a new discontent among poor whites. When federal military rule left Texas, the dormant Anglo elite reemerged with a new ideological strategy for maintaining political dominance. That strategy involved political and jurisprudential action that provided benefits to working-class whites and incorporated them within the dominant cultural identity by segregating "free" blacks and Hispanics as an underclass.[5] This left the existing economic order intact while allowing it to adjust to the new means of creating wealth generated by urbanization and industrialization. By the turn of the century, Texas' modern identity was incarnated as probusiness progressivism that was both racist and sensitive to the economic needs of middle-class and working-class whites, who received strong homestead protection, modest tort remedies, insurance and railroad regulation, public education, and racial preference in return for their allegiance.

Many in modern Texas had reason to celebrate this achievement. On a balmy evening in the spring of 1909, just four years after the Alamo came into the hands of Clara Driscoll's Daughters of the Republic of Texas, Chief Justice and Mrs. Reuben R. Gaines mingled with more than one hundred friends gathered to celebrate their fiftieth wedding anniversary in the grand ballroom of the Driskill Hotel.[6] Among the group were their Austin friends, some of Judge Gaines's colleagues on the bench, other important officials, and prominent members of the bar from distant parts of the state. These luminaries had responded to an engraved invitation to join "Judge and Mrs. R. R. Gaines at home at 8:30 p.m. March 31, 1909." Fortuity has preserved the signed guestbook from the soiree, a gift from Mr. and Mrs. H. D. McDonald of Paris, Texas, the Gaines's hometown. The book's few parchment pages are bound between yellow cardboard by a golden cord at the top. The cover is embellished with a small portrait of Louisa Gaines as a bride and bears an embossed monogram inscribing the letter "S" (for Shortbridge, her maiden name) within a larger "G."[7]

Chief Justice Gaines was a creature of routine. After work ended precisely at five o'clock, he visited the Austin Club almost every night where billiards, dominoes, and cards were played. This resulted in his developing a habit of coming home late, which discomfited Louisa. To emphasize her disapproval, one night she locked the judge out, and when he had to knock to gain entry to their apartment, she whispered, "Is that you, John?," to which, his name being Reuben, he responded, "Who the hell is John?" The clerk who told this tale has assured posterity that the judge, having enjoyed a happy marriage to Louisa for over fifty years, took the joke well and returned to the same good humor as ever. He was known to like his beer and his fishing, and his disposition was such that important matters never seemed to upset him, while small things would irritate him terribly. Most importantly, like Chief Justice Stayton before him, Gaines never had a political opponent, and according to a contemporary report, "in no instance was he ever known to deliver a speech in his own behalf or that of others."[8]

As Chief Justice and Mrs. Gaines moved among the well-wishers that spring night, they must have felt the absence of Reuben's predecessor as chief justice, the redoubtable John W. Stayton. It was Judge Stayton's sudden and untimely death in 1894 that had catapulted Gaines to the chief justiceship in his stead. While his judicial service was not as long as Gaines's, Stayton's thirteen years on the court, half of them as its chief, had by now still become legendary.[9]

Although the diligent Judge Stayton was conspicuous by his absence, another former colleague from the nineteenth century did share a glass of champagne that night with the happy Gaines couple. One of Reuben Gaines's closest associates on the bench was the man who had been appointed to replace him when he was elevated to chief justice in 1894, Leroy G. Denman. He had retired from the bench in 1899 to resume his lucrative law practice in San Antonio and had traveled to Austin that March night to toast his former chief.[10]

As they sipped champagne and reminisced over their time on the court, Gaines and Denman were joined by their old populist colleague, Justice Thomas Jefferson Brown, who upon Gaines's retirement in two years would replace him as chief justice. Even in this year of 1909, Brown was already handicapped by ill health and bent by age. He was a white-haired widower with a long beard and a gigantic walking staff that stabilized his tentative gait and compensated for failing eyes. He is said to have been a "venerable eccentric" who resembled Father Time, and whom lay observers were apt to regard with "general amusement," yet he was a formidable and respected member of the Hogg populist/progressive wing of the Democratic Party.[11] While neither Gaines nor Denman was known for being particularly religious, Brown was more reminiscent of T. J. "Stonewall" Jackson than of their mutual namesake Thomas Jefferson. It was said of him that "in a day of religious divide, for him there was no doubt; in a day when thousands are saying they do not know what lies beyond the grave, he, with an undimmed eye of faith, saw beyond its portals the Eternal City." The length of his tenure on the court was second only to Gaines's until well into the twentieth century.[12]

Although happy to be among the well-wishers at the Driskill, Brown did not drink anything stronger than milk, both because of his religious convictions and because of the pain he already felt in his belly. His years as the next chief would be hamstrung by what would become stomach cancer. Although very different in temperament, these two sages, Brown and Gaines, inspired deep affection and much whimsical lore among the court's staff.[13]

When the party had wound down and Gaines and Louisa walked toward the door of the ballroom after bidding their other guests good-night, perhaps the new electric lights on Austin's Sixth Street and the occasional sound of an automobile motoring along nearby Congress Avenue caused the judge to reflect upon themes of modernization and change. The capitol building at the end of Congress Avenue, and the very Driskill Hotel, the halls of which he now traversed, had been constructed during his term on the court. These were more than mere symbols; they were evidence of rapid social, political, and economic change.[14]

Fittingly, the Gaines's host that spring night was George Washington Littlefield, who had purchased the Driskill in 1895 and had begun the process of installing its first electric light system. Like Gaines, Littlefield, although not much of a drinker himself, was on the wet side of early-twentieth-century politics. This same George W. Littlefield fathered southern historical education at the University of Texas and erected on its South Mall a monument to the "men and women of the Confederacy." Within the original forty acres of the University of Texas and overshadowed by its main building tower, sit "the little six," six of the first classroom buildings of the school. Three buildings are arrayed on the east side and three buildings on the west side of the grass lawn of the South Mall at the edge of campus closest to the state capitol. Until 2015, among the "little six" stood six large statues on prominent pedestals, three on each side of the lawn. On the west side stood reminders of Texas' Confederate past; on the east side stood tributes to its new Southwestern future. On the west side atop the balustrade that separates the South Mall from the Main Mall and its Texas Tower stood Jefferson Davis, whose inscription read "(1808–1889), Colonel in the United States Army, United States Senator, Secretary of War of the United States, President of the Confederate States." But for the double-breasted cut of his frock coat, Davis's earnest, clean-shaven, bony countenance emerging from the stiff collar and wide flat bow tie could easily have been confused with popular portrayals of the young Abraham Lincoln. Staring southward toward the Texas capitol, Davis held a sheaf of documents in his left hand while his right hand, palm up, extended forward in an attempt to explain ... something. In August of 2015, after a court rebuffed attempts by the Sons of Confederate Veterans to stop it, the university removed the Davis statue from public view, relocating it inside the Briscoe Center for American History on campus.[15]

On this same west side and further southward toward the capitol, stood the next statute, that of Albert Sidney Johnston (1803–62), "Secretary of War of the Republic of Texas, Brigadier General in the United States Army, General in the Confederate States Army, Commander of the Army of the Mississippi."

Johnston was uniformed as a Confederate officer and clutched a sheathed saber in his left hand and his wide-brimmed hat in his gloved right. Next to him at the southern end on the western side stood Robert E. Lee (1807–70), "Colonel in the United States Army, Superintendent of the Military Academy at West Point, Commander of the Army of Northern Virginia, General in Chief of the Army of the Confederate States, President of Washington College." He, like General Johnston, was accoutered as a Confederate soldier. Both generals' statues were removed in 2017 to be housed with Davis's, leaving only pedestals wrapped in black plastic to cover the inscriptions where they once stood.

Tracing a horseshoe-shaped route across the southern edge of the South Mall and back northward, the southernmost statute on the east side, across from Lee's, was that of perhaps the least well-known member of this gallery of heroes. Standing in a frock coat with a modern Stetson hat in his bare left hand and a cane in his right, John H. Reagan, a typically clean-shaven man of the early twentieth century, looked toward the capitol to the south until his statue too was removed in 2017. The base of the statue, now also covered over, bore witness to his accomplishments: "(1818–1905), District Judge, Postmaster General of the Confederate States, United States Senator, First Chairman of the Railroad Commission."

The next statue northward was that of Governor James Stephen Hogg (1851–1906), Reagan's political ally. Of the statues removed in 2015 and 2017, only his is slated for re-erection in a different public location on campus. His inscription read: "Attorney General of Texas, The First Native Governor of Texas, The People's Governor of Texas." He and Reagan epitomized the modern Texas of the late nineteenth and early twentieth centuries, a state looking southward to its past and upward to its future. This horseshoe, until recently, was completed by the figure of Woodrow Wilson at the northeastern corner of the South Mall across from Jefferson Davis. Wilson was the primary national beneficiary of the political order forged in Texas by Hogg, Reagan, and their cohorts. An educated and sophisticated man of southern sensibilities, he represented the value of progressive learning in a new world that still rooted itself firmly in a southern past. Wilson's image, like that of Jefferson Davis, was removed by the university to be displayed elsewhere. All six statues and the monumental fountain at the southern, curved end of the South Mall "horseshoe" were erected at Littlefield's behest in the 1920s. Most telling, perhaps, is the fact that they stood proudly, openly, and unchanged for almost a century.[16]

The fountain at the base of this South Mall, on the edge of campus closest to the capitol, still includes a wide pool into whose higher northern edge thrusts a three-dimensional representation of winged Victory in the prow of a ship named *Columbia*. On either side of Victory stand classically nude but modestly draped representations of a twentieth-century American soldier and American sailor. In addition to the name *Columbia*, the hull of the ship bears the inscription of April 6, 1917, the date of America's entry into World War I. And along the retaining wall on the western side of the fountain complex was carved a dedication of the entire South Mall diorama: "To the men and women of the Confederacy who fought with valor and suffered with fortitude that States Rights would be maintained and who not dismayed by defeat nor discouraged by misrule builded [sic] from the ruins of a devastating war a greater South and to the men and women of the nation who gave of their possessions and of their lives that free government be made secure to the peoples of the earth this memorial is dedicated—The gift of George W. Littlefield, soldier in the Confederate Army, leader in Texas industry, Regent of The University." That inscription, recently, has also been removed.

Littlefield had been appointed to the Board of Regents of the University of Texas by Gov. Oscar B. Colquitt in 1911. At the time, he was one of the richest, if not the richest, man in Texas. A confirmed southerner, Littlefield complained bitterly of the northern bias he perceived in American history textbooks used at the university. Eugene C. Barker, then the preeminent historian at the university, explained to Littlefield that the problem was that southerners had insufficient library resources to write their own story, so in 1914 Littlefield established a fund to collect such material. As a result of his personal generosity, Barker and others rewrote the textbooks used to educate southern Texas gentlemen about the history of their country, and the pantheon of stone erected in Littlefield's memory was a testament to his influence on the university and on the young leaders of the early twentieth century it produced. The statues are gone. The influence is contested.[17]

As the Gaineses strolled on through the spacious lobby of Littlefield's Driskill Hotel toward the modern elevator, they might well have taken note of the many volumes kept on the Driskill's well-stocked shelves for the use of its guests. In this twilight era after the invention of electric streetcars but before radio and movies, reading was still the primary means of polite distraction. That, at least, had not changed. Two books, immensely popular in their day, were *The Theory of the Leisure Class* and *Looking Backward*.[18]

Thorstein Veblen's *The Theory of the Leisure Class* caused an instant stir when it was published in 1899. Veblen was an academic economist from the Midwest. The thesis of his book was simple, and was perhaps the most direct indictment of what came to be called "the Gilded Age." It was Veblen who invented the term "conspicuous consumption." He employed it to describe the process by which the wealthy spend their money on "superfluities" in order to demonstrate their exalted position in society. Indeed, it is precisely the superfluous, even the ridiculously impractical, character of their purchases that *guarantees* the perception of their status. The more profligate the spending, the more powerful the spender must be. Veblen's theory would hardly have been of interest to Americans before the huge accumulations of wealth that industrialization, urbanization, and oligopoly made possible late in the nineteenth century.[19]

Looking Backward, published in 1888, was even better known than *Theory of the Leisure Class*. One of the bestsellers of its era, it sold ten thousand copies a week for several years. In it, author Edward Bellamy, through the literary device of a modern Rip Van Winkle, described the world as it might be in one hundred years. In Bellamy's story, the main character Julian West falls asleep in 1887, only to awaken in the year 2000, where he finds a world without poverty, crime, or hardship of any kind.[20]

In Bellamy's imaginary year 2000, the very economic restructuring demanded by American populists and radicals of the 1890s had already produced a brave new world, and the book was so powerful among these constituencies that it led directly to the formation of "Nationalist clubs" all over the country. In the novel, as Bellamy's futuristic Doctor Leete explains to the newly awakened Julian West, Gilded Age Americans had simply "concluded to assume the conduct of their own business, just as one hundred odd years before they had assumed the conduct of their own government, organizing now for industrial purposes on precisely the same grounds that they had then organized for political purposes." What they produced was a world with no violence, no greed, and no ambition beyond national service, which became "the sole and certain way to public repute, social distinction and official power."[21]

In Bellamy's book, this transformation of society had arisen from a general realization that more and more capital had been concentrated in the hands of fewer and fewer people. As Dr. Leete continues, "Before this concentration began ... the individual workman was relatively important and independent in his relations to the employer. Moreover, when a little capital or a new idea

Looking Backward

was enough to start a man in business for himself, workingmen were constantly becoming employers and there was no hard and fast line between the two classes. Labor unions were needless then." Once society realized that the idyllic past no longer existed, ever-increasing labor agitation inevitably caused the organization of a nationwide labor movement, which then forced corporations to cede business functions to the people (i.e., the government). The result was a socialist utopia based upon the equality and brotherhood of man.[22]

This alternative future was very much what extreme radicals desired, what other populists hinted at, what progressives sought to bypass, and what conservatives most feared. It never materialized. Looking backward as he led his wife into the elevator of the Driskill Hotel, Chief Justice Reuben R. Gaines could be satisfied that the Texas Supreme Court had modernized the traditional rule of law just enough to avert the coming of this particular alternative future, but not enough to disturb the powers that be.

But Reuben Gaines was not the only government official looking backward at the turn of the century. In 1898, Dudley Wooten, a Dallas politician whose father was chairman of the board of regents of the University of Texas, published *A Comprehensive History of Texas 1685–1897*. A substantial portion of this watershed work was written by O. M. Roberts, the founder of the same university. And Roberts himself had been trying to form a Texas state historical society as early as 1874. In this he sought the help of equally iconic participants in the events to be chronicled, John H. Reagan, Elisha M. Pease, and Rip Ford among them. Due to various personal conflicts and turf battles extending over two decades, this effort did not reach fruition until 1897, the year before the publication of Wooten's book. In that year, the Texas State Historical Association was finally founded by the chief historian at Roberts's University of Texas, George Garrison. Garrison enlisted Roberts as the society's first president and the draftsman of its first constitution, one that in a sense might be viewed as Texas' eighth and final constitution. And in accordance with venerable tradition, that written constitution was preceded by a "call" to convene. Like the one demanding the 1861 Secession Convention, this call was also signed first by O. M. Roberts, who by that time had come to be called by the nickname "the Old Alcalde" in a nod to Texas' Hispanic roots now so far removed and quaintly remembered as to no longer require alienation or derision. Roberts was joined as signatory of the historical society's "call" by Garrison, Wooten, John H. Reagan, former secessionist Governor F. R. Lubbock, and two others. Among the charter members of the organization are also to be found the names of Rip Ford, Judge Leroy Denman, Judge Robert Simonton Gould, Col. Edward M. House, and ex-Governor James Stephen Hogg.[23]

In Roberts's constitution passed "in convention" by those answering the call, the objects of the association were held to be "the promotion of historical studies, and, in particular, the discovery, collection, preservation, and publication of historical material, especially such as relates to Texas." Professor Garrison became the association's first paid director serving under a board of trustees. The history building at the University of Texas that once overlooked the statues of John Reagan and Big Jim Hogg still bears his name.

Soon the association began publishing a quarterly journal to be named the *Southwestern Historical Quarterly*. In its pages and throughout the cultural reach of its readership, the modern political identity of Texas was embellished with appropriate myth and legend of the type reflected in George Littlefield's monument to the Confederacy and Clara Driscoll's renovated Alamo. The tropes inhabiting this late-nineteenth-century world of imagination propagated far and wide: the libertarian colonels of the Alamo fighting a revolution to defend the republican ideals of the Mexican Constitution of 1824, the Indians of the plains requiring extermination as incomprehensible barbarians obstructing the progress of western civilization, a "War between the States" made necessary not by slavery but by the need to protect "states' rights," Reconstruction as the tyranny of federal big government, the small yeoman farmer as backbone of democracy even though his class was vanishing, and a ruling "progressive" yet segregationist coalition made necessary not as a response to white populist discontent but by the imperatives of economic development and modernization. Separating complicated fact from these simple legends remains the work of historians.

Appendix

Theoretical Constitutional History

This brief essay is for the purpose of spelling out in greater detail for graduate students and other specialists the historiography and scholarly conversations into which this book seeks to enter.

The term "constitutional moment" is not one coined by the author. It is a term associated with Bruce Ackerman's theory of "constitutional moments," set out in his 1991 book *We the People: Foundations*. The term is used here to refer not only to a written constitution but also to the other documents that accompany it and give it political content. Ackerman argued that societies "reconstitute" their foundations by political means that include drafting and ratifying written constitutions. That means that studying constitutions and the conventions that drafted them should yield important insights into the surrounding circumstances. Although this thesis may give pause to some historians, it generates little controversy within political science, where comparative constitutionalism is as old as Aristotle and continues to be refined by scholars like Gary Jacobsohn, who argues for his notion of "Constitutional Identity" in Aristotelian terms:

> We can specify the features of a constitution so that we can identify that document as a constitution when we see certain attributes incorporated in a particular legal document. These traits enable us at least tentatively to affirm the existence of a constitution before engaging in

further analysis of the content of any specific constitutional identity. The certification is similar to our recognition of a table after seeing something that conforms to the criteria applicable to that particular object. We may then go on further to establish particular identities related to the general type, as when we distinguish a dining room table from, say, a pool table.[1]

The fact that most constitutions fail to definitively resolve the internal political and social conflicts they address is no obstacle to discerning the cultural identity they enshrine. Indeed, this "constitutional disharmony," as Jacobsohn puts it, "is critical to the development of constitutional identity, even as it may make more challenging the task of establishing the specific substance of that identity at any given point in time." Rather, "a vital component of the disharmony of the constitutional condition consists of identifiable continuities of meaning within which dissonance and contradiction play out in the development of constitutional identity." Political identity is never completely static.[2]

My own usage of Jacobsohn's theory of constitutional identity and Ackerman's "constitutional moments" also borrows from the work of intellectual and cultural historians and from modern legal historical methods epitomized by Morton Horwitz, who pioneered the study of common law liability rules as markers of fundamental politico-economic policy choices. This book looks not just at Texas's constitutional texts, but also at other formal political pronouncements and, after the rapid expansion of the judicial branch and the legal profession in the 1880s, at the activities of the judges who interpreted these texts and supplemented them to create a constitutional-legal regime. These legal and constitutional artifacts shed new light on the worldview of the political elite that dominated Texas by the early twentieth century. Like many of the other new perspectives recently catalogued by Walter Buenger, Robert Calvert, and Arnoldo Deleon, looking at history and politico-cultural identity through a constitutional lens tends to complicate the conventional view of Texas history.[3]

Similarly, this book's premise that Texas should be understood as an imagined community, an identity produced by ideological consensus among economic, cultural, and legal elites, is not new. Rather, it is an understanding of nationhood and identity popularized by Benedict Anderson in his 1983 book *Imagined Communities: Reflections on the Origins and Spread of Nationalism*.[4]

"Otherness," or its French cognate precursor *alterité* follows the theories of Emmanuel Levinas, Michael Taussig, Edward Said, and others who have argued for decades that the way in which cultural identity is produced is by defining those who are outsiders.[5]

Since it seeks to apply these relatively recent scholarly insights to Texas History, this book falls within the new historiography epitomized by Buenger's and Calvert's 1991 anthology *Texas through Time*—scholars applying new lenses to what has been a tradition-laden subject, Texas history, and asking questions like "Why does the macho myth of Anglo still reign?" This revisionist move was chronicled further in Buenger's and Arnoldo De Leon's 2011 sequel, *Beyond Texas through Time*, which explored the continuing expansion of these new historical perspectives. *Six Constitutions* adds yet another new perspective on the history of the quasi-mythical nation-state that is Texas.[6] Even for nonspecialists, the recent revisionist move within Texas history has become well-known, from the political fight of the early 2020s over Alamo architecture to the controversial claim of a recent book that slavery was a primary motivation for Texas independence, and that the Alamo legend should be reappraised.[7] While it shares revisionism's mistrust of taking myths for facts (and, after all, history is inherently revisionist or we wouldn't keep writing it), *Six Constitutions* is not a polemic, it is a history. Like Thucydides's *History of the Peloponnesian War*, it seeks to "take the trouble to find out the truth" rather than "accept[ing] the first story" heard.

I agree with R. G. Collingwood that history is an interpretation of evidence in a reflective way for the purpose of self-knowledge, not just knowledge of the individual self, but of the whole of human nature or at least portions of it. Its method in so doing is to answer questions about what happened in the past. However, this does not deny the subjective and dialectic aspect of the process between historians and evidence. History is the *interpretation* of evidence, not the evidence itself. Thus history is fundamentally a process of the mind, an encounter between the ideas of the historian and those of the actors who left evidence of their actions. The test of the historian is how well he or she interacts with and understands the ideas of the past and how comprehensibly he or she explains them. From this interplay, we seek to answer questions.[8]

One of this book's many questions is: How does republicanism coexist with an exclusivist political or cultural identity? Finding an answer requires an exercise in "historical anthropology"—that is, an effort to reconstruct the thought-worlds of historical actors, and thus both their self-images and the myths and stories that resonated well enough with their contemporaries to make a difference. This is an approach associated with G. W. F. Hegel among others, such as Clifford Geertz, and more recently, with Rhys Isaac.[9] However, this is also what Seth Jacobs and others have called "ideological history," the type of inquiry anticipated by Hegel and more recently refined by David Brion Davis and Christopher Brown. As Jacobs wrote, "Ideas matter. They can drive people to murder or martyrdom." The contention here is that the extent to which ideas divide, compete, synthesize and/or impregnate one another is crucial to understanding political, legal, and cultural history.[10]

In showing how they do so, this book borrows not only from the modern legal studies methodology and from cultural historians, but also from the ideological history of scholars like Davis, Brown, and Hegel. It seeks to apply Hegel's theory of intellectual dialectic to nineteenth-century Texas—by asking how competing ideas created new syntheses that exploded existing equilibriums, creating new dominant paradigms and then a new set of elemental tensions. An example would be how politico-economic radicalism, white racism, and growing social Victorianism all came to infiltrate the populist imagination, ultimately synthesizing into progressivism. Compound *geists* like these, to borrow and modify Hegel's terminology, are refined over time, and among the most telling artifacts to be examined in such an intellectual archaeology are the laws and constitutions that people leave behind. That, in any event, is the theory of this book. At the beginning of the twentieth century, the political controversies within Texas began to change. The passage of the 1907 Robertson Insurance Act regulating the insurance business and the subsequent establishment of a workers' compensation system in 1913 mollified much of the sentiment for economic and labor reform, and the state's then-entrenched one-party politics soon divided along different lines: wet versus dry, racist pro-klan versus racist but anti-klan.[11]

Gary Jacobsohn's notion of "constitutional disharmony" applies this same Hegelian dialectic. Calling upon Alasdair MacIntyre's theories of tradition and social stability, Jacobsohn explains that "I draw upon Alasdair MacIntyre's analysis of tradition to consider constitutional identity as an artifact of the dissonance in a nation's divided inheritance. Tradition for MacIntyre is more than a source of societal stability . . . ; rightly conceived it embodies an adversarial component—'continuities of conflict'—that connects it to the historical narrative within which it unfolds."[12]

These continuities of conflict unfolded in Texas in unique ways. The cultural and ideological contest during the Texas Republic and early statehood involved slavery, filibustering in Mexico, and government policy towards the Indians of the frontier. Political identity was established by whether one was a "Houston man" or a member of the firebrand opposition with reference to these issues, which ultimately gave way to new imperatives that culminated in Kansas-Nebraska and Secession. As the focus shifted to Secession in the late 1850s, the anti-Houston party came to be led by Oran Milo Roberts, an educated but bigoted man who would later adopt the consciously Tejano nickname "The Old Alcalde." Ironically, one of Texas's premier racists sought to find a place among the venerated heroes of the revolutionary past by connecting his very name to their frontier Spanish milieu. For scholars conversant with the vicissitudes of *alterité*, Roberts's adoptive or "mimetic" behavior is curiously characteristic.[13]

The sociologist Georg Simmel further refined the *alterité* argument. Simmel explained that establishing identity and excluding outsiders involves what he called the phenomenon of "the stranger." The "stranger" crystallizes "the unity of nearness and remoteness involved in every human relation." The more permanent a stranger becomes, the more he stands out. If he is merely a trader who facilitates interaction between the resident culture and outsiders, he generates less resentment. If he chooses to stay, or worse attempts to influence broader society, his strangeness is amplified, producing a greater need for norms defining him (and his associates) as outré.[14]

Both history and sociology, then, teach that it is human nature for groups threatened with control, infiltration, or subversion by powerful or numerous neighbors to protect their collective identity by morally marginalizing them. The intensity of the response is proportionate to the proximity (culturally and geographically) of the stranger and the perceived precariousness of the indigenous culture's position. These phenomena are strikingly present in Texas history. Early on, less cultural capital is expended defining blacks as others than in defining Catholics, Mexicans, Tejanos, and northerners as such. More expenditure is required only when blacks become citizens, and thus more "like" their oppressors. Conversely, less marginalization of Mexican Catholics is required once any threat of Mexican political intervention recedes. Instead, the attention focused on them is transferred, in the main, to northerners who increasingly appear on the cultural landscape as the principal threat to the Anglo-Texan slave economy.

Six Constitutions, then, stands at the intersection of scholarly conversations ancient and postmodern, from Aristotle to Horwitz, Jacobsohn, and Ackerman; from Thucydides to Hegel, Said, and Geertz. As Oliver Wendell Holmes said, "when men have realized that time has upset many fighting faiths, they may come to believe even more than they believe the very foundations of their own conduct that the ultimate good desired is better reached by free trade in ideas—that the best test of truth is the power of the thought to get itself accepted in the competition of the market, and that truth is the only ground upon which their wishes safely can be carried out."[15]

May the market remain ever-free and the conversations continue.

Notes

Introduction

1. Bruce Ackerman, *We the People: Foundations* (Cambridge: Belknap Press, 1991).

2. Leading works on the sociology and anthropology of *alterité* include Emmanuel Levinas, *Entre Nous: Thinking of the Other*, trans. Michael B. Smith (New York: Columbia University Press, 2000); Emmanuel Levinas, *Totality and Being: An Essay on Exteriority*, trans. Alphonso Lingis (Pittsburgh: Duquesne University Press, 1969); Emmanuel Levinas, *Otherwise than Being or Beyond Essence*, trans. Alphonso Lingis (Ithaca: Cornell University Press, 1998); Michael Taussig, *Mimesis and Alterity* (New York: Routledge, 1993); Edward Said, *Orientalism* (New York: Knopf Publishing Group, 1979); Edward Said, *Culture and Imperialism* (New York: Knopf Publishing Group, 1994). For "constitutional moments," see Bruce Ackerman, *We the People: Foundations* (Cambridge: Belknap Press, 1991). Ackerman's thesis is the subject of some dispute. See, for example, Michael J. Klarman, "Constitutional Fact/Constitutional Fiction: A Critique of Bruce Ackerman's Theory of Constitutional Moments," *Stanford Law Review* 44, no. 3 (February 1992): 759–97; Walter Dean Burnham, "Constitutional Moments and Punctuated Equilibria: A Political Scientist Confronts *We the People*," *Yale Law Journal* 108, no. 8 (June 1999): 2237–77; Daniel Taylor Young, "How Do You Measure a Constitutional Moment? Using Algorithmic Topic Modeling to Evaluate Bruce Ackerman's Theory of Constitutional Change," *Yale Law Journal* 122, no. 7 (May 2013): 1990–2055. A cultural self-conception is a necessary prerequisite to Benedict Anderson's nation or *polis* as an

"imagined community." Benedict Anderson, *Imagined Communities: Reflections on the Origin and Spread of Nationalism* (New York: W. W. Norton & Co., 1983). See also Bernard Bailyn, *The Ideological Origins of the American Revolution* (Cambridge: Harvard University Press, 1967).

3. Bruce Ackerman, *We the People: Foundations* (Cambridge: Belknap Press, 1991). Ackerman's thesis is the subject of some dispute. See, for example, Michael J. Klarman, "Constitutional Fact/Constitutional Fiction: A Critique of Bruce Ackerman's Theory of Constitutional Moments," *Stanford Law Review* 44, no. 3 (February 1992): 759–97; Walter Dean Burnham, "Constitutional Moments and Punctuated Equilibria: A Political Scientist Confronts *We the People*," *Yale Law Journal* 108, no. 8 (Jun 1999): 2237–77; Daniel Taylor Young, "How Do You Measure a Constitutional Moment? Using Algorithmic Topic Modeling to Evaluate Bruce Ackerman's Theory of Constitutional Change," *Yale Law Journal* 122, no. 7 (May 2013): 1990–2055.

4. Benedict Anderson, *Imagined Communities: Reflections on the Origin and Spread of Nationalism* (New York: W. W. Norton & Co., 1983); Bernard Bailyn, *The Ideological Origins of the American Revolution* (Cambridge: Harvard University Press, 1967).

5. Benedict Anderson, *Imagined Communities: Reflections on the Origin and Spread of Nationalism* (New York: W. W. Norton & Co., 1983); Bernard Bailyn, *The Ideological Origins of the American Revolution* (Cambridge: Harvard University Press, 1967); Emmanuel Levinas, *Entre Nous: Thinking of the Other*, trans. Michael B. Smith (New York: Columbia University Press, 2000); Emmanuel Levinas, *Totality and Being: An Essay on Exteriority*, trans. Alphonso Lingis (Pittsburgh: Duquesne University Press, 1969); Emmanuel Levinas, *Otherwise than Being or Beyond Essence*, trans. Alphonso Lingis (Ithaca: Cornell University Press, 1998); Michael Taussig, *Mimesis and Alterity* (New York: Routledge, 1993); Edward Said, *Orientalism* (New York: Knopf Publishing Group, 1979); Edward Said, *Culture and Imperialism* (New York: Knopf Publishing Group, 1994). Recently, historians of colonial America have come to similar conclusions about fears of an axis of enemies composed of Natives and slaves, and the importance of using this anxiety to fuse together otherwise disparate factions into a political consensus. It now seems clear that exploiting fear of a British-inspired Indian/slave revolt was a crucial tool in unifying the American patriot movement. See Robert G. Parkinson, *The Common Cause: Creating Race and Nation in the American Revolution* (Chapel Hill: University of North Carolina Press, 2016).

6. Robert Olwell, *Masters, Slaves, and Subjects: The Culture of Power in the South Carolina Low Country, 1740–1790* (Ithaca: Cornell University Press, 1998), 276–78; Michael Craton, *Testing the Chains: Resistance to Slavery in the British West Indies* (Ithaca: Cornell University Press, 1982), 81. See also Ellen and James Reily to Anna Raguet, December 5, 1839. Irion Family Collection, Special Collections Division, University of Texas at Arlington Libraries, in which it is documented that even

as far northeast as Nacogdoches, Indian wars, relations with the Cherokee, and disturbances and rebellion fomented by the Mexicans, "formed the all-engrossing theme" of polite Anglo conversation. See also Curtis Chubb, "Revisiting the Purpose of the 1855 Callahan Expedition," *Southwestern Historical Quarterly* 121, no. 4 (April 2018): 417–29; Jeff Guinn, *Our Land Before We Die: The Proud Story of the Seminole Negro* (New York: J. P. Tar/Putnam, 2005); Kevin Mulroy, *Freedom on the Border: The Seminole Maroons in Florida, the Indian Territory, Coahuila, and Texas* (Lubbock: Texas Tech University Press, 1993).

7. Gary Gerstle, *American Crucible: Race and Nation in the 20th Century* (Princeton: Princeton University Press, 2001) argues that late-nineteenth and early-twentieth-century political history has been a clash between ideas of racial nationalism and civic nationalism, the former being characterized by nativist movements and politicians, and the latter by the two Roosevelts and their followers. Kristin Hogansen, *Fighting for American Manhood: How Gender Politics Provoked the Spanish-American and Philippine-American Wars* (New Haven: Yale University Press, 1998) claimed that gendered arguments and ideologies were used by imperialist Americans to justify the American intervention into Cuba and the Philippines in the late nineteenth century.

8. A nice example of the second component of this world view can be found in the novels of Ian Fleming, who, in his first, described the attitude of his hero James Bond, British Secret Service Agent 007, thusly: "Bond reflected that good Americans were fine people and that most of them seemed to come from Texas." Ian Fleming, *Casino Royale* (1952).

9. This heroic view of Texas History is epitomized by George Garrison, Eugene Barker, and Walter Prescott Webb, among others.

10. G. W. F. Hegel, *The Philosophy of History*; Hegel, *The Phenomenology of Mind*; David Brion Davis, *The Problem of Slavery in the Age of Revolution* (Ithaca: Cornell University Press, 1975); Christopher Brown, *Moral Capital: Foundations of British Abolitionism* (Chapel Hill: University of North Carolina Press, 2006); Seth Jacobs, *America's Miracle Man in Vietnam* (Durham: Duke University Press, 2004), 5 (quote).

11. The encounter with Roberts is described in the official Texas Supreme Court memoriam of him and must have been a well-known vignette. Alexander Terrell, former clerk of the court, claimed that Roberts personally related the incident to him within "only a few days after" it happened. A. W. Terrell, "In Memoriam: Proceedings Touching the Death of Hon. Oran M. Roberts, Late Chief Justice of the Supreme Court," 92 *Texas Reports* vii–viii (1898). Yet Roberts mentions it nowhere in his vast corpus of autobiographical writings. The only reference to any meeting with Hamilton in Washington in 1866 or 1867 is rather obtuse and can be found in O. M. Roberts, "The Experiences of an Unrecognized Senator," *Quarterly of the Texas State Historical Association* 12, no. 2 (October 1908): 100–101. He says only that "a week or two after getting to Washington," he met with A. J. Hamilton and had two

hours' conversation in the Senate anteroom at the capitol, "much of which was not very agreeable, though nothing disrespectful occurred on either side."

12. The "white man's government quote is reported in many sources, the most recent of which is William C. Yancey, "The Old Alcalde: Texas's Forgotten Fire-Eater" (PhD diss., University of North Texas, 2016), 168.

Prologue

1. William Fairfax Gray, *At the Birth of Texas: The Diary of William Fairfax Gray, 1835–1838* (Ingleside, TX: Copano Bay Press, 2015), 167–94. Proceedings of the Convention at Washington, March 10, 1836, in H. P. H. Gammel, "Journals of the Convention of the Free, Sovereign, and Independent People of Texas in General Convention Assembled," *The Laws of Texas 1822–1897*, vol. 1 (Austin: Gammel Book Co., 1898), 837, 900; Ralph W. Steen, "Convention of 1836," *Handbook of Texas Online* (Texas State Historical Association), accessed August 10, 2017, http://www.tshaonline.org/handbook/online/articles/mjc12; *Handbook of Texas Online*, "Carbajal, Jose Maria Jesus," accessed August 10, 2017, http://www.tshaonline.org/handbook/online/articles/fca45. Gray's diary lists "Incarnation Bascus" and "***Carbejal" as present on March 1, but the official journal lists neither as credentialed delegates on that date. See Gray, *At the Birth of Texas*, 167–68; 1836 Convention Journal, 824–25. Bascus has disappeared from the historical record, unless he may have been the General Bascus who led Mexican troops that invaded Texas a mere six years later, which seems unlikely. John Frost, *A History of Mexico and Its Wars* (A. Hawkins, 1882), 174, available via Google and accessed August 10, 2017, https://books.google.com/books?id=3zoTAAAAYAAJ&dq=general+bascus&source=gbs_navlinks_s. Carbajal was a prominent Tejano who had known Austin since the 1820s and had risen to prominence as a surveyor, urban planner, and politician. See Joseph W. McKnight, "Texas's Earliest Legislation and Its Publication," *Laws and Decrees of the State of Coahuila and Texas, in Spanish and English* (Clark, NJ: The Lawbook Exchange, 2010). For de Zavala, see Raymond Estep, "Lorenzo de Zavala and the Texas Revolution," *Southwestern Historical Quarterly* 57, no. 3 (January 1954): 322–35; Raymond Estep, "Zavala, Lorenzo De," in *Handbook of Texas Online* (Texas State Historical Association), accessed April 17, 2014, http://www.tshaonline.org/handbook/online/articles/fza05. The journal of the 1836 convention is available electronically through the Tarlton Law Library at the University of Texas and was accessed in this fashion at https://tarltonapps.law.utexas.edu/constitutions/texas1836/journals. Hereafter, citations to this journal will follow the form "1836 Convention Journal," followed by the page number as indicated in the printed Gammel edition.

2. See Eric Hobsbawm, *The Age of Revolution 1789–1848* (London: Weidenfeld and Nicolson, 1962); David Brion Davis, *The Problem of Slavery in the Age of Revolution* (Ithaca: Cornell University Press, 1975).

3. Popular media reflect myth as much as reality. Much of the historical truth is left unsaid. Stephen Austin's pacifism seldom appears in movies and stories, but the war in Texas, most particularly the Battle of the Alamo, has been the subject of at least five Hollywood productions, featuring a variety of stars from Fess Parker to John Wayne to Billy Bob Thornton. While movies, fiction, and myth depict revolutionary Texians fighting and dying for classical liberty at Goliad, the Alamo, and San Jacinto, none of these media has identified a deeper, less trumpeted motivation of the Anglo rebels, the perpetuation and expansion of slavery. The inherent insecurity of a social system built on oppression made fertile ground for fear of outside influences that might ignite a slave revolt. See *The Martyrs of the Alamo* directed by William "Cristy" Cabanne (Fine Arts Film Co., 1915); *Davy Crockett, King of the Wild Frontier* directed by Norman Foster and starring Fess Parker (Hollywood: Walt Disney, 1955); *The Alamo* directed by and starring John Wayne (Brackettville, Texas: John Wayne, 1960); *Gone to Texas* directed by Peter Levin (Brackettville, Texas: Friedgen Productions, 1986); *The Alamo: Thirteen Days of Glory* directed by Burt Kennedy (Brackettville, Texas: Briggle, Hennessey, Carrothers and Associates, 1987); and *The Alamo* directed by John Lee Hancock (Dripping Springs and Bastrop, TX: Touchstone Pictures, 2004). For an account of the news received from the Alamo, see William Fairfax Gray, *At the Birth of Texas*, 179–94.

4. Robert Bruce Blake, "Guerrero Decree," in *Handbook of Texas Online* (Texas State Historical Association), accessed October 2, 2015, https://tshaonline.org/hand-book/online/articles/ngg01; Campbell, *Empire for Slavery*, 35–36.

5. Paul D. Lack, "Slavery and the Texas Revolution," 183, quoting Eugene C. Barker, "The Influence of Slavery in the Colonization of Texas," *Southwestern Historical Quarterly* 28 (July 1924), 1, 2 (Barker quotation). See also Lester G. Bugbee, "Slavery in Early Texas, I & II," *The Laws of Slavery in Texas*, ed. Randolph B. Campbell (Austin: University of Texas Press, 2010), 21–50.

6. "Republic of Mexico Decree of April 6, 1830," *The Laws of Slavery in Texas*, ed. Randolph B. Campbell (Austin: University of Texas Press, 2010), 19. Paul Lack less stridently explained away the claims of contemporary antislavery men in terms of bias: "Antislavery zealots (too) quickly attributed the Texas Revolution to a proslavery conspiracy." Barker, Campbell, and Lack epitomize what has now become the conventional historiography on the subject: that Mexican and abolitionist contemporary accounts are not to be trusted, that the rhetoric of the Texian rebels themselves is fragmentary or exaggerated, and that slavery was merely a minor irritant in Texian/Mexican relations. Campbell acknowledged that "logic supported the interpretation of the Texas Revolution presented by Tornel and Anglo-American abolitionists like Benjamin Lundy and John Scoble," but nevertheless concluded that "protecting slavery was not the *primary cause* of the Texas revolution, but it was certainly a *major result*" (emphasis added). Randolph B. Campbell, *An Empire for*

Slavery, 36 (second quotation); Paul D. Lack, "Slavery in Texas," 183, citing Barker (first quotation).

7. Torget's book, the most recent work on the subject, argues for a stronger nexus between the slavery issue and revolution, even while acknowledging that "there was ... no single position on slavery within Mexico, setting off a series of fierce debates among Mexicans and Americans over the institution's future in Texas." Andrew J. Torget, *Seeds of Empire: Cotton, Slavery, and the Transformation of the Texas Borderlands, 1800–1850* (Chapel Hill: University of North Carolina Press, 2015), 8. In support of Torget's more modern view, see Sean Kelley, "'Mexico In His Head': Slavery and the Texas-Mexico Border, 1810–1860," *Journal of Social History* 37, no. 3 (spring 2004): 709–23; Sarah E. Cornell, "Citizens of Nowhere: Fugitive Slaves and Free African Americans in Mexico, 1833–1857," *Journal of American History* 100, no. 2 (2013): 351–74.

8. Manuel de Mier y Teran, *Texas by Teran: The Diary Kept by General Manuel Mier y Teran on His 1828 Inspection of Texas*, ed. Jack Jackson, trans. John Wheat (Austin: University of Texas Press, 2000), http://web.b.ebscohost.com.ezproxy.lib.utexas.edu/ehost/ebookviewer/ebook/bmxlYmtfXzEwOTkzNF9fQU41?sid=0c4e5294-25fa-4a91-84dd-dd64aa4ed4f0@sessionmgr113&vid=0&format=EB&lpid=lp_41&rid=0, accessed November 16, 2014, 96 (ignorant quote), 97–98 (diminishing Mexican influence); Margaret Swett Henson, "Mier Y Teran, Manuel De," *Handbook of Texas Online* (http://www.tshaonline.org/handbook/online/articles/fmi02), accessed November 16, 2014. Uploaded on June 15, 2010. Published by the Texas State Historical Association; Margaret Swett Henson, "Anahuac Disturbances," *Handbook of Texas Online* (http://www.tshaonline.org/handbook/online/articles/jca01), accessed November 16, 2014. Uploaded on June 9, 2010. Published by the Texas State Historical Association.

9. Manuel de Mier y Teran, *Texas by Teran: The Diary Kept by General Manuel Mier y Teran on His 1828 Inspection of Texas*, ed. Jack Jackson, trans. John Wheat (Austin: University of Texas Press, 2000), 98–100 (indented quote).

10. Manuel de Mier y Teran, *Texas by Teran: The Diary Kept by General Manuel Mier y Teran on His 1828 Inspection of Texas*, ed. Jack Jackson, trans. John Wheat (Austin: University of Texas Press, 2000), 104 (quote on immigration).

11. Margaret Swett Henson, "Mier Y Teran, Manuel De," *Handbook of Texas Online* (http://www.tshaonline.org/handbook/online/articles/fmi02), accessed November 16, 2014. Uploaded on June 15, 2010. Published by the Texas State Historical Association.

12. Randolph B. Campbell, *Gone to Texas, a History of the Lone Star State* (Oxford: Oxford University Press, 2003), 132–33. A recent *military* history of the revolution that therefore does not treat slavery in detail is Stephen Hardin, *Texian Iliad* (Austin: University of Texas Press, 1994). The most recent books again deal hardly at all with slavery as a cause of the revolution. See H. W. Brands, *Lone Star Nation: How a Rag-*

ged Army of Volunteers Won the Battle for Texas Independence and Changed America (New York: Doubleday & Co., 2004); and William C. Davis, *Lone Star Rising* (The Free Press, 2003). Davis describes slavery in Texas and includes slave perspectives, but neither book argues that slavery was a primary motivation in the Texian revolt.

13. Manuel de Mier y Teran, *Texas by Teran: The Diary Kept by General Manuel Mier y Teran on His 1828 Inspection of Texas*, ed. Jack Jackson, trans. John Wheat (Austin: University of Texas Press, 2000), http://web.b.ebscohost.com.ezproxy.lib.utexas.edu/ehost/ebookviewer/ebook/bmxlYmtfXzEwOTkzNF9fQU41?sid=0c4e5294-25fa-4a91-84dd-dd64aa4ed4f0@sessionmgr113&vid=0&format=EB&lpid=lp_41&rid=0, accessed November 16, 2014, 97–98 (diminishing Mexican influence and quotes about North Americans), 99 (quote on slavery). No less a legal historian as former Texas Supreme Court Justice and current US senator John Cornyn accepts the influence of proslavery sentiment on the Texas Revolution. As he put the matter in 1995, "Ideology probably played a secondary role to the desires of many colonists for fortune and cheap land. A desire to preserve the institution of slavery, a perpetual source of irritation that had been barely tolerated under Mexican dominion, was no doubt on the minds of many." John Cornyn, "The Roots of the Texas Constitution: Settlement to Statehood," *Texas Tech Law Review* 26 (1995), 1089, 1122.

14. Randolph Campbell, *An Empire for Slavery*, 36, 39. A putative reduction in Texas' slave population over a short period in the mid-1830s and a reduction in armed agitation over the same period are often cited as evidence that slavery had become only a tangential issue by the time of the 1835–36 revolt, but these calmer circumstances could just as easily have magnified Texians' *perception* of a threat to slavery from Mexican authorities when they reasserted abolitionist policies and central control in 1835. For example, while Texas admittedly enjoyed looser rule from the Coahuila state government from 1833 to 1834, it was Santa Anna's crackdown of 1835 that precipitated the revolt. What is important, but often left unsaid, is that most of these 1835–36 measures amounted to little more than the reinstitution and intensification of the central control that had precipitated sporadic proslavery violence in 1832. This begs the question of why such measures would produce armed revolt in 1836, but not earlier. Campbell is less sure and restated the relevant question thus: "Did a Mexican threat to slavery prompt the revolt? Did the revolutionaries ever indicate that the protection of slavery was a primary cause of their actions?"

15. Donald E. Chipman and Harriet Denise Joseph, *Spanish Texas, 1519–1821: Revised Edition* (Austin: University of Texas Press, 1992), 49.

16. Donald E. Chipman and Harriet Denise Joseph, *Spanish Texas, 1519–1821: Revised Edition* (Austin: University of Texas Press, 1992), 1, 23–43. Interestingly, de las Casas was one of the first Spaniards to bring African slaves to the Americas in an attempt to ameliorate the situation of the native population. See *The Catholic Encyclopedia Online*, accessed April 24, 2004, http://www.newadvent.org. For a thorough discussion of the debate between de las Casas and Gines de Sepulveda, see

Lewis Hanke, *All Mankind Is One: A Study of the Disputation Between Bartolome De Las Casas and Juan Gines De Sepulveda in 1550 on the Intellectual and Religious and Intellectual Capacity of the American Indians* (DeKalb, Illinois, Northern Illinois University Press, 1994). Andrew J. Torget, *Seeds of Empire: Cotton, Slavery, and the Transformation of the Texas Borderlands, 1800–1850,* 44–47, 52 (quotation).

17. Gilbert C. Din, *Spaniards, Planters, and Slaves: The Spanish Regulation of Slavery in Louisiana, 1763–1803* (College Station, TX: Texas A&M University Press, 1999), 43 (quotation).

18. Two theorists who are relevant to evaluating the ideological impact of the Spanish legal tradition are David Brion Davis and Richard Tuck. David Brion Davis, *The Problem of Slavery in the Age of Revolution 1770–1823* (Ithaca, NY: Cornell University Press, 1975); Richard Tuck, *Philosophy and Government 1572–1651* (Cambridge University Press, 1993); and Richard Tuck, *The Rights of War and Peace: Political Thought and the International Order From Grotius to Kant* (Oxford: Oxford University Press, 1999). Davis and Tuck agree that ideology is a makeweight justifying political action. Davis, the historian, argues that England came by its antislavery (more particularly its "antislave trade") ideology as a matter of political expediency resulting from the Napoleonic wars. Having already lost the vast majority of its slave-holding colonies in the Western Hemisphere, Great Britain came to have no significant economic interest in the perpetuation of slavery. However, it did have an interest in destabilizing Spanish-American plantation agriculture and the slave economies of French colonies such as Haiti. British legislation against the slave trade was used as a pretext for policing the Atlantic and Caribbean and for fomenting rebellion among blacks in the New World. English-speaking abolitionism slowly grew out of this policy imperative as an unintended consequence, although religious leaders like John Wesley, the founder of Methodism, had already set the stage by preaching against slavery as an immoral institution as early as the 1750s. For a variation on Davis's theme, see Christopher Leslie Brown, *Moral Capital: Foundations of British Abolitionism* (Chapel Hill: University of North Carolina Press, 2006). Tuck, the political scientist, traced the origin of disputes over the proper treatment of American Native populations and, by implication of slaves, to theological conflicts within the Catholic Church between humanists and Thomists dating back as early as the fifteenth century. While the details of Tuck's work cannot be fully treated here, what he demonstrated is a dichotomy within Western European political thought during the period from the sixteenth through the early nineteenth centuries over the issues of conquest, subjugation, and slavery. Humanism ultimately helped produce several strands of the Protestant Reformation in Western Europe and dominated the theological and political thinking of the churches and governments of England and the Netherlands. Thomistic scholasticism ultimately held sway within the Catholic world, including Spain, as a result of the ascendancy of the Jesuits and Dominicans within the Counter-Reformation of the sixteenth and seventeenth centuries.

In consequence, the international political order also divided along theological and ideological lines, and as Tuck claimed, the Dutch legalist Grotius, the English philosophers Hobbes and Locke, and others in the Protestant world "argued for an aggressive and interventionary foreign policy," in the humanist tradition. Tuck, *The Rights of War and Peace: Political Thought and the International Order from Grotius to Kant*, 23–27, 78–79, 158–65.

19. Randolph B. Campbell, *An Empire for Slavery*, 14. As Campbell relates: "Mexican independence raised questions about slavery because Mexican revolutionaries had always voiced strong opposition to the institution. Father Miguel Hidalgo, the first leader of the revolt against Spain, issued several decrees in late 1810 demanding immediate manumission of all slaves on pain of death. And Jose Maria Morelos' 'Sentimientos de la Nacion' of September 14, 1813, proclaimed that 'slavery is forbidden forever.'" Andrew J. Torget, *Seeds of Empire: Cotton, Slavery, and the Transformation of the Texas Borderlands, 1800–1850*, 60, argues that Austin and the *Tejano* leadership in Texas were uniform in wanting slavery perpetuated in Texas and in lobbying Mexican officials to allow it.

20. Paul D. Lack, "Slavery and the Texas Revolution," 183–87; Randolph B. Campbell, *An Empire for Slavery*, 14–29. See also Eugene C. Barker, *The Life of Stephen F. Austin Founder of Texas 1793–1836* (Austin: Texas State Historical Association, 1949), 201–24. See also Lester G. Bugbee, "Slavery in Early Texas, I & II," *The Laws of Slavery in Texas*, ed. Randolph B. Campbell (Austin: University of Texas Press, 2010), 21–50. Writing in 1898, Bugbee argued, for example, that after the 1827 Coahuila-Texas constitution outlawed slavery, a decree of the state Congress of Coahuila-Texas Congress the following year that validated indentured service contracts yielded the necessary conclusion that the state government "after a harmless salvo in honor of abstract principles, quietly solved the practical difficulty by a decree which was intended to reopen Texas to negro bondage, now disguised under the more pleasing name of contract labor." Bugbee, "Slavery in Early Texas, I & II," 35.

21. Barker, *The Life of Stephen F. Austin*, 225–26.

22. William Ransom Hogan, *The Texas Republic: A Social and Economic History* (Norman: University of Oklahoma Press, 1946), 191–223.

23. See the "Texas Declaration of Independence," reprinted in William Carey Crane, *The Life and Select Literary Remains of Sam Houston of Texas*, 1885 reprint ed. (Philadelphia: J. B. Lippincott and Co., 1885 [orig. 1884]), 264–66. (All page citations are to the reprint edition.) Crane's book includes an appendix containing not only some of Houston's writings but also a copy of the *Texas Declaration of Independence* and other primary source material.

24. *The Laws of Slavery in Texas*, ed. Randolph B. Campbell (Austin: University of Texas Press, 2010), 8–9, 12–13; Sherie Marie Schuck-Hall, "Borderlands and Identities in Imperial Texas: The Alabamas and Coushattas in the Anti-Comanche Union, 1820–1840," *The International History Review* 25, no. 3 (September 2003):

563, 574–75, online version, accessed October 9, 2014, http://www.jstor.org/stable/40109399; Campbell, *An Empire for Slavery*, 15–17; Barker, *The Life of Stephen F. Austin*, 202–3.

25. Campbell, *An Empire for Slavery*, 19–22.

26. *The Laws of Slavery in Texas*, ed. Randolph B. Campbell (Austin: University of Texas Press, 2010), 27; Titles I–IV, "Federal Constitution of the United Mexican States (1824)," in *Texas Constitutions 1824–1876* (Austin: Tarlton Law Library, Jamail Center for Legal Research at the University of Texas School of Law), electronic version, accessed July 7, 2018, http://tarlton.law.utexas.edu/c.php?g=813224&p=5802557. Further references to this document will follow the form: "1824 Constitution, Title __, Article __."

27. 1824 Constitution, Title V, Articles 125–38, 140–44.

28. 1824 Constitution, Title V, Article 148–53; Miguel Gonzales Oropeza and Jesus F. de la Teja, *Actas del Congreso Constituyente de Coahuila y Texas de 1824 a 1827: Primera Contitucio Bilingue* (Mexico: Tribunal Electoral del Poder Judicial de la Federacion: 2016), 16.

29. 1824 Constitution, Title VI, Articles 157–61, Oropeza and de la Teja, *Actas del Congreso Constituyente de Coahuila y Texas de 1824 a 1827: Primera Contitucio Bilingue* (Mexico: Tribunal Electoral del Poder Judicial de la Federacion: 2016), 23, 165–66; *The Laws of Slavery*, 27–30.

30. "Constitution of Coahuila and Texas Article 13," Oropeza and de la Teja, *Actas del Congreso Constituyente de Coahuila y Texas de 1824 a 1827*, 165–66, 228; *Texas Slavery Laws*, 14; Campbell, *An Empire for Slavery*, 19–22. Further references to the 1827 state constitution as found in Oropeza and de la Teja will follow the form: 1827 Constitution, Article __.

31. 1827 Constitution, Articles 2, 11, 12, 18, and 22; Oropeza and de la Teja, *Actas del Congreso Constituyente de Coahuila y Texas de 1824 a 1827*, 17.

32. Campbell, "State of Coahuila and Texas Decree No. 56," *Texas Slavery Laws*, 18.

33. Lester G. Bugbee, "Slavery in Early Texas, II," *The Laws of Slavery in Texas*, ed. Randolph B. Campbell (Austin: University of Texas Press, 2010), 38–43; Campbell, *An Empire for Slavery*, 25–26; Barker, *The Life of Stephen F. Austin*, 213–14.

34. Bugbee, "Slavery in Early Texas, II," 38–39; Barker, *The Life of Stephen F. Austin*, 215–16; Campbell, *An Empire for Slavery*, 25–26; Durst to Austin 10 November 1829, in ed. Eugene C. Barker, *Annual Report of the American Historical Association for the Year 1922, in Two Volumes and a Supplemental Volume*, vol. 2, *The Austin Papers* (Washington, DC: Government Printing Office, 1928), 280–87 (first quote); Austin to Durst 17 November 1829, in ed. Barker, *Annual Report of the American Historical Association for the Year 1922*, 288–89 (second quote). The multivolume set of Austin's papers are located in the Texas A&M University Special Archives. The volumes were published serially. The first volume was published in 1924 as an annual report of the American Historical Association for 1919. It covers documents from 1789 through

1827. The volume referenced here contains the Austin correspondence from 1828 to 1834. Correspondence after September 1834 appears in Eugene C. Barker, ed., *The Austin Papers October 1834-January 1837* (Austin: University of Texas Press, 1926). Further references to this collection will identify the date and participants, followed by the shortened designation *Austin Papers*.

35. For Barker's quotation from this letter (without emphasis), see Barker, *The Life of Stephen F. Austin*, 215. It is surprising that Barker's analysis of this letter in *The Life of Stephen F. Austin* ignores the emphasis on the word "all" in the original. Yet failure to notice such details can often lead to misinterpretation. Indeed, this particular elision may account for much confusion over the meaning of the statements later made by Austin and other Texian leaders.

36. Robert Bruce Blake, "Guerrero Decree," in *Handbook of Texas Online* (Texas State Historical Association), accessed October 2, 2015, https://tshaonline.org/handbook/online/articles/ngg01; Campbell, *An Empire for Slavery*, 25–26; Barker, *The Life of Stephen F. Austin*, 213–16.

37. Even Austin's admiring biographer Barker acknowledged that "the legal status of slavery in Texas . . . probably caused Austin more anxiety during the early years of the colony than any other . . . Austin's own views of slavery underwent several changes. Until 1830 he thought it indispensable to the rapid progress of Texas and exerted himself to safeguard it." As for the proslavery declaration of 1832 mentioned below, Barker claimed that it occurred "probably during the convention of October, though it does not appear in the journal—and thereafter Austin reluctantly but finally accepted the inevitable and returned to the earlier doctrine that Texas must be a slave state." Barker, *The Life of Stephen F. Austin*, 201–2.

38. Paul Lack, for example, has argued that the state legislature's crackdown on indentured servitude "helped spur a movement in Texas for separate statehood that originated in that year." Lack, "Slavery and the Texas Revolution," 184–86; Campbell, *An Empire for Slavery*, 27.

39. Barker, *The Life of Stephen F. Austin*, 220.

40. Campbell, *An Empire for Slavery*, 29, 36–38; Margaret Swett Henson, *Juan Davis Bradburn a Reappraisal of the Mexican Commander of Anahuac* (College Station: Texas A&M University Press, 1982), 94–95 (quote), 104–9 (events of 1832 in Anahuac). See also James L. Haley, *The Texas Supreme Court* (Austin: University of Texas Press, 2013), 13, and n. 33; and Edna Rowe, "The Disturbances at Anahuac in 1832," *Quarterly of the Texas State Historical Ass'n* 6, no. 4 (April 1903): 265–99. Haley seems to argue that slavery was only an instigator of these riots as an instance or example of a "general distaste for taxation" that predisposed Texians to protest the installation of Bradburn as collector of port duties at Anahuac. He describes Rowe's as a "traditional account of the disturbances" and Henson's as "highly revisionist." If by this he means to imply that Rowe was closer to the true causes of the conflict than Henson, I disagree.

41. Andrew Torget, *Seeds of Empire: Cotton, Slavery, and the Transformation of the Texas Borderlands, 1800–1850*, 44 (quotation), 48 (Austin and Kirkham).

42. Margaret Swett Henson, *Juan Davis Bradburn A Reappraisal of the Mexican Commander of Anahuac*, 132–34 (citing Bradburn report on the need to watch for slave smuggling and early rumors of revolt), 137–38 (quoting Bradburn on the fugitive slaves and their role in bringing about his ouster). An interesting Mexican account of the Anahuac disturbances can be found in Vicente Filisola, *Memoirs for The History of the War in Texas*, trans. Wallace Woolsey (Austin: Eakin Press, 1985), 72–123.

43. Stephen Austin, Address to the Convention, April 1, 1833, in *Austin Papers*, 934.

44. Campbell, *An Empire for Slavery*, 38.

45. "Constitution or Form of Government of the State of Texas (1833)," in *Texas Constitutions 1824–1876* (Austin: Tarlton Law Library, Jamail Center for Legal Research at the University of Texas School of Law), electronic version, accessed October 11, 2008, http://tarlton.law.utexas.edu/constitutions/text/cah3gp.html; Barker, *The Life of Stephen F. Austin*, 223–24; Campbell, *An Empire for Slavery*, 38; Austin to Henry Austin, April 9, 1833, in *Austin Papers*, 953; Austin to Wiley Martin, May 30, 1833, in *Austin Papers*, 981.

46. Barker, *The Life of Stephen F. Austin*, 370–94; Jesus F. de la Teja, ed., *A Revolution Remembered: The Memoirs and Selected Correspondence of Juan N. Seguin*, 20–24, 129–32; Sherie Marie Schuck-Hall, "Borderlands and Identities in Imperial Texas: The Alabamas and Coushattas in the Anti-Comanche Union, 1820–1840," *International History Review* 25, no. 3 (September 2003): 563, 577–78, online version, accessed October 9, 2014, http://www.jstor.org/stable/40109399, citing Tenorio to Perfecto de Cos April 9, 1835, in *Military Papers of the Texas Revolution 1835–6*, ed., J. H. Jenkins (Austin: 1973).

47. Schuck-Hall, "Borderlands and Identities in Imperial Texas"; Barker, *The Life of Stephen F. Austin*, 356–409.

48. Campbell, *An Empire for Slavery*, 39–41; Lack, "Slavery and The Texas Revolution," 187.

49. William B. Travis to David G. Burnet, February 6, 1835, in John Jenkins, ed., *The Papers of the Texas Revolution, 1835–1836*, vol. 1 (Austin: Presidial Press, 1973), 100 (first quote). Travis to Burnet, May 21, 1835, in Jenkins, ed., *The Papers of the Texas Revolution, 1835–1836*, vol. 1, 121–22 (indented quote).

50. Ben Milam to Francis Johnson, July 5, 1835, *Austin Papers 1834–1837*, 83 (first quote); Matagorda Safety Committee Resolutions of 1835, *Austin Papers 1834–1837*, 143.

Chapter 1

1. Barker, *The Life of Stephen F. Austin*, 408–20; Mary Whatley Clarke, *David G. Burnet* (Austin: Pemberton Press, 1969), 50–52; William Barrett Travis to David G. Burnet, May 21, 1835, in John Jenkins, ed., *The Papers of the Texas Revolution, 1835–1836*, vol. 1 (Austin: Presidial Press, 1973), 121–22 (quote).

2. Ben H. Procter, "Texas Rangers," in *Handbook of Texas Online* (Texas State Historical Association), accessed September 6, 2014, http://www.tshaonline.org/handbook/online/articles/met04; Paul D. Lack, "Consultation," in *Handbook of Texas Online* (Texas State Historical Association), accessed September 6, 2014, and August 5, 2018, http://www.tshaonline.org/handbook/online/articles/mjc08; 1836 Convention Journal, 823.

3. Stephen F. Austin to David G. Burnet, January 1836, in John Jenkins, ed., *The Papers of the Texas Revolution, 1835–1836*, vol. 1 (Austin: Presidial Press, 1973), 100.

4. Barker, *The Life of Stephen F. Austin*, 348–51; Barker, *The Life of Stephen F. Austin*, 350 (1832 petition quote); Stephen John Hartnett, *Democratic Dissent and the Cultural Fictions of Antebellum America* (Urbana: University of Illinois, 2002), 47–49; James David Miller, *South by Southwest: Planter Emigration and Identity in the Slave South* (Charlottesville: University of Virginia Press, 2002), 56–57.

5. Barker, *The Life of Stephen F. Austin*, 360–64; Randolph B. Campbell, *An Empire for Slavery*, 38, 46; "Journal of the Convention (1833)," in *Austin Papers*, 941–42.

6. Mary Whatley Clarke, *David G. Burnet*, 62; John Quincy Adams, *Speech of John Quincy Adams of Massachusetts . . . Relating to the Annexation of Texas to This Union Delivered in the House of Representatives of the United States, in Fragments of the Morning Hour, from the 16th of June to the 7th of July, Inclusive* (Washington, DC: Gales and Seaton, 1838), electronic copy at the John Quincy Adams Library at the Boston Public Library, accessed August 27, 2013, http://archive.org/details/speechofjohnquin00adam; John Quincy Adams, *Address of John Quincy Adams to His Constituents of the Twelfth Congressional District at Braintree, September 17, 1842* (Boston: J. H. Eastburn, 1842).

7. Anson Jones, *Memoranda and Official Correspondence Relating to the Republic of Texas, Its History and Annexation* (Chicago: Rio Grande Press, 1859; republished by the Texas State Historical Survey Committee, 1966).

8. Lack, *Slavery and the Texas Revolution*, 187; Frances W. Johnson to William Martin, May 6, 1835, in John H. Jenkins, ed., *The Papers of the Texas Revolution, 1835–1836*, vol. 1 (Austin: Presidial Press, 1973), 100; William B. Travis to Burnett, May 21, 1835, in Jenkins, ed., *The Papers of the Texas Revolution, 1835–1836*, vol. 1, 122 (Travis quote).

9. R. M. Williamson, Address of June 22, 1835, in Jenkins, ed., *The Papers of the Texas Revolution, 1835–1836*, vol. 1, 199.

10. William H. Wharton, "Texas: A Brief Account of the Origin, Progress and Present State of the Colonial Settlements of Texas Together with an Exposition of the Causes Which Have Induced the Existing War With Mexico," in Jenkins, ed., *The Papers of the Texas Revolution, 1835–1836*, vol. 9, 240.

11. William Fairfax Gray, *At the Birth of Texas: The Diary of William Fairfax Gray, 1835–1838* (Ingleside, TX: Copano Bay Press, 2015), 167–69; 1836 Convention Journal, 823–38; Rupert Richardson, "Framing the Constitution of the Republic of Texas," *Southwestern Historical Quarterly* 31, no. 3 (Texas State Historical Association, 1928),

192–93; William Carey Crane, *The Life and Select Literary Remains of Sam Houston of Texas* (Philadelphia: J. B. Lippincott and Co., 1885), 264–66. Crane's book includes an appendix containing not only some of Houston's writings but also a copy of the *Texas Declaration of Independence* and other primary source material. Digital versions of the documents are available at *Texas Constitutions 1824–1876* (Tarlton Law Library, Jamail Center for Legal Research at the University of Texas School of Law), http://tarlton.law.utexas.edu/constitutions/text/cah3gp.html.

12. *1836 Convention Journal*, 900. General Provisions, Section 9, "Constitution of the Republic of Texas (1836)," in *Texas Constitutions 1824–1876* (Tarlton Law Library, Jamail Center for Legal Research at the University of Texas School of Law), electronic version, accessed October 11, 2008, http://tarlton.law.utexas.edu/constitutions/text/cah3gp.html; Randolph B. Campbell, *An Empire for Slavery*, 47. Further citation to the 1836 Constitution will follow the form Constitution of the Republic of Texas (1836), Article __, Section __.

13. Report Concerning the African Slave Trade, Proceedings of the Convention at Washington, March 15, 1836, in H. P. H. Gammel, ed., "Journals of the Convention of the Free, Sovereign, and Independent People of Texas in General Convention Assembled," *The Laws of Texas 1822–1897*, vol. 1 (Austin: Gammel Book Co., 1898), 896.

14. National Archives, "Struggles over Slavery: the Gag Rule," https://www.archives.gov/exhibits/treasures_of_congress/text/page10_text.html#:~:text=In%20May%20of%201836%20the,rule%20passed%20in%20succeeding%20Congresses.&text=In%201844%20the%20House%20rescinded,made%20by%20John%20Quincy%20Adams (accessed July 9, 2021).

15. "Declaration of Independence by the Republic of Texas, 1836," in *Texas Constitutions 1824–1876* (Tarlton Law Library, Jamail Center for Legal Research at the University of Texas School of Law), accessed October 11, 2008, http://tarlton.law.utexas.edu/constitutions/text/cah3gp.html.

16. "Declaration of Independence by the Republic of Texas, 1836," in *Texas Constitutions 1824–1876*, accessed October 11, 2008, http://tarlton.law.utexas.edu/constitutions/text/cah3gp.html.

17. "Declaration of Independence by the Republic of Texas, 1836," in *Texas Constitutions 1824–1876*, accessed October 11, 2008, http://tarlton.law.utexas.edu/constitutions/text/cah3gp.html.

18. *Constitution of the Republic of Texas* (1836) (first quote); Proceedings of the Convention at Washington, March 10, 1836, in H. P. H. Gammel, "Journals of the Convention of the Free, Sovereign, and Independent People of Texas in General Convention Assembled," *The Laws of Texas 1822–1897*, vol. 1 (Austin: Gammel Book Co., 1898), 896 (second quote); Gerald W. Mullin, *Flight and Rebellion: Slave Resistance in 18th Century Virginia* (New York: Oxford University Press, 1972), 160–64; Robert Olwell, *Masters, Slaves, and Subjects: The Culture of Power in the South Carolina Low*

Country, 1740–1790 (Ithaca: Cornell University Press, 1998), 276–79. In revolutionary Texas, Ben Milam had already made the explicit connection as cited previously. See Ben Milam to Francis Johnson, July 5, 1835, *Austin Papers 1834–1837*, 83.

19. Gary Clayton Anderson, *The Conquest of Texas: Ethnic Cleansing in the Promised Land, 1820–1875* (Norman: University of Oklahoma Press, 2005),76–79.

20. Anderson, *The Conquest of Texas*, 108–25. See the Alamo website, "The Alamo: History: Myths and Misconceptions," accessed November 3, 2008, http://www.thealamo.org/myths.html.

21. *1836 Convention Journal*, 829, 832 (committee of the whole references), 834 (Constitution "for Texas" and committee appointments), 839–41 (additions to committee, Rangers, flag resolution), 843–44 (Houston made commander).

22. *Handbook of Texas Online*, Joe E. Ericson, "Collinsworth, James," accessed August 8, 2018, http://www.tshaonline.org/handbook/online/articles/fco97; Rupert Richardson, "Framing the Constitution of the Republic of Texas," 195–96; *Handbook of Texas Online*, Joe E. Ericson, "Potter, Robert," accessed August 8, 2018, http://www.tshaonline.org/handbook/online/articles/fpo31; *Handbook of Texas Online*, Joe E. Ericson, "Childress, George Campbell," accessed August 8, 2018, http://www.tshaonline.org/handbook/online/articles/fch28; *Handbook of Texas Online*, Ingrid Broughton Morris and Deolece M. Parmelee, "Gaines, James Taylor," accessed August 8, 2018, http://www.tshaonline.org/handbook/online/articles/fgao4; *Handbook of Texas Online*, David M. Vigness, "Fisher, William S.," accessed August 8, 2018, http://www.tshaonline.org/handbook/online/articles/ffi24; *Handbook of Texas Online*, Mrs. Patrick H. Welder, "Power, James," accessed August 8, 2018, http://www.tshaonline.org/handbook/online/articles/fpo36; *1836 Convention Journal*, 847–48 (Potter and the military committee).

23. Rupert Richardson, "Framing the Constitution of the Republic of Texas," 198–204; *1836 Convention Journal*, 854–59; William Fairfax Gray, *At the Birth of Texas: The Diary of William Fairfax Gray, 1835–1838*, 169, 171 (embarrassment of Council and Smith in disarray), 175 (number of officers), 174–75 (long tedious debates over land titles and "much log rolling").

24. Gray, *At the Birth of Texas*, 173–74 (Smith behind the bar). Gray also claimed that Lorenzo de Zavala was chair of the subcommittee on the executive article but gives no other names for any of the subcommittee members or chairs. Gray, *At the Birth of Texas*, 170, 173 (constitution report and de Zavala), 180–82 ("boyish" and "disgusted" quotes), and 184 (adjournment and dispersal). See also Rupert Richardson, "Framing the Constitution of the Republic of Texas," 198.

25. *1836 Convention Journal*, 859–74 (March 9 report); *Constitution of the Republic of Texas* (1836); Rupert Richardson, "Framing the Constitution of the Republic of Texas," 205–7 (land question). Rusk and Collinsworth were prominent lawyers who were among the first justices of the Texas Supreme Court, and they possessed two

of the most voluminous law libraries in early Texas. See John Cornyn, "The Roots of the Texas Constitution: Settlement to Statehood," *Texas Tech Law Review* 26 (1995): 1089, 1116.

26. Richardson, "Framing the Constitution of the Republic of Texas" 205–7 (the land question); Gray, *At the Birth of Texas*, 173–86, 176 ("business drags" quote), 183 (loan quotes).

27. Rupert Richardson, "Framing the Constitution of the Republic of Texas," 206; *Constitution of the Republic of Texas* (1836), "General Provisions," Section 10.

28. *1836 Convention Journal*, 860 (voting and senatorial districts), 870 (immigrant restrictions); *Constitution of the Republic of Texas* (1836), "General Provisions," Section 10 (definition of citizenship), Article I, Section 7 (final definition of senatorial districts); "General Provisions," Section 9 (prohibition on free Africans).

29. Cornyn says that "the Constitution of the Republic was a composite of the United States Constitution and that of several southern states, although no one single state constitution appears to have been the model." John Cornyn, "The Roots of the Texas Constitution: Settlement to Statehood," *Texas Tech Law Review* 26 (1995): 1089, 1122. Richardson says that "the constitution of the Republic of Texas is a composite structure of portions of the constitutions of the United States and of several of the state constitutions in effect at the time," and the idea that "free negroes and Indians are not to be counted in determining apportionment in congress, may have been taken from any one of the several southern state constitutions," and the plan followed for the judiciary was "commonly in use in the southern and western states." In support of this, he cites the constitutions of Tennessee, South Carolina, Arkansas, Alabama, Missouri, and North Carolina. Rupert Richardson, "Framing the Constitution of the Republic of Texas," 209–10, 212. For an interesting study of Texian identity formation during the period of the revolution and republic, see Andrea Kokeny, "The Construction of Anglo-American Identity in the Republic of Texas as Reflected in the 'Telegraph and Texas Register,'" *Journal of the Southwest* 46, no. 2, (summer 2004): 283–308.

30. For the survival unscathed of the open courts provision, see *LeCroy v. Hanlon*, 713 S.W.2d 335, 339 (Tex. 1986).

31. *Constitution of the Republic of Texas (1836)*, Article I (powers of government), Article II (Congress), Article III (executive), Article IV (judicial branch), Article: General Provisions, Section 9 (slavery), Article I, Section 25 (prohibition on private subsidies), Article: Declaration of Rights, Section 17 (monopolies), Article V, Section 1 (prohibition on clerical office holding); Hogan, *The Texas Republic: A Social and Economic History*, 194–95.

32. Richardson, writing almost one hundred years ago, completely missed the significance of what he seems to have admitted to be the main oddity in the declaration of rights, the prohibition on clerical office-holding. He described the provision as

"sandwiched in with little purpose." Rupert Richardson, "Framing the Constitution of the Republic of Texas," 213. This is why historians keep rewriting history: because prior works and insights are never complete and need revision based upon new information and new perspectives.

33. Proceedings of the Convention at Washington, March 10, 1836, in H. P. H. Gammel, "Journals of the Convention of the Free, Sovereign, and Independent People of Texas in General Convention Assembled," *The Laws of Texas 1822–1897*, vol. 1 (Austin: Gammel Book Co., 1898), 875.

Chapter 2

1. T. R. Fehrenbach, *Lone Star: A History of Texas and the Texans* (New York: Macmillan Co., 1968), 452.

2. Ronald Takaki, *A Different Mirror: A History of Multi-Cultural America* (Boston: Back Bay Books, 1993), 184–90; David Montejano, *Anglos and Mexicans in the Making of Texas: 1836–1900* (Austin: University of Texas Press, 1987), 1–100. Jesus F. de la Teja, *A Revolution Remembered: The Memoirs and Correspondence of Juan N Seguin*, viii. In the case of Seguin, de la Teja describes him after the revolution as "betrayed. Having defended the land of his birth against Mexico City, he was subsequently confronted by newcomers who treated him as an alien in Texas." De la Teja emphasizes the common interests and experiences of Tejanos and Texians in Jesus F. de la Teja, "Discovering the Tejano Community in 'Early' Texas," *Journal of the Early Republic* 18, no. 1 (spring 1998): 73–98, and this is a unique and enlightening approach to remedying the oversimplification of Tejano society, but I do not regard it as a denial of Montejano's argument or my thesis here about prejudice against Tejanos.

3. Randolph B. Campbell, *Gone to Texas*, 160; Sam W. Haynes, *Soldiers of Misfortune: The Somervell and Mier Expeditions* (Austin: University of Texas Press, 1990), 169; Stanley Siegel, *A Political History of The Texas Republic, 1836–1845* (Austin: University of Texas Press, 1956), 40–41; Joseph M. Nance, *After San Jacinto: The Texas-Mexican Frontier, 1836–1841* (Austin: University of Texas Press, 1963), 45–67; Samuel Augustus Mitchell and James H. Young, *A New Map of Texas, with the Contiguous American and Mexican States* (Philadelphia: James H. Mitchell, 1836). David Rumsey Historical Map Collection, accessed 15 August 2013, http://www.davidrumsey.com/luna/servlet/detail/RUMSEY~8~1~216~20055:A-New-Map-Of-Texas,-With-The-Contig.

4. Stanley Siegel, *The Poet President of Texas: Mirabeau B. Lamar* (Austin: Jenkins Publishing Co., 1977), 51–90; Stanley Siegel, *A Political History of The Texas Republic, 1836–1845* (Austin: University of Texas Press, 1956), 100–36, 173; Campbell, *Gone to Texas*, 160.

5. Campbell, *Gone to Texas*, 161; Siegel, *A Political History of the Texas Republic, 1836–1845*, 76–91; Mary Bell Hart, "Preface," *Journals of the Convention Assembled*

at the City of Austin on the 4th of July 1845 for the Purpose of Framing a Constitution for the State of Texas, facsimile reprod. of 1845 ed. (Austin: Shoal Creek Publishers, 1974), ii.

6. Sam Houston, "Inaugural Address as President of the Republic of Texas, Delivered before the Texan Congress," in William Carey Crane, *Life and Select Literary Remains of Sam Houston of Texas* (Philadelphia, J. B. Lippincott, 1885), 279.

7. Benjamin Lundy, *The War in Texas: A Review of Facts and Circumstances, Showing That the Contest is the Result of a Long Premeditated Crusade against the Government, Set on Foot by Slaveholders, Land Speculators, etc. with a View of Re-establishing, Extending, and Perpetuating the System of Slavery and the Slave Trade in the Republic of Mexico* (Philadelphia: Merrihew and Gunn, 1836); John Quincy Adams, *Speech of John Quincy Adams of Massachusetts . . . Relating to the Annexation of Texas to This Union Delivered in the House of Representatives of the United States, in Fragments of the Morning Hour, from the 16th of June to the 7th of July, Inclusive* (Washington, DC: Gales and Seaton, 1838), electronic copy at the John Quincy Adams Library at the Boston Public Library, accessed August 27, 2013, http://archive.org/details/speechofjohnquin00adam; Campbell, *Gone to Texas*, 162–63; Siegel, *A Political History of The Texas Republic, 1836–1845*, 76–105. See also John Quincy Adams, *Address of John Quincy Adams to His Constituents of the Twelfth Congressional District at Braintree, September 17, 1842* (Boston: J. H. Eastburn, 1842).

8. Britain was hesitant to disturb its lucrative trade relations with the Mexicans and, because it had just abolished slavery in 1833, was reluctant to approve of it when practiced by others. However, the chaotic political situation in Mexico (which would soon return Santa Anna to power) convinced British merchants and government ministers that there was little to be gained in mollifying Mexico, while an independent Texas presented the prospect of a growing market for English manufactures and an excellent opportunity to confine America's western territorial ambitions. Campbell, *Gone to Texas*, 165; Christopher Brown, *Moral Capital*, 243–44; David Brion Davis, *Slavery and Human Progress* (Oxford: Oxford University Press, 1984), 174–79. Slavery was finally abolished in the British Empire in 1833 by Parliament's Slavery Abolition Act, which involved government indemnity payments to slave owners in compensation for the loss of the value of their human property. A detailed account of the Texian/British negotiations can be found in Ephraim Douglass Adams, *British Interests and Activities in Texas* (Baltimore: Johns Hopkins Press, 1910), 36–122.

9. Campbell, *Gone to Texas*, 167–69.

10. For Lamar, see Houston to Dr. Robert Anderson Irion, Irion Papers, Special Collections, Jenkins Garrett Library, University of Texas at Arlington. The quote about Burnet was published recently in Jill Harris, "What's in a Name: Burnet Road," *Austin Monthly* (December, 2008): 48. See also Richard Bruce Winders, *Crisis in the Southwest: The United States, Mexico, and the Struggle over Texas* (Wilmington: Scholarly Resources, 2002), 40–44.

11. James L. Haley, *The Texas Supreme Court: A Narrative History, 1836–1986* (Austin: University of Texas Press, 2013), 50–51.

12. Houston had begun his policy of accommodation toward the Indians by negotiating his own treaty with some of the Cherokees in the fall of 1836, in order to keep them out of alliance with Mexico. In this he used his personal good offices as a friend and adopted member of the tribe. However, the newly elected Texas Congress refused to ratify this treaty, and one member even called for an investigation of Houston because of the rumors that some Indians had conspired with Mexico during the revolution. Houston nonetheless proposed employment of Indian rangers to help protect the frontier, negotiation of further Indian treaties, and the erection of trade houses to establish permanent economic contacts. Richard Bruce Winders, *Crisis in the Southwest: The United States, Mexico, and the Struggle over Texas*, 40–44; Gary Clayton Anderson, *The Conquest of Texas*, 121–35. According to Anderson, Houston was perfectly willing to overplay rumors of an Indian War and of Cherokee and Comanche cooperation with the Mexicans in order to lure the US troops in Louisiana under General Gaines into Texas to protect white settlers. He thought that this might force President Andrew Jackson's hand with respect to annexation. When the scheme failed, Houston quickly reverted to his old pacifistic ways. Anderson sees in this more support for a ruthless and politically flexible Houston than one enamored with the Indians.

13. Anderson, *The Conquest of Texas*, 134. See also F. Todd Smith, *From Dominance to Disappearance: The Indians of Texas and the Near Southwest, 1786–1859* (Lincoln: University of Nebraska Press, 2006), which parallels in some respects Anderson's narrative, but deals mainly with tribes in Louisiana and Northeast Texas, while Anderson's focus is further west and hence more relevant here.

14. Anderson, *The Conquest of Texas*, 155–61.

15. Anderson, *The Conquest of Texas*, 172; Stanley Siegel, *The Poet President of Texas: The Life of Mirabeau B. Lamar, President of Texas* (Austin: Jenkins Publishing, 1977), 9–13; Mary Whatley Clarke, *Chief Bowles and the Texas Cherokees* (Norman: University of Oklahoma Press, 2001), 77–91; James L. Haley, *The Texas Supreme Court: A Narrative History, 1836–1986* (Austin: University of Texas Press, 2013), 47, quoting Mirabeau Lamar, Inaugural Address, December 13, 1838, as follows: "How long shall this cruel inhumanity, this murderous sensibility for the sanguinary savage be practiced? Until other oceans of blood, the blood of our wives and children shall glut their voracious appetite? . . . The white man and the red man cannot dwell in harmony together . . . [we must have] war to the knife." See also S. C. Gwynne, *Empire of the Summer Moon: Quanah Parker and the Rise and Fall of the Comanches, the Most Powerful Indian Tribe in American History* (New York: Scribner, 2011).

16. Anderson, *The Conquest of Texas*, 173; McCleod to Lamar, December 1, 1838, *Lamar Papers*, vol. 2 (Austin: Texas State Library), 308–10, cited in Anderson, *The Conquest of Texas*, 172.

17. Anderson, *The Conquest of Texas*, 174; President Lamar's December 21 address to Congress, *Lamar Papers*, vol. 2, eds. Charles Adams Gulick and Katherine Elliott (Austin: Texas State Library, 1922), 346–69, https://archive.org/stream/papersmirabeauboolibrgoog#page/n6/mode/2up. Most famously, in 1839 Lamar accomplished moving the capital of Texas to Waterloo on the upper Colorado River at the foot of the Balcones Escarpment and next to Comanche settlements. The town was soon renamed Austin, after the famous colonial empresario, reluctant revolutionary leader, and erstwhile secretary of state, who had died of pneumonia in December 1836. The whole purpose of the relocation was as a symbolic gesture encouraging rapid westward expansion. See John G. Johnson, "Capitals," in *Handbook of Texas Online* (Texas State Historical Association), accessed September 6, 2014, http://www.tshaonline.org/handbook/online/articles/mzc01; Harriet Smither and Jane Carefoot, "Texas State Archives," in *Handbook of Texas Online* (Texas State Historical Association), accessed September 6, 2014, http://www.tshaonline.org/handbook/online/articles/lct06; Eugene C. Barker, "Austin, Stephen Fuller," in *Handbook of Texas Online* (Texas State Historical Association), accessed September 6, 2014, http://www.tshaonline.org/handbook/online/articles/fau14.

18. Gary Clayton Anderson, *The Conquest of Texas*, 177; Campbell, *Gone to Texas*, 166–67; Nance, *After San Jacinto: The Texas-Mexican Frontier, 1836–1841*, 113–22.

19. Gary Clayton Anderson, *The Conquest of Texas*, 178–81. Mary Whatley Clark, *Chief Bowles and the Texas Cherokees*, 91–96; Ben H. Procter, "Reagan, John Henninger," in *Handbook of Texas Online* (Texas State Historical Association), accessed September 12, 2013, http://www.tshaonline.org/handbook/online/articles/fre02. See also Ben H. Procter, *Not without Honor: The Life of John H. Reagan* (Austin: University of Texas Press, 1962).

20. Sam Houston to Anna Raguet, May 15, 1838, Irion Family Collection, Special Collections Division, University of Texas at Arlington Libraries.

21. See Ellen and James Reily to Anna Raguet, December 5, 1839, Irion Family Collection, Special Collections Division, University of Texas at Arlington Libraries. These anti-Mexican and anti-Tejano sentiments were not new. Nacogdoches businessman Henry Raguet, in an 1836 letter to his wife, Marcia, who was with family in the United States at the time, reported that "the largest proportion of the American troops and citizens here consider the native Mexicans here their enemies . . . In the same light did Mexicans here consider the troops here." Raguet described himself as having "always been a friend of our Mexican neighbors here," and proclaimed that he had "always advocated their rights and reprimanded those of our countrymen whose conduct toward them was improper." Henry Raguet to Marcia Raguet, April 17, 1836, Henry Raguet Family Papers, 1786–1835, Center for American History, the University of Texas at Austin. Meanwhile, by 1837, the recently appointed Texas Secretary of War, Thomas Rusk, claimed to have received some information "from a source entitled to great credit of the undoubted hostility of the Cherokee Indi-

ans and of some matters going on between them and the Mexican Government." Thomas J. Rusk to Robert A. Irion, April 30, 1837, Irion Family Collection, Special Collections Division, University of Texas at Arlington Libraries. But Texas Senator Robert A. Irion, in an 1837 letter to Memucan Hunt, then serving as minister to Washington, DC, indicated that it was the Caddos who "seemed to be the principal leaders among the hostile bands." Irion asked Hunt to solicit aid from the United States in combating this danger, although it is clear from his letter that the Texas government, more than anything else, wanted Hunt to concentrate on attempting to effectuate annexation to the United States. In another 1837 Irion letter, this one to Henry Raguet, Irion indicated that the Texas Congress was planning on reporting a bill "authorizing an expedition against those who are known to be hostile, namely the Caddos, Wacos, Tiwoicanees, Creeks &c &c." Although the bill was likely to be reported, according to Irion President Houston disagreed with any policy of sending an expedition against "any of the Indians, and whether this measure will meet his approbation I think doubtful." Irion was of the opinion that the reason Houston opposed this kind of expedition was because it might "bring on a general war," which he considered unlikely to "ever take place unless the Mexican Army advanced of which now, there is not the least prospect." Nonetheless, it seems that many in the government were ready to consider all the tribes as in league with Mexico, and once Lamar took the governor's chair their views were given full rein. Robert A. Irion to Henry Raguet, May 12, 1837, Irion Family Collection, Special Collections Division, University of Texas at Arlington Libraries.

22. Sam Houston to Anna Raguet, December 10, 1839, Irion Family Collection, Special Collections Division, University of Texas at Arlington Libraries.

23. Houston to Irion, January 27, 1840, Irion Family Collection, Special Collections Division, University of Texas at Arlington Libraries.

24. Gary Clayton Anderson, *The Conquest of Texas*, 158–61, 181–82; Thomas W. Cutrer, "Karnes, Henry Wax," *Handbook of Texas Online* (Texas State Historical Association), accessed September 6, 2014, http://www.tshaonline.org/handbook/online/articles/fka02; Richard Bruce Winders, *Crisis in the Southwest: The United States, Mexico, and the Struggle over Texas*, 44–47.

25. Anderson, *The Conquest of Texas*, 181–82; Thomas W. Cutrer, "Karnes, Henry Wax," in *Handbook of Texas Online* (Texas State Historical Association), accessed September 6, 2014, http://www.tshaonline.org/handbook/online/articles/fka02; Joseph M. Nance, *After San Jacinto: The Texas-Mexican Frontier, 1836–1841*, 291; Richard Bruce Winders, *Crisis in the Southwest: The United States, Mexico, and the Struggle over Texas*, 45, 59. The Council House Fight began when Karnes and the other authorities escorted the Comanche delegation recently arrived in San Antonio to the meeting or "council" room in a building adjacent to the jail. Unfortunately, these Indian leaders only represented a small contingent of the Comanche tribes in the area, and Karnes had ordered Colonel William S. Fisher, the officer in command

of his Texas Army bodyguard, to seize the Comanche leaders if they failed to bring in the full complement of Anglo captives. When the Anglo leaders discovered through their Tejano translator that the Comanches had brought only one Anglo captive to trade, a mutilated teenage girl, Fisher ordered all of the Indians jailed. When they resisted, he then ordered his troops to fire on the Comanches, who were bolting for the door. Outside the Council House, the other Comanche men began to run, and several were shot down by Texian troops present. Many were killed, and the remaining Comanches were incarcerated. The Council House Fight was a major public relations victory for the Lamar administration's policy of ethnic cleansing. The few Comanches who escaped assured their friends and neighbors that the Texians could not be trusted. Anderson, *The Conquest of Texas*, 182–84; Nance, *After San Jacinto: The Texas-Mexican Frontier*, 291. The Comanches withdrew to the west and held a council with their former enemies the Kiowa, as well as some Cheyenne and Arapahoe. The upshot of the Council House Fight was a treaty between these four tribes creating a lasting alliance that continued raiding the Texas frontier. For example, a raiding party of braves from these allied tribes attacked as far into the heart of Anglo settlement as Victoria in August of 1840 and rustled more than a thousand horses and cattle. They moved farther southeast and burned Linnville while the Texians assembled a militia from the neighboring towns. Burleson and Felix Huston, another old Indian fighter, led this force, which attacked the Indian army at Plum Creek. Anderson, *The Conquest of Texas*, 188–90; Richard Bruce Winders, *Crisis in the Southwest: The United States, Mexico, and the Struggle over Texas*, 45, 59.

26. Anderson, *The Conquest of Texas*, 194–95; Ford Dixon, "Cayton Erhard's Reminiscences of the Texan Santa Fe Expedition, 1841," *Southwestern Historical Quarterly* 66, no. 3 (April 1963): 424–38; H. Bailey Carroll, "Texan Santa Fe Expedition," in *Handbook of Texas Online* (Texas State Historical Association), accessed August 23, 2013, http://www.tshaonline.org/handbook/online/articles/qyt03; Richard Bruce Winders, *Crisis in the Southwest: The United States, Mexico, and the Struggle over Texas*, 49–50. For a somewhat revisionist account, see also Paul N. Spellman, *Forgotten Texas Leader: Hugh McLeod and the Texan Santa Fe Expedition* (College Station: Texas A&M University Press, 1999).

27. Anderson, *The Conquest of Texas*, 196–99; Sam W. Haynes, *Soldiers of Misfortune: The Somervell and Mier Expeditions* (Austin: University of Texas Press, 1990). The Vasquez and Woll invasions and other events are described by Juan Seguin in Juan N Seguin, *A Revolution Remembered: The Memoirs and Correspondence of Juan N Seguin*, ed. Jesus F de la Teja (Austin: Texas State Historical Association, 2002), 92–100. William Campbell Binkley, "The Last Stage of Texan Military Operations against Mexico, 1843," *Southwestern Historical Quarterly* 22, no. 3 (January, 1919): 260–71 gives a background summary of these events and proceeds to a narrative of the 1843 Warfield and Snively expeditions into New Mexico and the northwestern frontier.

28. Gary Clayton Anderson, *The Conquest of Texas*, 200–206, 210–11. Samuel Colt first manufactured a revolving pistol at his plant in Paterson, New Jersey, in 1842, and the Texas Rangers were among the first to use them in earnest. This was the now famous and highly collectable 1842 Colt Paterson Revolver.

29. Nance, *After San Jacinto: The Texas-Mexican Frontier*, 238, n. 142, citing Gammel, ed., *Laws of Texas*, vol. 2, 325–26.

30. Madeleine Stern, "Stephen Pearl Andrews, Abolition, and the Annexation of Texas," *Southwestern Historical Quarterly* 67, no. 4 (1964): 491–523. For Tappan, see Ronald Walters, *American Reformers 1815–1860* (New York: Hill & Wang, 1978); and Ronald Walters, *The Anti-Slavery Appeal: American Abolitionism after 1830* (New York: W. W. Norton & Co., 1984), 5–6, 12.

31. Madeleine Stern, "Stephen Pearl Andrews, Abolition, and the Annexation of Texas," 501.

32. Stern, "Stephen Pearl Andrews, Abolition, and the Annexation of Texas," 502–4.

33. Charles Shively, "An Option for Freedom in Texas," *Journal of Negro History* 50, no. 2 (April 1965): 77–96.

34. Shively, "An Option for Freedom in Texas," 85–86.

35. Randolph B. Campbell, *An Empire for Slavery: The Peculiar Institution in Texas, 1821–1865* (Baton Rouge: Louisiana State University Press, 1989), 214–15.

36. Mary Bell Hart, "Preface," *Journals of the Convention Assembled at the City of Austin on the 4th of July 1845 for the Purpose of Framing a Constitution for the State of Texas* (Austin: Shoal Creek Publishers, 1974 [orig. ed., 1845]), ii–iii. The proceedings were also published in 1846 by J. W. Cruger under the title "Debates of the Texas Convention" with additional materials included. All citations to the *Debates* will follow the form *Debates of the 1845 Convention* ___. See *Debates of the Texas Convention*, William F. Weeks, reporter (Houston: J. W. Cruger, 1846), accessed August 22, 2013, http://tarlton.law.utexas.edu/constitutions/texas1845/debates. Further references to the convention journal will follow the Hart reprinted edition in the format *Journals of the Convention* (1845) ___.

37. *Journals of the Convention* (1845), i, iii; *Joint Resolution for Annexing Texas to the United States Approved March 1, 1845* (Texas State Library and Archives Commission), accessed August 24, 2013, https://www.tsl.state.tx.us/ref/abouttx/annexation/march1845.html; Anson Jones, "Proclamation of President Anson Jones, May 8, 1845," *National Register* (May 8, 1845), E. L. R. Wheelock Jr. Collection, Archives and Information Services Division, Texas State Library and Archives Commission, electronic version, accessed August 30, 2013, https://www.tsl.state.tx.us/exhibits/annexation/part5/anson_jones_may8_1845_proclamation.html.

38. *Journals of the Convention* (1845), v; "James Knox Polk," *American President: A Reference Resource* (Charlottesville: University of Virginia Miller Center) website, accessed August 30, 2013, http://millercenter.org/president/polk/essays/biography/5; "John Slidell's Mission to Mexico," *A Continent Divided: The U.S.–Mexico War*

(Arlington: University Texas at Arlington), UTA Library website, accessed August 30, 2013, http://library.uta.edu/usmexicowar/essaysresult.php?content_id=180; Murphy Givens, "Corpus Christi: Training Ground for the War with Mexico," *Corpus Christi Caller-Times*, August 28, 2013.

39. James L. Haley, *The Texas Supreme Court*, 20–21, 54; *Journals of the Convention Assembled at the City of Austin on the 4th of July 1845 for the Purpose of Framing a Constitution for the State of Texas*, v–vi, ix; Rose M. Harris, "Love, James," in *Handbook of Texas Online* (Texas State Historical Association), accessed August 22, 2013, http://www.tshaonline.org/handbook/online/articles/flo27; Alice Duggan Gracy, "Caldwell, John," in *Handbook of Texas Online* (Texas State Historical Association), accessed August 22, 2013, http://www.tshaonline.org/handbook/online/articles/fca11.

40. *Journals of the Convention* (1845), vii–ix; James L. Haley, *The Texas Supreme Court*, 44–45.

41. *Journals of the Convention* (1845), 3–11.

42. *Journals of the Convention* (1845), 12–13.

43. *Journals of the Convention* (1845), 12–21.

44. *Journals of the Convention* (1845), 22–23 (report), 33–35 (contents of bill of rights), 264 (passage).

45. John Cornyn, "The Roots of the Texas Constitution," 1091–92, 1098, 1137–41; *Journals of the Convention* (1845), 35–39. Again, the proposed article on the executive was considered sufficiently important to require that five hundred copies of it be printed and distributed showing the work of the convention.

46. Patrick T. Conley, "The People's Constitution," in the Dorr Rebellion (Phillips Memorial Library), accessed August 14, 2018, http://library.providence.edu/dps/projects/dorr/pcon.php; John Cornyn, "The Roots of the Texas Constitution," 1091–92, 1098, 1137–41; *Journals of the Convention* (1845), 35–39. Again, the proposed article on the executive was considered sufficiently important to require that five hundred copies of it be printed and distributed showing the work of the convention.

47. *Journals of the Convention* (1845), 46–49. Again, five hundred copies of Hemphill's report were printed and distributed.

48. *Constitution of the State of Texas* (1861), Article IV, note between Sections 5 and 6, as reflected in digital version found within the collection *Texas Constitutions 1824–1876* (Tarlton Law Library, University of Texas School of Law), accessed August 21, 2014, http://tarlton.law.utexas.edu/constitutions/texas1861/a4.

49. *Journals of the Convention* (1845), 53–54, 63.

50. *Journals of the Convention* (1845), 54.

51. *Debates of the 1845 Convention*, 156–59 ("white" debate), 157 (Rusk quotes), 158 (Jones quote), 159 (Navarro quote and final action); *Journal of the 1845 Convention*, 341 (final passage). Jones is not listed in the credentialing of delegates in either the *Journal* or the *Debates*, but "Oliver Jones" is listed as having signed the conven-

tion's resolution of July 4th in favor of annexation. *Journal of the 1845 Convention*, 10; *Handbook of Texas Online*, Carolyn Hyman, "Jones, Oliver," accessed August 14, 2018, http://www.tshaonline.org/handbook/online/articles/fjo61. See also John Cornyn, "The Roots of the Texas Constitution," 1142–45; David McDonald, *Jose Antonio Navarro: In Search of the American Dream in Nineteenth-Century Texas* (Denton: Texas State Historical Association Press, 2010), 208–15, 205 (intense animosity quote), 207 (Tejanos highly suspect quote).

52. *Journals of the Convention* (1845), 66, 85.

53. See, for example, Joseph W. McKnight, "Protection of the Family Home from Seizure by Creditors: The Sources and Evolution of a Legal Principle," *Southwestern Historical Quarterly* 86, no. 3 (January 1983): 369; *Journals of the Convention* (1845), 109–16.

54. *Journals of the Convention* (1845), 116–17; Winthrop D. Jordan, *The White Man's Burden, Historical Origins of Racism in the United States* (Oxford: Oxford University Press, 1974), 61–68, 79, 87; Peter H. Wood, *Black Majority: Negroes in Colonial South Carolina from 1670 through the Stono Rebellion* (New York: W. W. Norton & Co., 1974), 271–84, 308–30; John W. Blassingame, *The Slave Community: Plantation Life in the Antebellum South* (Oxford: Oxford University Press, 1972), 192–248. While slave codes in older states like South Carolina and Virginia date to the early and mid-1700s, after Nat Turner's well publicized rebellion of 1831 in Virginia newer states of the Cotton South nearer to Texas began enacting their own (e.g., Alabama in 1833). See John G. Akin, *Digest of the Laws of Alabama* (Philadelphia: Alexander Towar, 1833), 391–98, accessed August 28, 2013, http://www.archives.state.al.us/teacher/slavery/lesson1/doc1.html.

55. *Journals of the Convention* (1845), 120–27.

56. *Journals of the Convention* (1845), 126–27.

57. *Journals of the Convention* (1845), 262, 270; James W. Paulsen, "A Short History of the Supreme Court of the Republic of Texas," *Texas Law Review* 65, no. 2 (December, 1986): 237–304; James L. Haley, *The Texas Supreme Court: A Narrative History, 1836–1986*, 36–43.

58. *Journals of the Convention* (1845), 170.

59. *Journals of the Convention* (1845), 279–84.

60. *Journals of the Convention* (1845), 294–95.

61. *Journals of the Convention* (1845), 337–38.

62. Constitution of the State of Texas, in *Journals of the Convention* (1845), 338–67. Further citations to the constitution will follow the format Constitution of the State of Texas (1845), Article___, Sec. ____; "Texas Governor Edmund Jackson Davis: An Inventory of Governor Edmund Jackson Davis Records at the Texas State Archives, 1869–1874," *Texas Archival Resources Online* (Texas State Library and Archives Commission, 2018), https://legacy.lib.utexas.edu/taro/tslac/40016/tsl-40016.html (accessed July 11, 2018); Constitution of the State of Texas (1845), Articles IV, XIII.

63. Constitution of the State of Texas (1845).

64. Constitution of the State of Texas (1845), Article III, Sec. 1 & 2.

65. Constitution of the Republic of Texas (1836), Article II, Sec. 3, Declaration of Rights, Sec. 17; Constitution of the State of Texas (1845), Article VII, Sec. 30–31.

66. Constitution of the Republic of Texas (1836), "Declaration of Rights," Sec. 12; Constitution of the State of Texas (1845), Article I, Sec. 15; Article VII, Sec. 22, 28.

67. Constitution of the State of Texas (1845), Article III, Sections 1–2, Article V, Section 2, "Bill of Rights," Sections 1–2.

68. Constitution of the State of Texas (1845), Article III, Section; 1–2; Constitution of the State of Texas (1845), Article V, Section 2; Constitution of the State of Texas (1845), "Bill of Rights," Sections 1–4, 15; Constitution of the State of Texas (1845), Article VII, Sections 22, 28, 30–31.

69. Constitution of the Republic of Texas (1836), "General Provisions," Section 9.

70. Constitution of the State of Texas (1845), Article XIII, Section 1.

71. Constitution of the State of Texas (1845), Article VIII, Section 1–3.

72. Constitution of the State of Texas (1845), Article VIII, Section 1–3; Winthrop D. Jordan, *The White Man's Burden, Historical Origins of Racism in the United States* (Oxford: Oxford University Press, 1974), 61–68, 79, 87; Peter H. Wood, *Black Majority: Negroes in Colonial South Carolina from 1670 through the Stono Rebellion* (New York: W. W. Norton & Co., 1974), 271–84, 308–30; John W. Blassingame, *The Slave Community: Plantation Life in the Antebellum South* (Oxford: Oxford University Press, 1972), 192–248. See generally Randolph B. Campbell, ed., *The Laws of Slavery in Texas: Historical Documents and Essays* (Austin: University of Texas Press, 2010).

73. Campbell, *Gone to Texas*, 186–91; Claude Elliott, "Henderson, James Pinckney," in *Handbook of Texas Online* (Texas State Historical Association), accessed August 31, 2013, http://www.tshaonline.org/handbook/online/articles/fhe14; Matthew Ellenberger, "Horton, Albert Clinton," in *Handbook of Texas Online* (Texas State Historical Association), accessed August 30, 2013, http://www.tshaonline.org/handbook/online/articles/fho62; Campbell, *Gone to Texas*, 186–91.

74. Randolph B. Campbell, *An Empire for Slavery*, 217–30. One response to Campbell's critique is that it is hard to ignore the incidents of later anti-German violence justified on the grounds of German unionism. See James L. Haley, *Passionate Nation An Epic History of Texas* (New York: Free Press, 2006), 299–300; James L. Haley, *The Texas Supreme Court: A Narrative History, 1836–1986* (Austin: University of Texas Press, 2013), 70; Rodman I. Underwood, *Death on the Nueces: German Texans Treue der Union* (Austin: Eakin Publishing Co., 2002). With respect to true antislavery sentiment, Campbell well summarized the conventional wisdom on the subject thus:

> A few articulate Germans expressed anti-slavery views, but, in fact, the proslavery consensus encompassed Texas' largest non-Anglo immigrant population as well. . . . In reality, Texans had little basis for concern over

German opposition.... Germans were hardly the enemies of slavery that Olmsted and a few historians have made them.
—Randolph B. Campbell, *An Empire for Slavery*, 215–17.

75. Olmsted's admiration for the participants in the 1848 radical German revolts was so profound as to cause him twice to ride the long and rocky trail from San Antonio out to the German settlements around Sisterdale, where veterans of these clashes resided. Dr. Adolf Douai, a local German newspaper editor, accompanied the Olmsted brothers and their third partner (known only as "B") on these trips. Douai and a Dr. Froebel also mentioned by Olmsted were political refugee "forty-eighters." According to James Howard, Olmstead's modern reeditor, like many Hill Country German immigrants,

> Douai was a Forty-eighter, a participant in the 1848 revolutions in Germany [who had] founded on July 5, 1853 the San Antonio *Zeitung*, a "social democratic" newspaper for the Germans of West Texas ... [and] he had worked for five years in Russia as a tutor ... arrested during the 1848 uprising.... He served a prison term for the unwritten crime of political radicalism. He first came to New Braunfels where he opened a private school in 1852. The next year he moved to S. A. to begin editing.

Douai claimed to be a "radical democrat" and a Free-Soiler, and ultimately, he was forced to flee from Texas to Boston and then to Hoboken in 1856. Before that, the Olmsteds raised money to help Douai keep running his San Antonio paper, whose stockholders withdrew their support after Douai's support for the 1854 national Free-Soil convention and its platform statement condemning slavery as immoral. As Howard described it in his afterword to the 1962 edition of Olmsted's journal, "The Olmsteds had done what they could to rescue the ... *Zeitung* ... in the interest of forwarding a free-soil organ in the camp of the opposition. Besides obtaining capital for Douai, Frederick Olmsted persuaded Theodore Parker and other anti-slavery advocates to subscribe for the *Zeitung*, and he promised to write for it himself." Frederick Law Olmsted, *Journey through Texas: A Saddle Trip on the Southwestern Frontier*, ed. James Howard (Austin: Von Boeckmann-Jones Press, 1962, [orig. ed. 1857]), ix, 261–74 (all page references are to the 1962 Howard edition); Olmsted, *Journey through Texas*, 261–74. (This is part of James Howard's editorial "Afterward.")

76. Olmsted, *Journey through Texas*, 18.

77. Olmsted, *Journey through Texas*, 200–201.

78. Olmsted, *Journey through Texas*, 201.

79. Olmsted, *Journey through Texas*, 68.

80. Olmsted, *Journey through Texas*, 204; Sean Kelley, "'Mexico in His Head': Slavery and the Texas-Mexico Border, 1810–1860," *Journal of Social History* 37, no. 3 (spring 2004): 709–23; Sarah E. Cornell, "Citizens of Nowhere: Fugitive Slaves

and Free African Americans in Mexico, 1833–1857," *Journal of American History* 100, no. 2 (2013): 351–74. See also Curtis Chubb, "Revisiting the Purpose of the 1855 Callahan Expedition," *Southwestern Historical Quarterly* 121, no. 4 (April 2018): 417–29; Jeff Guinn, *Our Land before We Die: The Proud Story of the Seminole Negro* (New York: J. P. Tar / Putnam, 2005); Kevin Mulroy, *Freedom on the Border: The Seminole Maroons in Florida, the Indian Territory, Coahuila, and Texas* (Lubbock, Texas Tech University Press, 1993). See also James McDonald, *Jose Antonio Navarro: In Search of the American Dream in Nineteenth-Century Texas* (Denton: Texas State Historical Association Press, 2010), 212, who says, "As we have seen already, a community tolerant of mixed-race persons was a social reality in the Tejano regions of Texas."

81. Olmsted's friend Douai described his own enemies and the controversy surrounding his professed abolitionism. Olmsted made note of this in the journal, and before leaving for New Braunfels to see German Texas for himself, he conferred in San Antonio with future unionist governor Elisha M. Pease, who told him that "as to slavery, as fast as [the Germans] acquired property, they followed the customs of the country and purchased slaves like other white people, even Northern men, who invariably conquered their prejudices when they came here to settle and found their practical inconvenience." Olmsted knew (and acknowledged) that some Germans were more antislavery than others. Olmsted, *Journey through Texas*, 66. Unionism thrived in the German hill country for a decade after Olmsted's visit and well into the Civil War itself. See Frank Wilson Kiel, "Treue der Union: Myths, Misrepresentations, and Misinterpretations," *Southwestern Historical Quarterly* 115, no. 3 (January 2012): 282–94. Once he arrived in German settlements, however, Olmsted asked the Germans themselves about this subject and got varying reports. He concluded that when a slave was on the run, "negro cabins he generally approaches with confidence, and in the hovels of the Mexicans, while he is in the settled country, he often obtains food and shelter. Any man who harbors a negro in Texas is liable to fine and long imprisonment. Most of the Germans, I presume, would refuse to take in a negro whom they knew to be running away. Once, however, I happened to learned that a poor, ignorant Roman Catholic immigrant, happening to find a half-starved fugitive when looking after his cattle, melted in compassion, took pains to prevail upon him to come to his cabin, bound up his wounds, clothed him, gave him food and whisky, and set him rejoicing on his way again." Frederick Law Olmsted, *Journey through Texas*, 203. Olmsted went on to admit that most accusations of Germans actually harboring slaves were false, but they were unjustly persecuted anyway merely because of their antislavery sentiments. As he put it, "The slaveholders who have the least acquaintance with Germans, knowing their sympathy with the slaves, are very much afraid to have them settle near their plantations, but as far as I can judge, their apprehensions are without good foundation."

Chapter 3

1. Two additional factors that lessened fears of Indians and Mexicans were (1) the refusal of state authorities to create Indian reservations out of unoccupied public lands in West Texas, and (2) a new series of reassuring but undermanned army forts constructed during the Fillmore and Pierce administrations of the late 1840s and early 1850s. Robert Wooster, *Fort Davis: Outpost on the Texas Frontier* (Austin: Texas State Historical Association, 1994); Robert Wooster, *The Military and United States Indian Policy, 1865–1903* (New Haven: Yale University Press, 1988); Robert Wooster, "U.S. Army on the Western Frontier," in "Texas Frontier Forts: Nineteenth Century Forts and the Clash of Cultures on the Texas Frontier," *Texas Beyond History: The Virtual Museum of Texas Cultural History* (Austin: College of Liberal Arts of the University of Texas at Austin), accessed December 20, 2008, http://www.texasbeyondhistory.net/forts/military.html.

2. Wesley Norton, "The Methodist Episcopal Church and the Civil Disturbances in North Texas 1859–1860," *Southwestern Historical Quarterly* 68, no. 3 (1965): 317–41.

3. Norton, "The Methodist Episcopal Church and the Civil Disturbances in North Texas 1859–1860," 331 (Bewly quote).

4. David B. Chesebrough, *Clergy Dissent in the Old South 1830–1865* (Carbondale: Southern Illinois University Press, 1996), 33–34.

5. James Marten, *Texas Divided* (Lexington: University Press of Kentucky, 1990), 29 (quoting *Corpus Christi Ranchero*, September 3, 1863), 53–55, 63–66.

6. Marten, *Texas Divided*, 222–23.

7. Marten, *Texas Divided*, 64–65.

8. Dale Baum, *The Shattering of Texas Unionism* (Baton Rouge: Louisiana State University Press, 1998), 71–72, 74–79. Baum also relates that in southeastern Texas, "at least thirty German immigrants at Frelsburg in Colorado County apparently avoided the polls because they hoped to 'escape the consequences' of voting against secession or believed their votes would be of no consequence." Baum, *The Shattering of Texas Unionism*, 79. One emblematic story concerns James H. Bell, the unionist member of the Texas Supreme Court about whom more is said in the pages that follow. When Bell went to cast his vote in the secession election, he was handed a colored paper ballot already printed as "For Secession." When it became clear that this was the only ballot available, he took it and calmly struck through these words, wrote in "Against," and handed back the ballot. The election judge responded, "Judge Bell, I am very sorry to see you cast that vote, and you will regret it." James L. Haley, *The Supreme Court of Texas; A Narrative History, 1836–1986* (Austin: University of Texas Press, 2013), 66–67.

9. Frank H. Smyrl, "Unionism in Texas, 1856–1861," *Southwestern Historical Quarterly* 68, no. 2 (1964): 172–95, citing *The Washington American*, January 4, 1856.

10. Frank H. Smyrl, "Unionism in Texas, 1856–1861," 184–89. Walter Buenger's 1979 "Secession and the Texas German Community: Editor Lindheimer vs. Editor Flake" foreshadows Baum's argument that, with a few exceptions like Douai and the Sisterdale bunch, Germans were pretty much a reflection of the state as a whole, politically speaking, but they split for different reasons between Union and Confederacy. Buenger claims that "except for the absence of rabid secessionists, the divisions in the German community mirrored the divided reactions in the rest of the state." In a later passage, however, Buenger acknowledges the existence of some Germans further to the left. "There were some influential Germans who stoutly opposed slavery and supported the union," he says, although many apparently left the state. Walter L Buenger Jr., "Secession and the Texas German Community: Editor Lindheimer vs. Editor Flake," *Southwestern Historical Quarterly* 82, no. 4 (1979): 379–402.

11. Buenger, "Secession and the Texas German Community"; Crystal Sasse Ragsdale, "Lindheimer, Ferdinand Jacob," in *Handbook of Texas Online* (Texas State Historical Association), accessed September 6, 2014, http://www.tshaonline.org/handbook/online/articles/fli04.

12. Campbell, *An Empire for Slavery*, 214–15.

13. For an interesting study of one way in which abolitionists took on "blackness" as a cultural characteristic, see John Stauffer, *The Black Hearts of Men, Radical Abolitionists and the Transformation of Race* (Cambridge: Harvard University Press, 2002).

14. Treatments of Texas secession are numerous. See Walter L. Buenger, *Secession and the Union in Texas* (Austin: University of Texas Press, 1984); James Marten, *Texas Divided: Loyalty and Dissent in the Lone Star State* (Lexington: University Press of Kentucky, 1990); Walter Buenger, "The Riddle of Secession," *Southwestern Historical Quarterly* 87, no. 2 (1983): 151–53; J. J. Bowden, *The Exodus of Federal Forces from Texas, 1861* (Austin: Eakin Press, 1986); Dale Baum, *The Shattering of Texas Unionism: Politics in the Lone Star State during the Civil War Era* (Baton Rouge: Louisiana State University Press, 1998); Randolph B. Campbell, "Political Conflict within the Southern Consensus: Harrison County, Texas 1850–1880," *Civil War History* 26, no. 3 (1980): 218–39; Roy Sylvan Dunn, "The KGC in Texas, 1860–1861," *Southwestern Historical Quarterly* 70, no. 4 (1967): 543–73; John Moretta, "William Pitt Ballinger and the Travail of Texas Secession," *Houston Review* 11, no. 1 (1989): 3–26; Phillip Rutherford, "Texas Leaves the Union," *Civil War Times Illustrated* 20, no. 3 (1981): 12–23; Frank H. Smyrl, "Unionism in Texas, 1856–1861," *Southwestern Historical Quarterly* 68, no. 2 (1964): 172–95. David P. Smith, "Civil War Letters of Sam Houston," *Southwestern Historical Quarterly* 81, no. 4 (1978): 417–26; Marilyn McAdams Sibley, "Letters From Sam Houston to Albert Sidney Johnson," *Southwestern Historical Quarterly* 66, no. 2 (1962/63): 252–61; Sam Houston, *The Personal Correspondence of Sam Houston*, edited by Madge Thornall Roberts (Denton, TX: University of North Texas, 1996). There have also been several books and theses

written on the political history of Texas secession. See, for example, Robert Kingsley Peters, "Texas: Annexation to Secession" (PhD diss., University of Texas at Austin, 1977). However, references within these works to the formal rhetoric of the protagonists in the dispute are rare. Those in search of the actual rhetoric of the debate are more likely to find it in biographies of the participants than in scholarly articles. Unfortunately, these biographies are overwhelmingly of only one participant in the debate, Sam Houston. There are also several articles on Houston's writings, as well as on those of other pre–Civil War politicians from Texas and elsewhere in the South. See Bob Garner, "Let Us Be Patriots and Texans—A Content Analysis of the Secession Rhetoric of Sam Houston: 1854–1861," *Texana* 12, no. 1 (1974): 1–19; Donna R. Tobias, "The States' Rights Speaking of Oran Milo Roberts 1850–1861: A Study in Agitational Rhetoric" (PhD diss., Louisiana State University and Agricultural and Mechanical Col., 1982. DAI 43(8) (1983): 2497-A). Kenneth Wayne Howell, "When the Rabble Hiss, Well May Patriots Tremble: James Webb Throckmorton and the Secession Movement in Texas," *Southwestern Historical Quarterly* 109, no. 4 (2006): 431–64; Donald Braider, "Solitary Star: A Biography of Sam Houston," *Journal of Southern History* 40 (November 1974): 658–59; Robert A. Calvert, "In Search of Sam Houston," *Locus* 6, no. 2 (1994): 159–61; Gregg Cantrell, "Whither Sam Houston?," *Southwestern Historical Quarterly* 97, no. 2 (1993): 345–57; Gilbert Cuthbertson, "Sam Houston's Neighbors: A Record of Early Montgomery County," *Texana* 9, no. 3 (1971): 260–69; Marshall DeBruhl, *Sword of San Jacinto—A Life of Sam Houston* (New York: Random House, 1993); Joe B. Frantz, "Texas Giant of Contradictions: Sam Houston," *American West* 17, no. 4 (1980): 4–13, 61–65; Marquis James, *The Raven: A Biography of Sam Houston* (Garden City, NY: Blue Ribbon Books, Halcyon House, 1929); F. N. Boney, "The Raven Tamed: An 1845 Sam Houston Letter," *Southwestern Historical Quarterly* 68, no. 1 (1964): 90–92; Joe B. Frantz, "The Sam Houston Letters: A Corner of Texas in Princeton," *Princeton University Library Chronicle* 33, no. 1 (1971): 18–29; Margaret Hutton, "The Houston-Fisher Controversy," *Southwestern Historical Quarterly* 76, no. 1 (1972): 38–57; David P. Smith, "Civil War Letters of Sam Houston," *Southwestern Historical Quarterly* 81, no. 4 (1978): 417–26; Marilyn McAdams Sibley, "Letters From Sam Houston to Albert Sidney Johnson," *Southwestern Historical Quarterly* 66, no. 2 (1962/63): 252–61; Sam Houston, *The Personal Correspondence of Sam Houston*, edited by Madge Thornall Roberts (Denton, TX: University of North Carolina Press, 1996). For examples of work on others besides Houston, see, for example, C. Alwyn Barr, "The Making of a Secessionist: The Antebellum Career of Roger Q. Mills," *Southwestern Historical Quarterly* 79, no. 2 (1975): 129–44; William S. Hitchcock, "Southern Moderates and Secession: Senator Robert M. T. Hunter's Call for Union," *Journal of American History* 59, no. 4 (March 1973): 871–84; James Marten, "The Lamentations of a Whig: James Throckmorton Writes a Letter," *Civil War History* 31, no. 2 (1985): 163–70; John Moretta, "William Pitt Ballinger and the Travail of Texas Secession," *Houston Review* 11, no. 1 (1989): 3–26; Edmund Ruffin,

The Diary of Edmund Ruffin (Baton Rouge: Louisiana State University Press, 1972). See also James E. Crisp, "Sam Houston's Speechwriters: The Grad Student, the Teenager, the Editors, and the Historians," *Southwestern Historical Quarterly* 97, no. 2 (1993): 203–27. See Barr, "The Making of a Secessionist: The Antebellum Career of Roger Q. Mills"; Marten, "The Lamentations of a Whig: James Throckmorton Writes a Letter"; Moretta, "William Pitt Ballinger and the Travail of Texas Secession." Thomas E. Shuford, "Three Texas Unionist Editors face the Secession Crisis: A Case Study on Freedom of the Press" (PhD diss., University of Texas at Austin, 1979).

15. For Houston's rhetoric, see Susan F. Wiltshire, "Sam Houston and the Iliad." *Tennessee Historical Quarterly* 32, no. 3 (1973): 249–54; James, *The Raven*; Charles Edward Lester, *The Life of Sam Houston* (New York: J. C. Derby, 1855). Lester's book is a later reediting of his original *Sam Houston and His Republic* (New York: Burgess, Stringer, 1846). This book is reportedly based heavily on the author's actual conversations with Houston, who was then the fifty-three-year-old first president of the Republic of Texas. Marshall De Bruhl, *Sword of San Jacinto: A Life of Sam Houston*, 364. On this subject, DeBruhl quotes David G. Burnet, an inveterate Houston detractor, as having told Houston's associate Thomas J. Rusk that "I entertain no doubt that Houston is himself, the real author of that volume of lies." Wiltshire says merely that Lester "worked closely with Houston for three months," and she concludes, correctly in my view, that Lester wrote the 1846 book and later embellished it as part of Houston's possible "Know-Nothing" US presidential campaign of 1856, producing *The Life of General Sam Houston* in 1855. "Campaign biographies" were, at that time, a common literary genre. See also George Creel, *Sam Houston: Colossus in Buckskin* (New York: Cosmopolitan Book Corporation, 1928); M. K. Wisehart, *Sam Houston: American Giant* (Washington: R. B. Luce, 1962). William Carey Crane made the same point about Houston long before Wiltshire: "It is said that he could repeat Pope's Homer's Iliad almost verbatim. His anxiety to study the languages of Greece and Rome became intense . . . at last his family learned that he was sojourning, more according to his existing taste, with the Cherokee Indians. . . . Questioned by relatives as to his motives for such a wild choice, he replied, that . . . if he could not study Latin in the Academy, he could, at least, read a translation from the Greek in the woods, and read it in peace." William Carey Crane, *The Life and Select Literary Remains of Sam Houston of Texas* (Philadelphia: J. B. Lippincott and Co., 1885 [orig. ed., 1884]), 18–19 (all page citations are to the 1885 reprint edition).

16. Walter Buenger, "The Riddle of Secession," *Southwestern Historical Quarterly* 87, no. 2 (1983): 151–53, 153 (quote).

17. Marshall De Bruhl, *Sword of San Jacinto: A Life of Sam Houston* (New York: Random House, 1993), 352–56, 401; Donna Tobias, "The States Rights Speaking of Oran Milo Roberts: A Study in Agitational Rhetoric" (PhD diss., Louisiana State University and Agricultural and Mechanical Col., 1982, DAI 43(8) (1983): 2497-A), 139–41.

18. *Journal of the House of Representatives, 8th Legislature State of Texas* (Austin: John Marshall & Company, 1860), 25–51 (November 10th Speech), 259–63 (December 21 Speech), in *State Secession Debates, 1859–1862* (New Haven: Krause-Thomson Organization, 197–?), microfilm.

19. Runnels also engaged in a four-page tirade against corporate and railroad interests. In this latter section, he used characteristic agrarian populist rhetoric to urge the legislature to prevent railroad companies from defaulting on loans from the state secured by two million dollars of corporate railroad bonds. The scheme was for the interest due the state on the bonds to be used for public education. Apparently, the notion of providing government assistance to unpopular industries (e.g., gambling) and justifying it in the name of generating revenue for education is not a new development.

20. *Journal of the Texas House of Representatives, 8th Legislature State of Texas*, 25–43.

21. *Journal of the Texas House of Representatives, 8th Legislature State of Texas*, 43–51 and 43 (first quote); 48 (second quote); 50 (third quote).

22. *Journal of the Texas House of Representatives, 8th Legislature State of Texas*, 50–51.

23. *Journal of the Texas House of Representatives, 8th Legislature State of Texas*, 51.

24. *Journal of the Texas House of Representatives, 8th Legislature State of Texas*, 45.

25. *Journal of the Texas House of Representatives, 8th Legislature State of Texas*, 48.

26. *Journal of the Texas House of Representatives, 8th Legislature State of Texas*, 48 (first quote), 49 (second and third quotes).

27. *Journal of the Texas House of Representatives, 8th Legislature State of Texas*, 261.

28. *Journal of the Texas House of Representatives, 8th Legislature State of Texas*.

29. Tobias, "The State's Rights Speaking of Oran Milo Roberts," 24–30.

30. Tobias, "The State's Rights Speaking of Oran Milo Roberts," 30–36, 46, quoting James D. Lynch, *The Bench and Bar of Texas* (St. Louis: Nixton-Jones Printing Co., 1885), 280; Tobias, "The State's Rights Speaking of Oran Milo Roberts," 43–46.

31. Tobias, "The State's Rights Speaking of Oran Milo Roberts," 42, cites as an example "In Defense of the University at San Augustine: Criticism Upon the Pedantry and Presumption of M. A. Montrose's Articles Published in the Redlander Under Signature of 'AVE' and Strictures upon Refusal of Canfield to Publish Articles Answering Montrose" (1843). A better example might be O. M. Roberts, "Primitive Christian Education," O. M. Roberts Papers, Center for American History, University of Texas at Austin, 35–37.

32. O. M. Roberts, "Essay on Mormonism," O. M. Roberts Papers, Center for American History, University of Texas at Austin.

33. Tobias, "The States Rights Speaking of Oran Milo Roberts," 100.

34. *Galveston News*, July 24, 1855.

35. "Speech in Opposition to Know Nothingism," Oran Milo Roberts Papers, Center of American History, University of Texas at Austin.

36. "Speech in Opposition to Know Nothingism," Oran Milo Roberts Papers, Center of American History, University of Texas at Austin. Other writers have chronicled the parallels between antipapism and antipuritanism in the rhetoric of Texas politicians throughout the nineteenth century. See Joseph Locke, "Conquering Salem: The Triumph of the Christian Vision in Turn-of-the-Twentieth-Century Texas," *Southwestern Historical Quarterly* 115, no. 3 (January 2012): 232–57.

37. See Tobias, "The States Rights Speaking of Oran Milo Roberts," 139–41.

38. O. M. Roberts, "The Political, Legislative, and Judicial History of Texas," in *A Comprehensive History of Texas 1685–1897*, vol. 2, ed. Dudley G. Wooten (Dallas: William G. Scarff, 1898), 91; James L. Haley, *The Texas Supreme Court: A Narrative History, 1836–1986*, 65–66; Walter Buenger, "The Riddle of Secession," *Southwestern Historical Quarterly* 87, no. 2 (1983): 153. In Buenger's words, "Secession was both a spontaneous popular movement present in most counties of the state and a process openly led by pillars of the community."

39. O. M. Roberts, "The Impending Crisis," original manuscript of speech of Judge O. M. Roberts of the Supreme Court of Texas at the capital, December 1, 1860, O. M. Roberts Collection, Center for American History, University of Texas at Austin (speech quotes); Tobias, "The States Rights Speaking of Oran Milo Roberts," 159–209 (circumstances and content of the speeches of Roberts and Bell). The original handwritten draft of Roberts's speech is written in ink on lined sheets of very thick light blue paper from a legal pad manufactured by John C. Clark & Son, 230 Dock Street, Philadelphia. The speech fills an entire legal pad and is written in a close antique hand. Fortunately, Roberts's speech was self-published shortly after it was given, as was that of Judge Bell. All of these speeches are located in Box 2F473 of the O. M. Roberts Collection, Center for American History, and the University of Texas at Austin. Roberts bound most of them together in a scrapbook (bearing the label "MSS #8211"), with the essay on Mormonism and some other essays, as well as the original handwritten draft of the "1860—The First Call upon the People of Texas to Assemble in Convention."

40. James H. Bell, "Speech at the Capitol-December 1, 1860," O. M. Roberts Collection, Center for American History, University of Texas at Austin. See also William Shakespeare, *Henry VI*, Part 2. Clearly, "First let's kill all the lawyers" was not first used as a political slogan in the late twentieth century. It is equally clear that while some, in agreement with the hackneyed contemporary lawyer joke, regard this as a "good start," there have always been others to remind us of the context in which Shakespeare penned this line: "It is the battle cry of rabble-rousers, brigands, and tyrants." Those societies in which it has actually been practiced include Nazi Germany, Stalinist Russia, Maoist China, Castro's Cuba, and virtually every other regime of extreme repression in modern history. Judge Bell apparently knew his Shakespeare and his history well enough to know this. Unlike modern politicians, Judge Bell

understood that Jack Cade and Wat Tyler, not lawyers, were the bad guys, and that this is one of the points Shakespeare sought to make.

41. O. M. Roberts, "The Impending Crisis" (quotes from Roberts' speech); Tobias, "The State's Rights Speaking of Oran Milo Roberts," 183 (Tobias' conclusion); Tobias, "The State's Rights Speaking of Oran Milo Roberts," 186 (regarding the Declaration of Independence).

42. Marshall DeBruhl, *Sword of San Jacinto*, 396; Donna Tobias, "The State's Rights Speaking of Oran Milo Roberts," 174; David Minor, "Throckmorton, James Webb," in *Handbook of Texas Online* (Texas State Historical Association), accessed August 19, 2014, http://www.tshaonline.org/handbook/online/articles/fth36; Bob Garner, "Let Us Be Patriots and Texans—A Content Analysis of the Secession Rhetoric of Sam Houston: 1854–1861," 1–19. Edward Maher, Secession in Texas (PhD book, Fordham University, 1960), 89, lists Houston, Hamilton, and Paschal as the most important unionists in pre–Civil War Texas. Prof. James Paulsen, "Challenges to Confederate Conscription in the Texas Supreme Court" (unpublished draft of February 25, 2005), 10, at note 17 echoes this view.

43. DeBruhl, *Sword of San Jacinto*, 391–92.

44. DeBruhl, *Sword of San Jacinto*, 391–92 (Throckmorton actions); Claude Elliott, *Leathercoat, the Life of James W. Throckmorton* (San Antonio: Standard Printing Co., 1938); David Minor, "Throckmorton, James Webb," in *Handbook of Texas Online* (Texas State Historical Association), accessed August 19, 2014, http://www.tshaon-line.org/handbook/online/articles/fth36; *The Campaign Intelligencer*, July 23, 1859 (*Intelligencer* quote).

45. *Southern Intelligencer*, August 4, 1858.

46. *Southern Intelligencer*, August 4, 1858, 2.

47. *Southern Intelligencer*, May 25, 1859, 2. See also John L. Waller, *Colossal Hamilton of Texas: A Biography of Andrew Jackson Hamilton, Militant Unionist and Reconstruction Governor* (El Paso: Texas Western Press, 1968), 18.

48. *Southern Intelligencer*, July 27, 1859, 2. See also Waller, *Colossal Hamilton of Texas*, 19–20.

49. *Congressional Globe*, 36th Congress, 1st Session, Part I, 603–4, quoted in Waller, *Colossal Hamilton of Texas*, 23.

50. Paschal was listed as editor of the paper in the December 3, 1856, issue of the *Southern Intelligencer*, 2. No other official listing of an editor is found in the issues extant on microfilm from 1856 to 1860. It appears from the issues read and cited here that Paschal had certainly ceased regularly editing the paper once he stood for the Electoral College in 1860 and began touring the state to give speeches in favor of the "uncommitted" Union ticket. This corresponds with the appearance of H. H. Raven as "publisher" in the late summer / early fall of 1860. See *Southern Intelligencer*, September 5, 1860. Raven apparently returned to Austin in May 1859 from

an absence elsewhere, since he was described then by Paschal as his "printer friend, H. H. Raven." *Southern Intelligencer,* May 11, 1859. By October 1860, A. B. Norton had taken over as publisher. *Southern Intelligencer,* October 10, 1860. It appears that at this point Paschal was campaigning and providing pieces to the paper, but someone else was actually editing it for the printer and owner, A. B. Norton. Shuford cites Norton's essay in *A History of the Texas Press Association,* ed. E. B. Baillio (Dallas: Southwestern Printing Co., 1916), and the March 28, 1860, issue of the *Dallas Herald* for the proposition that Norton had become editor by earlier that month, March 1860. See Shuford, "Three Texas Unionist Editors face the Secession Crisis: A Case Study on Freedom of the Press," 31, and accompanying note 37.

51. See James Paulsen, "Challenges to Confederate Conscription in the Texas Supreme Court" (unpublished draft of February 25, 2005).

52. *Southern Intelligencer,* November 19, 1856. In the same issue, Paschal excoriated Houston and his "three thousand vice-gerents [sic] and their deluded [Know-Nothing] followers," who threatened to "destroy the South" and the Union. He also wrote vehemently in favor of religious freedom and equal treatment of (presumably white) immigrants, considering the Democratic Party the true champion of the little (white) man. His racism toward blacks is evident in the *Southern Intelligencer,* October 21, 1857, which argued for the right of states to let blacks vote, but only because of principles of states' rights. In response to the charge that he was an egalitarian, Paschal responded that "no one has a greater horror of this political black equality allowed in some States, than the writer. But it is a privilege which concerns the States alone where it exists." *Southern Intelligencer,* October 21, 1857.

53. *Southern Intelligencer,* May 25, 1859, 1.

54. *Southern Intelligencer,* October 10, 1860, 1. When A. B. Norton took over from Paschal as editor just before the 1860 campaign, the *Intelligencer*'s platform did not change. It republished from the *New York Day Book* letters purporting to be from East Texas and Fort Worth, each of which exaggerated the danger of abolitionists urging a slave revolt. "J.W.S." from Fort Worth claimed that "we will hang every man who does not live above suspicion. . . . Necessity now reverses the rule, for it is better to hang ninety-nine innocent [suspicious] men than to let one guilty one pass." Alluding to the French Revolution and the Romantic poet Lord Byron, Norton (or perhaps Paschal—it is difficult to be sure) replied that "Byron's old pirate Lambro—'as mild a man as ever scuttled a ship or cut a throat,' was a babe in the woods compared to this Ft. Worth man. J. W. S. should have lived in the time of the bloody butchers, Marat and Robespierre." Alluding to more ancient history and literature, the editor continued by criticizing secessionists on the ground that their exaggerated scare stories encouraged disloyalty and contempt for law and order, leading people to believe "their lives, their property, their women, and their children are in imminent danger." Then, according to the *Intelligencer,* "when the Constitution and the laws

are overthrown, when the powers of the Judiciary are usurped by the mob, then every man carries his life in his hands.... It is the reign of Nero with the horrible feature of a multitude of fiddlers, instead of a single tyrant."

Another letter published in the same issue, this one from a friendly correspondent signed "Union," added another aspect to the *Intelligencer*'s attempt to paint itself as the voice of conservatism, wisdom, and reason. "Union" particularly criticized the performance of one N. W. Shannon at a September 18th secessionist meeting in Washington County. It claimed that Shannon, a young lawyer, "always has been a disruptionist.... He is the flower of the Democracy here.... He is the chevalier of the young South. Keen, shrewd and insinuating, he always stands behind the curtains to bring about the doctrine of the 'Young South.' He curses the old people as 'fogies' and boldly asserts the young men of the South as the regenerators of the country" (*Southern Intelligencer*, October 10, 1860, 1, 2).

55. O. M. Roberts, "1860—The First Call Upon the People of Texas to Assemble in Convention," O. M. Roberts Collection, Center for American History, University of Texas at Austin. This document, handwritten by Roberts, is attached to his personal description of the events surrounding it, from which the quotes in this paragraph are taken. It was a slightly amended version written by George Flournoy that was printed and published in December 1860, according to Roberts's notes.

56. *Journal of the Secession Convention of Texas 1861*, edited from the original in the Department of State by Ernest William Winkler, State Librarian (Austin: Austin Printing Co., 1912), accessed September 26, 2014, http://tarlton.law.utexas.edu/constitutions/slider/constitution/texas1861/journals/, 24–26, 36–, 38, 46–48. See also *Journal of the House of Representatives, 8th Legislature State of Texas*. Hereafter, Winkler's *Journal of the Secession Convention 1861*, pdf images of which are available in print form but have been microfilmed and scanned for internet use, will be cited in the following shortened form: *Journal of the Secession Convention of Texas*, _____.

57. *Journal of the House of Representatives—8th Legislature State of Texas*; *Journal of the Secession Convention of Texas*, 48–49; Donna Tobias, "The State's Right Speaking of Oran Milo Roberts 1850–1861: A Study in Agitational Rhetoric," 213.

58. *Journal of the Secession Convention of Texas*, 58–65.

59. *Journal of the Secession Convention of Texas*, 61–65.

60. *Journal of the Secession Convention of Texas*, 58–59.

61. *Journal of the Secession Convention of Texas*, 79–85.

62. *Journal of the Secession Convention of Texas*, 68; Walter L. Buenger, "Secession," in *Handbook of Texas Online* (Texas State Historical Association), accessed September 1, 2013, http://www.tshaonline.org/handbook/online/articles/mgs02; Dale Baum, *The Shattering of Texas Unionism* (Baton Rouge: Louisiana State University Press, 1998), 71–72, 74–79; James L. Haley, *The Texas Supreme Court: A Narrative History, 1836–1986*, 66–67.

63. *Journal of the Secession Convention of Texas*, 86–98

64. *Journal of the Secession Convention of Texas*, 90–98, 113–14 (Houston's reply to the convention), 119 (Roberts' response), 125–36 (gun purchase ordinance).

65. *Journal of the Secession Convention of Texas*, 128–29.

66. *Journal of the Secession Convention of Texas*, 133–34.

67. *Journal of the Secession Convention of Texas*, 159–86.

68. Walter L. Buenger, "Constitution of 1861," in *Handbook of Texas Online* (Texas State Historical Association), accessed September 1, 2013, http://www.tshaonline.org/handbook/online/articles/mhc04; Constitution of the State of Texas (1845), Article VIII; Constitution of the State of Texas (1861), Article VIII.

69. See, for example, Diane Miller Sommerville, *Rape and Race in the Nineteenth Century South* (Chapel Hill: University of North Carolina Press, 2004); Martha Hodes, *White Women, Black Men: Illicit Sex in the Nineteenth Century South* (New Haven: Yale University Press, 1997); William Faulkner, *Light in August* (New York: Random House, 1959); Elizabeth Fox Genovese, *Within the Plantation Household* (Chapel Hill: University of North Carolina Press, 1988).

70. Pryor Lea, John Henry Brown, and John D. Stell, "Address to the People of Texas," in *Journal of the Secession Convention of Texas*, 252–61.

71. DeBruhl, *Sword of San Jacinto*, 394–96.

72. DeBruhl, *Sword of San Jacinto*, 396–97.

73. "Genealogical Notes and Anecdotes: Sam Houston as Caius Marius," website, accessed September 21, 2013, http://www.crosswinds.net/~marlerjc/houston.html.

74. James, *The Raven*, 410–11.

75. James H. Bell, letter to M. C. Hamilton et al., cover letter transmitting printed copy of "Speech at the Capitol-December 1, 1860," O. M. Roberts Collection, Center for American History, University of Texas at Austin. Indeed, it was for this reason that Walter Buenger titled his book "Stilling the Voice of Reason."

76. See, for example, James W. Paulsen and James Hambleton, "Confederates and Carpetbaggers: The Precedential Value of Decisions from the Civil War and Reconstruction Era," *Texas Bar Journal* 51, no. 9 (October 1988): 916.

77. Cicero, *Pro Milone*, chapter 4, online version at the Perseus Project of Tufts University, accessed September 1, 2013, http://www.perseus.tufts.edu/hopper/text?doc=Perseus%3Atext%3A1999.02.0011%3Atext%3DMil.%3Achapter%3D4; Alwyn Barr, ed., "Records of the Confederate Military Commission in San Antonio, July 2–October 10, 1862," *Southwestern Historical Quarterly* 70, no. 3 (October 1966): 289–313.

Chapter 4

1. Carl H. Moneyhan, *Republicanism in Reconstruction Texas* (College Station: Texas A&M University Press, 2001 [orig. ed., Austin: University of Texas Press, 1980]), 3 (citations are to the Texas A&M 2001 edition); Ronald Norman Gray, "The

NOTES TO PAGES 92–94

Abortive State of West Texas" (thesis, Texas Technical College, 1969), online version, accessed November 19, 2013, http://repositories.tdl.org/ttu-ir/bitstream/handle/2346/14201/31295004608377.pdf?sequence=1.

2. Andrew Johnson: Proclamation 134—Granting Amnesty to Participants in the Rebellion, with Certain Exceptions (May 29, 1865), in Gerhard Peters and John T. Woolley, eds., the American Presidency Project, online version, accessed August 19, 2014, http://www.presidency.ucsb.edu/ws/?pid=72392 (quote); Andrew Johnson, Proclamation 139—Reorganizing a Constitutional Government in Texas (June 17, 1865), in Gerhard Peters and John T. Woolley, eds., the American Presidency Project, online version, accessed August 19, 2014, http://www.presidency.ucsb.edu/ws/?pid=71947.

3. *Journal of the Texas State Convention: Assembled at Austin, Feb. 7, 1866. Adjourned April 2, 1866.* (Austin: Southern Intelligencer, 1866), pdf book online at *Texas Constitutions 1824–1876*, accessed August 19, 2014, http://tarlton.law.utexas.edu/constitutions/, 3; Carl H. Moneyhan, *Republicanism in Reconstruction Texas*, 23, 32–33. Although Moneyhan says the proclamation was dated November 17th, the convention journal says the 15th. Further citations to the 1866 journal will be abbreviated: "*Journal of the 1866 Texas Convention*, (page number)."

4. *Journal of the 1866 Texas Convention*, 5–8; Claude Elliott, *Leathercoat, the Life of James W. Throckmorton* (San Antonio: Standard Printing Co., 1938); David Minor, "Throckmorton, James Webb," in *Handbook of Texas Online* (Texas State Historical Association), accessed August 19, 2014, http://www.tshaonline.org/handbook/online/articles/fth36; L. W. Kemp, "Latimer, Albert Hamilton," in *Handbook of Texas Online* (Texas State Historical Association), accessed August 19, 2014, http://www.tshaonline.org/handbook/online/articles/fla44; "Hon. William M. Taylor," *U.S. Biographies Project*, website, accessed August 19, 2014, http://www.usbiographies.org/texas/houston/taylor.html. Throughout this chapter, I have referred to the lists of delegates within the 1866 and 1868–69 *Journals* of the conventions, as well as Appendices 3 and 4 (tables of delegates) in Moneyhon's book for biographical and political information on delegates. Carl H. Moneyhon, *Republicanism in Reconstruction Texas*, 226–47.

5. Janice C. May, *The Texas State Constitution* (Oxford: Oxford University Press, 2011), 18; Carl H. Moneyhon, *Republicanism in Reconstruction Texas* (College Station: Texas A&M University Press, 2001), 34. For the organization of the Union Caucus, see Moneyhon, *Republicanism in Reconstruction Texas*, 42–43. Although Moneyhon says that Throckmorton won the runoff with Latimer by 44 to 24, the convention journal records the vote was 41 to 24 with another three votes cast for "scattering," perhaps an indication of a smattering of minor candidates. *Journal of the 1866 Texas Convention*, 6. Runnels's application for pardon is discussed at *Journal of the 1866 Texas Convention*, 42. The ordinance on Houston's salary is found at "Ordinance 21," *The Constitution, as Amended, and Ordinances of the Convention*

of 1866, Together with the Proclamation of Governor Declaring the Ratification of the Amendments to the Constitution, and the General Laws of the Regular Session of the Eleventh Legislature of the State of Texas (Austin: Printed at the Gazette office, by Jo. Walker, state printer, 1866), accessed August 23, 2014, http://tarlton.law.utexas.edu/constitutions/download/texas1866/texas1866.pdf, 49. The last quote in the paragraph is from *The Constitution, as Amended, and Ordinances of the Convention of 1866, Together with the Proclamation of Governor Declaring the Ratification of the Amendments to the Constitution, and the General Laws of the Regular Session of the Eleventh Legislature of the State of Texas* (Austin: Printed at the Gazette office, by Jo. Walker, state printer, 1866), accessed August 23, 2014, http://tarlton.law.utexas.edu/constitutions/download/texas1866/texas1866.pdf, 3. The actions on the Houston salary ordinance are at *Journal of the 1866 Texas Convention* 221 (proposed and referred to Committee on Finance), 258 (passed to the orders of the day), 288 (ordinance passed by vote of 62 to 1), 266 (resolution on Houston's death and portrait passed unanimously). See also "Bradshaw, Amzi," in *Handbook of Texas Online* (Texas State Historical Association), accessed August 23, 2014, http://www.tshaonline.org/handbook/online/articles/fbryv (last quote). By implication, O. M. Roberts acknowledged taking President Johnson's loyalty oath when describing his travails as a senator who would not be seated by the US Congress. He does not mention the loyalty oath but says he could not take the "test oath" later prescribed by Congress (a version of which became known as the "ironclad oath") swearing the affiant had not assisted in the rebellion. O. M. Roberts, "The Experiences of an Unrecognized Senator," *Quarterly of the Texas State Historical Association* 12, no. 2 (October 1908): 94–95.

6. *Journal of the 1866 Texas Convention*, 6–7 (Throckmorton speech), 16–27 (Hamilton message), 22 (Hamilton quote).

7. *Journal of the 1866 Texas Convention*, 21–27, 24–25 (first quote), 25 (second quote), 26 (third quote), 31 (Bumpass resolution).

8. *Journal of the 1866 Texas Convention*, 30–31.

9. *Journal of the 1866 Texas Convention*, 31.

10. *Journal of the 1866 Texas Convention*, 37.

11. Constitution of the State of Texas (1866), Article IV; cf. Constitution of the State of Texas (1861), Article IV; *Journal of the 1866 Texas Convention*, 132–33 (Roberts committee report).

12. *Journal of the 1866 Texas Convention*, 38–39.

13. *Journal of the 1866 Texas Convention*, 38–40 (Roberts proposal), 81 (Degener proposal).

14. *The Constitution as Amended and Ordinances of the Convention of 1866, Together with the Proclamation of the Governor Declaring the Ratification of the Amendments to the Constitution, and the General Laws of the Regular Session of the 11th Legislature of the State of Texas* (Austin: J. O. Walker, State Printer, 1866), 35–40.

15. *Journal of the 1866 Texas Convention*, 66, 102, 166, 203.

16. "Ordinance 13," *The Constitution, as Amended, and Ordinances of the Convention of 1866, Together with the Proclamation of Governor Declaring the Ratification of the Amendments to the Constitution, and the General Laws of the Regular Session of the Eleventh Legislature of the State of Texas* (Austin: Printed at the Gazette Office, by Jo. Walker, State Printer, 1866), 45–46; *Journal of the 1866 Texas Convention*, vol. 1, 357–59 (vote and protest on division and quotes therefrom); Carl H. Moneyhon, "Appendix 3: Delegates to the Constitutional Convention of 1866," in *Republicanism in Reconstruction Texas*, 226–35 (identifying political information on members of the Union Caucus and other delegates). Ronald Norman Gray, "The Abortive State of West Texas" (thesis, Texas Technical College, 1969): 16–18, accessed August 27, 2014, http://repositories.tdl.org/ttu-ir/bitstream/handle/2346/14201/31295004608377.pdf?sequence=1 states that the final vote on division that precipitated Bumpass's protest was on Flanagan's original proposal, but this is incorrect as indicated by the ordinance on division actually passed and enrolled, which was the version reported by A. B. Norton and supported by E. J. Davis. See *Journal of the 1866 Texas Convention*, 357; Ernest Wallace, *The Howling of Coyotes: Reconstruction Efforts to Divide Texas* (College Station: Texas A&M University Press, 1979), 20.

17. *Journal of the 1866 Texas Convention*, 33–35.

18. *Journal of the 1866 Texas Convention*, 35, 60, 146–52, 156–59, 161–64; Carl Moneyhan, *Republicanism in Reconstruction Texas*, 38–39; "Ordinance 11," *The Constitution, as Amended, and Ordinances of the Convention of 1866, Together with the Proclamation of Governor Declaring the Ratification of the Amendments to the Constitution, and the General Laws of the Regular Session of the Eleventh Legislature of the State of Texas* (Austin: Printed at the Gazette office, by Jo. Walker, state printer, 1866), 41–44.

19. Constitution of the State of Texas (1845), Article VII, Sections 30–31; Constitution of the State of Texas (1861), Article VII, Sections 30–31.

20. Carl Moneyhon, *Republicanism in Reconstruction Texas*, 39–40, 227; Claude Elliott, "Paschal, Isaiah Addison," in *Handbook of Texas Online* (Texas State Historical Association), accessed August 22, 2014, http://www.tshaonline.org/handbook/online/articles/fpa47; *Journal of the 1866 Texas Convention*, 141–42, 336–37; Constitution of the State of Texas (1866), Article VII, Sections 33 and 36, cf. Constitution of the State of Texas (1861), Article VII, Sections 30, 31, 33.

21. Constitution of the State of Texas (1866), Article VII, Section 36 (including note concerning repeal of previous laws); Constitution of the State of Texas (1866), Article X, Section 3. See also *Journal of the Reconstruction Convention which Met at Austin, Texas, June 1, A.D., 1868* (Austin: Tracy, Siemering & Co., 1870), 66–73, reporting to the 1868 convention the history of the relationship between railroad subsidies and public education, and the donation of public lands toward the foundation of a state university.

22. "Ordinance 29," *The Constitution, as Amended, and Ordinances of the Convention of 1866, Together with the Proclamation of Governor Declaring the Ratification of the Amendments to the Constitution, and the General Laws of the Regular Session of the Eleventh Legislature of the State of Texas* (Austin: Printed at the Gazette office, by Jo. Walker, state printer, 1866), 52–53, 46 (proposal), 243–44 (vote); Thomas W. Cutrer, "Waul, Thomas Neville," in *Handbook of Texas Online* (Texas State Historical Association), accessed August 23, 2014, http://www.tshaonline.org/handbook/online/articles/fwa76; J. L. Bryan, "Bradshaw, Amzi," in *Handbook of Texas Online* (Texas State Historical Association), accessed August 23, 2014, http://www.tshaonline.org/handbook/online/articles/fbryv; Hobart Huson, "Phillips, Alexander H.," in *Handbook of Texas Online* (Texas State Historical Association), accessed August 23, 2014, http://www.tshaonline.org/handbook/online/articles/fph06.

23. *Journal of the 1866 Texas Convention*, 41 (Ireland proposal), 45 (committee report), 58 (committee report read and adopted on voice vote).

24. *Journal of the 1866 Texas Convention*, 119 (Roberts proposal).

25. *Journal of the 1866 Texas Convention*, 51, 59 (Committee on the Legislative Department reports); Constitution of the State of Texas (1866), Article III, Sections 1–10, cf. Constitution of the State of Texas (1861), Article III, Sections 1–11.

26. *Journal of the 1866 Texas Convention*, 81–91, 89 (quotes).

27. *Journal of the 1866 Texas Convention*, 89 (quotes), 91 (read to come up in order), 185–87 (final passage Article III).

28. *Journal of the 1866 Texas Convention*, 51–52 (initial committee proposal), 61 (proposal read again to be taken up in special order), 68 (taken up by special order and considered by committee of the whole), 93 (Roberts amendment proposed in committee of the whole adopted by convention with Throckmorton support), 94–100 (debate and proposals leading to final adoption of Article VIII with final engrossment at 100); Constitution of the State of Texas (1866), Article III, Section 1.

29. Constitution of the State of Texas (1866), Article III, Section 1.

30. Constitution of the State of Texas (1866), Article III, Section 2; *Journal of the 1866 Texas Convention*, 51–52 (initial committee proposal), 93 (Roberts amendment proposed in committee of the whole adopted by convention with Throckmorton support; Davis and W. E. Jones amendments proposed), 94 (Mabry's motion and its tabling), 95 (Degener proposal tabled), 97 (Throckmorton amendment), 98 (Norton proposal), 100 (final adoption of Article VIII with final engrossment); Douglas Hale, "Mabry, Hinche Parham," in *Handbook of Texas Online* (Texas State Historical Association), accessed August 24, 2014, http://www.tshaonline.org/handbook/online/articles/fma02.

31. Constitution of the State of Texas (1866), Article X; *Journal of the 1866 Texas Convention*, 199 (McCormack proposal), 215 (Davis amendment).

32. Carl Moneyhon, *Republicanism in Reconstruction Texas*, 37, citing contemporary observer Benjamin Truman (most liberal constitution), 49–50 (1866 election);

James Baggett, "The Rise and Fall of the Texas Radicals: 1867–1883" (PhD diss., North Texas State University, 1972; Ann Arbor: University Microfilms, 1973), 50–54 (1866 election), 58 (election of Roberts and Burnet); *Journal of the 1866 Texas Convention*, 318 (quotes); Andrew Johnson, Presidential Proclamation Declaring a State of Peace between Texas and the United States, in *Narrative History of Texas Secession and Readmission to the Union: Related Readmission Documents* (Austin: Texas State Library and Archives Commission), accessed August 24, 2014, https://www.tsl.texas.gov/ref/abouttx/secession/20aug1866.html.

33. Baggett, "The Rise and Fall of the Texas Radicals: 1867–1883," 56–57; Carl Moneyhon, *Republicanism in Reconstruction Texas*, 51–57.

34. Baggett, "The Rise and Fall of the Texas Radicals: 1867–1883," 51–53 (Throckmorton election), 58–62 (anti-African legislation and Fourteenth Amendment); Moneyhon, *Republicanism in Reconstruction Texas*, 51–52; James Baggett, "The Rise and Fall of the Texas Radicals: 1867–1883," 59, quoting H. Gammel, ed., *Laws of Texas*, vol. V, 995–97 (quotes); Michael Ariens, *Lone Star Law* (Lubbock: Texas Tech University Press, 2011), 39–40 (black codes); Carl H. Moneyhon, "Reconstruction," in *Handbook of Texas Online* (Texas State Historical Association), accessed August 27, 2014, http://www.tshaonline.org/handbook/online/articles/mzr01.

35. The new Congress was the Fortieth Congress, which took over from the Thirty-Ninth Congress on March 4, 1867. The First Reconstruction Act was passed March 2nd, so only the Second Act was passed by the new congress, on March 23, 1867, but it is logical to assume that the Republicans in the 39th Congress were affected by the outcome of the 1866 elections where Johnson campaigned strenuously against the radicals and lost badly.

36. Congress of the United States, Chapter CLIII: An Act to Provide for the More Efficient Government of the Rebel States, in *Narrative History of Texas Secession and Readmission to the Union: Related Readmission Documents: Reconstruction Acts 1867* (Austin: Texas State Library and Archives Commission), webpage, accessed August 25, 2014, https://www.tsl.texas.gov/ref/abouttx/secession/reconstruction.html); US Constitution, Amendment XIV, Section 3.

37. James Baggett, "The Rise and Fall of the Texas Radicals: 1867–1883," 62 (Sheridan); Congress of the United States, Chap. VI, An Act Supplementary to an Act Entitled "An Act to Provide for the More Efficient Government of the Rebel States," passed March Second, Eighteen Hundred and Sixty-Seven, and to Facilitate Restoration, in *Narrative History of Texas Secession and Readmission to the Union: Related Readmission Documents: Reconstruction Acts 1867* (Austin: Texas State Library and Archives Commission), accessed August 25, 2014, https://www.tsl.texas.gov/ref/abouttx/secession/reconstruction.html.

38. Janice C. May, *The Texas State Constitution* (Oxford: Oxford University Press, 2011), 19–20; James Baggett, "The Rise and Fall of the Texas Radicals: 1867–1883," 72–73, 80; Congress of the United States, Chap. VI. An Act Supplementary to an Act

Entitled "An Act to Provide for the More Efficient Government of the Rebel States," passed March Second, Eighteen Hundred and Sixty-Seven, and to Facilitate Restoration, in *Narrative History of Texas Secession and Readmission to the Union: Related Readmission Documents: Reconstruction Acts 1867* (Austin: Texas State Library and Archives Commission), accessed August 25, 2014, https://www.tsl.texas.gov/ref/abouttx/secession/reconstruction.html; Joseph G. Dawson III, "Hancock, Winfield Scott," in *Handbook of Texas Online* (Texas State Historical Association), accessed August 25, 2014, http://www.tshaonline.org/handbook/online/articles/fha48.

39. *Journal of the Reconstruction Convention which Met at Austin, Texas, June 1, A.D., 1868* (Austin: Tracy, Siemering & Co., 1870), vol. 1, 3; Charles Christopher Jackson, "Caldwell, Colbert," *Handbook of Texas Online (Texas State Historical Association)*, accessed August 25, 2014, http://www.tshaonline.org/handbook/online/articles/fca10. Although most official and scholarly sources spell the judge's name "Caldwell," the alternate spelling of "Coldwell" is correct and is used by his descendants. See Colbert N. Coldwell, "Setting the Record Straight: Colbert Coldwell's Quest for Justice," *Journal of the Texas Supreme Court Historical Society* 3, no. 3 (spring 2014): 21–26, stating that "much of what has been written about Justice Coldwell is wrong." The 1868 convention journal was published in two volumes, one covering the first session from June 1 to August 31, and the second covering the second session from December 8, 1868, to February 5, 1869. Further citations to the 1868 convention journal will follow the form *Texas Reconstruction Convention Journal* (1868), vol. ___, (p) ___. See also Baggett, "The Rise and Fall of the Texas Radicals: 1867–1883," 92; Moneyhon, *Republicanism in Reconstruction Texas*, 83–86. Moneyhon makes the unsubstantiated assertion that because Coldwell was seen as a rabble rouser, Davis at least appeared the more moderate candidate and the Democrats voted for him, although they later denied it. Moneyhon, *Republicanism in Reconstruction Texas*, 86. I choose to ignore this assertion in favor of the more credible view concurred in by Baggett that Coldwell, a close friend of Andrew Hamilton, was put up by his moderate faction as a candidate who might appeal to some radicals, while no one could have been operating under the misimpression that Davis, a South Texan former Whig who always opposed secession, who went north to meet with Lincoln and request a commission in the Union Army, who raised and commanded the First Texas (US) Cavalry, and who fought hard against the Confederacy in the recent war, was anything but radical by any contemporary southern political metric. Moreover, Davis was known to favor the extreme ab initio position and Coldwell to oppose it. See, for example, James Baggett, "The Rise and Fall of the Texas Radicals: 1867–1883," 92, 94–96; "Davis, Edmund Jackson," in *Handbook of Texas Online* (Texas State Historical Association), accessed August 25, 2014, http://www.tshaonline.org/handbook/online/articles/fda37.

40. Moneyhon, *Republicanism in Reconstruction Texas*, 83–86, 248–49.

41. *Texas Reconstruction Convention Journal* (1868), vol. 1, 12–13 (early quotes), 14 (quote on Fourteenth Amendment).

42. *Texas Reconstruction Convention Journal* (1868), vol. 1, 15.

43. *Texas Reconstruction Convention Journal* (1868), vol. 1, 14 (Pease proposals), 149–50 (report on payment by railroads in worthless Confederate money); Moneyhon, *Republicanism in Reconstruction Texas*, 83–84, 87.

44. *Texas Reconstruction Convention Journal* (1868), vol. 1, 25–26 (committee appointments), 28, 126, 128, 138, 143, 154, 157, 189, 241 (deliberations and proposals on ab initio), 797 (final vote on ab initio), 851–52 (proposals and vote to recess); *Texas Reconstruction Convention Journal* (1868), vol. 2, 326–29 (final vote on state division); Baggett, "The Rise and Fall of the Texas Radicals: 1867–1883," 93–94 (summary of first session); Ronald Norman Gray, "The Abortive State of West Texas" (thesis, Texas Technical College, 1969), 23–45, online version, accessed August 27, 2014, http://repositories.tdl.org/ttu-ir/bitstream/handle/2346/14201/31295004608377.pdf?sequence=1; Ernest Wallace, *The Howling of Coyotes: Reconstruction Efforts to Divide Texas* (College Station: Texas A&M University Press, 1979), 46–124.

45. *Texas Reconstruction Convention Journal* (1868), vol. 1, 31 (Flanagan proposal), 56–57 (majority committee report), 57–58 (minority report), 115–16 (vote), 181–80 (homestead protection).

46. *Texas Reconstruction Convention Journal* (1868), vol. 1, 641–42. The Committee on the Political and Legislative Department's report was taken up again on August 23rd and acted upon. *Texas Reconstruction Convention Journal* (1868), vol. 1, 853–59.

47. *Texas Reconstruction Convention Journal* (1868), vol. 1, 232–43 (initial report), 238–340 (general provisions report), 766–67 (mechanic liens), 816–18 (action taken).

48. *Texas Reconstruction Convention Journal* (1868), vol. 1, 232–43 (initial report), 238–40 (general provisions report), 766–67 (mechanic liens), 816–18 (action taken).

49. Constitution of the State of Texas (1866), Article VII, Section 22; Constitution of the State of Texas (1869), Article XII, Section 15.

50. Constitution of the State of Texas (1866), Article XII; Constitution of the State of Texas (1869), Article X.

51. Constitution of the State of Texas (1869), Article XII.

52. Constitution of the State of Texas (1869), Article X, Section 8; Article XII, Section 15; Article XII, Section 44.

53. *Texas Reconstruction Convention Journal* (1868), vol. 1, 162–69 (Degener report and proposal for Immigration Bureau), *Texas Reconstruction Convention Journal* (1868), vol. 1, 168 (quotes about Europeans); Constitution of the State of Texas (1869), Article XI (Immigration article of new constitution).

54. *Texas Reconstruction Convention Journal* (1868), vol. 1, 168.

55. *Texas Reconstruction Convention Journal* (1868), vol. 1, 610–11 (first two quotes), 613 (last quote).

56. Constitution of the State of Texas (1869), Article IX.

57. *Texas Reconstruction Convention Journal* (1868), vol. 1, 609–14 (committee report), 896–99 (segregation proposals), 911–18 (further deliberations).

58. *Texas Reconstruction Convention Journal* (1868), vol. 1, 609–14, 896–99, 911–18; Constitution of the State of Texas (1869), Article IX, Section 9.

59. Constitution of the State of Texas (1869), Article I, Sections 21–22; Constitution of the State of Texas (1866), Article I.

60. Constitution of the State of Texas (1869), Article III, Sections 1, 5, 13.

61. *Texas Reconstruction Convention Journal* (1868), vol. 1, 569 (additional categories of disenfranchised); *Texas Reconstruction Convention Journal* (1868), vol. 2, 481–83 (final vote rejecting radical committee proposal on registration in favor of A. J. Hamilton substitute); Constitution of the State of Texas (1869), Article III, Section 1; Constitution of the State of Texas (1869), Article XII, Section 1.

62. Constitution of the State of Texas (1869), Article IV; cf. Constitution of the State of Texas (1866), Article V; Constitution of the State of Texas (1869), Article V; cf. Constitution of the State of Texas (1866), Article IV; *Texas Reconstruction Convention Journal* (1868), vol. 1, 296–302 (initial Executive Committee report), 477–78 (modified report on Executive by Committee of the Whole), 527–30, 557–58 (deliberations on Executive Article), 572, 595–97, 623–25, 645–47 (votes on Executive Article by section), 465–70 (Committee on the Judiciary report), 818–25 (Judicial Article adopted by sections).

63. *Texas Reconstruction Convention Journal* (1868), vol. 1, 193–203 (report of Committee on Lawlessness and Violence claiming a "war of races" by "whites against the blacks" with rampant murder of freedmen and white union men by ex-rebels); Ernest Wallace, *The Howling of Coyotes: Reconstruction Efforts to Divide Texas*, 64–66, 69 (reasons for recess), 73 (division predominating second session); Carl Moneyhon, *Republicanism in Reconstruction Texas*, 100–101 (division predominating second session), 97–100 (Republican disputes during intermission). The Texas GOP had its state political convention in mid-August, where the Davis faction was so incensed by moderate control over the platform on issues such as ab initio, that it bolted and held its own rump convention. This also contributed to the radicals' increased efforts to accomplish division. Moneyhon makes the interesting argument that the ab initio question had been resolved between the sessions by the US Supreme Court decision in *Texas v. White*, which held that Texas remained a state during the rebellion, but one with a dysfunctional government, and only those acts taken by the illegitimate rebel government that aided the insurrection were null and void. However, this makes no sense given that the decision was not announced until April 12, 1869. Carl Moneyhon, *Republicanism in Reconstruction Texas*, 100; *Texas v. White*, 74 U.S. 700 (1869).

64. *Texas Reconstruction Convention Journal* (1868), vol. 1, 14 (committee created), 51 (committee appointed), 135 (Mills resolution to cede El Paso to the United States to

be combined with Santa Fe into new territory), 136 (Democrat proposed ordinance to authorize legislature to divide state referred to special committee), 106 (request of committee for copy of Beaman Bill), 143–48 (committee reports; majority endorses Beaman Bill), 160–62 (action on committee report postponed), 174–75 (more proposals for ceding western lands), 205–6 (division issue again recommitted to committee), 391 (Thomas resolution), 409–11 (convention vote to stop considering division by 47–37); Wallace, *The Howling of Coyotes: Reconstruction Efforts to Divide Texas*, 47 (balance of power in committee), 48–51 (Beaman proposal and Committee report, including maps).

65. *Texas Reconstruction Convention Journal* (1868), vol. 2, 4, 21–27, 38–43, 72, (proposals, counterproposals, and parliamentary maneuvers), 95–98 (Coldwell proposal narrowly defeated), 147–48 (vote repealing Thomas resolution), 534–35 (identifying information on delegates Kuchler, Varnell, and Jordan); Wallace, *The Howling of Coyotes: Reconstruction Efforts to Divide Texas*, 73–84 (deliberations of winter session on division, Canby arrival and discussion of West Texas constitution), 84–90 (press and public agitation). On the circumstances of the West Texas constitution's drafting, Wallace cites the personal correspondence of radical delegate J. P. Newcomb, the *Dallas Herald*, December 17, 1868, and Betty J. Sandlin, "The Texas Reconstruction Convention of 1868–1869" (PhD diss., Texas Tech University, 1970). See *Constitution of the State of West Texas* (Austin: n.p., 1869), accessed August 31, 2014, http://tarlton.law.utexas.edu/constitutions/texas1868. There were no fewer than nine military commanders of the Fifth Military District from 1867 to 1870. See Carl H. Moneyhon, "Reconstruction," *Handbook of Texas Online* (Texas State Historical Association), accessed August 30, 2014, http://www.tshaonline.org/handbook/online/articles/mzr01.

66. Wallace, *The Howling of Coyotes: Reconstruction Efforts to Divide Texas*, 73–84 (deliberations of winter session on division, proposed map, Canby arrival and discussion of West Texas constitution), 84–90 (press and public agitation), 91–108 (final actions of convention and Congress on division). On the circumstances of the West Texas constitution's drafting, Wallace cites the personal correspondence of radical delegate J. P. Newcomb, the *Dallas Herald*, December 17, 1868, and Betty J. Sandlin, "The Texas Reconstruction Convention of 1868–1869" (PhD diss., Texas Tech University, 1970).

67. *Texas Reconstruction Convention Journal* (1868), vol. 2, 267–68 (Davis proposal); Wallace, *The Howling of Coyotes: Reconstruction Efforts to Divide Texas*, 79–89 (West Texas Constitution, Degener and Hamilton speeches, debate, map, and press and public reaction), 91–108 (final actions of convention and Congress on division); *Texas Reconstruction Convention Journal* (1868), vol. 1, 193–203 (report of Committee on Lawlessness and Violence); *Constitution of the State of West Texas* (Austin: n.p., 1869), accessed August 31, 2014, http://tarlton.law.utexas.edu/constitutions/texas1868, Article VIII (voter registration; Article III (Legislature; qualified

electors; Public Schools), Article VII, Sections 2–3 (General Provisions re: voter disqualification and invalidity of laws supporting rebellion or racial inequality).

68. *Texas Reconstruction Convention Journal* (1868), vol. 2, 301–3, 326–27 (votes passing Davis proposal), 343–45 (addition of two more commissioners and election of commissioners), 255–56 (passage of resolution by B. H. Gray to appoint eleven man committee to revise provisions already engrossed, report a text of the constitution and prepare an ordinance for holding an election), 260 (committee appointed by Davis), 382–88 (report of drafting committee), 394–416, 481–91 (votes on constitution, section by section), 512–18 (final actions on constitution); Wallace, *The Howling of Coyotes: Reconstruction Efforts to Divide Texas*, 99–108 (convention's final days and actions of Davis and Canby); Moneyhon, *Republicanism in Reconstruction Texas*, 101–3 (convention's final days and actions of Davis and Canby); *Constitution of the State of Texas, Adopted by the Constitutional Convention Convened under the Reconstruction Acts of Congress Passed March 2, 1867, and the Acts Supplementary Thereto; to be Submitted for Ratification or Rejection at an Election to Take Place on the First Monday of July 1868* (Austin: Printed at the *Daily Republican* Office, 1869), 44–45, accessed August 31, 2014, http://tarlton.law.utexas.edu/constitutions/download/texas1869/texas1869.pdf (Election Declaration).

69. Wallace, *The Howling of Coyotes: Reconstruction Efforts to Divide Texas*, 109–28 (activities of commissioners and congressional refusal to divide); Moneyhon, *Republicanism in Reconstruction Texas*, 104–28 (state division and election of 1869); Carl H. Moneyhon, "Reconstruction," in *Handbook of Texas Online* (Texas State Historical Association), accessed August 31, 2014, http://www.tshaonline.org/handbook/online/articles/mzr01; Alwyn Barr, *Reconstruction to Reform: Texas Politics 1876–1906* (Austin: University of Texas Press, 1971), 8–9.

70. Carl H. Moneyhon, "Reconstruction," in *Handbook of Texas Online* (Texas State Historical Association), accessed August 31, 2014, http://www.tshaonline.org/handbook/online/articles/mzr01; Alwyn Barr, *Reconstruction to Reform: Texas Politics 1876–1906* (Austin: University of Texas Press, 1971), 8–9.

71. Barr, *Reconstruction to Reform: Texas Politics 1876–1906*, 8–9; Michael Ariens, *Lone Star Law* (Lubbock: Texas Tech University Press, 2011), 44; Carl H. Moneyhon, *Republicanism in Reconstruction Texas*, 133–45.

72. Carl H. Moneyhon, *Republicanism in Reconstruction Texas*, 145–51 (12th Legislature), 152–65 (congressional elections of 1871), 168–91 (elections of 1872 and 1873); James R. Norvell, "The Reconstruction Courts of Texas, 1867–1873," *Southwestern Historical Quarterly* 62, no. 2 (October 1958): 148–50.

73. Moneyhon, *Republicanism in Reconstruction Texas*, 145–51 (12th Legislature), 168–91 (elections of 1872 and 1873); Ariens, *Lone Star Law*, 45; Payne Jr., "Coke, Richard," in *Handbook of Texas Online* (Texas State Historical Association), accessed September 1, 2014, http://www.tshaonline.org/handbook/online/articles/fco15; James R. Norvell, "The Reconstruction Courts of Texas, 1867–1873," *Southwestern Historical Quarterly* 62, no. 2 (October 1958): 148–50.

74. Moneyhon, *Republicanism in Reconstruction Texas*, 192–96; Ariens, *Lone Star Law*, 44–47; Alwyn Barr, "Alexander, William [1819–1882]," in *Handbook of Texas Online* (Texas State Historical Association), accessed September 1, 2014, http://www.tshaonline.org/handbook/online/articles/fal13; Carl H. Moneyhon, "Ex Parte Rodriguez," in *Handbook of Texas Online* (Texas State Historical Association), accessed September 1, 2014, http://www.tshaonline.org/handbook/online/articles/jreo1; George E. Shelley, "The Semicolon Court of Texas," *Southwestern Historical Quarterly* 48, no. 4 (April 1945): 449–68; James R. Norvell, "The Reconstruction Courts of Texas, 1867–1873," *Southwestern Historical Quarterly* 62, no. 2 (October 1958): 150–55; Lance A. Cooper, "'A Slobbering Lame Thing?': The Semicolon Case Reconsidered," *Southwestern Historical Quarterly* 101, no. 3 (January, 1998): 321–39.

75. Moneyhon, *Republicanism in Reconstruction Texas*, 192–96; Ariens, *Lone Star Law*, 44–47; Alwyn Barr, "Alexander, William [1819–1882]," in *Handbook of Texas Online* (Texas State Historical Association), accessed September 1, 2014, http://www.tshaonline.org/handbook/online/articles/fal13; Carl H. Moneyhon, "Ex Parte Rodriguez," in *Handbook of Texas Online* (Texas State Historical Association), accessed September 1, 2014, http://www.tshaonline.org/handbook/online/articles/jreo1; George E. Shelley, "The Semicolon Court of Texas," *Southwestern Historical Quarterly* 48, no. 4 (April 1945): 449–68; James R. Norvell, "The Reconstruction Courts of Texas, 1867–1873," *Southwestern Historical Quarterly* 62, no. 2 (October 1958): 150–55; Lance A. Cooper, "'A Slobbering Lame Thing?': The Semicolon Case Reconsidered," *Southwestern Historical Quarterly* 101, no. 3 (January, 1998): 321–39; *Ex Parte Rodriguez*, 39 Tex. 705 (1874).

76. Moneyhon, *Republicanism in Reconstruction Texas*, 192–96; Ariens, *Lone Star Law*, 44–47; Shelley, "The Semicolon Court of Texas," 449–68; Norvell, "The Reconstruction Courts of Texas, 1867–1873," 150–55; Cooper, "'A Slobbering Lame Thing?': The Semicolon Case Reconsidered, 321–39; T. B. Wheeler, "Reminiscences of Reconstruction in Texas," *Quarterly of the Texas State Historical Association* 11, no. 1 (July 1907): 56–63.

Chapter 5

1. Nell Irvin Painter, *Standing at Armageddon: The United States, 1877–1919* (New York: W. W. Norton & Company 1987), 7.

2. Arnold M. Paul, *Conservative Crisis and the Rule of Law: Attitudes of Bar and Bench 1887–1895* (Harper and Roe: New York, New York, 1969), 1–2.

3. Nell Irvin Painter, *Standing at Armageddon: The United States, 1877–1919* (New York: W. W. Norton & Company 1987), 8–18, 18 (commune quote).

4. Seth Shepard McKay, "*Making the Texas Constitution of 1876*" (Philadelphia: University of Pennsylvania, 1924), 69, citing *Galveston News*, May 11, 1875, quoting the *Sherman Courier*.

5. Seth Shepard McKay, *Making the Texas Constitution of 1876* (Philadelphia: University of Pennsylvania, 1924), 68, quoting *State Gazette* (Austin), August 24, 1875;

Frank M. Stewart and Joseph L. Clark, *The Constitution and Government of Texas* (Boston: D. C. Heath & Co., 1933), 15.

6. O. M. Roberts, "The Political, Legislative, and Judicial History of Texas during Its Fifty Years of Statehood," in ed. Dudley G. Wooten, *A Comprehensive History of Texas 1685–1897*, vol. 2 (Dallas: William G. Scarff, 1898), 247.

7. Lawrence Goodwyn, *Democratic Promise: The Populist Moment in America* (New York: Oxford University Press, 1976), 45–49.

8. Joe E. Ericson and Ernest Wallace, "Constitution of 1876," in *Handbook of Texas Online* (Texas State Historical Association), accessed September 5, 2013, http://www.tshaonline.org/handbook/online/articles/mhc07; Seth Shepard McKay, *Making the Texas Constitution of 1876* (Philadelphia: University of Pennsylvania, 1924), 95–99; Patrick G. Williams, "Of Rutabagas and Redeemers: Rethinking the Texas Constitution of 1876," *Southwestern Historical Quarterly* 106, no. 2 (October 2002): 230–35. Williams studied Republican voting strength in these counties and concluded that "the key to voting on this issue seems not to have been Grange (or any other economic interest group) affiliation, but instead the size of the non-Democratic vote in delegates' home districts. The greater tendency of Grange delegates to vote against suffrage restriction is most likely to be attributed to the greater tendency of Grangers to come from securely Democratic, white-majority counties."

9. McKay, *Making the Texas Constitution of 1876* (Philadelphia: University of Pennsylvania, 1924), 47–48; Seth Shepard McKay, ed., *Debates in the Texas Constitutional Convention of 1875* (Austin: University of Texas, 1930). The Debates will henceforward be cited in the format "Debates____." The remainder of my commentary on the convention relies on McKay's seminal works often oversimplified by later historians, but is fundamentally based on my own analysis of the primary source material that he cited, and the *Debates* he collated. The *Debates* is more useful than his book and I treat it as essentially a primary source. Cross citations are also provided to the official *Journal of the Constitutional Convention of the State of Texas Begun and Held in the City of Austin, September 6th, 1875* (Galveston: Galveston News, 1875). These will be in the form of *Journal* ____." Examples of unjustified extrapolation of some of McKay's book can be found in S. D. Myres, "Mysticism, Realism, and the Texas Constitution of 1876," *Political and Social Science Quarterly* 9, no. 2 (1928): 166–84; Benjamin Hervey Good, *"John Henninger Reagan"* (Philadelphia: University of Pennsylvania, 1924), 351; and Frank M. Stewart and Joseph L. Clark, *The Constitution and Government of Texas* (Boston: D. C. Heath & Co., 1933), 13–17, although each contains useful source material. Their conclusions have passed largely unquestioned into the later historiography. Other examples of overgeneralization are listed in Patrick G. Williams, "Of Rutabagas and Redeemers: Rethinking the Texas Constitution of 1876," *Southwestern Historical Quarterly* 106, no. 2 (October 2002): 233–34, including J. Morgan Kousser, *The Shaping of Southern*

Politics: Suffrage Restriction and the Establishment of the One-Party South, 1880–1910 (New Haven: Yale University Press, 1974). Other treatments of the Grange and its influence on state constitutions include Alwyn Barr, *Reconstruction to Reform: Texas Politics, 1876–1906* (Austin: University of Texas Press, 1971); Dale Baum and Robert A. Calvert, "Texas Patrons of Husbandry: Geography, Social Contexts, and Voting Behavior," *Agricultural History* 63, no. 4 (Autumn, 1989): 36–55, 49; Robert Calvert and Arnoldo De Leon, *The History of Texas* (2nd ed.; Wheeling, IL: Harlan Davidson, 1996), 148–49; John Walker Mauer, "State Constitutions in a Time of Crisis," *Texas Law Review* 68, no. 7 (June 1990): 1615–48; and Lawrence D. Rice, *The Negro in Texas 1874–1900* (Baton Rouge: Louisiana State University Press, 1971). For Grange membership numbers, see *Walsh & Pilgrim's Directory of the Officers and Members of the Constitutional Convention of the State of Texas, A. D. 1875* (Austin: Democratic Statesman Office, 1875), and J. E. Ericson, "The Delegates to the Convention of 1875: A Reappraisal," *Southwestern Historical Quarterly* 67 (July, 1963): 22–27, both cited in Williams, "Of Rutabagas and Redeemers: Rethinking the Texas Constitution of 1876," 234, n. 5. Mauer's article argues that the 1876 constitution should be understood as an example of "restrictive constitutions" among five postwar southern states that departed from prior traditions of liberality toward legislative prerogative. This conclusion is an overgeneralization. Mauer understates the support for industry allowed in the 1876 constitution, for example.

10. Seth Shepard McKay, *Making the Texas Constitution of 1876* (Philadelphia: University of Pennsylvania, 1924): 105–7; Ford Dixon, "Erhard, Cayton," in *Handbook of Texas Online* (Texas State Historical Association), accessed September 12, 2013, http://www.tshaonline.org/handbook/online/articles/fer09; "Waelder, Jacob," in *Handbook of Texas Online* (Texas State Historical Association), accessed September 12, 2013, http://www.tshaonline.org/handbook/online/articles/fwa04; Seymour V. Connor, "Ford, John Salmon [Rip]," in *Handbook of Texas Online* (Texas State Historical Association), accessed September 12, 2013, http://www.tshaonline.org/handbook/online/articles/ffo11; Frank Wagner, "Murphy, John Bernard," in *Handbook of Texas Online* (Texas State Historical Association), accessed September 12, 2013, (http://www.tshaonline.org/handbook/online/articles/fmu37).

11. Ben Procter, Reagan's most recent biographer, relates that in the 1870s, "his enemies attempted to smear him, because of his activities in bringing the International and Great Northern to Palestine, by referring to him as a prominent lobbyist and lawyer for railroad rings," and in Reagan's early speeches on what would become the Interstate Commerce Act, he made clear that his aim was to control railroad excesses "without abridging any of their necessary and legitimate rights and privileges." Ben H. Proctor, *Not Without Honor: The Life of John H. Reagan* (Austin: University of Texas Press, 1971), 207, 219. For Reagan's political tactics and fights against those to the right and left, see Proctor, *Not Without Honor*, 228–31, 252–53, 292–93, 296–97. See also Benjamin Hervey Good, "John Henninger Reagan" (Philadelphia: University

of Pennsylvania, 1924); Ben H. Procter, "Reagan, John Henninger," in *Handbook of Texas Online* (Texas State Historical Association), accessed September 12, 2013, http://www.tshaonline.org/handbook/online/articles/freo2.

12. *Debates*, 381, n. 101 (quote about Reagan). At least one scholar has independently arrived at the same conclusion regarding the shifting alliances in the 1875 convention. See Patrick G. Williams, "Of Rutabagas and Redeemers: Rethinking the Texas Constitution of 1876," *Southwestern Historical Quarterly* 106, no. 2 (October 2002): 230-53, where he argues that "the convention's actions with respect to education, taxation, and suffrage not only challenge the notion that Grange delegates were exclusively or even primarily responsible for key aspects of the constitution but also make clear that Grangers rarely voted as a bloc. Instead, they divided amongst themselves on a whole range of vital issues addressed by the convention." The other recent article on the 1875 convention is not relevant here. It argues that the 1876 Texas constitution falls within a pattern of alternating "contractive and expansive" constitutional development nationwide posited by Morton Keller in *Affairs of State: Public Life In Late Nineteenth Century America* (Cambridge: Belknap Press, 1977), 112-13. See John Walker Mauer, "State Constitutions in a Time of Crisis," *Texas Law Review*, 1615.

13. Seth Shepard McKay, *Making the Texas Constitution of 1876* (Philadelphia: University of Pennsylvania, 1924), 45-66; Lewis L. Gould, *Alexander Watkins Terrell: Civil War Soldier, Texas Lawmaker, American Diplomat* (Austin: University of Texas Press, 2004), 64.

14. *Debates*, 1; Barbara H. Fisher, "Pickett, Edward Bradford," in *Handbook of Texas Online* (Texas State Historical Association), accessed September 12, 2013, http://www.tshaonline.org/handbook/online/articles/fpio5.

15. S. D. Myres, "Mysticism, Realism, and the Texas Constitution of 1876," *Political and Social Science Quarterly* 9, no. 2 (1928): 166, 174-76, quoting *Daily Herald* (San Antonio), September 5, 1875, and September 7, 1875, and citing *Daily Herald* (San Antonio), October 16, 1875. In his work, McKay identified several contemporary newspapers as organs of the Democratic Party. Among these were the *Houston Telegraph*, San Antonio *Daily Herald*, and Austin *State Journal*. See McKay, *Making the Texas Constitution of 1876*, 42, notes 89, 90, 91.

16. *Debates*, 178-90; *Journal*, 305-12.

17. *Debates*, 190-93; *Journal*, 320-22; Kristl Knudsen Penner, "Whitfield, John Wilkins," in *Handbook of Texas Online* (Texas State Historical Association), accessed September 16, 2013, http://www.tshaonline.org/handbook/online/articles/fwh38; "Lynch, Francis J.," in *Handbook of Texas Online* (Texas State Historical Association), accessed September 16, 2013, http://www.tshaonline.org/handbook/online/articles/flyo2.

18. *Debates*, 168-78, 203-11, 808-9; *Journal*, 320-22; Worth Robert Miller, "Martin, Francis Marion," in *Handbook of Texas Online* (Texas State Historical Association),

http://www.tshaonline.org/handbook/online/articles/fma56; Aragorn Storm Miller, "Chambers, Edward," *Handbook of Texas Online* (Texas State Historical Association), accessed September 16, 2013, http://www.tshaonline.org/handbook/online/articles/fchaa; Robert Miller, "Nugent, Thomas Lewis," *Handbook of Texas Online* (Texas State Historical Association), accessed September 16, 2013, http://www.tshaonline.org/handbook/online/articles/fnu02; Malcolm D. McLean, "Robertson, Elijah Sterling Clack," *Handbook of Texas Online* (Texas State Historical Association), accessed September 16, 2013, http://www.tshaonline.org/handbook/online/articles/fro24. Williams, who studied records of Grange membership, claimed that Nugent was not a Granger. See Williams, "Of Rutabagas and Redeemers: Rethinking the Texas Constitution of 1876," 238.

19. McKay concluded that "perhaps the most talked about single argument against the proposed constitution was the one originated by the *Galveston News* . . . that Texas would have a 'Senegambia' on the eastern coast (because of) . . . the action of the convention in refusing to provide a poll tax prerequisite for voting, and in providing for an elected judiciary." He described the *Galveston News* as "the most widely circulated newspaper in the state" and "conservative and almost non-partisan, but professed to have a Democratic leaning." Seth S. McKay, *Making the Texas Constitution of 1876*, 151, 169, 177–82; *Galveston News*, January 28, 1876; *Galveston News*, January 30, 1876.

20. *Debates*, 207–11, 459 (Johnson quotes); "Stockdale, Fletcher Summerfield," in *Handbook of Texas Online* (Texas State Historical Association), accessed September 17, 2013, http://www.tshaonline.org/handbook/online/articles/fst60.

21. *Journal*, 237–38. For Democratic reliance on boss rule, see Godfrey Hodgson, *Woodrow Wilson's Right Hand Man* (New Haven: Yale University Press, 2006), 31–42; and Evan Anders, *Boss Rule in South Texas* (Austin: University of Texas Press, 1982), 3–25, 65–81.

22. *Journal*, 304–9; *Debates*, 167–76; Erma Baker, "Brown, John Henry," in *Handbook of Texas Online* (Texas State Historical Association), accessed September 17, 2013, http://www.tshaonline.org/handbook/online/articles/fbr94.

23. *Journal*, 395–401, 511–21; McKay, *Making the Texas Constitution of 1876*, 104–5; Ernest Wallace, "Demorse, Charles," in *Handbook of Texas Online* (Texas State Historical Association), accessed September 30, 2013, http://www.tshaonline.org/handbook/online/articles/fde36; Constitution of the State of Texas (1876), Article VII; Constitution of the State of Texas (1869), Article III, Section 1.

24. *Debates*, 356–57 (Stockdale quote); *Journal*, 245–46 (Sansom quote), 400 (Robertson quote).

25. *Debates*, 326–69; *Journal*, 243–45; McKay 106–9; S. S. McKay and Doug Johnson, "Dohoney, Ebenezer Lafayette," in *Handbook of Texas Online* (Texas State Historical Association), accessed September 18, 2013, http://www.tshaonline.org/handbook/online/articles/fdo07; Constitution of the State of Texas (1876), Article VII.

26. *Journal*, 243–45; Constitution of the State of Texas (1876), Article VII.

27. *Journal*, 64, 125–28, 228–34, 371–72; Constitution of the State of Texas (1876), Article III, Section 5; Seth S. McKay, *Making the Texas Constitution of 1876*, 76–78, 84–86; "Crawford, William Lyne," in *Handbook of Texas Online* (Texas State Historical Association), accessed September 19, 2013, http://www.tshaonline.org/handbook/online/articles/fcr14.

28. *Debates*, 116.

29. Constitution of the State of Texas (1866), Article VII, Section 36; Constitution of the State of Texas (1869), Article XII, Sections 6; Constitution of the State of Texas (1869), Article X, Sections 5 and 7; Constitution of the State of Texas (1876), Article XIV, Section 3; *Journal*, 144, 226–27, 376, 616–24, 629–30, 632–45; *Debates*, 117–33, 267–70, 400–421 (the debate on railroads and subsidies); Seth S. McKay, *Making the Texas Constitution of 1876*, 111; Donna J. Kumler, "German, James Lafayette," in *Handbook of Texas Online* (Texas State Historical Association), accessed September 24, 2013, http://www.tshaonline.org/handbook/online/articles/fge10. Patrick Williams argues that this was not a moderate position but actually progrowth because the original committee report did not advocate anything but land subsidies for railroads because "amidst the enormous controversy generated by the subsidies that both Republicans and Democrats in the Reconstruction legislature had voted to the Texas and Pacific and the International railways, both parties had as early as 1872 formally forsworn such promises of money or bonds." However, he admits that there were a "very few Democrats of any stripe argued for continuing a policy of paying railroads to build." His conclusion is that "the decision the convention had to make with respect to state subsidy of economic growth was not between rewarding private companies with public money or merely with public land, as some historians seem to assume, but between granting land or nothing at all. No one argued for money subsidies at the convention (and, as noted above, few Democrats were arguing for them in the broader public arena), while forceful and eloquent voices were heard denouncing the granting even of land to railroads." I think his admission that there were at least a few delegates and others who favored nonland subsidies "in the broader public arena," and his failure to account for the provision of the 1869 constitution allowing this (albeit by a two-thirds vote of the legislature) undercut his argument, although the difference between us is only one of emphasis. Patrick Williams, "Of Rutabagas and Redeemers: Rethinking the Texas Constitution of 1876," 236–37, 240; Constitution of the State of Texas (1869), Article XII, Section 6.

30. *Journal*, 263–64; Constitution of the State of Texas (1869), Article X, Section 8; Article XII, Section 15; Constitution of the State of Texas (1876), Article XIV, Sections 6 and 7; Constitution of the State of Texas (1876), Article XVI, Section 50.

31. *Journal*, 44, 240–41, 275; *Debates*, 272–86.

32. *Journal*, 84 (Reagan chairman), 406–13 (majority report of Ballinger); Seth S. McKay, *Making the Texas Constitution of 1876*, 123–24; *Debates*, 381 (Ballinger's criticism of Reagan).

33. *Journal*, 413 (minority report quote), 95–97 (Ford moves resolution prohibiting judges from "taking an active part in the discussion of political questions. . . ." Norvell moves judicial article w/supreme court of 3 elected to serve for 6 yrs), 413–22 (minority report of Reagan), 437–46 (minority report by DeMorse reducing juries from 12 to 5 and removing jury trial for petty offenses, and except in cases of "extreme punishment" not using penitentiaries but sentencing convicts to hard labor for use of counties); *Debates*, 379–87, 421–34; Constitution of the State of Texas (1876), Article V; Constitution of the State of Texas (1876), Article XVI, Section 26.

34. Constitution of the State of Texas (1876), Article XII, Sections 3 and 4; Article X, Section 2.

35. Alwyn Barr, *Reconstruction to Reform: Texas Politics 1876–1906*, 25–26.

36. Richard Hofstadter, *The Age of Reform: From Bryan to FDR* (New York: Alfred A. Knopf, 1955).

37. Hofstadter, *The Age of Reform*, 47–50.

38. *The Age of Reform*, 58–59.

39. *The Age of Reform*, 62, 80–89.

40. Robert H. Wiebe, *The Search for Order, 1877–1920* (New York: Hill and Wang, 1967), 37 (coarse leadership quote), 42–43 (alien context quote), 45–47.

41. Wiebe, *The Search for Order, 1877–1920*, 45–60; Steven Hahn, *The Roots of Southern Populism: Yeoman Farmers and the Transformation of the Georgia Upcountry, 1850–1890* (New York: Oxford University Press, 1983), 1, 9–10, 109–28, 141–65.

42. Lawrence Goodwyn, *Democratic Promise: The Populist Moment in America* (New York: Oxford University Press, 1976), vii, 25 (humiliating conditions quote), 30–33, 31 (tenant quote); Steven Hahn, *The Roots of Southern Populism: Yeoman Farmers and the Transformation of the Georgia Upcountry, 1850–1890* (New York: Oxford University Press, 1983).

43. Goodwyn, *Democratic Promise: The Populist Moment in America*, 36–43, 104.

44. Painter, *Standing at Armageddon*, 60–67; Goodwyn, *Democratic Promise: The Populist Moment in America*, 45–49.

45. Goodwyn, *Democratic Promise: The Populist Moment in America*, 51–58, 60–61, 73–75.

46. Goodwyn, *Democratic Promise: The Populist Moment in America*, 78–86.

47. Ben H. Proctor, *Not Without Honor: The Life of John H. Reagan* (Austin: University of Texas Press, 1971); Ben H. Procter, "Reagan, John Henninger," in *Handbook of Texas Online* (Texas State Historical Association), accessed September 12, 2013, http://www.tshaonline.org/handbook/online/articles/fre02.

48. Goodwyn, *Democratic Promise: The Populist Moment in America*, 166–69.

49. Goodwyn, *Democratic Promise: The Populist Moment in America*, 177–78.

50. Alwyn W. Barr, *Reconstruction to Reform: Texas Politics, 1876–1906*, 27–31, 39 (Coke and Hubbard); *Texas Capitol* (Austin), November 13, 1881; Frederick W. Rathjen, "The Texas State House," in *The Texas State Capitol*, ed. Robert C. Cotner (Austin: Pemberton Press, 1968), 5. For more on the Capitol fire, see Austin Library

website, accessed April 29, 2007, http://www.ci.austin.tx.us/library/ahc/capitol/early.htm; O. M. Roberts, "The Political, Legislative, and Judicial History of Texas during Its Fifty Years of Statehood," in *A Comprehensive History of Texas 1685–1897*, ed. Dudley G. Wooten, vol. 2 (Dallas: William G. Scarff, 1898), 239, 249; and "Capitol" in *Handbook of Texas* (Texas State Historical Association), accessed October 14, 2014, http://www.tshaonline.org/handbook/online/articles/ccc01. I am grateful to Bill Pugsley, Executive Director of the Texas Supreme Court Historical Society, for his editorial suggestions on the first several paragraphs of this introduction, most of which were incorporated in one way or another in the text. A prior and differently worded version of six paragraphs of my account of the 1881 capitol fire and the Willie/Stayton court were published in the summer/fall 2007 "Member Update" of the Texas Supreme Court Historical Society.

51. Alwyn W. Barr, *Reconstruction to Reform: Texas Politics, 1876–1906*, 27–31, 39 (Coke and Hubbard); *Texas Capitol* (Austin), November 13, 1881; Frederick W. Rathjen, "The Texas State House," in *The Texas State Capitol*, ed. Robert C. Cotner (Austin: Pemberton Press, 1968), 5. For more on the Capitol fire, see Austin Library website, accessed April 29, 2007, http://www.ci.austin.tx.us/library/ahc/capitol/early.htm; O. M. Roberts, "The Political, Legislative, and Judicial History of Texas during Its Fifty Years of Statehood," in *A Comprehensive History of Texas 1685–1897*, ed. Dudley G. Wooten, vol. 2 (Dallas: William G. Scarff, 1898), 239, 249; and "Capitol" in *Handbook of Texas* (Texas State Historical Association), accessed October 14, 2014, http://www.tshaonline.org/handbook/online/articles/ccc01; *Texas Siftings* (Austin), November 12, 1881; *Texas Siftings* (Austin), November 13, 1881.

52. Hans Baade, "Law at Texas: The Roberts-Gould Era, 1883–1893," *Southwestern Historical Quarterly* 86, no. 2 (1982): 175–79, citing (Robert S. Gould?), "Autobiographical Sketch" in "Robert Simonton Gould," Part 1, Robert S. Gould Papers, Center for American History, University of Texas at Austin, 137; R. L. Batts, "Robert Simonson Gould," *The Alcalde* 2 (August, 1914): 883, 888; R. L. Batts, "The Study of Law," *The University Record* 1 (October 1899), 334; R. L. Batts, "Memorial Address" in the bound typewritten manuscript, John Gould, ed., "Robert Simonton Gould (1826–1904): Autobiographical and Biographical Material," Part 1, Robert S. Gould Papers, Center for American History, University of Texas at Austin, 276. Longtime court reporter and Austin State Senator Alexander W. Terrell attested that Gould and Roberts knew each other "long and intimately." See Alexander W. Terrell, "Address at the Presentation of the Resolutions of the Austin Bar Association to the Supreme Court (memorializing Justice Gould)" in the bound typewritten manuscript, ed., John Gould, "Robert Simonton Gould (1826–1904): Autobiographical and Biographical Material," Part 1, *Robert S. Gould Papers*, Center for American History, University of Texas at Austin, 287. See also T. U. Taylor, *Fifty Years on Forty Acres* (Austin, 1938), 86.

53. Judge W. D. Wood, "Biographical Sketch" in the bound typewritten manuscript, ed. John Gould, "Robert Simonton Gould (1826–1904): Autobiographical and

Biographical Material," Part 1, *Robert S. Gould Papers*, Center for American History, University of Texas at Austin, 245 (Southern man quote); R. L. Batts, "Memorial Address" in the bound typewritten manuscript, John Gould, ed., "Robert Simonton Gould (1826–1904): Autobiographical and Biographical Material," Part 1, *Robert S. Gould Papers*, Center for American History, University of Texas at Austin, 276 (differences between Roberts and Gould quotes). John C. Townes, "Judge Gould as a Member of the Supreme Court," in ed. John Gould, "Robert Simonton Gould (1826–1904): Autobiographical and Biographical Material," part 1, *Robert S. Gould Papers*, Center for American History, University of Texas at Austin, 284 (conservatism quote).

54. Jeanette H. Flachmeier, "Bonner, Micajah Hubbard," in *Handbook of Texas Online* (Texas State Historical Association), accessed September 21, 2014, http://www.tshaonline.org/handbook/online/articles/fbo19; Roy L. Swift, "West, Charles Shannon," in *Handbook of Texas Online* (Texas State Historical Association), accessed September 21, 2014, http://www.tshaonline.org/handbook/online/articles/fwe29.

55. Craig H. Roell, "Stayton, John William," in *Handbook of Texas Online* (Texas State Historical Association), accessed September 21, 2014, http://www.tshaonline.org/handbook/online/articles/fst23; "In Memoriam of John W. Stayton," 87 Tex. Reports, v–xvii.

56. Act of February 29, 1879, in H. P. N. Gammel, ed., *The Laws of Texas, 1823–1897*, vol. 7 (Austin: n.p., 1898), 1309; Frederick W. Rathjen, "The Texas State House," in *The Texas State Capitol*, ed. Robert C. Cotner (Austin: Pemberton Press, 1968), 2–6.

57. Act of April 18, 1882, in *Laws of Texas*, ed., H. P. N. Gammel, vol. 8 (Austin, 1898), 1411–15. Also see O. M. Roberts, "The Political, Legislative, and Judicial History of Texas during Its Fifty Years of Statehood," in *A Comprehensive History of Texas 1685–1897*, ed. Dudley G. Wooten, vol. 2 (Dallas: William G. Scarff, 1898), 239, 249; "Capitol," in *Handbook of Texas* (Texas State Historical Association), accessed October 14, 2014, http://www.tshaonline.org/handbook/online/articles/ccc01; and Frederick W. Rathjen, "The Texas State House," in Robert C. Cotner, ed., *The Texas State Capitol* (Austin: Pemberton Press, 1968), 2–6.

58. Act of April 1, 1882, in *Laws of Texas*, ed. H. P. N. Gammel, vol. 8 (Austin, 1898), 1411–15. Also see O. M. Roberts, "The Political, Legislative, and Judicial History of Texas during its Fifty Years of Statehood," 239, 249; and "Capitol," in *Handbook of Texas* (Texas State Historical Association), accessed October 14, 2014, http://www.tshaonline.org/handbook/online/articles/ccc01; James L. Haley, *The Texas Supreme Court* (Austin: University of Texas Press, 2013), 97, 105–6.

59. *Austin Statesman*, September 8, 1882; *Austin Statesman*, March 16, 1883 (quote); Frederick W. Rathjen, "The Texas State House," in *The Texas State Capitol*, ed. Robert C. Cotner (Austin: Pemberton Press, 1968), 7. Texas Legislative Council, ed., *The Texas Capitol, Symbol of Accomplishment* (Austin: Texas Legislative Council, 1986), 36.

60. "Capitol," in *Handbook of Texas* (Texas State Historical Association), accessed October 14, 2014, http://www.tshaonline.org/handbook/online/articles/ccc01; O. M.

Roberts, "The Political, Legislative, and Judicial History of Texas during Its Fifty Years of Statehood," 254, 263; James L. Haley, *The Texas Supreme Court* (Austin: University of Texas Press, 2013), 230.

61. Claude Elliott, "Ireland, John," in *Handbook of Texas Online* (Texas State Historical Association), accessed September 21, 2014, http://www.tshaonline.org/handbook/online/articles/firo1.

62. John Gould, ed., "Robert Simonton Gould (1826–1904): Autobiographical and Biographical Material," Part 1, *Robert S. Gould Papers*, Center for American History, University of Texas at Austin, 104–5. After an unknown named Don Yarbrough (who would ultimately be forced to resign office) defeated sitting Justice Charles Barrow in the 1976 Democratic primary under circumstances where Barrow received 90% of the lawyers' votes in the State bar poll and all the newspaper endorsements, and Yarbrough claimed to have made only one speech and spent only $350 on his entire campaign, many concluded that this unusual result must be attributed to Justice Yarbrough sharing a similar last name with popular Texas politicians Ralph and Don Yarborough (two O's), and many also concluded that "this episode proved that almost anyone could be elected to the Texas Supreme Court, if they had a popular name." Anthony Champaign and Kyle Cheek, "The Cycle of Judicial Elections: Texas as a Case Study," *Fordham Urb. L. J.* 29, no. 3 (2001): 907, 910. See also William J. Chriss, "Chief Justice Jack Pope and the End of the Non-Partisan Court, 1964–1985" (Austin: Texas Supreme Court Historical Society Symposium, unpublished, April 11, 2013).

63. John Henry Brown, *Indian Wars and Pioneers of Texas* (Austin: State House Press, 1988 [orig. ed. Austin: L. E. Daniell, 1892?]), 186, 382–83 (all page citations are to the 1988 reprint edition); Thomas W Cutrer, "Willie, Asa Hoxie," in *Handbook of Texas Online* (Texas State Historical Association), accessed September 21, 2014, http://www.tshaonline.org/handbook/online/articles/fwi43.

64. Craig H. Roell, "Stayton, John William," in *Handbook of Texas Online* (Texas State Historical Association), accessed September 21, 2014, http://www.tshaonline.org/handbook/online/articles/fst23; "In Memoriam of John W. Stayton," 87, Tex. Reports, v–xvii.

65. "Proceedings of the Organizational Session of the Texas Bar Association," *Proceedings of the Texas Bar Association* (Galveston: By Order of the Association, 1882), 8.

66. "Proceedings of the Organizational Session of the Texas Bar Association," *Proceedings of the Texas Bar Association* (Galveston: By Order of the Association, 1882), 16.

67. *Proceedings of the First and Second Annual Sessions of the Texas Bar Association* (Houston: By Order of the Association, 1884), 11–12.

68. "Report of A. W. Terrell," *Proceedings of the First and Second Annual Sessions of the Texas Bar Association* (Houston: By Order of the Association, 1884), 24–25.

69. O. M. Roberts, "The Political, Legislative, and Judicial History of Texas during its Fifty Years of Statehood," in *A Comprehensive History of Texas 1685–1897*, ed. Dudley G. Wooten, vol. 2 (Dallas: William G. Scarff, 1898), 269–70. Appellate judicial service was a serious financial hardship on successful private attorneys. The Supreme Court, at this time, split its sessions between three courthouses, one in Austin, one in Tyler, and one in Galveston. Prior to his appointment, Willie had been a prominent and politically influential Galveston attorney. Although he was elected to serve in the US House of Representatives, he chose to serve only one term and then returned to Galveston where he resumed private practice and earned additional income as the City Attorney. Once the new capitol was completed, and with judicial institutional reform and backlog reduction already a hot topic, it was undoubtedly becoming clear to Willie that not only would further service on the Court continue to drain his financial reserves, but it would probably also require him to soon spend substantially more time away from his wife and family. When he retired, Willie had been married for almost thirty years, and he and his wife Bettie had ten children, five of whom lived to maturity in Galveston. See Thomas W. Cutrer, "Willie, Asa Hoxie," *Handbook of Texas Online* (Texas State Historical Association), accessed September 21, 2014, http://www.tshaonline.org/handbook/online/articles/fwi43.

70. 56 Tex. 452 (Tex. 1882).

71. 58 Tex. 27 (Tex. 1882).

72. 57 Tex. 465 (Tex. 1882).

73. 57 Tex. 215 (Tex. 1882).

74. William Pitt Ballinger noted a conversation with the federal judge in Galveston, former Texas Supreme Court Chief Justice Amos Morrill, where Ballinger called to Morrill's attention a new book on trials of land titles, and in response, "the old fellow said he could name four men who knew all that is to be known on that subject Willie, West, himself, and myself!!!" William Pitt Ballinger, "Diary 1883," Box 2Q427, *William Pitt Ballinger Diaries*, Center for American History, University of Texas at Austin (diary entry of March 3, 1883), 55.

75. For example, in *Houston & Texas Central Railway Company v. Simpson*, 60 Tex. 103 (Tex. 1883), Simpson, a teenager living in Denison, Texas, had his right leg caught and crushed in a turntable on the railroad's property. Turntables were generally located at the end of a rail line and their function was to allow railroad employees to turn a locomotive around 180 degrees. On arriving at a turntable, a locomotive was detached from its train, turned in its desired direction, and headed either for a new destination or to the roundhouse for repair. Turntables were balanced so precisely that as few as two people could turn the heaviest locomotives. The trial of the case resulted in a verdict of $3,500 for Simpson's injuries. The turntable was unenclosed and near a pond that Simpson and his friends were accustomed to fish in. Under these circumstances, Justice Stayton held that it was "not a trespass in a child which would deprive it of the right to recover for an injury resulting from the attempted

use of a dangerous machine to which children would be attracted for sport or pastime."

76. *Houston and Texas Central Railway Company v. Simpson*, 60 Tex. 103, 106 (Tex. 1883). "Greenfield Village Memories," website, accessed November 10, 2006, http://www.wrenscottage.com/gvm/transportation/turn-table.php.

77. See Joseph M. Hawes and N. Ray Hiner, eds., *American Childhood: A Research Guide and Historical Handbook* (Westport, CT: Greenwood Press, 1985), 6–11; Lloyd DeMause, ed., *The History of Childhood* (New York: Psychohistory Press, 1974), 52; Bruse Belligham, "The History of Childhood Since the 'Invention of Childhood': Some Issues in the Eighties," *Journal of Family History* 13, no. 3 (1988): 347–58; C. Goldin, "Family Strategies and the Family Economy in the Late Nineteenth Century: The Role of Secondary Workers," in *Philadelphia: Work, Space, Family, and Group Experience in the Nineteenth Century*, ed. Theodore Herschberg (New York: Oxford University Press, 1981); M. R. Haines, "Poverty, Economic Stress, and Family in a Late Nineteenth Century American City: White Philadelphia, 1880," in *Philadelphia: Work, Space, Family, and Group Experience in the Nineteenth Century*, ed. Theodore Herschberg (New York: Oxford University Press, 1981). My statement here would probably be controversial among modern historians of the family. Philippe Aries, *Centuries of Childhood: A Social History of Family Life* (New York: Knopf Pub. Group, 1962) is the seminal work arguing that childhood was "invented" in the early modern era. However, his view that this somehow deprived children of "freedom" and "equality" they had in mingling with adults in ancient and medieval times is now viewed with derision by DeMause and other more recent scholars who argue that increased protection and nurturing of children in the eighteenth, nineteenth, and twentieth centuries was a good thing. Nonetheless, all of these scholars agree that a significant change in the status and perception of children, socially and legally, occurred in the mid-nineteenth century.

78. Cecil Harper Jr., "Henry, John Lane," in *The Handbook of Texas Online* (Texas State Historical Association), accessed September 21, 2014, http://www.tshaonline.org/handbook/online/articles/fhe21.

79. See Randolph B. Campbell, "Gaines, Reuben R.," in *Handbook of Texas Online* (Texas State Historical Association), accessed September 21, 2014, http://www.tshaonline.org/handbook/online/articles/fga06. Craig H. Roell, "Stayton, John William," in *Handbook of Texas Online* (Texas State Historical Association), accessed September 21, 2014, http://www.tshaonline.org/handbook/online/articles/fst23; "In Memoriam of John W. Stayton," 87 Tex. Reports, v–xvii.

80. *Gulf, Central, & Santa Fe Railway Co. v. Levy*, 59 Tex. 542 (Tex. 1883); *Gulf, Central, & Santa Fe Railway Co. v. Levy*, 59 Tex. 563 (Tex. 1883).

81. *So Relle v. Western Union Tel Co.*, 55 Tex. 308, 313–14 (Tex. Comm. App., 1881).

82. 66 Tex. 580, 18 S. W. 351 (Tex., 1885).

83. Another example of how the court applied existing remedial doctrines to new fact situations is the 1884 case of *Jones v. George,* 61 Tex. 345 (Tex., 1884). In this

case, Jones sued George on a theory of "breach of warranty." Jones was a cotton farmer, and George was a druggist who sold him a patent medicine for killing worms. George told Jones that this medicine contained "Paris green," a substance that Jones was satisfied had killed worms in the past. Justice Stayton reasoned that under these circumstances, "No warranty arises, but there is an implied contract that the thing sold and delivered is of the kind which the parties contract with reference to." While the case did not specifically recognize an implied warranty, Stayton did so by implication, holding that whether the action is denoted as one on an implied warranty or on a breach of contract "the relief would be the same." This case gave rise to an entire jurisprudence of implied warranty liability in impure food, drug, and commodity situations.

84. Roberts, "The Political, Legislative, and Judicial History of Texas during Its Fifty Years of Statehood," 252–53.

85. Roberts, "The Political, Legislative, and Judicial History of Texas during Its Fifty Years of Statehood," 256.

86. Roberts, "The Political, Legislative, and Judicial History of Texas during Its Fifty Years of Statehood," 258.

87. Roberts, "The Political, Legislative, and Judicial History of Texas during Its Fifty Years of Statehood," 247–47.

88. Thomas Lloyd Miller, *The Public Lands of Texas, 1519–1970* (Norman: University of Oklahoma Press, 1972), vii; Wilson Elbert Doleman, "The Public Lands of Western Texas 1870–1900" (PhD diss., University of Texas at Austin, 1974), 9; Paul Kens, "Wide Open Spaces? The Texas Supreme Court and the Scramble for the State's Public Domain, 1876–1898," *Western Legal History* 16, no. 2 (Summer/Fall, 2003): 160–87.

89. Kens, "Wide Open Spaces? The Texas Supreme Court and the Scramble for the State's Public Domain, 1876–1898," 160. *Summers v. Davis*, 49 Tex. 541 (Tex. 1878) (citing *Cannon's Administrator v. Vaughn*, 12 Tex. 399 (Tex. 1854)).

90. Kens, "Wide Open Spaces? The Texas Supreme Court and the Scramble for the State's Public Domain, 1876–1898," 163.

91. *Poston v. Blanks*, 14 S. W. 67 (Tex. Com. App., 1890); *Swetman v. Sanders*, 20 S. W. 124 (Tex. Com. App., 1892). For example, in the 1884 case of *Gammage v. Powell*, 61 Tex. 629 (Tex. 1884), the court had to evaluate Powell's claim to 160 acres in Nolan County. Powell had settled on the land in 1880 but had failed to file an application for the homestead within thirty days of occupation as required by law. Within a few months, a man named Gammage claimed title to Powell's homestead based upon a headright certificate that he held to a substantial block of land including the parcel claimed by Powell. A headright certificate was generally used to by the state to convey large chunks of land without the requirement of occupation. Only after Gammage received a patent based on his headright did Powell file his homestead application, well beyond the statutory thirty-day time limit. Meanwhile, Gammage's patent from the state was prima facie evidence of *legal* title. While the Court acknowledged that a patent was generally proof of superior title, it nonetheless ruled

that Powell, the yeoman in actual occupation of the land, obtained *equitable* title to it from the moment of his occupation. Under these circumstances, the speculator Gammage's patent would have to give way to homesteader Powell's prior equitable claim to title. Because Powell's claim was prior in time, the decision in the case ripened his equitable title into full legal title.

92. For example, in *Garrett v. Weaver*, 70 Tex. 463; 7 S. W. 766 (Tex. 1888), Justice Stayton refused to acknowledge the homestead claims of Weaver as against a valid patent purchased by Garrett from the General Land Office. A patent is the legal document accomplishing conveyance of land from the public domain to a private owner. Patents were issued upon submittal of a survey and fulfillment of any other conditions, such as payment of a purchase price. The Court vindicated Garrett's patent for the simple reason that neither Weaver nor the homesteader from whom he had purchased the land "ever lived upon the land."

93. *Hogue v. Baker*, 92 Tex. 58; 45 S. W. 1004 (Tex. 1898).

94. Constitution of the State of Texas (1876), Article XIV, Section 3.

95. "Message of Governor O. M. Roberts to the Texas Legislature, January 10, 1883," as quoted in O. M. Roberts, "The Political, Legislative, and Judicial History of Texas during Its Fifty Years of Statehood," in *A Comprehensive History of Texas 1685–1897*, ed. Dudley G. Wooten, vol. 2 (Dallas: William G. Scarff, 1898), 252–53.

96. Roberts, "The Political, Legislative, and Judicial History of Texas during Its Fifty Years of Statehood," 257, quoting the Inaugural Message of Governor John Ireland, 1883.

97. See, for example, *Galveston, Harrisburg, & San Antonio Railway Company v. State*, 77 Tex. 367; 12 S. W. 988 (Tex., 1889).

98. Hamilton, *The Federalist #78*.

Chapter 6

1. Charles E. Neu, "House, Edward Mandell," in *Handbook of Texas Online* (Texas State Historical Association), accessed September 21, 2014, http://www.tshaonline.org/handbook/online/articles/fho66; Godfrey Hodgson, *Woodrow Wilson's Right Hand Man* (New Haven: Yale University Press, 2006), 31–42.

2. Godfrey Hodgson, *Woodrow Wilson's Right Hand Man* (New Haven: Yale University Press, 2006), 31–42; Evan Anders, *Boss Rule in South Texas* (Austin: University of Texas Press, 1982), 3–25, 65–81. Anders demonstrates that the South Texas bosses or *padrones* of the late nineteenth and early twentieth centuries were conservative machine politicians intensely loyal to the Democratic Party. Their tactics and ideology resembled those of other Democratic machines in other regions. Although they were ideologically part of the Cleveland/Clark hard-money wing of the party, they supported House's progressive candidates, beginning with Hogg, out of expediency and because of reciprocal arrangements with state and national party regulars who could provide benefits and demanded strict party loyalty in exchange. Moreover, the

local *padrones* could not adulterate the simple message of strict party loyalty that bound their own dependents to themselves. See also Randolph B. Campbell, *Gone to Texas* (Oxford: Oxford University Press, 2003), 313–20; Neu, "House, Edward Mandell," in *Handbook of Texas Online*.

3. For the Federalist general theory, see, for example, Daniel Hulsebosch, "Writs to Rights: The Transformation of the Anglo-American Common Law, 1790–1850" (unpublished draft reviewed in Transnational Legal Histories Colloquium, University of Texas School of Law, spring 2007).

4. After Culberson's service as governor from 1895 to 1899, he was elected to the US Senate and served until 1923. He was succeeded as governor by Joseph D. Sayers, elected in 1898 and reelected in 1902. Both Culberson and Sayers were Hoggist progressives who supported the national party's bimetallism. Although Culberson opposed the Ku Klux Klan on grounds of public order, he never challenged segregation. Interestingly, Reagan challenged Culberson for the nomination in 1894 but lost due to House providing a well-organized campaign effort to Culberson, who pitched himself as a bimetallist, while Reagan attempted to paint him as insufficiently prosilver. Godfrey Hodgson, *Woodrow Wilson's Right Hand: The Life of Colonel Edward M. House* (New Haven: Yale University Press, 2006), 34–39; Robert L. Wagner, "Culberson, Charles Allen," in *Handbook of Texas Online* (Texas State Historical Association), accessed September 15, 2013, http://www.tshaonline.org/handbook/online/articles/fcu02; Ben H. Proctor, *Not without Honor: The Life of John H. Reagan* (Austin: University of Texas Press, 1971), 292–98.

5. James L. Roark, "Behind the Lines," in *Writing the Civil War*, ed. James M. McPherson and William J. Cooper (Columbia: University of South Carolina Press, 1998), 223.

6. See, for example, Philip Shaw Paludan, "What Did the Winners Win," in *Writing the Civil War*, ed. James M. McPherson and William J. Cooper (Columbia: University of South Carolina Press, 1998), 175–87; Patricia Everidge Hill, *Dallas: The Making of a Modern City* (Austin: University of Texas Press, 1996); Eric H. Monkkonen, *America Becomes Urban: The Development of U.S. Cities & Towns, 1780–1980* (Berkeley: University of California Press, 1988); Char Miller and Heywood T. Sanders, eds., *Urban Texas: Politics and Development* (College Station: Texas A&M University Press, 1990), 3–112.

7. James Green, *Death in the Haymarket: A Story of Chicago, the First Labor Movement and the Bombing that Divided Gilded Age America* (Random House: New York, 2006); Ben H. Proctor, *Not without Honor: The Life of John H. Reagan* (Austin: University of Texas Press, 1971), 292–98; Dallas History website, accessed March 26, 2006, http://www.dallashistory.org/cgi-bin/webbs_config.pl?noframens;reedequals15399.

8. Railroad Commission of Texas, *History of the Railroad Commission: Chronological Listing of Key Events in the History of the Railroad Commission of Texas*

(*1866-1939*), website, accessed September 12, 2013, http://www.rrc.state.tx.us/about/history/chronological/chronhistory01.php.

9. Arnold M. Paul, *Conservative Crisis and the Rule of Law: Attitudes of Bar and Bench 1887-1895* (Harper and Roe: New York, New York, 1969), 1-2, 76-78. Paul cites John Randolph Tucker, "British Institutions and American Constitutions," *Report of the Fifteenth Annual Meeting of the American Bar Association* (1892), pp. 213-44; John W. Cary, "Limitations of the Legislative Power in Respect to Personal Rights and Private Property," *Report of the Fifteenth Annual Meeting of the American Bar Association* (1892), pp. 245-86; and John F. Dillon, "Address of the President," *Report of the Fifteenth Annual Meeting of the American Bar Association* (1892), pp. 167-211.

10. Lief H. Carter and Christine B. Harrington, *Administrative Law and Politics: Cases and Comment* (Longman: New York, 2000), 70, citing "Proceedings of the New York State Bar Association" (1893), 37.

11. *Budd v. New York*, 143 U.S. 517, 551 (1892), Brewer, j. dissenting.

12. Seymour D. Thompson, "Government by Lawyers," in *Proceedings of the 15th Annual Session of the Texas Bar Association* (1896), 64-85.

13. Walter F. Murphy et al., *Courts Judges and Politics: An Introduction to the Judicial Process* (Boston: McGraw Hill, 2006), 88.

14. Murphy, *Courts Judges and Politics*, 300.

15. G. Allen Tarr, *Judicial Process and Judicial Policy Making* (Belmont, CA: Thomson/Wadsworth, 2003), 30; Owen M. Fiss, *Troubled Beginnings of the Modern State, 1888-1910*, volume 8 in *The Oliver Wendell Holmes Devise History of the United States* (Cambridge, MA: Cambridge University Press, 2006).

16. *Acts of 16th Legislature of Texas*, July 9, 1879, 30; J. H. Davenport, *The History of the Supreme Court of the State of Texas* (Austin, TX: Southern Law Book Publishers, 1917), 139. See also "Interpretive Commentary," *Vernon's Annotated Texas Statutes*, Constitution, vol. 2 (West Publishing Co.: St. Paul, 1993), 23.

17. Murphy, *Courts Judges and Politics: An Introduction to the Judicial Process*, 125-26.

18. Murphy, *Courts Judges and Politics*, 125.

19. "Interpretive Commentary," *Vernon's Annotated Texas Statutes*, Constitution, vol. 2 (West Publishing Co.: St. Paul, 1993), 23; J. H. Davenport, *The History of the Supreme Court of the State of Texas*, 209-10; Kathy Cochran, "The Court of Criminal Appeals of Texas," *Texas Bar Journal* 69, no. 3 (March 2006): 218-23. On January 15, 1891, House Resolution #2 with respect to these amendments was introduced by Rep. William F. Adkins of Columbus and referred to the Committee on Constitutional Amendments. *House Journal*, Texas Legislature (22nd Regular Session, 1891), 30. On April 2, 1891, Senate Joint Resolution 16 arising from the House resolution and proposing to amend the Constitution with respect to the judicial branch was reported to the House as having passed by a 26-0 vote. *House Journal*, Texas Legislature (22nd

Regular Session, 1891), 806. This Senate Joint Resolution 16, pursuant to its terms, was submitted to the people and adopted at an election held on August 11, 1891. The vote was 37,445 for to 35,695 against. Ibid. While there were a total of less than 75,000 votes cast in the 1891 referendum, there were, for example, more than 400,000 cast in the 1894 Supreme Court elections and more than 500,000 in the same "down ballot" races in 1896. See Thomas R. Phillips, "Popular Elections for the Texas Supreme Court" (unpublished manuscript, 2010), 26–27.

20. "Interpretive Commentary," *Vernon's Annotated Texas Statutes*, Constitution, vol. 2 (West Publishing Co.: St. Paul, 1993), 23; Leila Clark Wynn, "A History of the Civil Courts in Texas," *Southwestern Historical Quarterly* 60, no. 1 (July, 1956): 9. See also "Commission of Appeals," in *Handbook of Texas Online*, accessed March 26, 2006, http://www.tsha.utexas.edu/handbook/online/articles/cc/mdc5.html.

21. These statistics, and those that follow, are a result of my own research and tabulations utilizing the LexisNexis computerized legal research system and the *Southwestern Reporter* published by West Publishing Company.

22. Wynn, "A History of the Civil Courts in Texas," 11.

23. William Pitt Ballinger, "Diary 1883," Box 2Q427, *William Pitt Ballinger Diaries*, Center for American History, University of Texas at Austin (diary entry of January 2, 1883), 2.

24. Leila Clark Wynn, "A History of the Civil Courts in Texas," 22.

25. "Interpretive Commentary," *Vernon's Annotated Texas Statutes*, Constitution, vol. 2 (West Publishing Co.: St. Paul, 1993), 24.

26. Leila Clark Wynn, "A History of the Civil Courts in Texas," 21.

27. "In Memoriam of Leroy G. Denman," 107 Tex. 672–76; Leroy G. Denman, "Denman, Leroy Gilbert," in *The Handbook of Texas Online* (Texas State Historical Association), accessed September 21, 2014, http://www.tshaonline.org/handbook/online/articles/fde40.

28. "In Memoriam of Thomas J. Brown," 107 Tex. 662–70; J. H. Davenport, *The History of the Supreme Court of Texas* (Austin: Southern Law Book Publishers, 1917), 218 (quote concerning Justice Brown's appointment); David Minor, "Brown, Thomas Jefferson," in *Handbook of Texas Online* (Texas State Historical Association), accessed September 8, 2014, http://www.tshaonline.org/handbook/online/articles/fbr97.

29. Leila Clark Wynn, "A History of the Civil Courts in Texas," *Southwestern Historical Quarterly* 60, no. 1 (July, 1956): 10.

30. H. L. Clamp, Deputy Clerk of Texas Supreme Court, "In Retrospect" (personal memoir in the possession of the Texas Supreme Court Historical Society), 5. For E. M. House, see Charles E. Neu), "House, Edward Mandell," in *Handbook of Texas Online* (Texas State Historical Association), accessed September 21, 2014, http://www.tshaonline.org/handbook/online/articles/fho66.

31. "In Memoriam of Reuben R. Gaines," 107 Tex. Rep. 658, 661.

32. Willie's older brother James was Attorney General of Texas, and Willie himself was elected to Congress from his home district of Galveston in 1874, and after one term returned there, only to be elected city attorney. Brown served as a political *consigliere* of sorts within the state Democratic Party and became so prominent within the party that Colonel House suggested he run for governor in 1901. Brown declined, preferring his position on the bench. See Thomas W. Cutrer, "Willie, Asa Hoxie," in *Handbook of Texas Online* (Texas State Historical Association); and David Minor, "Brown, Thomas Jefferson," in *Handbook of Texas Online* (Texas State Historical Association).

33. J. H. Davenport, *The History of the Supreme Court of Texas* (Austin: Southern Law Book Publishers, 1917), 149.

34. See Joe B. Frantz, *The Driskill Hotel* (Austin: Encino Publishing, 1973), 6–8. For details of this development and the electrification of Austin, see Joseph Jones, *Life on Waller Creek* (Austin: AAR/Tantalus, 1982), 155–58.

35. O. M. Roberts, "The Political, Legislative, and Judicial History of Texas during its Fifty Years of Statehood," 296–306; Randolph B. Campbell, *Gone to Texas: A History of the Lone Star State* (New York: Oxford University Press, 2003), 321–26.

36. O. M. Roberts, "The Political, Legislative, and Judicial History of Texas during Its Fifty Years of Statehood," 320.

37. Charles L. Miller, *Bounty and Donation Land Grants in Texas 1835–1888* (Austin: University of Texas Press, 1967), 3, citing J. T. Robison, Commissioner, "Report of the Commissioner of the General Land Office, September 1, 1910," in *Reports of the Commissioner, 1889–1952*, 25.

38. 86 Tex. 128 (1893).

39. *Busk v. Lowrie*, 86 Tex. 128, 129–30 (1893).

40. *Busk v. Lowrie*, 86 Tex. 128, 31–132.

41. *Galveston, Harrisburg, and San Antonio Railway Company v. State*, 89 Tex. 340; 34 S. W. 746 (Tex. 1896).

42. 90 Tex. 163; 38 S. W. 21 (Tex. 1896).

43. 90 Tex. 607; 40 S. W. 402 (Tex. 1897).

44. 89 Tex. 356; 34 S. W. 738 (Tex. 1896).

45. *Quinlan v. Houston and Texas Central Railway Company*, 89 Tex. 356, 374 (Tex. 1896).

46. *Texas & Pacific Railway Company v. Gay*, 86 Tex. 571; 26 S. W. 599 (Tex. 1894); *Texas & Pacific Railway Company v. Gay*, 88 Tex. 111; 30 S. W. 543 (Tex. 1895).

47. *Texas Pacific Railway Company v. Gay*, 88 Tex. 111, 116; 30 S. W. 543 (Tex. 1895).

48. *Texas Pacific Railway Company v. Gay*, 88 Tex. 111, 117.

49. 91 Tex. 574; 44 S. W. 1059 (Tex., 1898).

50. *Joske v. Irvine* at 581. Justice Denman acknowledges that this rule has been "generally admitted" and goes back to at least 1780.

51. *Joske v. Irvine* at 581.

52. *Joske v. Irvine* at 582, citing *Lee v. Int'l & Great Northern Rwy.Co.*, 89 Tex. 583; 36 S.W 63 (Tex. 1896).

53. 91 Tex. 221; 42 S. W. 850 (Tex., 1897).

54. 65 Tex. 281 (Tex., 1886).

55. 67 Tex. 665; 4 S. W. 357 (Tex. 1887).

56. 92 Tex. 168; 46 S. W. 629 (Tex. 1898).

57. *Wright v. Tipton*, at 171.

58. *Plessy v. Ferguson*, 163 U.S. 537 (1896); *Sweatt v, Painter*; 339 U.S. 629 (1950); *Brown v Board of Education*, 347 U.S. 483 (1954); *Cisneros v. Corpus Christi Independent School District*, 324 F. Supp. 599 (SDTex., 1970); Michael Ariens, *Lone Star Law* (Lubbock: Texas Tech University Press: 2011), 59–61, citing Act of Apr. 5, 1889, 21st Leg., R.S., ch. 108, 109 *Gammel's Laws of Texas* 1160; Act of March 19, 1891, 22nd Leg., R. S. ch. 10 *Gammel's Law of Texas* 46; Act of Apr. 11, 1891, 22nd Leg., R. S. ch., 103, in *Gammel's Law of Texas*, 167; Jason J. McDonald, "Confronting Jim Crow in the 'Lone Star' Capital: The Contrasting Strategies of African-American and Ethnic-Mexican Political Leaders in Austin, Texas, 1910–1930," *Continuity and Change* 22, no. 1 (May 2007): 143–69; Guadalupe San Miguel Jr., "The Struggle against Separate and Unequal Schools: Middle Class Mexican Americans and the Desegregation Campaign in Texas, 1929–1957," *History of Education Quarterly* 23, no. 3 (Autumn 1983): 343–59; Carlos M. Alcala and Jorge C. Rangel, "Project Report: De Jure Segregation of Chicanos in Texas Schools," *Harvard Civil Rights–Civil Liberties Law Review* 7 (March 1972): 307–91; Arnoldo De Leon, *They Called Them Greasers: Anglo Attitudes toward Mexicans in Texas, 1821–1900* (Austin: University of Texas Press, 1983); Gilbert G. Gonzales, "Segregation of Mexican Children in a Southern California City: The Legacy of Expansionism and the American Southwest," *Western Historical Quarterly* 16, no. 1 (January 1985): 469–71; Martha Menchaca, "Chicano Indianism: A Historical Account of Racial Repression in the United States," *American Ethnologist* 20, no. 3 (August 1993): 583–603. For a general discussion, see also "Texas Jim Crow Laws," Bringing History Home, website, accessed September 20, 2013, http://www.bringinghistoryhome.org/assets/bringinghistoryhome/3rd-grade/unit-2/activity-5/3_Texas_Jim%20Crow.pdf.

59. *Pullman-Palace-Car Co. v. Cain*, 40 S. W. 220 (Tex. Civ. App. 1897); Craig H. Roell, "Pleasants, Henry Clay," *Handbook of Texas Online* (Texas State Historical Association), accessed September 22, 2013, http://www.tshaonline.org/handbook/online/articles/fpl03. One other court case indicating challenges by blacks to segregation is the federal district court railroad case of *U.S. v. Dodge*, 25 Fed. C. 882 (WDTX 1877), where the government prosecuted railroad employees under the federal Civil Rights Act of 1875 for segregating black passengers. The government lost at trial because of the "separate but equal" doctrine, which the judge used to

instruct the jury. Michael Ariens, *Lone Star Law* (Lubbock: Texas Tech University Press, 2011), 60.

60. *Gulf C.& S. F. Ry. Co. v. Sharman*, 158 S. W. 1045 (Tex. Civ. App.—Austin 1913).

61. Articles 6746 and 6753, Texas Revised Civil Statutes.

62. *Gulf C.& S. F. Ry. Co. v. Sharman*, 158 S. W. 1045 (Tex. Civ. App.—Austin 1913).

63. *Gulf C.& S. F. Ry. Co. v. Sharman*, 158 S. W. 1045 (Tex. Civ. App.—Austin 1913); *Brown v. Board of Education of Topeka*, 347 U.S. 483 (1954). For a good summary of the connections between racism and progressivism, see David Bernstein and Thomas C. Leonard, "Excluding Unfit Workers: Social Control Versus Social Justice in the Age of Economic Reform," *Law and Contemporary Problems* 72, no. 3 (summer 2009): 177–204.

64. *Ewing v. State of Texas*, 81 Tex. 172, 177, 179; 16 S. W. 872 (Tex., 1891).

65. 88 Tex. 458; 31 S. W. 52 (Tex., 1895).

66. 58 Tex. 545 (Tex., 1883).

67. Constitution of the State of Texas (1876), Article 16, Section 50.

68. *Higgins v. Bordages*, 88 Tex. 458, 464; 31 S. W. 52 (Tex., 1895).

69. *Queen Insurance Company v. State*, 86 Tex. 250, 266; 24 S. W. 397 (Tex., 1893), citing *Beach on Private Corporations*, vol. 2, Section 856.

70. *Queen Insurance Company v. State*, 86 Tex. 250, 266; 24 S. W. 397 (Tex., 1893), citing *Beach on Private Corporations*, vol. 2, Section at 266.

71. 88 Tex. 184; 30 S. W. 869 (Tex. 1895).

72. *Queen Insurance Company v. State*, 86 Tex. 250; 24 S. W. 397 (Tex., 1893).

73. *Queen Insurance Company v. State*, 86 Tex. 250; 24 S. W. 397 (Tex., 1893), at 266.

74. 68 Tex. 361; 4 S. W. 633 (Tex., 1887).

75. *Price v. Supreme Lodge*, 68 Tex. 361, 368 (Tex. 1887). Similarly, the court was faced with interpreting the "total loss doctrine" in connection with fire insurance policies in *Royal Insurance Company v. McIntyre*, 90 Tex. 170; 37 S. W. 1068 (Tex. 1896).

76. James A. Tinsley, "Texas Progressives and Insurance Regulation," *Southwestern Social Science Quarterly*, vol. 36, no. 3 (December 1955), 237–47; *Handbook of Texas Online*, Seymour V. Connor, "Robertson, James Harvey," accessed August 22, 2018, http://www.tshaonline.org/handbook/online/articles/fro27; *Handbook of Texas Online*, Laurie E. Jasinski, "Texas Workers' Compensation Commission," accessed August 22, 2018, http://www.tshaonline.org/handbook/online/articles/mdtkz.

Epilogue

1. Benjamin F. Cardozo, *The Nature of the Judicial Process* (New Haven: Yale University Press, 1921), excerpted in *Courts, Judges, and Politics: An Introduction to the Judicial Process*, 6th ed., ed. Walter F. Murphy (Boston: McGraw Hill, 2006), 33.

2. William Blackstone, *Commentaries on the Laws of England*, Legal Classics Library ed. (Birmingham, AL: Gryphon Editions Ltd., 1983), vol. 1, 70.

3. Hamilton, *The Federalist* #78.

4. Goodwyn argues persuasively that in Texas, efforts by Populist Party officials to integrate the populist movement were almost totally unsuccessful because the cultural inheritance of racism was more powerful than issues of economic reform. Democrats kept luring away support of the People's Party by using race-baiting as the criticism of choice. Lawrence Goodwyn, *Democratic Promise: The Populist Moment in America* (New York: Oxford University Press, 1976), 289–99.

5. Evan Anders, *Boss Rule in South Texas* (Austin: University of Texas Press, 1982), 3–25, 65–81; Neil Foley, *The White Scourge: Mexicans, Blacks, and Poor Whites in Texas Cotton Culture* (Berkeley: University of California Press, 1997), 1–45. Foley argues that even extreme lower class or politically radical whites were marginalized by, in essence depriving them culturally of their "whiteness," an argument with which I agree, but which is beyond my scope, since he uses it to explain events after the period under discussion here.

6. Roxanne Williamson, "Driskill Hotel," in *Handbook of Texas Online* (Texas State Historical Association), accessed September 8, 2014, http://www.tshaonline.org/handbook/online/articles/ccd01. See also Joe B. Frantz, *The Driskill Hotel* (Austin: Encino Publishing, 1973). It appears that the Driskill was originally four stories tall with "sixty steam heated guest rooms with four elaborate suites on the second floor." Roxanne Williamson, "Driskill Hotel," in *Handbook of Texas Online*. Frantz says that instead of four suites, the second floor had two large parlors and two bridal suites in addition to the ballroom or "dining room." Frantz, *The Driskill Hotel*, 9. The reception invitation did not specify the exact location of the party, so I have deduced that the large number of guests present would have required use of one of the ballroom/dining rooms, and that although the invitation indicates "Judge and Mrs. Gaines at home," the reception could not have been held in their apartment at the Driskill, which was most likely one of the steam heated guest rooms, even though they were also unusually large for their genre. Since electric lights, automobiles, and elevators were common in Austin by 1909, and since the Gaines would have been quite old for stair climbing, I have further surmised that they often used the Driskill's elevator to reach their apartment, as described below. Electric lights were added to the Driskill's guest rooms in 1895, and by 1923, two-thirds of the guest rooms had indoor baths. What Frantz called "special chambers," which were evidently suites, had indoor baths from the beginning. Frantz, *The Driskill Hotel*, 49. Frantz relates a story about a party for a "group of dignitaries" hosted by Chief Justice and Mrs. Gaines in the dining room, where he was carving a turkey and then fell to the floor when a waiter pulled his chair out from under him to give him more room to carve. This story is repeated in H. L. Clamp, Deputy Clerk of Texas Supreme Court, "In Retrospect" (personal memoir in the possession of the Texas Supreme Court Historical Society). Clamp first began clerking in 1902, so the story presumably happened in the twentieth century, but I conclude it was not at the fiftieth anniversary party

because 8:30 would have been quite late for dinner and a carved turkey would not have fed over one hundred guests. The clerk says that Gaines chased the waiter all the way to the stairwell. Frantz says he chased him all the way out in the street with the carving knife. Frantz appears to be relating a legend current at the hotel that had been told and retold a number of times. Clamp's account is probably closer to the literal truth of the incident.

7. See Randolph B. Campbell, "Gaines, Reuben R.," in *Handbook of Texas Online*; "Guestbook for 50th Anniversary Party, Wednesday, March 31, 1909"; Box 2D186, *Louisa Shortridge Gaines Papers*, Center for American History, University of Texas at Austin. When the Austin Bar Association appeared before the Supreme Court on October 19, 1914, to present resolutions in memoriam of Justice Gaines, who died earlier that year, the memory of this party figured prominently. "It is a most pleasing and grateful recollection to the members of the bar of Austin, and to the members of the courts resident here, that Judge Gaines and his wife celebrated their golden wedding in Austin at which so many of us were guests at that enjoyable occasion." See "In Memoriam of Reuben R. Gaines," 107 Tex. Rep. 658.

8. Leila Clark Wynn, "A History of the Civil Courts in Texas," *Southwestern Historical Quarterly* 60, no. 1 (July, 1956): 1–23; H. L. Clamp, Deputy Clerk of Texas Supreme Court, "In Retrospect" (personal memoir in the possession of the Texas Supreme Court Historical Society) (first quote); and J. H. Davenport, *The History of the Supreme Court of Texas* (Austin: Southern Law Book Publishers, 1917), 171–72 (last quote). Although prohibition was a major issue in Texas from the 1880s through the early twentieth century, Gaines and his wife were known to occasionally imbibe. In fact, Mrs. Gaines's recipe collection encourages bakers to "pour a little rum" on fruitcake, and her papers include an enticing recipe for a champagne cocktail written on the Supreme Court stationary of "R. R. Gaines, Chief Justice." Box 2D186, *Louisa Shortridge Gaines Papers*, Center for American History, University of Texas at Austin. See also Randolph B. Campbell, "Gaines, Reuben R.," *Handbook of Texas Online*.

9. Craig H. Roell, "Stayton, John William," *Handbook of Texas Online* (Texas State Historical Association), accessed September 8, 2014, http://www.tshaonline.org/handbook/online/articles/fst23; "In Memoriam of John W. Stayton," 87 Tex. Reports v–xvii.

10. "In Memoriam of Leroy G. Denman," 107 Tex. 672–76; Leroy G. Denmon, "Denman, Leroy Gilbert," *The Handbook of Texas Online* (Texas State Historical Association), accessed September 8, 2014, http://www.tshaonline.org/handbook/online/articles/fde40.

11. The description of Brown is taken from Leila Clark Wynn, "A History of the Civil Courts in Texas," *Southwestern Historical Quarterly* 60, no. 1 (July, 1956): 11.

12. "In Memoriam of Thomas J. Brown," 107 Tex. 662, 668.

13. David Minor, "Brown, Thomas Jefferson," *Handbook of Texas Online* (Texas State Historical Association), accessed September 8, 2014, http://www.tshaonline.org/handbook/online/articles/fbr97, describes Brown's health problems. In response to his memoriam presented to the Supreme Court, Justice Gaines was said by his friend and successor Justice T. J. Brown, to have been unselfish and impartial, "a devoted friend to those with whom he associated, but he was not a bitter enemy to anyone. On the bench he was neither friend nor foe to any man, nor in any way interested in the matter to be decided." These remarks are different in tone than those offered in memory of the firm but fair scholar Stayton, or of Brown himself, who would die only a few months after Gaines.

14. An electric power plant was built in Austin in the 1890s and there were already telephone lines in place in 1886. See Frantz, *The Driskill Hotel*, 6–8. Electric streetcars ran in downtown Austin from 1891 to 1940. For details of this development and the electrification of Austin, see Joseph Jones, *Life on Waller Creek* (Austin: AAR/Tantalus, 1982), 155–58.

15. "Jefferson Davis Statue Comes Down at University of Texas," *The Two-Way: Breaking News from NPR* (National Public Radio), accessed December 2, 2015, http://www.npr.org/sections/thetwo-way/2015/08/30/436072805/jefferson-davis-statue-comes-down-at-university-of-texas.

16. Rebekah Allen, "UT to Re-erect Statue of James Hogg, after Removing It in 2017 because of Confederate Ties," *Dallas Morning News* (December 6, 2018), https://www.dallasnews.com/news/higher-education/2018/12/06/ut-re-erect-statue-james-hogg-after-removing-2017-confederate-ties (accessed April 9, 2019).

17. Littlefield died in 1920, three years before the fountain was dedicated. David B. Gracey II, "Littlefield, George Washington," in *Handbook of Texas Online* (Texas State Historical Association), accessed September 4, 2014, http://www.tshaonline.org/handbook/online/articles/fli18.

18. See Joe B. Frantz, *The Driskill Hotel* (Austin: Encino, 1973); Joseph Jones, *Life on Waller Creek* (Austin: AAR / Tantalus, 1982), 155–58.

19. Thorstein Veblen, *The Theory of the Leisure Class*, Easton Press 1994 edition (Norwalk, CT: Easton Press, 1994 [orig. ed. New York, 1899]). See, in particular, the 1973 introduction to this edition by John Kenneth Galbraith at pp. xv–xxv. See also H. W. Brands, *The Murder of Jim Fisk for the Love of Josie Mansfield: A Tragedy of the Gilded Age* (New York: Anchor Books, 2011), and Brands, *American Colossus: The Triumph of Capitalism, 1865–1900* (New York: Doubleday, 2010).

20. See A. T. Mason and Gordon Baker, eds., *Free Government in the Making* (New York: Oxford University Press, 1949, 4th edition 1985), 502–9, 536–44.

21. Edward Bellamy, *Looking Backward: 2000–1887*, 1992 Easton Press collectors' edition (Norwalk, CT: Easton Press, 1992 [orig. ed. Boston, 1887]) (all page citations

are to the 1992 Easton edition), e–f (Nationalist clubs), 58 (first quote from Bellamy), 105 (second quote from Bellamy).

22. Bellamy, *Looking Backward*, 53 (quote).

23. Richard B. McCaslin, *At the Heart of Texas: 100 Years of the Texas State Historical Association, 1897–1997* (Austin: Texas State Historical Association, 2007), 6–19.

Appendix

1. Gary Jacobsohn, *Constitutional Identity* (Cambridge: Harvard University Press, 2010), 5–6. A recent example of the kind of constitutional history this book attempts is Frank Cicero Jr., *Creating the Land of Lincoln: History and Constitutions of Illinois, 1778–1870* (Champaign: University of Illinois Press, 2018). Cicero does for Illinois what this book does for Texas.

2. In this, Jacobsohn relies on works as diverse as those of political theorist Hanna Pitkin and constitutional scholars Donald Lutz, Walter Murphy, Laurence Tribe, and Stanley N. Katz. Cicero Jr., *Creating the Land of Lincoln*, 4–5; Hanna Fenichel Pitkin, "The Idea of a Constitution," *Journal of Legal Education* 37, no. 2 (1987), 167–69; Donald S. Lutz, *Principles of Constitutional Design* (Cambridge: Cambridge University Press, 2006); Walter F. Murphy, *Constitutional Democracy: Creating a Just Political Order* (Baltimore: Johns Hopkins University Press, 2007); Laurence H. Tribe, "A Constitution We Are Amending: In Defense of a Restrained Judicial Role," *Harvard Law Review* 97, no. 2 (December 1983): 433–45; Stanley N. Katz, "Constitutionalism in East Central Europe: Some Negative Lessons from the American Experience," in Vicki C. Jackson and Mark Tushnet, eds., *Comparative Constitutional Law* (New York: Foundation Press, 1999).

3. Walter L. Buenger and Robert A. Calvert, eds., *Texas through Time: Evolving Interpretations* (College Station: Texas A&M University Press, 1991); Walter L. Buenger and Arnoldo DeLeon, eds., *Beyond Texas through Time: Breaking Away from Past Interpretations* (College Station: Texas A&M University Press, 2011). The heroic view of Texas History criticized by the new revisionists is epitomized by George Garrison, Eugene Barker, and Walter Prescott Webb, among others.

4. Benedict Anderson, *Imagined Communities: Reflections on the Origin and Spread of Nationalism* (New York: W. W. Norton & Co., 1983). See also Bernard Bailyn, *The Ideological Origins of the American Revolution* (Cambridge: Harvard University Press, 1967).

5. Leading works on the sociology and anthropology of *alterité* include Emmanuel Levinas, *Entre Nous: Thinking of the Other*, trans. Michael B. Smith (New York: Columbia University Press, 2000); Levinas, *Totality and Being: An Essay on Exteriority*, trans. Alphonso Lingis (Pittsburgh: Duquesne University Press, 1969); Levinas, *Otherwise than Being or Beyond Essence*, trans. Alphonso Lingis (Ithaca: Cornell University Press, 1998); Michael Taussig, *Mimesis and Alterity* (New York: Routledge, 1993); Edward Said, *Orientalism* (New York: Knopf Publishing Group, 1979); Said, *Culture and Imperialism* (New York: Knopf Publishing Group, 1994). Recently,

historians of colonial America have come to similar conclusions about fears of an axis of enemies composed of Natives and slaves, and the importance of using this anxiety to fuse together otherwise disparate factions into a political consensus. It now seems clear that exploiting fear of a British inspired Indian/slave revolt was a crucial tool in unifying the American patriot movement. See Robert G. Parkinson, The Common Cause: Creating Race and Nation in the American Revolution (Chapel Hill: University of North Carolina Press, 2016).

6. Walter L. Buenger and Robert A. Calvert, eds., *Texas through Time: Evolving Interpretations* (College Station: Texas A&M University Press, 1991); Walter L. Buenger and Arnoldo DeLeon, eds., *Beyond Texas through Time: Breaking Away from Past Interpretations* (College Station: Texas A&M University Press, 2011). A critical description of the first book and the questions it raises can be found on Amazon at https://www.amazon.com/Texas-through-Time-Evolving-Interpretations/dp/0890964904/ref=tmm_hrd_swatch_0?_encoding=UTF8&qid=&sr=; accessed April 9, 2019 (macho quote).

7. Stephen Harrigan, Carlos Kevin Blanton, Christopher Hooks, and John Phillip Santos, "The New Texas History: In an Era of Political Polarization, Is It Possible for Texans to Settle on a 'Usable Past' We Can All Agree On," *Texas Monthly* (October 2019), pp. 72–85; Bryan Burrough, Chris Tomlinson, and Jason Stanford, *Forget the Alamo: The Rise and Fall of an American Myth* (New York: Penguin Press, 2021).

8. R. G. Collingswood, *The Idea of History* (Oxford: Oxford University Press, 1946).

9. Clifford Geertz, *The Interpretation of Cultures* (New York: Basic Books, 1973); Geertz, *Works and Lives: The Anthropologist as Author* (Palo Alto: Stanford University Press, 1989); Rhys Isaac, *Landon Carter's Uneasy Kingdom* (Oxford: Oxford University Press, 2004); Isaac, "Stories of Enslavement: A Person Centered Ethnography from an Eighteenth Century Plantation," in Bruce Clayton and John Salmond, eds., *Varieties of Southern History: New Essays on a Region and its People* (New York: Greenwood Press, 1996), 3–21.

10. G. W. F. Hegel, *The Philosophy of History*; Hegel, *The Phenomenology of Mind*; David Brion Davis, *The Problem of Slavery in the Age of Revolution* (Ithaca: Cornell University Press, 1975); Christopher Brown, *Moral Capital: Foundations of British Abolitionism* (Chapel Hill: University of North Carolina Press, 2006); Seth Jacobs, *America's Miracle Man in Vietnam* (Durham: Duke University Press, 2004), 5 (quote).

11. Lewis L. Gould, "Progressive Era," *Handbook of Texas Online*, accessed August 14, 2017, http://www.tshaonline.org/handbook/online/articles/npp01; Laurie E. Jasinski, "Texas Workers' Compensation Commission," *Handbook of Texas Online*, accessed August 14, 2017, http://www.tshaonline.org/handbook/online/articles/mdtkz. Obviously the allusion to imagined communities again refers to Anderson, *Imagined Communities: Reflections on the Origin and Spread of Nationalism*.

12. Gary Jacobsohn, *Constitutional Identity* (Cambridge: Harvard University Press, 2010), 19 (quote), 89–117 citing: Alasdair MacIntyre, *After Virtue: A Study in Moral Theory* (South Bend: Notre Dame University Press, 1981).

13. For example, after accomplishing conquest of the Persian Empire, Alexander the Great promptly adopted the Persian court customs most amenable to his exercise of power and most likely to obscure the strangeness of his own presence on the physical and cultural landscape of Asia. The conqueror exerts his will upon the landscape; when the danger of resistance has receded, he seeks to take on the most useful and comforting aspects of that landscape. Partly because of their creation of the term *barbarian* and partly because they are seen as characteristically western, the Greeks have been particularly fruitful subjects of research on *alterité* and how it works in Western culture. Any treatment must account for the fact that Anglo-Texan identity and ideology can be explained in part as a phenomenon of *alterité*—national or ethnic self-identification by reference to "the other." For some historical applications of this theory, see, for example, Francois Hartog, *The Mirror of Herodotus: The Representation of the Other in the Writing of History*, trans. Janet Lloyd (Berkeley: University of California Press, 1988); Paul Cartledge, *Greeks: A Portrait of Self and Others* (Oxford: Oxford University Press, 2002). A similar study with specific reference to early Texas is David Montejano, *Anglos and Mexicans in the Making of Texas 1836–1986* (Austin: University of Texas Press, 1987). For a fascinating literary application, see Edith Hall, *Inventing the Barbarian: Greek Self-Definition through Tragedy* (Oxford: Oxford University Press, 1991). See also Francois Hartog, *The Mirror of Herodotus: The Representation of the Other in the Writing of History*, trans. Janet Lloyd (Berkeley: University of California Press, 1988); Paul Cartledge, *Greeks: A Portrait of Self and Others* (Oxford: Oxford University Press, 2002); Edith Hall, *Inventing the Barbarian: Greek Self-Definition through Tragedy* (Oxford: Oxford University Press, 1991). For works on *alterité* and the medieval world, see Timothy (Kallistos) Ware, *Eustratios Argenti: A Study of the Greek Church under Turkish Rule* (Oxford: Clarendon Press, 1964); and Tia M. Kolbaba, *The Byzantine Lists-Error of the Latins* (Urbana and Chicago: University of Illinois Press, 2000).

14. Georg Simmel, "The Stranger," in *The Sociology of Georg Simmel*, trans. and ed. Kurt H. Wolff (New York: The Free Press, 1950), 402–8. While history describes these phenomena and sociology can explain how they work, those seeking to know *why* humans seem to need group identities and perceived enemies turn to anthropology and psychoanalysis. Although the details are beyond the scope of this study, it is worthwhile to note that both disciplines put forth explanations. Where the disciplines intersect, at Jung's theory of universal archetypes, the explanation is stated thus by Joseph Campbell:

> Throughout life all enemies are symbolical (to the unconscious) of the father.... Hence... the irresistible compulsion to make war: the impulse to destroy the father is continually transforming itself into public violence. The old men of the immediate community or race protect themselves from their growing sons by the psychological magic of their totem ceremonies. They

enact the ogre father, and then reveal themselves to be the feeding mother too. A new and larger paradise is thus established. But this paradise does not include the traditional enemy tribes, or races, against whom aggression is still systematically projected. All of the "good" father-mother content is saved for home, while the "bad" is flung abroad and about: "For who is this uncircumcised Philistine, that he should defy the armies of the living God." ... Instead of clearing his own heart the zealot tries to clear the world. The laws of the City of God are applied only to his in-group ... while the fire of perpetual holy war is hurled (with good conscience, and indeed a sense of pious service) against whatever uncircumcised, barbarian, heathen, "native," or alien people happens to occupy the position of neighbor.

Joseph Campbell, *The Hero with a Thousand Faces* (Princeton: Princeton University Press, 1949, 2nd edition, 1968), 155–56, quoting 1 Samuel 17:26.

15. *Abrams v. U.S.*, 250 U.S. 616 (1919), Holmes, j., dissenting.

Index

Note: Page numbers in italics indicate illustrative material

ab initio dispute, 97–98, 109–10, 120, 268n63
abolition. *See* antislavery sentiment
Ackerman, Bruce, 217
Adams, Henry, 84
Adams, John Quincy, 37
Adkins, William F., 286n19
Africans and descendants. *See* blacks; slavery
Agricultural Wheel, 152
A. H. Belo & Company v. Smith, 196–97
Alabama Indians, 15–16, 26
Alamo, Battle of the (1836), 27, 28, 30, 216, 219
The Alamo Express (newspaper), 65
Alexander, William, 124
alterité ("otherness"), xiii, 219, 221, 296n13
American Bar Association, 176
Americanism, Texas as ultimate expression of, xv, 225n8
amnesty, 91–92. *See also* Reconstruction
Ampudia, Pedro de, 42
Anders, Evan, 284n2
Anderson, Benedict, 218
Anderson, Gary Clayton, 241n12
Andrews, Stephen Pearl, 43–45
Anglo immigration, Mexican policy on, 2, 3–4, 6–7, 8, 12–13, 14, 19, 26
annexation: diplomatic negotiations with United States, 36, 37–38, 44; joint resolution for, 45–46, 48; Texian support for, 36–37
anticlericalism, 22, 32
antislavery sentiment: domestic, 16, 20, 34, 43–45, 59, 61, 63–65, 248–49n74, 250n81; in England, 44, 230n18, 240n8; of German immigrants, 35, 59, 61, 63–64, 66, 248–49nn74–75, 250n81; in Mexico, 2–3, 6–8, 10–14, 16–17, 19–20, 21–22, 229n14, 231n19; on the political spectrum, 65–67; and religion, 5, 6, 63–64, 71, 72–73, 230–31n18; of Tejanos, 20, 34, 59, 63–64, 66; in United States, as threat to Texan proslavery identity, 32, 43–44, 63–65, 69–74, 79, 81–82, 85–86, 88–89; in United States, Texan attempts to mollify, 21, 24, 37
antitrust law, 202–3
appellate court structure, 95, 145, 146, 162, 178–81
Arapahoe Indians, 244n25
Aries, Philippe, 282n77
Arizpe, Miguel Ramos, 9
Atcheson, Daniel, 181–82
attractive nuisance doctrine, 164–65, 281–82n75
Austin, Brown, 10
Austin, Henry, 15, 20
Austin, John, 13
Austin, Moses, 5, 13–14
Austin, Stephen F.: independence sentiment, 14–15, 18, 19, 20; mentioned, 86; shifting views on slavery, 12, 233n37; slavery disputation with Mexican government, 7, 8, 10, 11–12, 231n19; US diplomacy, 36
Austin Statesman (newspaper), 136–37, 139, 158

Ballinger, William Pitt, *133*; *vs.* abolitionists, 64; in blue ribbon committee, 162; in

299

convention for 1876 constitution, 132, 139, 141, 142, 143, 144–45; and land title court cases, 281n74; on Terrell, 181
banks: in 1845 constitution, 55–56; in 1876 constitution, 146; and racist conspiracies, 148
Barker, Eugene C., 213, 225n9, 227n6, 233n35, 233n37
Barrow, Charles, 280n62
Bascus, "Incarnation," 1, 226n1
Batts, R. L., 156
Baum, Dale, 66, 251n8
Beaman, Fernando, 118
Bell, James H., 73–74, *75*, 76–78, 79, 80, 88, 251n8, 256–57n40
Bell, John, 65–66
Bellamy, Edward, *Looking Backward*, 214–15
Bewly, Anthony, 63–64, 65
Bexar, Siege of (1835), 17, 18, 19
bills of rights: and 1836 constitution Declaration of Rights, 31; in 1845 constitution, 49, 55; in 1869 constitution, 116; in US Constitution, 14
Black Bean Episode (1843), 42
blacks: citizenship of, 30–31, 50–51, 100; education rights, 104; expulsion from Texas, 43; and Fourteenth Amendment, 90, 105, 106, 116, 122; and intermarriage, 99–100; limited "equal" rights for, 94, 99, 101–3, 199; and political alliances in 1875 convention, 138, 147; segregation of, 104, 115–16, 123, 141, 198–201, 289–90n59; voting rights, 55, 94, 100–101, 116, 131, 136, 139, 258n52. *See also* slavery
Blackstone, William, 207
Blount (Methodist minister), 63
Bolivar, Simon, 6
Bonner, Micajah, *154*, 155, 156–57, 161, 163
Bowie, James, 16, 18
Bowles (Cherokee chief), 40
Bradburn, John D., 13–14, 233n40
Bradshaw, Amzi, 93, 99
Brands, H. W., 228–29n12
Breckinridge, John C., 78, 80
Brewer, David, 176–77
Britain. *See* England
Brown, Christopher, 220
Brown, John, 63
Brown, John Henry, 81, 85, 139

Brown, Thomas Jefferson, *185*; cases overseen by, 187, 189–90, 192, 198, 202; on Gaines, 293n13; judicial career, 182–83, 186, 210, 288n32; nomination for reelection, 187–88
Brown v. Board of Education, 200
Bryan, William Jennings, 173, 174
Buckley, Constantine W., 74, 78, 79
Buenger, Walter, 68, 218, 219, 252n10, 256n38
Bugbee, Lester G., 231n20
Bumpass, John K., 95, 97
Burke, Edmund, 74
Burleson, Edward, 38, 40, 244n25
Burnet, David G.: antislavery sentiment, 16, 20–21; and Houston, 38, 254n15; as interim president of Texas republic, 35–36; and pacifism, 18, 19; and US Senate seat, 105, 106
Burnett, James R., 121
business progressivism, 165, 174–75, 176–78, 207–8, 209
Busk v. Lowrie, 188–90
Butts, William, 63

Caddo Indians, 39, 41, 43, 243n21
Caldwell, John, 46, 47, 48
California Supreme Court, 178–79
Calvert, Robert, 218, 219
Campbell, Joseph, 296–97n14
Campbell, Randolph B., 227n6, 229n14, 231n19, 248–49n74
Canby, Edward, 119, 121
capital building, 153–55, 157–58
Carbajal, Jose Maria Jesus, 1, 226n1
Cardozo, Benjamin, 207
Casas, Bartolomé de las, 5, 6, 229n16
Catholicism: antislavery sentiment, 5, 6, 230–31n18; conversion to, 7; Protestant criticism of, 22, 32, 56–57
certiorari, 178, 179
Chambers, Edward, 137, 139, 141
Chambers, William, 147
Charles V, King of Spain, 5
Cherokee Indians, 27, 39, 40, 41, 43, 241n12, 242–43n21
Cheyenne Indians, 244n25
children, legal protection of, 163, 165, 282n77

INDEX

Childress, George, 27, 28
Choctaw Indians, 39
citizenship: in 1833 constitution, 14; in 1836 constitution, 26, 30–31; in 1845 constitution, 50–51; in 1866 constitution, 100; in 1869 constitution, 116. *See also* voting and elections
Civil Rights Act (1875), 289n59
Civil War (1861–65), 83–84, 86–87, 89. *See also* Confederacy; Reconstruction; Secession
Clamp, H. L., 291–92n6
Clark, Edward, 51, 69
class: and political demarcation, 127–28, 130; and race, 32–33. *See also* Grangers; populism
Cleveland, Grover, 173, 175
Coahuila y Texas (Mexican state), 9–13, 14, 19, 25, 231n20
Coke, Richard, *124*; and convention for 1876 constitution, 135; judiciary appointments, 126, 129, 145; political elections, xvii, 123, 125, 147; US Senate seat, 153
Coldwell, Colbert, 108, 111, 119, 266n39
Collingwood, R. G., 219
Collinsworth, James, 27, 28, 29, 237–38n25
Colquitt, Oscar B., 213
Colt revolvers, 43, 83–84, 245n28
Columbia Declaration (1835), 21. *See also* Declaration of Independence (1836)
Comanche Indians, 39, 41, 43, 243–44n25
combinations in restraint of trade, 203
Commission of Appeals, 145, 162, 178, 179, 180
comparative constitutionalism, xiii
Confederacy: and amnesty, 91–92; martial law against unreconstructed states, 106–7, 122; monuments, 211–13; Texas admission to, 83, 84. *See also* Reconstruction; Secession
Congressional Reconstruction, 90–91, 105–7. *See also* Constitution of 1869
conservative Anglo progressivism and conservative modern Texas, as concept, xv
conspicuous consumption, 214
conspiracy theory of history, 148
constitution, defined, xiii
constitutional disharmony, 218, 220

constitutional identity, 217–18, 220
constitutional moments, xiii, 217
Constitution of 1824 (Mexico), 8–9, 12, 13, 16, 20, 21
Constitution of 1827 (Coahuila-Texas), 9–10, 20, 231n20
Constitution of 1833, 14, 20
Constitution of 1836: approval of, 36–37; citizenship provision, 26, 30–31; convention delegates, 27; debt provisions, 56; and Declaration of Independence, 21–26, 82; Declaration of Rights, 31; influenced by 1824 Mexican constitution, 9; influenced by US Constitution, 31, 238n29; land title provisions, 29–30; political chaos surrounding, 28–29; slavery provisions, 31–32, 57; and Texan identity formation, 31–33
Constitution of 1845: overview of contents, 55; amendments to, 84–85; and annexation resolution, 45–46, 48; approval of, 53–54, 58–59; Bill of Rights, 49, 55; citizenship provisions, 50–51; convention delegates, 46–47; corporation and bank provisions, 52, 55–56, 98; debt provisions, 49, 56; education provisions, 51, 103; general provisions, 51–52, 55, 57; government branches, 49–50, 54, 55; land grant provisions, 47, 50, 52–53; religion provisions, 49, 56–57; slavery provisions, 52, 57–58; and Texan identity formation, 59; voting provisions, 55, 56
Constitution of 1861: as amendment to 1845 constitution, 84; corporation provisions, 98; education provisions, 103; slavery provisions, 84–85; and Texan identity formation, 67, 87. *See also* Secession
Constitution of 1866: approval of, 104–5; citizenship provisions, 100; convention delegates, 92–93; convention ordinances, 93–94, 96, 97; convention proposals for reform, 94–95; corporation and railroad provisions, 98–99, 143; education provisions, 103–4, 198; freedmen provisions, 102–3; judiciary provisions, 95; land grant provisions, 99; and state division proposal, 96–97; voting provisions, 100–101

Constitution of 1869: ab initio dispute, 109–10, 120, 268n63; amendments to, 123, 126; approval of, 121; Bill of Rights, 116; calls for repeal of, 135; citizenship provisions, 116; convention delegates, 108; convention proposals for reform, 108–9; corporation and railroad provisions, 109–10, 112–13, 143, 146, 192; debt provisions, 110–12; education provisions, 113, 114–16; immigration provisions, 113–14; judiciary provisions, 117, 123; land grant provisions, 111, 112–13, 192; and state division proposal, 118–21; voting provisions, 116, 140

Constitution of 1876: approval of, 147; convention delegates, 131–32; convention faction disputes, 135–39, 140–41, 142, 143, 144; convention proposals for reform, 135; corporation and railroad provisions, 143–44, 146–47, 170, 276n29; debt provisions, 144; education provisions, 140–42, 199; executive and legislative provisions, 142–43; immigration provisions, 144; judiciary provisions, 144–46, 178; land grant provisions, 130, 141, 142, 143–44, 157–58, 168, 276n29; and Texan identity formation, 127, 147; voting provisions, 131, 136, 139–40

– 1891 amendments: approval of, 179–80, 286–87n19; judicial reorganization, 155, 174, 179–80, 181; railroad regulations, 175–76

Constitution of the Texas State Historical Association, 215–16

Constitution of the United States, 8, 14, 28, 31, 49, 238n29

Consultation (*Consultado*) Convention (1835), 18–19, 24, 29

continuities of conflict, 220–21

Cook, W. D. S., 140

Cooke, G. B., 137

Cooper, Washington Bogart, 87

cooperatives (farmers), 151, 153

Cordova, Vicente, 39

Cornyn, John, 229n13, 238n29

corporations: in 1836 constitution, 32, 55–56; in 1845 constitution, 52, 55–56, 98; in 1861 constitution, 98; in 1866 constitution, 98–99; in 1869 constitution, 109–10, 112–13, 146; in 1876 constitution, 143–44, 146–47; and antitrust law, 202–3; insurance companies, 203–5; in populist rhetoric, 148–49; in secessionist rhetoric, 255n19. *See also* railroads

Cortina, Juan, 127

Cos, Perfecto de, 15–16, 17, 22

Council House Fight (1840), 41, 42, 243–44n25

court of appeals, 95, 145, 146, 162, 178–81

court system. *See* judicial branch

Coushatta Indians, 15–16, 26

Crane, William Carey, 254n15

Crawford, William L., 142

Creek Indians, 39

criminal appellate court structure, 95, 145, 146, 178, 179

Cruger, J. W., 245n36

Cuba, and slave plantation system, 79

Culberson, Charles, 173, 188, 192, 204, 285n4

Culbertson, D. B., 74

Cunningham, A. S., 50

Daily Herald (newspaper), 136
Daily State Gazette (newspaper), 131
Dallas News (newspaper), 196
Davidson, W. L., 161
Davis, David Brion, 220, 230n18
Davis, Edmund J.: in convention for 1866 constitution, 103, 104; in convention for 1869 constitution, 107, 108, 110, 113, 117, 118–21, 266n39; political elections, 122, 123, 125–26, 128; reforms as governor, 122–23; as unionist, 105
Davis, Jefferson, 211
Davis, William C., 229n12
Daws, S. O., 150, 151
De Bruhl, Marshall, 254n15
debt: in 1836 constitution, 56; in 1845 constitution, 49, 56; in 1869 constitution, 110–12; in 1876 constitution, 144; repudiation of state, 97, 109–10
Declaration of Independence (1776, US), 22, 25, 70, 82
Declaration of Independence (1836, Texas), 21–26, 82
Degener, Edward, 101, 103, 113–14, 118, 119, 120

INDEX

Delaware Indians, 39
De Leon, Arnoldo, 218, 219
DeMause, Lloyd, 282n77
Democratic Party: dominance during Reconstruction, 123–26, 127–28; and factional disputes in 1875 convention, 131, 134, 135–38, 140–41, 142, 143, 144, 147; overthrow during Reconstruction, 106, 107, 121–22; and *padron* system, 173, 284–85n2; and populism, 153, 173–74, 176; and populism-progressivism fusion, xviii, 173, 174–75, 207–8; split of, 187. *See also* Grangers; Secession
DeMorse, Granger Charles, 140, 141
Denman, Leroy G., *185*; cases overseen by, 187, 193, 194–96, 202, 288n50; judicial career, 182, 186, 210; mentioned, 216; nomination for reelection, 187–88
depression of the mid-1890s, 175
Devine, Thomas J., 81
dialectics, process of, xvii
Dillard, W. W., 137
Dillon, John F., 176
Din, Gilbert, 6
Dixon, David C., 73
Dohoney, Ebenezer, 137, 139, 140, 141
Donelly, Ignatius, *Caesar's Column*, 148
Douai, Adolf, 65, 249n75, 250n81
Dred Scott decision, 69
Driscoll, Clara, 209, 216
Driskill Hotel, 209, 211, 291n6
Duboise de Saligny, Alphonse, 38
Dunlap, Andrew, 152
Durst, John, 11

economic and financial interests: business progressivism, 165, 174–75, 176–78, 207–8, 209; and conspicuous consumption, 214; depression of the mid-1890s, 175; federal regulatory measures, 176–77; and socialist utopia, 214–15. *See also* banks; corporations; land grants and titles; railroads; slavery
education: in 1845 constitution, 51, 103; in 1861 constitution, 103; in 1866 constitution, 103–4, 198; in 1869 constitution, 113, 114–16; in 1876 constitution, 140–42, 199

Edwards, Monroe, 12
electorate. *See* voting and elections
Ellis, Richard, 22, 27, 28, 30
England: antislavery sentiment in, 44, 230n18, 240n8; recognition of Texas republic, 38, 44, 240n8
Epperson, Ben, 65, 74, 76, 80
Erhard, Cayton, 132, 141, 144
executive branch: in 1845 constitution, 49; in 1876 constitution, 142
Ex Parte Rodriguez, 124–25, 128, 129, 135

Fannin, James W., 12, 16, 18
farmers: protections for, 110–11, 128–29, 130–31, 144; yeoman ideal, 31, 55, 59, 78, 111, 146, 148, 168, 171. *See also* Grangers; homesteads; populism
Farmers' Alliance, 150–53, 173
Farmer's Mutual Benefit Association, 152
federal government. *See* United States
Federalists, 37, 69, 70, 72–73. *See also* Whigs and Know-Nothingism
Field, Steven J., 176
Fifteenth Amendment, 122
Filisola, Vicente, 39
Fillmore, Millard, 68
financial interests. *See* economic and financial interests
Fisher, George, 48
Fisher, Samuel Rhoads, 23
Fisher, William S., 28, 42, 243–44n25
Flake, Ferdinand, 66
Flanagan, James W., 108, 110–11, 115, 121, 122
Flanagan, Webster, 138
Fleming, Ian, 225n8
Flournoy, George, 80, 81, 141, 142
Foley, Neil, 291n5
Ford, John S. "Rip," 80, 132, 139, 141, 143, 215, 216
Fourteenth Amendment, 90, 105, 106, 116, 122
France, recognition of Texas republic, 38
Frantz, Joe B., 291–92n6
Frazier, C. A., 95
freedmen. *See* blacks
freedom of religion, 49, 56–57
freedom of speech and press, 31, 49

Gaines, James, 28, 241n12
Gaines, Mrs. Reuben Reid, 209, 292n8
Gaines, Reuben Reid, *184*; cases overseen by, 166, 182, 183, 186, 187, 190, 191, 192, 196–97, 201–2, 203; fiftieth wedding anniversary, 209, 291–92nn6–7; judicial career, 166, 182, 183, 186, 293n13
Galveston News (newspaper), 138, 196, 275n19
Galveston Weekly News (newspaper), 65
Gamble, William G., 89
Gammage v. Powell, 283–84n91
Garrison, George, 215, 216, 225n9
Garwin, W. L., 150
Gay, John M., 193
Geertz, Clifford, 220
George, Milton, 152
German immigrants: antislavery sentiment, 35, 59, 61, 63–64, 66, 248–49nn74–75, 250n81; and unionism, 66, 251n8, 252n10
Gerstle, Gary, 225n7
Ginés de Sepúlveda, Juan, 5
Glasscock v. Shell, 163
Gonzales, Battle of (1835), 17, 18
Goodwyn, Lawrence, 150, 291n4
Gould, Jay, 160
Gould, Robert S., *154*; cases overseen by, 163; judicial career, 156, 158; mentioned, 155, 216; and Texas Bar Association, 161
Graham, M. D., 81
Grand State Farmers' Alliance, 150
Grangers: assimilation into Alliance populism, 150–51; and factional disputes in 1875 convention, 131, 134, 136–39, 141, 142, 143, 144, 147, 274n12; ideology of, 130, 149; movement development and growth, 128–29; reform impulse, 149–50. *See also* populism
Grant, Ulysses S., 119, 121, 122, 123, 125–26, 128
Gray, Peter W., 81
Gray, William Fairfax, 28–30, 237n24
Great Southwestern Strike (1886), 151
Greeley, Horace, 123
Greenback Party, 172. *See also* People's Party
Gregg, John, 82–83
Guadalupe Hidalgo, Treaty of (1848), 62
Guerrero, Vicente, 11, 12

Gulf, Central, & Santa Fe Railway Co. v. Levy, 166
Gulf C.& S. F. Ry. Co. v. Sharman, 199–200

Haley, James L., 233n40
Hamilton, Alexander, 171, 207
Hamilton, Andrew Jackson "Colossal," *93*; and convention for 1866 constitution, 94–95, 101–2; in convention for 1869 constitution, 107–8, 111–12, 120; political elections, 122; as provisional governor of Reconstruction Texas, 92; and Roberts, xvii, 225–26n11; and Rodriguez suit, 124–25; as unionist, 74, 76–78, 105
Hamilton, Morgan, 107–8, 119, 121, 122
Hamilton, Robert, 27
Hancock, John, 65, 95, 100
Hancock, Winfield S., 107
Hardin, Stephen, 228n12
Harper, Thomas C., 204
Harrer, James, 63
Haynes, John L., 66
Hays, Jack, 41, 43
Hegel, G. W., xvi, xvii, 220
Hemphill, John, 46–47, 48, 50, 52–53, *54*, 82
Henderson, James Pinckney, 46, 59, 69, 71–72, *77*, 157
Henderson, James W., 100
Henry, John Lane, 146, 166, 182
Henson, Margaret Swett, 233n40
heroic view of Texas history, xvi, 2, 225n9, 227n3
Hidalgo, Miguel, 6, 231n19
Higgins v. Bordages, 202
Hispanics. *See* Mexicans; Tejanos
historical anthropology, xvi, 219–20
Hobbesian social theory, 6, 25
Hofstadter, Richard, 148
Hogansen, Kristin, 225n7
Hogg, James Stephen, *184*; and antitrust law, 202; judiciary appointments, 182; mentioned, 201, 216; monument of, 212; and *padron* system, 173, 284n2; political elections, 172, 173; and populism-progressivism fusion, xviii, 207; as progressive, 174; and Railroad Commission, 176; retirement, 187
Holmes, Oliver Wendell, 222

homesteads: land claims, 111, 112, 144, 168–70, 188–90, 283–84nn91–92; protection from creditors, 51–52, 56, 112, 130, 144; taxes, 56, 112, 202
Horton, Albert Clinton, 59
Horwitz, Morton, 218
Houck and Dieter v. Anheuser-Busch Brewing Association, 202–3
House, Edward Mandell: and Brown, 183; and Culberson, 173, 285n4; mentioned, 216; and populism-progressivism fusion, xviii, 173, 207; as progressive, 174
Houston, Margaret, 93
Houston, Sam: biographies on, 253n14, 254n15; and convention for secession, 80, 81, 83; criticism of Lamar, 38, 40–41, 42–43; death of, 93; independence sentiment, 14, 18, 20; Indian alliance efforts, 27, 37, 38–39, 40, 43, 241n12, 243n21; mentioned, 47; military command, 19, 27–28, 35; opposition to Confederacy, 83, 84; political elections, 36, 42, 68, 73, 78, 80, 132; as unionist, 65, 68, 74, 76, 86–87
Houston & Texas Central Railway Company v. Simpson, 164–65, 281–82n75
Houston & Texas Central Railway Company v. State, 192
Houston & Tex. Ry Co. v. Fowler, 163
Howard, James, 249n75
Hubbard, Richard B., 153, 156
humanists *vs.* Thomists, 5, 6, 230–31n18
Hunt, Memucan, 38, 243n21
Huston, Felix, 244n25

ideological history, xvi, 220
Illinois Supreme Court, 179
imagined community, 218
immigration: in 1869 constitution, 113–14; in 1876 constitution, 144; of Indians into Texas, 39; and industrialization, 175; Mexican policy, 2, 3–4, 6–7, 8, 12–13, 14, 19, 26. *See also* German immigrants
Immigration Law of 1830 (Mexico), 12–13, 14, 19, 26
indentured servitude, 10–11, 12–13, 24, 231n20, 233n38
Independence Convention (1836), 7

Indians: citizenship of, 26, 30, 50–51, 116; enslavement of, 5; and federal protection of the frontier, 48, 84, 96, 243n21, 251n1; land grants, 15–16, 26–27, 68; Mexican-Tejano alliance with, 17, 26, 34, 39–40, 242–43n21; in secessionist rhetoric, 82; as term, xiv; territorial relocation, 39; Texian aggression toward, 38, 39–42, 241n15, 243–44n25, 243n21; Texian alliance with, 37, 38–39, 40, 43, 241n12; voting rights, 55
Industrial Accident Board, 205
industrialization, 128, 148, 149, 171, 175, 201. *See also* railroads
insurable interest doctrine, 204
insurance companies, 203–5
intermarriage and miscegenation, 99–100, 199
Interstate Commerce Act (1887), 152, 176
Ireland, "Oxcart" John, 98, 99, 158, *159*, 166, 167–68, 170–71
Irion, Robert, 40, 243n21
Isaac, Rhys, 220
Iturbide, Agustín de, 3, 8

Jack, Patrick H., 13, 15
Jackson, Andrew, 36, 37, 68, 241n12
Jacksonianism, 32, 49, 73, 79
Jacobs, Seth, 220
Jacobsohn, Gary, 217–18, 220
Jeffersonianism, 31, 59, 150, 168. *See also* yeoman farmer ideal
Johnson, Andrew, 90, 91–92, 104, 105
Johnson, John H., 136–37, 138, 139, 141
Johnson, Middleton T., 97
Johnston, Albert Sidney, 211–12
Jones, Anson, 21, 43, 46, 48, 54
Jones, Evan, 152
Jones, Oliver, 51, 246–47n21
Jones, W. E., 95, 96, 103
Jones v. George, 282–83n83
Jordan, A. P. H., 119
Joske v. Irvine, 195–96
judicial branch: in 1845 constitution, 50, 54; in 1866 constitution, 95; in 1869 constitution, 117, 123; in 1876 constitution, 144–46; in 1891 constitutional amendments, 155,

174, 179–80, 181; appointment *vs.* election of judges, 50, 54, 95, 117; calls for reform of, 129, 155, 161–62, 178; liberalizing approach during populist era, 164–65, 166, 177–78; and Texan identity formation, 155–56, 171, 188. *See also* Supreme Court (Texas)

Kansas-Nebraska Act (1854), 68
Karnes, Henry Wax, 41, 243–44n25
Kearby, Jerome C., 173
Kens, Paul, 168
Kent, James, 174
Kickapoo Indians, 41
Kiowa Indians, 244n25
Kirkham, James, 13–14
Knights of Labor, 149, 150–51
Knights of the White Camellia, 117
Know-Nothingism and Whigs, 37, 65, 66, 68, 70, 71–73, 76
Kuechler, Jacob, 119, 122
Ku Klux Klan, 117, 122, 285n4

laborers. *See* farmers; working class
labor movement: northern, 149; and socialist utopia, 215. *See also* populism
Lack, Paul, 227n6, 233n38
Lacy, Martin, 40
Lamar, Mirabeau B.: criticized by Houston, 38, 40–41, 42–43; and Indian aggression, 39–41, 43, 241n15, 243n21, 244n25; mentioned, 46, 47; military background, 36; relocation of capital, 242n17
Lamb, William, 150–51
land grants and titles: in 1836 constitution, 29–30; in 1845 constitution, 47, 50, 52–53; in 1866 constitution, 99; in 1869 constitution, 111, 112–13, 192; in 1876 constitution, 130, 141, 142, 143–44, 157–58, 168, 276n29; diminishing supply of uninhabited lands, 167, 188, 191, 192–93; homestead claims, 111, 112, 144, 168–70, 188–90, 283–84nn91–92; for Indians, 15–16, 26–27, 68; railroad claims, 170–71, 190–92
Latimer, Albert H., 92
Lea, Pryor, 85
Lee, Robert E., 212

legislative branch: in 1845 constitution, 50, 55; in 1861 constitution, 84; in 1876 constitution, 142–43
Lester, Edward, 254n15
Levinas, Emmanuel, 219
Lincoln, Abraham, 66, 73, 80, 87, 90, 91
Lindheimer, Ferdinand, 66
Lindsay, Livingston, 115
Lipscomb, Abner S., 46–47, 48
literacy tests, 101
Littlefield, George Washington, 211, 213, 216, 293n17
Lochner v. New York, 165, 176, 177
Lockean social theory, 22, 25, 32, 57
Louis-Philippe, King of France, 38
Love, James, 46, 47
Lubbock, F. R., 71–72, 215
Lufkin v. City of Galveston, 202
Lynch, Francis J., 136, 141, 143

Mabry, Hinche, 103
MacIntyre, Alasdair, 220
Macune, Charles W., 151–53
Maher, Edward, 257n42
Maltby, Henry, 64
Manifest Destiny, 35
marriage: intermarriage and miscegenation, 99–100, 199; and property, 53, 112; and tort law, 197–98
Marshall, John, 174
martial law, 106–7, 122, 123
Martin, Frances Marion, 137, 138
Martin, Wiley, 15
Mauer, John Walker, 273n9
Mayfield, James S., 46, 53
McCormack, Andrew, 104
McCormick, George, 141
McCulloch, Ben, 83–84
McDonald, James, 250n80
McFaddin, J. N., 129
McIntyre, Hugh, 86
McKay, Seth Shepard, 131, 272n9, 275n19
McKinney, Solomon, 63
McMurray v. McMurray, 197–98
McNeil, Sterling, 12
Methodists, 32, 63–64
Mexican government: and annexation of Texas, 38, 46; antislavery legislation, 2–3,

INDEX

6–8, 10–14, 16–17, 19–20, 21–22, 229n14, 231n19; constitution of 1824, 8–9, 12, 13, 16, 20, 21; immigration policy, 2, 3–4, 6–7, 8, 12–13, 14, 19, 26; Indian alliance with, 17, 26, 34, 39–40, 242–43n21; and Indian land grants, 15–16, 26–27; military aggression against Texas republic, 42, 44; protection of slave runaways from Texas, 59–61; and Texian Declaration of Independence, 24–26; and Texian petition for statehood, 14–15, 19, 24, 25. *See also* Texas Revolution (1835–36)

Mexicans: in secessionist rhetoric, 82; as term, xiv. *See also* Tejanos

Mexican War of Independence, 3

Mier Expedition (1842), 42

Mier y Teran, Manuel de, 2, 3–4, 11

Milam, Ben, 17, 237n18

Mills, William, 118, 139

miscegenation and intermarriage, 99–100, 199

Moneyhon, Carl, 108, 110, 266n39, 268n63

monopolies and perpetuities, 32, 49, 56

Moore, George F., 125

Moore, Littleton W., 140

Morelos, José María, 3, 6, 231n19

Morrill, Amos, 281n74

Morse, Charles S., 182

Morse carbine rifles, 84

municipal authority, 201–2

Munn v. Illinois, 176

Munroe, Armisted, 118, 120

Murphy, J. B., 132

Myers, E. E., 153

National Farmers' Alliance, 152–53

nationalism: racial *vs.* civic, 225n7; *vs.* unionism, 65

Native Americans. *See* Indians

natural harmony theory, 148

Navarro, José Antonio, 27, 46, 48, 51

Neu Braunfelser Zeitung (newspaper), 66

Newcomb, James P., 65, 119, 120

New York Bar Association, 176

Nickerson v. Nickerson, 197

northerner antislavery sentiment: Texan attempts to mollify, 21, 24, 37; as threat to Texan proslavery identity, 32, 43–44, 63–65, 69–74, 79, 81–82, 85–86, 88–89

Northwestern Alliance, 152

Norton, A. B., 95, 103, 258n50, 258n54

Nueces Strip (Wild Horse Desert), 36

Nugent, Thomas L., 137, 141

Ochiltree, William B., 82

office-holding requirements, 32, 57, 100, 116, 120

Oldham, W. S., 82

Olmsted, Frederick Law, 249n75; *Journey through Texas*, 59–61, 64, 249n74, 250n81

"otherness" (*alterité*), xiii, 219, 221, 296n13

padron system, 173, 284–85n2

Painter, Nell Irvin, 128

Panic of 1837, 37

papism, 72–73

Parker, Theodore, 249n75

Paschal, George W., 74, 76, *77*, 78, 79–80, 105, 257–58n50, 258n52

Paschal, Isaiah, 98

patents, 189, 283n91, 284n92

Patrons of Husbandry, 128. *See also* Grangers

Patten, Nathan, 111, 121

Paul, Arnold, 128

Pease, Elisha M., 105, 107–9, 215, 250n81

People's Party, 172, 173–75. *See also* populism

perpetuities and monopolies, 32, 49, 56

Phillips, Alec, 183

Phillips, Alexander, 99

Pickett, E. B., 135

P. J. Willis Bros. v. McNeil, 163

Pleasants, Henry Clay, 199

Plessy v. Ferguson, 199

police, state, 122, 123

Polk, James K., 45, 46

poll taxes, 131, 136, 139–40, 142

populism: and 1875 convention, 131; fusion with progressivism, xviii, 173, 174–75, 207–8; and Grangers, 130, 149, 150; ideology of, 148–50; movement development and growth, 150–52, 173–74; movement marginalization and decline, 174–75, 176–78; political office

gains, 158; and racism, 148–49, 150, 291n4; and socialist utopia, 214–15
Potter, Robert, 27, 29, 30
Power, James, 28
Presidential Reconstruction, 90, 91–92. *See also* Constitution of 1866
press and speech, freedom of, 31, 49
Price v. Supreme Lodge of the Knights of Honor, 204
prisoners of war: Mexican, 32; Texian, 42
progressivism: conservative Anglo, xv; fusion with populism, xviii, 173, 174–75, 207–8; and judicial pragmatism, 177–178, 206–7; movement development and growth, 165, 174–75, 176–78
Prohibition, 183, 198, 292n8
property: and debt, 56, 111–12, 144; and marriage, 53, 112; slaves as, 4, 11–12, 13, 20, 22–23, 53, 69. *See also* land grants and titles
Protestants: *vs.* Catholics, 5, 22, 32, 56–57, 230–31n18; Fundamentalism, 149
psychoanalysis, 296–97n14
public lands. *See* land grants and titles
public schools. *See* education
Pullman-Palace-Car Co. v. Cain, 199
Puritans, 72–73

Queen Insurance Company v. State, 203
Quinlan v. Houston & Texas Central Railway Company, 192

race and racism: and citizenship, 26, 30–31, 50–51, 100; and class, 32–33; in convention for 1876 constitution, 138, 147; and "otherness," xiii, 219, 221, 296n13; and populism, 148–49, 150, 291n4; segregation, 104, 115–16, 123, 141, 198–201, 289–90n59; and voting, 55, 56, 65, 94, 100–101, 131. *See also* blacks; Indians; Tejanos; whiteness
Raguet, Anna, 40
Raguet, Henry, 242n21, 243n21
Raguet, Marcia, 242n21
railroads: in 1866 constitution, 98–99, 143; in 1869 constitution, 109–10, 111, 112–13, 143, 192; in 1876 constitution, 143–44, 146, 147, 170, 276n29; Interstate Commerce Act, 152, 176; land claims, 170–71, 190–92; regulation of, 175–76; in secessionist rhetoric, 255n19; and segregation, 199–200, 289–90n59; strikes, 128; Texas Railroad Commission, 176, 183; and tort law, 163, 164–65, 166, 193–95, 281–82n75; transcontinental, 99
Raven, H. H., 257–58n50
Reagan, John H.: in convention for 1876 constitution, 132, 134, 137, 139, 141, 142, 143, 144–45; in convention for secession, 81, 82; and Culberson, 285n4; flexible political leanings, 72, 74–76, 79, 132–34, 156; and Indian diplomacy, 40; mentioned, 201, 215; monument of, 212; and populism-progressivism fusion, 207; as progressive, 174; in Railroad Commission, 176; railroad legislation, 152, 273n11
real-estate disputes, 163–64
Reconstruction: collapse of, 122–26, 128; Congressional, 90–91, 105–7 (*see also* Constitution of 1869); and disenfranchisement of ex-Confederates, 106–7, 116–17, 120; Presidential, 90, 91–92 (*see also* Constitution of 1866); and readmission to Union, 122
Reeves, S. J., 182
religion: and antislavery sentiment, 5, 6, 63–64, 71, 72–73, 230–31n18; constitutional freedom, 49, 56–57; and populism, 149; Protestants *vs.* Catholics, 5, 22, 32, 56–57, 230–31n18
Rentfro, R. B., 138, 139
Republican Party: development of, 105; dominance during Reconstruction, 107, 121–22 (*see also* Constitution of 1869); and factional disputes in 1875 convention, 131, 134, 136–39, 141, 142, 143, 144, 147; factions, 107–8; overthrow during Reconstruction, 123–26, 127–28; reduced influence following Redemption, 172
revisionist history, 219
revolutionary age, 1–2
Reynolds, Joseph J., 121, 122
Richardson, Rupert, 238–39n32, 238n29
right to bear arms, 31
Rio Grande, as Texas-Mexico boundary, 36

INDEX

Roark, James L., 175
Roberts, Oran Milo, 75; background, 71; and capital building fire, 153–55; in convention for 1866 constitution, 93, 95, 99, 100, 102; in convention for secession, 80, 81–82, 83; and Gould, 156, 163; and Hamilton, xvii, 225–26n11; influence on Texas political history, xvii–xviii, 215–16, 221; political elections, 153, 158; and politicization of judge nominations, 188; public lands rhetoric, 130, 167–68, 170; and railroad land claims, 130, 170, 190; secessionist rhetoric, 71–74, 81–82; state Supreme Court appointment, 126, 129; and Texas Bar Association, 161; and US Senate seat, 105, 106, 262n5
Robertson, Elijah S. C., 137, 140–41
Robertson Insurance Law (1907), 204–5
Robinson, Henry, 84
Robinson, James, 28
Robson, John H., 80
Robson, W. S., 161
Rodriguez, Joseph, 124–25
Rogers, William P., 80, 81
Roosevelt, Theodore, 165
Ross, Lawrence Sullivan "Sul," 146, 161, 162
Rowe, Edna, 233n40
Ruby, George, 108, 118
Ruiz, Francisco, 41
Runnels, Hardin R.: in convention for 1866 constitution, 92, 93; and Houston, 68–69, 80; political elections, 68, 132; secessionist rhetoric, 69–71, 72, 74, 255n19
Runnels, Hiram G., 46, 50, 51
Rusk, Thomas Jefferson: in convention for 1836 constitution, 27, 28, 29; in convention for 1845 constitution, 46–47, 48, 51; death of, 69; on Indian aggression, 242–43n21; legal background, 237–38n25; mentioned, 254n15; military command, 36, 40; secessionist rhetoric, 72
Russell, S. H., 137, 139

Said, Edward, 219
San Antonio de Bexar, Siege of (1835), 17, 18, 19
San Jacinto, Battle of (1836), 35, 36
Sansom, Richard, 140, 141

Santa Anna, Antonio Lopez de: centralized government under, 16, 24, 25, 26, 229n14; and civil war, 15; coup led by, 13; return to power, 42, 240n8; and Texas Revolution, 19, 35–36
Saunders, X. B., 161
Sayers, Joseph D., 285n4
schools. *See* education
Schuetze, Julius, 115
Scoble, John, 44
Secession: constitutional amendments, 84–85; convention called for, 80; convention delegates, 81; Declaration of Causes, 81–82; declared null and void ab initio, 97–98, 109–10, 120, 268n63; rhetoric of, 67, 68, 69–74, 81–82, 85–86, 88–89; *vs.* unionist rhetoric, 67–68, 74, 76–80, 88; and unionist supporters, 65–66, 74–76, 80; voter approval of, 83. *See also* Reconstruction
segregation, 104, 115–16, 123, 141, 198–201, 289–90n59
Seguin, Juan, 1, 15, 239n2
semicolon decision, 124–25, 128, 129, 135
Seminole Indians, 39
separate but equal doctrine, 115, 199, 289–90n59
sexuality, fear of black male, 85
Shakespeare, William, 74, 256–57n40
Shannon, N. W., 259n54
Shawnee Indians, 39, 40, 41
Shelley, Percy Bysshe, 74
Sheridan, Philip, 107
Sherman Antitrust Act (1890), 175
Sherman Silver Purchase Act (1893), 175
Sherwood, Lorenzo, 64, 162
Shively, Charles, 44
Simmel, Georg, 131, 221
slavery: in 1836 constitution, 31–32, 57; in 1845 constitution, 52, 57–58; in 1861 constitution, 84–85; in 1866 constitution, 102; in 1869 constitution, 116; in British legal tradition, 230n18, 240n8; and citizenship, 14, 26; fears of revolt, 2, 17, 21, 26, 34, 43, 52, 58, 79–80, 85, 247n54; historiography, 2–3, 227–28nn6–7, 228–29nn12–14; and indentured servitude, 10–11, 12–13, 24, 231n20,

233n38; and labor competition, 35, 66, 78; and revisionist history, 219; runaways, 13, 59–61, 250n81; in Spanish legal tradition, 5–6, 53, 230–31n18; in Texian constitution proposals, 9–10, 14–15, 20; in Texian Declaration of Independence (1836), 22–23; Texian-Mexican dispute over, 2–3, 4, 6–8, 10–14, 16–17, 19–20, 21–22, 231n19; and Texian-US diplomatic negotiations, 37; and Thirteenth Amendment, 90, 106. *See also* antislavery sentiment
slave trade, 8, 20, 22, 23, 38, 66, 67, 78
Smith, Benjamin Fort, 12
Smith, Henry, 19, 28, 29
Smyrl, Frank, 65–66
socialist utopia, 214–15
social struggle theory, 148
Somervell, Alexander, 42
So Relle v. Western Union Tel Co., 166
Southern Intelligencer (newspaper), 65, 76, 78, 79–80, 257–58n50, 258–59n54, 258n52
southern nationalism *vs.* unionism, 65
Southwestern Historical Quarterly (journal), 216
South Western Reporter, 181
Spanish legal tradition, 5–6, 53
speech and press, freedom of, 31, 49
Spencer, Frank M., 124
"Spirit of 1776" rhetoric, 22, 70
states' rights rhetoric, 65. *See also* Secession
Stayton, Robert W., *154*; and appellate court restructuring, 180; cases overseen by, 163–65, 193–94, 198, 281–82n75, 283n83, 284n92; judicial career, 157, 160–61, 166, 186, 210; mentioned, 155, 182; and Texas Bar Association, 161
Steadman, William, 80
Stedman, Nathan A., 188
Stell, John D., 81, 85
Stern, Madeleine, 44
Stockdale, Fletcher S., 138, 140, 142, 143
Stuart, Hamilton, 99
Stuart v. Western Union Telegraph Company, 166
suffrage. *See* voting and elections
Supreme Court (California), 178–79
Supreme Court (Illinois), 179

Supreme Court (Mexico), 9
Supreme Court (Texas): in 1845 constitution, 50; in 1866 constitution, 95; in 1869 constitution, 117, 123; in 1876 constitution, 145–46, 178; in 1891 constitutional amendments, 155, 179, 180, 181; antitrust law, 202–3; calls for reform of, 161, 162; caseload of, 162–64, 180–81, 187; collegiality following 1891 constitutional amendments, 181, 186–87; facilities for, 155, 158, 181–82, 281n69; insurance cases, 203–4; liberalizing approach during populist era, 164–65, 166; membership changes, 156–57, 160–61, 163, 166, 182–83; municipal authority cases, 201–2; and politicization of judge nominations, 187–88; pragmatic approach following 1891 constitutional amendments, 177–78, 206–7; public lands cases, 168–70, 171, 188–93, 283–84nn91–92; reporters of, 161, 181; segregation cases, 199–201; and the semicolon decision, 125, 135; tort law, 163, 164–65, 166, 193–98, 281–82n75
Supreme Court (United States): and business progressivism, 165, 176–77; caseload of, 178, 179; segregation rulings, 199, 200, 289–90n59; slavery rulings, 69

Taft, William Howard, 165
Tappan, Lewis, 43, 44
Taussig, Michael, 219
taxes: for education fund, 104, 114, 140; homestead, 56, 112, 202; poll, 131, 136, 139–40, 142; in Republican program, 123
Taylor, William M., 92, 93
Taylor, Zachary, 46
Teja, Jesus F. de la, 239n2
Tejanos: antislavery sentiment, 20, 34, 59, 63–64, 66; citizenship of, 51; and increase in Anglo immigration, 3–4, 41; at Independence Convention, 1, 226n1; Indian alliance with, 39–40, 41; office-holding requirements, 57; prejudice against, 35, 239n2, 242n21; and segregation, 199; as term, xiv; and unionism, 66; voting rights, 55, 65
telegraph operators, 164, 166
temperance, 183, 198, 292n8

INDEX

Tenorio, Antonio, 15–16
Terrell, Alexander W., xvii, 125, 161, 162, 181, 225n11
territory: confiscation of Indian, 39, 68; expansion under Texas republic, 36, 38, 41, 242n17; federal protection of Texas frontier, 48, 84, 96, 243n21, 251n1; and Kansas-Nebraska Act, 68; state division proposals, 96–97, 118–21; in Texas annexation provisions, 45. *See also* land grants and titles
Texans, as term, xiv
Texas A&M University, 142
Texas Bar Association, 161, 177
Texas & Pacific Railway Company v. Gay, 193
Texas Railroad Commission, 176, 183
Texas Revolution (1835–36): causes of, overview, 1–4; Consultation (*Consultado*) Convention (1835), 18–19, 24, 29; conventions leading to (1832 and 1833), 14, 19–20; Declaration of Independence, 21–26, 82; end of, 35–36; historiography, 2–3, 227–28nn6-7, 228–29nn12-14; Independence Convention (1836), 7; and Mexican prisoners of war, 32; military establishment and operations, 19, 27–28; opening of hostilities, 16–17, 18; petition for statehood prior to, 14–15, 19, 24, 25. *See also* Constitution of 1836
Texas State Historical Association, 215–16
Texas v. White, 268n63
Texians, as term, xiv
Thirteenth Amendment, 90, 106
Thomas, David, 27, 28
Thomas, James W., 119
Thomists *vs.* humanists, 5, 6, 230–31n18
Thompson, Seymour D., 177
Thompson v. Baker, 191
Throckmorton, James: in convention for 1866 constitution, 92, 93, 94, 100, 102, 103; political elections, 105, 106; removal from office, 107; as unionist, 76
Torget, Andrew, 2–3, 4, 5–6, 13–14, 228n7, 231n19
Tornel, José María, 2, 11
tort law, 163, 164–65, 166, 193–98, 281–82n75
Townes, John C., 188

T. & P. Ry. Co. v. O'Donell, 163
transcontinental railroad, 99
Travis, William Barret, 13, 15, 16–17, 18, 21, 26, 27
Tuck, Richard, 230–31n18
Turner, Frederick Jackson, 148, 149
Turner, Nat, 26, 247n54
Tyler, John, 44, 45

Ugartechea, Domingo de, 15, 22
unionism: development of, 65; and development of Republican Party, 105; influential supporters of, 65–66, 74–76, 80, 257n42; rhetoric of, 67–68, 74, 76–80, 88
uniqueness rhetoric, 11
United States: annexation of Texas, 36, 37–38, 44, 45–46, 48; antislavery sentiment in, as threat to Texan proslavery identity, 32, 43–44, 63–65, 69–74, 79, 81–82, 85–86, 88–89; antislavery sentiment in, Texan attempts to mollify, 21, 24, 37; ban on slave trade, 8, 67; Constitution, 8, 14, 28, 31, 49, 238n29; Declaration of Independence, 22, 25, 70, 82; Indian policy, 39; Interstate Commerce Act, 152, 176; martial law against unreconstructed Confederate states, 106–7, 122; protection of Texas frontier from Indians, 48, 84, 96, 243n21, 251n1; and state division proposals, 96–97, 118–21; and transcontinental railroad, 99. *See also* Supreme Court (United States)
University of Texas, 142, 167, 211–13; School of Law, 161, 163
urbanization, 175, 201
US-Mexican War (1846–48), 59, 62
U.S. v. Dodge, 289–90n59

Van Buren, Martin, 37–38, 39
Van Zandt, Isaac, 49, 51, 52
Varnell, William M., 119, 121
Vasquez, Rafael, 42
Veblen, Thorstein, *The Theory of the Leisure Class*, 214
Velasco, Treaty of (1836), 35–36
Victoria, Guadalupe, 3
Viesca, Augustine, 15
Viesca, J. M., 11, 12

voting and elections: in 1845 constitution, 55, 56; in 1866 constitution, 100–101; in 1869 constitution, 116, 140; in 1876 constitution, 131, 136, 139–40; and literacy tests, 101; and poll taxes, 131, 136, 139–40, 142; and race, 55, 56, 65, 94, 100–101, 131; residency requirements, 100, 120; and the semicolon decision, 125, 128, 135

Wade, H. W., 137, 139
Waelder, Jacob, 132, 141, 144, 146
Wahl, Thomas N., 78
Waite, Morrison R., 178
Walker, A. S., 166, 181
Walker, Joseph, 94
Wallace, Ernest, 118
The Washington American (newspaper), 65
Waul, T. N., 82, 99
weaponry rights, 31
Webb, Walter Prescott, 225n9
Wesley, John, 32, 230n18
West, Charles S., *133*; cases overseen by, 125, 163–65; in convention for 1876 constitution, 132, 142, 143; judicial career, 157; and Texas Bar Association, 161
West, John B., 181
West Texas, proposed state of, 97, 118–21
Wharton, William H., 22
Whigs and Know-Nothingism, 37, 65, 66, 68, 70, 71–73, 76
whiteness: and citizenship, 30, 50–51; and cultural superiority, xv, 37; and education, 104; and intermarriage, 100; and political rights, 82; and segregation, 200–201; and Texan identity formation, 67, 147, 208–9

Whitfield, John W., 136, 137, 140, 141
Whitmore, G. W., 121
Wichita Indians, 39, 41, 43
Wiebe, Robert H., 149
Wigfall, Louis T., 71–72, 82
Wilcox, John, 81
Wild Horse Desert (Nueces Strip), 36
Wiley, A. P., 81
Wilkinson, Alfred E., 181
Willette, Thomas, 63
Williams, George H., 125–26
Williams, Patrick G., 272n8, 274n12, 276n29
Willie, Asa Hoxie, *159*; cases overseen by, 163–65, 204; judicial career, 158, 160, 162, 186, 281n69, 288n32; and Texas Bar Association, 161
Willie, James, 160, 288n32
Wilson, Woodrow, 165, 174, 183, 212
Wiltshire, Susan F., 254n15
Woll, Adrian, 42
women's rights, 53, 55, 112, 197–98
Wooten, Dudley, *A Comprehensive History of Texas 1685–1897*, 215
working class: protections for, 56, 110–11, 144; social protests, 128. *See also* populism
Wright v. Tipton, 198
writ of certiorari, 178, 179
wrongful death claims, 193

Yarbrough, Don, 280n62
Yates, Andrew J., 44
yeoman farmer ideal, 31, 55, 59, 78, 111, 146, 148, 168, 171. *See also* homesteads

Zavala, Lorenzo de, 1, 9, 27, 237n24